Facts On File

BIOGRAPHICAL

ENCYCLOPEDIA OF

ARTISTS

SIR LAWRENCE GOWING
GENERAL EDITOR

VOLUME 3
LIMBURG BROTHERS – FRANCISCO RIBALTA

☑®

Facts On File, Inc.

Published in North America by:
Facts On File, Inc.
132 West 31st Street
New York, NY 10001

The Brown Reference Group plc
(incorporating Andromeda Oxford Ltd)
8 Chapel Place
Rivington Street
London EC2A 3DQ

Library of Congress Cataloging-in-Publication Data

LC Control Number: 2005040500
    Type of Material: Text
        Main Title: Biographical encyclopedia of artists / edited by Lawrence Gowing.
    Published/Created: New York: Facts On File, c2005.
    Projected Pub. Date: 0504
    Related Names: Gowing, Lawrence.
        Description: p. cm.
            ISBN: 0816058032
        Contents: v. 1. Alvar Aalto–Paul Durand-Ruel -- v. 2. Albrecht Dürer–Jan
                  Lievensz -- v. 3. Limburg Brothers–Francisco Ribalta -- v. 4.
                  Jusepe de Ribera–Francisco de Zurbarán.
        Subjects: Artists--Biography.
                  Artists--Encyclopedias.
    LC Classification: N40 .B535 2005
    Dewey Class No.: 709/.2/2 B 22

Volume 3 ISBN   0-8160-5806-7
Set ISBN   0-8160-5803-2

Facts On File books are available at special
discounts when purchased in bulk quantities
for businesses, associations, institutions, or
sales promotions. Please call our Special Sales
Department in New York at (212) 967-8800
or (800) 322-8755.

You can find Facts On File on the World Wide
Web at http://www.factsonfile.com

Cover design by Cathy Rincon

Printed in China

10 9 8 7 6 5 4 3 2 1

The publisher wishes to thank the following individuals and institutions for
their help in the preparation of this work:

INDIVIDUALS: Margaret Amosu, Professor Manolis Andronikos, Janet
Backhouse, Claudia Bismarck, John Boardman, His Grace the Duke of
Buccleugh, Richard Calvocoressi, Lord Clark, Curt and Maria Clay, James
Collins, Bryan Cranstone, Mrs E.A. Cubitt, Mary Doherty, Judith Dronkhurst,
Rosemary Eakins, Mark Evans, Claude Fessaguet, Joel Fisher, Jean-Jacques
Gabas, Dr Oscar Ghez, Paul Goldman, G. St G.M. Gompertz, Zoë Goodwin,
Toni Greatrex, A.V. Griffiths, Victor Harris, Barbara Harvey, Maurice
Howard, A.D. Hyder, Jane Jakeman, Peg Katritzky, Moira Klingman,
Andrew Lawson, Betty Yao Lin, Christopher Lloyd, Jean Lodge, Richard
Long, Lorna McEchern, Eunice Martin, Shameem Melluish, Jennifer
Montagu, Sir Henry Moore, Richard Morphet, Elspeth O'Neill, Alan
Peebles, Professor Dr Chr. Pescheck, Pam Porter, Professor P.H. Pott, Alison
Renney, Steve Richard, Andrew Sherratt, Richard Shone, Lawrence Smith,
Don Sparling, Graham and Jennifer Speake, Annamaria Petrioli Tofani, Mary
Tregear, Jim Tudge, Betty Tyers, Ivan Vomáčka, Tom Wesselmann.

INSTITUTIONS: Ashmolean Museum, Oxford; Bibliothèque Nationale, Paris;
Bodleian Library, Oxford; British Library, London; British Museum,
London; Courtauld Institute of Art, London; Gulbenkian Foundation,
Lisbon; Louvre, Paris; Merseyside County Museums, Liverpool;
Metropolitan Museum, New York; Museum of Modern Art, New York;
Museum of Modern Art, Oxford; Oriental Institute, Oxford; Oxford City
Library; Petit Palais, Geneva; Phaidon Press, Oxford; Pitt Rivers Museum,
Oxford; Sainsbury Centre for the Visual Arts, Norwich; Sotheby Parke
Bernet & Co., London; Tate Gallery, London; Victoria and Albert Museum,
London; Warburg Institute, London.

The publisher wishes to thank the numerous individuals, agencies, museums,
galleries, and other institutions who kindly supplied the illustrations for this
book.

The publisher also wishes to acknowledge the important contributions of
Judith Brundin, Ann Currah, Bernard Dod, Herman and Polly Friedhoff, Juliet
Grindle, Jonathan Lamède, Giles Lewis, Andrew McNeillie, Penelope Marcus,
and Louise Pengelley.

Limburg brothers late 14th–early 15th century

The Limburgs were a family of French illuminators. There were at least three brothers: Paul (Polequin), Jean (Jacquemin), and Herman. There may also have been a fourth brother, Arnold. They are exceptionally well documented for their period: between 1399 and 1416 some 35 records are preserved, which refer to them and their activities. We know their parentage and origin: their father was a sculptor in Nijmegen (Netherlands), who called himself "Limburg", where he came from. Their mother was the sister of the well known painter Jean Malouel.

Early in 1399 two of the brothers, Jean and Herman, were apprenticed to a Parisian goldsmith, when they are called "jonnes enfans". Because of an epidemic in Paris, they were sent back to their native country, but a conflict between Brabant and Guelders delayed them; they were imprisoned and held for ransom in Brussels. The Duke Philip the Bold of Burgundy advanced the money to free the boys after they had been in prison for about six months. Early in 1402 another document records that Philip the Bold engaged Paul and Jean to illuminate a "très belle et notable Bible" for him. They are now called "enlumineurs" and are requested to paint the miniatures in this codex as quickly as possible.

After the death of their first patron in 1404, the brothers entered the service of Duc Jean de Berry, for whom they undertook the illuminations of two splendid books of hours: the *Belle Heures* (Cloisters, New York) which were completed in 1408 or 1409 and are described in the inventory of the Duc de Berry of 1413; and the most famous *Très Riches Heures du Duc de Berry* (Musée Condé, Chantilly). This manuscript was only half finished when the Duc de Berry died in 1416. The brothers died in the same year.

Although not recorded, from internal evidence it can be deduced that one or two, perhaps all three of the brothers, visited northern Italy, most likely Florence, Padua, and possibly Siena. *The Presentation of Christ* in the *Très Riches Heures*, modeled after the well known fresco in S. Croce, Florence, by Taddeo Gaddi, is one of the undeniable proofs of such a voyage. The first recorded work by the Limburgs, made for Philip the Bold between 1402 and 1404, is a *Bible moralisée* (now in the Bibliothèque Nationale, Paris, MS. Fr.

166). The Limburgs completed only the first three gatherings of this manuscript and started on the fourth. Their model is preserved: a *Bible moralisée* of c1350–70 (now also in the Bibliothèque Nationale, Paris; MS. fr. 167) which was then owned by Philip the Bold. The Limburgs followed the prototype closely; they also framed the miniatures in quatrefoils alternating with architectural borders as in the earlier *Bible moralisée*. The same texts in Latin, followed by a French translation, are inscribed in the wide margins.

The miniatures reproduce the compositions of the earlier Bible faithfully, but, as is usual in such cases, the Limburgs updated the style into that of their own period and altered details. Notable differences in the execution of these make it possible to distinguish two "hands", the two brothers Paul and Jean. Paul, the more gifted, displays a remarkably subtle range of colors; he often models his rather voluminous figures in delicate white on a light background. Jean, whose figures as a rule are slimmer, is inclined to fill his scenes with a greater number of people.

The *Bible moralisée* was far from being finished when Philip the Bold died in 1404. The brothers later entered the service of the Duc de Berry; at what exact date is not known. Jean, Duc de Berry was the greatest French patron of the arts at this period and he proved to be a most appreciative and inspiring Maecenas to the Limburgs. The first commission the brothers undertook for him is a Book of Hours, the so-called *Belles Heures* (Cloisters, New York). It is conjectured that the brothers—in this case all three of them were involved—started on this manuscript c1405. About the ownership of the Duc there can be no doubt. There are two portraits of him and one of his wife in the manuscript, as well as a superb inscription on the first folio by Jean Flamel, the Duc's secretary, which states explicitly that the Duc commissioned this Book of Hours. Furthermore, the script is mentioned in the fourth account of the Duc's collection drawn up by Robinet d'Estampes in 1412/13.

In contrast to the *Bible moralisée*, where the Limburgs had to follow closely an existing model, this Book of Hours provided ample opportunity for fresh innovations. No less than seven novel cycles are included in the manuscript. After the calendar it starts with 11 scenes from the legend of St Catherine; this unusually extended length can be attributed to St

Catherine's being one of the patron saints of the Duc de Berry's wife, Jeanne of Boulogne. The 11 scenes chosen leave out some of the best known incidents from her life, such as her mystical marriage to Christ, in favor of others that are only rarely shown—such as Catherine in prison tended by angels and visited by Queen Faustina, who in the next miniature is beheaded for her devotion to Catherine.

This cycle is followed by a shorter one, which is not only unprecedented in a Book of Hours, but is altogether new in art: four miniatures illustrate the Great Litany, of which only one scene, that of St Michael sheathing his sword, is at all customary. The third exceptional cycle tells in nine scenes the story of the 11th-century theologian Raymond Diocrès and of the foundation of the Carthusian Order by his pupil St Bruno: no earlier representations of Diocrès exist and of St Bruno only a few single scenes. Perhaps the most impressive of the nine miniatures is the last one, depicting from above, at an odd angle, the building of the Grand Chartreuse, while monks are fishing in a pool in the foreground.

The story of St Jerome is told at even greater length in 12 scenes. This cycle stresses Jerome's scholarship. Again the last one is of special interest: during the Saint's burial procession hermits emerge from caves to pay homage, and the blind and lame approach to be healed by touching the corpse. The hermits Paul and Anthony are the subjects of the next cycle with eight illustrations. Among them are some very attractive scenes, especially those in the "wilderness": in one scene St Anthony is looking for St Paul's hermitage and encounters a snake, while in the next one he is guided by a centaur to the Saint, who is sitting in front of his hut. The inventiveness of the brothers in these new cycles is matched by their unsurpassed delicate handling of color and contour, including some early attempts at perspective.

The last and the most important commission the brothers undertook for Jean de Berry is the *Très Riches Heures*, now in the Musée Condé at Chantilly. At the death of the patron and the artists in 1416 the manuscript was still unbound, and only about half finished. All three brothers worked on this, their masterpiece. The book starts, as Books of Hours do, with calendar pictures, though it is likely that the miniaturists did not begin their work

with this cycle. The calendar is normally illustrated with 24 small medallions, one each for the zodiac sign and the occupation of the month. The Limburgs for the first time combined these two, enlarged them and filled the entire space of the page, incorporating an equally wide arch above, enclosing in addition astronomical information such as the days of the week and phases of the moon. In the inner lobe Apollo, holding the blazing sun, rides in his chariot drawn by winged horses.

The 11 pictures underneath (November was not finished by the Limburgs but by Jean Colombe) show four courtly scenes: January, a banquet with the Duc de Berry presiding; April, the betrothal of a courtly pair; May, an outing on horseback; and August, hawking. The other seven depict peasant activities such as plowing in March, haymaking in June, sheepshearing in July. January and February show indoor scenes. The other nine portray, as a backdrop against a brilliant blue sky, contemporary buildings such as castles, ones either in the possession of the Duc de Berry or of the King or of a nephew, Louis II of Anjou. Of these buildings only one is still in existence, but all can be identified with the help of early drawings and etchings. The one for June with the Sainte Chapelle on the right and the Palais de la Cité on the left is perhaps the most enchanting. To these should be added the Mont St Michel illustrating the Mass for St Michael towards the end of the book, as well as some smaller background silhouettes.

These unique backdrops are combined with minutely observed representations of seasonal work on the land which are rendered with delicate precision. Outstanding single pictures such as the Zodiac Man and the Map of Rome are rarities in a Book of Hours. Even the customary sequence of the Life of the Virgin and the Passion of Christ are presented with new and unexpected touches: Christ in Gethsemane stands against a black sky, relieved only by stars and a couple of torches; and the Crucifixion is plunged, as the biblical text describes, into an overall bluish-gray haze. In all these the Limburgs surpass any contemporary Italian—and herald Netherlandish—panel painting. The *Très Riches Heures* is a masterpiece of the first order, and as such fully deserves the popularity it

has recently acquired thanks to color reproductions.

Further reading. Meiss, M. and Beatson, E.H. *The Belles Heures of Jean, Duke of Berry*, New York (1974). Meiss, M. with Longnon, J. and Cazelles, R. *The Très Riches Heures of Jean, Duke of Berry*, New York (1969). Meiss, M. with Smith, S.O.D. and Beatson, E.H. *The Limburgs and their Contemporaries*, London (1974).

Lin Maya 1959–

The American sculptor and architect Maya Lin was born in Athens, Ohio. In 1981, while still an undergraduate student at Yale University, she gained immediate fame when she won the nationwide competition to design the Vietnam Veterans' Memorial in Washington, D.C. Her proposal consisted of a V-shaped, black granite wall inscribed with the names of all the Americans who died or went missing during the Vietnam War. The Minimalist nature of her design caused controversy among the American public. Upon visiting the finished work, however, many acknowledged its subtle power, as the nearly 58,000 inscribed names make the enormous loss of life a deeply moving reality.

Lin has created other memorials, notably the Civil Rights Memorial in Montgomery, Alabama (1989). She has also applied her Minimalist aesthetic to large-scale sculpture made of unexpected materials such as grass-covered mounds of earth and crushed glass.

Lipchitz Jacques 1891–1973

The French sculptor Jacques Lipchitz (originally Chaim Jacob) was born in Druskieniki in Lithuania. He settled in Paris in 1909 and lived there until emigrating to America in 1941. For the last ten years of his life he also lived in Italy.

Lipchitz was one of the major sculptors associated with Cubism. His response to Cubism in this early formative period was not unlike that of his friend Juan Gris: sober and with a tight-lipped discipline. Made in stone or bronze, Lipchitz's Cubist sculptures consisted of figures and still lifes composed from simple, rather static inclined planes and curves, enlivened by simple changes of texture (for example, *Man with Mandolin*, 1917; Yale University Art Gallery, New Haven). They reflect their origins in Cubist painting in their

Maya Lin: The Vietnam Veterans' Memorial; black granite; 1982. Washington, D.C.

Jacques Lipchitz: Mother and Child; bronze; 120×73×72cm (47×29×28in); 1940. Wilhelm-Lehmbruck-Museum, Duisberg

concern with shallow surface relationships and frequent use of the low-relief form.

He later recalled a period of crisis *c*1916 to 1918 when he had to struggle free from "ossification". Although a few later sculptures (like *Figure*, 1926–30; Museum of Modern Art, New York) echo the frontal solemnity of the Cubist pieces, most of his subsequent works are dramatically different in form and mood. They are more muscular than architectural, with a baroque sense of drama and scale and a full-blooded expressive romanticism.

In 1925 he invented some small maquettes which he called "Transparents" (for example, *Pierrot Escapes*, 1927; Kunsthaus, Zurich). A few inches high, they are pierced-form pieces made of thin sheets or ribbons, modeled in wax then cast in bronze. Whimsical in mood (pierrots, harlequins, acrobats) and increasingly open and curvilinear in form, they liberated his own thinking and anticipated the linear iron constructions of Picasso and González in the 1930s.

Their vitality and energetic arabesque quality was assimilated into the scale and mass of his early work, producing the characteristic, restless heavyweight rhythms of his mature style (seen in *Song of the Vowels*, 1932; private collection).

In the early 1950s he evolved another small-scale idiom: the "semi-automatic". Hand-size improvisations in warm wax were allowed to suggest a theme or configuration that was then consciously developed. These often inspired the monumental public sculptures that he had made from the 1940s onwards. Some of them are on an enormous scale.

He thought that the smaller works were the real power-house behind his own sculpture and considered modeling as his natural technique. It is the smaller pieces, fingered and squeezed by the hand, that best express that characteristic Lipchitz energy, vitality, and spontaneity; qualities that are sometimes diluted in the transfer to the massive public scale of his many commissions. The typical form of his mature work is Baroque and muscular, with a complex of heavyweight forms, curves, and hollows caught up in restless interaction—often streaming out laterally in a manner reminiscent of Daumier's figure groups.

He never became involved in modern art's inbred self-analysis and by the time of his death was firmly established as one of the century's major figure-sculptors.

Further reading. Hammacher, A.M. *Jacques Lipchitz, his Sculpture*, New York (1961). Lipchitz, J. and Arnason, H.H. *My Life in Sculpture*, New York (1972).

Lippi 15th and 16th centuries

Fra Filippo (*c*1406–69) and Filippino Lippi (*c*1457–1504) were Italian painters of the Florentine school, Filippino being the illegitimate son of Fra Filippo, a monk in holy orders. Filippo Lippi was placed as an orphan in the care of the monks of the Carmine, Florence, in 1421. He is first mentioned as a painter in 1431. Masaccio's presence in the Carmine during the 1420s, while he was decorating the Brancacci Chapel, meant that Filippo had closer contact with this artist than any other painter of his generation. Filippo's first

Fra Filippo Lippi: Virgin and Child; panel; 80×51cm (32×20in); 1440–5. National Gallery of Art, Washington, D.C.

Filippino Lippi: Tobias and the Angel; oil on panel; 33×23cm (13×9in); c1480. National Gallery of Art, Washington, D.C.

of St Bernard (Badia, Florence), we can easily trace the mystical and delicate quality of his father's late works. The style achieved great popularity in the patrician circles of Rome and Florence; and in 1498 Filippino signed important contracts to decorate the interiors of two private chapels—the Caraffa Chapel in S. Maria sopra Minerva, Rome (completed 1493) and the Strozzi Chapel in S. Maria Novella, Florence (completed 1502). Each has an elaborate decorative system, incorporating walls, ceiling, and altarpiece into one program, with many tricks to deceive the beholder. In these schemes and in the great *Adoration of the Magi* (1496; Uffizi, Florence), the influence of his father and of Botticelli, to whom his earlier work is so close, recedes. Filippino develops a more substantial portrayal of the human form, with close and brilliant attention to detail.

Lipton Seymour 1903–86

The American sculptor Seymour Arthur Lipton was born in New York. His original profession was dentistry. A self-taught artist, he turned seriously to sculpture in 1932 but continued to practice as a dentist for some years. His early works were Expressionist figurative wood carvings; but from 1945, when he began working sheet lead, his sculptures became more abstract. In the early 1950s he developed his mature style, working with bronze on sheet metal and Monel alloy, for which he invented a unique brazing process to texture his surfaces. His sculptures derive from natural imagery and the human figure, in which rounded skins of metal often enclose other forms. Lipton was a pioneer of direct-metal sculpture, and his many public commissions include *Archangel* (1964) for the Lincoln Center, New York.

Liss Johann c1590–1629

The German painter Johann Liss (or Lys) was a native of Oldenburg (Holstein), but was active in Venice for most of his short career. After an early visit to the Netherlands, where he was in contact with Jordaens, Liss moved to Italy, and established himself in Venice before 1624. Like his friend Domenico Feti, he did much to infuse new vigor into local tradition with his warm palette and animated brushwork. He first painted small-scale cabinet pictures, and later larger-scale altarpieces,

dated work, the *Tarquinia Madonna* of 1437 (Galleria Nazionale, Florence), reveals the additional influences of the sculpture of Donatello, and of the contemporary Flemish paintings that were then making their way to Italy. The Barbadori Altarpiece (Louvre, Paris), commissioned in 1437, shows a mastery of spatial construction; in the virtual elimination of framing divisions, it marks an important step in the development of the *sacra conversazione*.

Filippo's frescoes in the choir of Prato Cathedral (1452–65) show a new feature: a prettifying and sweetening of forms which was probably derived from a study of Fra Angelico's works. In Filippo's late works—particularly the group of panels representing the *Adoration of the Christ*

Child (Staatliche Museen, Berlin; Uffizi, Florence; etc) a new mystical interpretation of the subject matter is adopted. With this, any attempt at relating in depth the scales of the major figures to one another is abandoned. Filippo's last commission was for a series of frescoes in Spoleto Cathedral, on which he was involved at the time of his death in 1469. These were completed by his assistants, who probably included Filippino and Botticelli.

Filippino's earliest certain independent work does not occur until 1483. His first major commission came a year later, when he was asked to complete Masaccio's unfinished frescoes in the Brancacci Chapel, S. Maria del Carmine, Florence. In this work, and in paintings such as *The Vision*

developing towards the end of his life a style that anticipates the Rococo in its extreme freedom of handling, and its lightness and softness of color.

Lissitzky El 1890–1941

The Russian artist and architect El Lissitzky was born Eleazar Markovich Lissitsky in Polschlindk, Smolensk. He studied architecture at the Technische Hochschule, Darmstadt, Germany (1909–14) and engineering and architecture in Riga and Moscow (1914–15). He qualified as an engineer in Germany and as an architect in Moscow. Invited by Chagall, Director of the Vitebsk School of Art, he joined the School as Professor of Architecture and Graphic Arts (1919–21). He painted his first *Proun* painting in Vitebsk in 1919, after contact with the ideas of Malevich. In the several *Proun* paintings he combined Suprematist and Constructivist elements to link art and architecture (as in *Construction—Proun 2*, 1920; Philadelphia Museum of Art). By 1920 he used these elements in experimental typographical design, as in his *Story of Two Squares* (six drawings published in Holland in 1922). He moved to Moscow to become professor at the State Art School, Vkhutemas. During the 1920s he was extremely important in propagating new Russian art in Western Europe, through visits, writings, and organizing exhibitions. He collaborated with Jean Arp on *The Isms of Art* (published 1925) and created the ingeniously adaptable exhibiting rooms in the Landesmuseum, Hannover (1924; destroyed by the Nazis in 1936). His activities during the 1930s were limited by ill health.

Further reading. Barr, A.H. *Cubism and Abstract Art*, New York (1936). Gray, C. *The Great Experiment: Russian Art 1863–1922*, London (1962). Lissitzky, El. *Russia: an Architecture for World Revolution*, Vienna (1930). Lissitzky, El. and Arp, J. *Die Kunstismen*, Zurich (1925). Lissitzky-Küppers, S. *El Lissitzky: Life, Letters, Texts*, London (1968). Malevich, K. *The Non-Objective World*, Chicago (1959).

Lochner Stefan c1400–51

The German painter Stefan Lochner was probably born at Meersburg, south Baden. He was the most distinguished master of the Cologne school, and it is in Cologne that many of his surviving paintings can now be seen. A new naturalism in his style of painting anecdotal subjects, peopled with soft featured figures in glowing colors on a gold ground, implies that he served his apprenticeship in the Low Countries. The influence of the Master of Flémalle and of Jan van Eyck is very likely.

Lochner is first documented in Cologne in 1442; he later represented his guild as a City Councillor in 1447 and 1450. Most of his works are attributed to him merely by stylistic comparison, and only two are dated: *The Presentation in the Temple* (1447; Hessisches Landesmuseum, Darmstadt) and *The Adoration of the Child* of 1447, also at Darmstadt.

Lochner's earliest paintings, *St Jerome in his Cell* and the *Madonna in the Rose Bower* still betray the influence of earlier miniature painters such as the Limburg brothers, particularly in his treatment of space. However, already they hint at the greater animation of the figures and the keen observation of nature that Lochner developed in his later works. About 1440 he probably began the *Last Judgment*, a triptych altarpiece for the church of St Laurence, Cologne, the panels of which are

El Lissitzky: a reconstruction of the artist's "Abstract Room", an exhibition room of Abstract paintings originally arranged in Hanover in 1927; Niedersächsische Landesgalerie und Städtische Galerie, Hannover

Stefan Lochner: Madonna in the Rose Bower; panel; 51×40cm (20×16in); c1440. Wallraf-Richartz-Museum, Cologne

Lohse Richard 1902–88

The Swiss painter Richard Paul Lohse was born in Zurich. Although he was little known to the wider public, his view of geometric abstraction as a progressive attempt to systematize the elements of art had a decisive influence on artists working in this field. His paintings after 1943 were based on a horizontal-vertical grid, the proportions of which were determined mathematically, diagonal rhythms being introduced by predetermined progressions of color. Unlike many earlier geometric abstractionist painters, he did not wish to enter the field of applied art; the paintings were justified as the manifestation of an internal law.

Lombardo family
15th and 16th centuries

Born and trained in Lombardy, Pietro Lombardo (c1435–1515) was a sculptor and architect who moved to Venice in the

Pietro Lombardo: an angel in the vaulting of S. Giobbe, Venice; marble; c1475

now separate and dispersed (center panel, Wallraf-Richartz-Museum, Cologne; inner wings, Städelsches Kunstinstitut, Frankfurt am Main; outer wings; Alte Pinakothek, Munich). The central inner panel has all the drama of Bruegel or Bosch as the myriad little naked resurrected figures are led by angels to the Gate of Heaven or by demons to the Gate of Hell. Above them, the larger figure of Christ presides with the intercessors, John the Baptist and the Virgin Mary. The side wings depict the martyrdom of saints in 12 separate scenes, while their outer sides are painted with six saintly figures and two kneeling donors.

Another triptych, the *Patron Saints of Cologne* (painted before 1447), now in Cologne Cathedral, is Lochner's masterpiece. The outside of the wings shows the Annunciation in a domestic interior set against a richly brocaded curtain, reminiscent of van Eyck. The inside of all three

panels portrays figures offering homage to the Christ Child, seated on the Virgin's knee. The Magi occupy the center panel, to the left is St Ursula and her escort of Virgins, and to the right St Gereon with his men-at-arms. These two are the patron saints of the city. The figures are composed into a solemn semicircle around Christ, those at the back in darker shades to highlight the main characters. They are an elegant group, with faces full of individuality. The soft forms of their features contrast with the brilliant detailing of their clothes and the ground on which they stand.

The Cologne triptych is closely related to the Darmstadt *Adoration* in style, indicating that it was a product of Lochner's maturity. Albrecht Dürer wrote how it cost him two silver pennies to have the painting shown to him in the cathedral; he regarded it as the city's most important panel picture.

mid 1460s and was responsible for introducing a Renaissance style into the city. A series of wall tombs of Doges establishes the new architectural forms, which also appear in the frames of paintings by Giovanni Bellini and the Vivarini, creating, for the first time, a Renaissance context for their work. Working on a large scale Pietro, with his contemporary Codussi, gave a Renaissance reformulation to the traditional Venetian palace facade, and built the marble-encrusted church of S. Maria dei Miracoli (1481–9): the most perfect example of coloristic, neo-Byzantine, Venetian Renaissance architecture.

His sons developed their father's work as a monumental sculptor (for example the Vendramin Monument, SS. Giovanni e Paolo, Venice) in a more Classical direction, imitating the Antique. Tullio (c1460–1532) was a major sculptor in this "Neoclassical" mode, and the humanist cast of his work can be seen in his now scattered reliefs of antique subjects executed for Alfonso d'Este c1508 (Hermitage Museum, St Petersburg).

Long Richard 1945–

The English artist Richard Long was born in Bristol. He studied at Bristol School of Art (1962–4) and St Martin's School of Art, London, from 1966 to 1968, the year of his first solo exhibition in Düsseldorf. He represented Britain in the 1976 Venice Biennale. The foremost British "land artist" from 1968 onwards, Long has made art works during, or in response to, walks through the countryside in Britain and throughout the world. The pieces can take the form of captioned photographs, sometimes combined with maps, or else sculptures made in the country or on the gallery floor from natural materials—for instance stones or wood, arranged in simple forms such as circles, lines and spirals (for example, *119 Stones*, 1976; Tate Gallery, London).

Further reading. Seymour, A. *Richard Long: Walking in Circles*, London (1991).

Longhena Baldassare 1598–1682

Baldassare Longhena was the only architect of the Venetian Baroque to create a

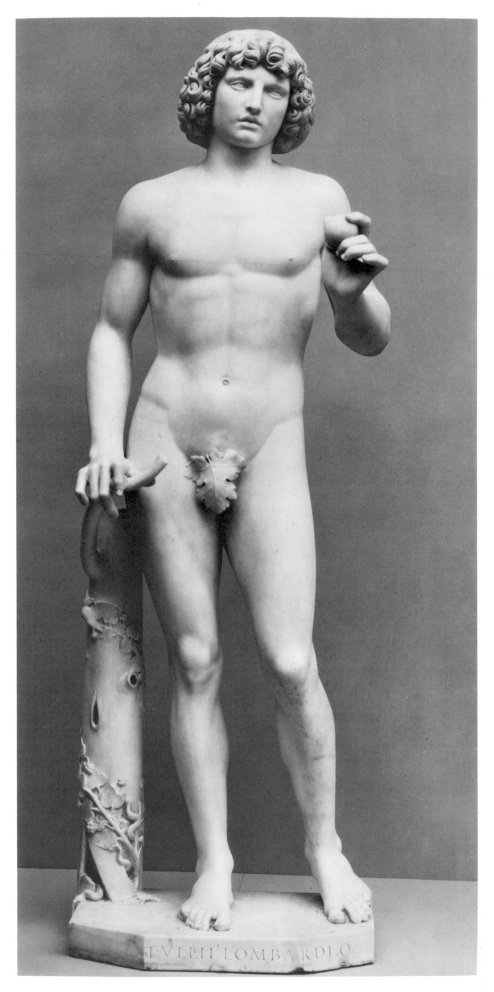

Tullio Lombardo: Adam from the Vendramin Monument, SS. Giovanni e Paolo, Venice; marble; height 193cm (76in); c1493. Metropolitan Museum, New York

style comparable in quality to the great Baroque architecture of Rome. Trained by the neo-Palladian Vincenzo Scamozzi, he quickly moved to a style more or less antithetical to that of his master; but the influence of Sansovino and of Palladio himself is ever present in his buildings, and it was to this specifically Venetian tradition that he gave Baroque expression.

Thus the sumptuous plastic richness of his palace facades on the Grand Canal (Ca' Pesaro and Ca' Rezzonico, both begun in the 1630s) comes from a magnificent marriage between the rather flat, three-tiered facade of Sansovino's already monumental Palazzo Corner Ca' Grande and the same architect's deeply cut, sculpturally enriched Library. From the Library, Longhena learned the importance of light as a means of giving substance and warmth to architecture. By means of ever richer variations of texture (including colossal rustication) and a vigorous profusion of forcefully carved sculptural detail, he intensified the chiaroscuro effects of Sansovino's building. Interacting with the changing light and the reflections from the Canal, his facades thus became full of movement and drama.

Longhena's main monument is the church of S. Maria della Salute (begun 1631), which was commissioned by the State as an ex voto offering for deliverance from the plague. The church is now so essential a feature of Venice that it is almost impossible to imagine the entrance to the Grand Canal without it; Longhena's domed octagonal structure perfectly fits its triangular site, spreading outwards by means of a patterned pavement to the very steps of the canal.

The plan of the church has been brilliantly analyzed as a fusion between the centralized, geometric plans of the Renaissance and the progressive scenographic space of the Baroque. Longhena's design owes something both to the Baroque theater and to Palladio's Redentore.

Theatrical too is the use of sculpture. Giant figures of Apostles placed above the columns enliven the space of the central octagon. On the exterior the volutes, which make the dynamic transition between the octagon and the dome, are topped by statues who ride above them as on the crest of a wave and seem about to bowl outwards into space.

The greater exuberance of Longhena's architecture as a whole shows the increasing tendency towards display in both public and private patronage in Venice from 1600: a grandiloquence that is perhaps a symptom of a city in decline.

Longhi Pietro 1702–85

The Italian painter Pietro Longhi was born Pietro Falca, the son of the silversmith Alessandro Falca, in Venice. He was apprenticed to Antonio Balestra (1666–1740). He visited Bologna in 1719; there he studied under Giuseppe Maria Crespi, who exerted a great influence upon him as a genre painter. It is possible that he also came into contact there with the genre painter, Gamberini. Longhi's early genre paintings reflect Crespi's manner in color range and in subject matter.

Before 1730 Longhi was back in Venice where he became successful as a painter of small-scale canvases showing everyday Venetian life. Human activities, such as the taking of afternoon tea, a visit to nearby friends, or a game of blind man's buff, were recorded with laconic fidelity. His attention was drawn equally to the daily lives of both the aristocracy and the peasantry; he depicted the whole social hierarchy of Venice and recorded his subjects dispassionately, without condemnation or comment, recording life as a photographer might today, highlighting the spontaneity of ordinary events.

Only rarely did Longhi paint major religious compositions for churches. His art received official recognition nonetheless, and he was a founding-member of the Accademia; in 1763 he was made Director of the Academy in the Palazzo Pisani. Longhi's genre paintings may be compared with those by Hogarth in England and by Lancret and de Troy in France; Longhi would have known these works through prints. A large number of paintings by Longhi still survive in Venice: important groups are to be found in the Museo Correr, the Galleria Querini Stampalia, and in the Gallerie dell'Accademia.

Loos Adolf 1870–1933

The Austrian architect and polemicist Adolf Loos was born at Brno, Moravia. An early visit to the U.S.A. made a lasting impression upon him. He worked mainly in Vienna, where he became Chief Architect of the Housing Estates Movement (1920–2), but also in Paris (1923–8) and Prague.

Loos was an ally of the moralist and critic

Pietro Longhi: A Lute-Player; chalk and pencil on paper; 1752. Museo Correr, Venice

Karl Kraus and a friend of other revolutionary artists and intellectuals—the painter Oskar Kokoschka, the composer Arnold Schoenberg, and the philosopher Ludwig Wittgenstein. He also wrote on a variety of social and cultural topics, but is remembered for his crusade against decoration in such essays as "The Poor Rich Man" (1900) and the notorious "Ornament and Crime" (1908). He attacked the Vienna Secession, the Wiener Werkstätte (run by Josef Hoffmann), and later the Bauhaus, for their concept of total design. He believed in the unselfconscious, anonymous products of the ordinary craftsman, as opposed to the artist-craftsman—a theme that Le Corbusier later adopted. As an architect, his most important building for the modern movement and its apologists was the deliberately plain-looking and cuboid Steiner house (Vienna, 1910).

Loos' particular type of multilevel open planning, which can be experienced in his houses of the 1920s (for example the Moller house, Vienna, 1928), was arguably his most significant contribution to modern architecture. But this aspect has been overlooked in favor of an image of him as a pioneer father of the International style—a label he would have despised. He was a classicist, and he had a passion for using luxury materials like marble in his buildings. Building without ornament was a doctrine which, Loos wrote in 1924, "the purists have pushed to absurdity".

Lorenzetti brothers
13th and 14th centuries

The Lorenzetti brothers Pietro (*c*1280–1348) and Ambrogio (*c*1290–1348) were Italian painters of the Sienese School. With Simone Martini, the Lorenzetti brought Sienese painting to its finest flowering and European renown. While Pietro's earliest works show Ducciesque influence, Ambrogio's *Madonna of S. Angelo* of 1319 (in Vico l'Abate, near Florence) reveals an independence of both Duccio and Pietro. Pietro's early activity took him to Assisi (Passion Cycle, lower church of S. Francesco) and to Arezzo (polyptych, 1320; church of S. Maria della Pieve). Ambrogio is twice documented as being in Florence (1321 and 1327).

The brothers' respective experiences undoubtedly formed their artistic personalities. Their periods of collaboration, first in the mid 1320s (when they produced frescoes in the church of S. Francesco, Siena; now mainly lost) and then in 1335 (to paint frescoes in the Spedale di S. Maria della Scala, Siena; now destroyed) account for the influence of one upon the other. Late in their careers they may have had a joint workshop.

Pietro's development increasingly emphasized the realization of volumes in space. Throughout his work there is a continuing exploration of the psychological states of his figures which was the special mark of his genius. He had a fine feeling for discursive narrative (seen in the Assisi frescoes and his predella, the Carmelite Altarpiece, 1329; Pinacoteca Nazionale, Siena). He shared with his brother an interest in problems of pictorial space (*Birth of the Virgin*, 1342; Museo dell'Opera del Duomo, Siena).

Ambrogio, by temperament calmer and more speculative, produced a body of work remarkable for its variety of innovations. His *Maestà*, painted for the cathedral of Massa Marittima (*c*1330) is the first work of his mature style; spatially and iconographically it elaborates Duccio's prototype (1308–11; Museo dell'Opera del Duomo, Siena). His *Scenes from the life of Saint Nicholas of Bari* (*c*1332; Uffizi, Florence) display great sensitivity for setting narrative within convincing spaces. *The Presentation in the Temple* (1342; Uffizi,

Pietro Lorenzetti: Deposition from the Cross; fresco; c1329. Lower church of S. Francesco, Assisi

Pietro Lorenzetti: The Last Supper; fresco; c1329. Lower church of S. Francesco, Assisi

Florence) and the *Annunciation* (1344; Pinacoteca Nazionale, Siena) combine monumentality and perspectival experiment. For its developments in composition, the evocation of space, and its realization of landscape, his political *Allegory of Good and Bad Government* (fresco, 1338–9; Palazzo Pubblico, Siena) is his best known work and certainly his masterpiece.

Further reading. Starn, R. *Ambrogio Lorenzetti: the Palazzo Pubblico, Siena*, New York (1994).

Lorenzo di Credi 1459?–1536

The Florentine painter Lorenzo di Credi trained under Verrocchio whose workshop, the most important in its day, also included the young Leonardo da Vinci. About 1485 Credi completed to Verrocchio's design an altarpiece for Pistoia Cathedral; in 1486 he took charge of his master's workshop, inheriting it on Verrocchio's death in 1498. For the period from 1491 until he entered a hospice in 1531, documents give a good picture of the activities of an unexceptional but professionally respected painter of his time. He restored paintings, sat on committees supervising and valuing the work of other artists, and arbitrated in disputes between them and their patrons. He died in 1536.

Many paintings are ascribed to him but few are documented. Essentially a workshop painter producing for the market, his paintings tend to be repetitions of particular types. Thus there are Madonnas for private devotion of which the London (National Gallery) version is typical, *tondi* showing the Virgin adoring the Child (Metropolitan Museum, New York), paintings of single saints, and a number of *sacra conversazione* altarpieces. Several portraits have been attributed to him, including a self-portrait (1488; National Gallery of Art, Washington, D.C.), and many drawings, including preparatory studies of heads of youths and old men (for example in the Louvre, Paris).

Credi's style changed little during his lifetime. Formed while a pupil of Verrocchio, and deeply influenced by the early work of Leonardo, it was largely unaffected by the advances of Leonardo, Raphael, and Sarto in the early 16th century. His compositions and figure-poses are monotonously conventional. However, the paintings are technically competent, their colors pleasantly bright, and their

Lorenzo di Credi: Self-portrait; panel; transferred to canvas; 46×32cm (18×13in); 1488. National Gallery of Art, Washington, D.C.

linear qualities typically Florentine. His figures can lack characterization, a shortcoming compensated for by the clarity of perception and delicate beauty of his drawings. Credi had a large number of pupils, none of whom became artists of significance.

Lorenzo Monaco c1370–1425

The Italian artist Lorenzo Monaco was born Piero di Giovanni. Although he had been born in Siena, he was considered a Florentine painter and miniaturist in his mature period. In 1391 he took vows in the Camaldolese monsastery of S. Maria degli Angeli, Florence. We have no certain information about his training but his first

works display a fusion of Sienese and Florentine elements, the latter deriving from the tradition of the Cioni and Gaddi. There is also a striving to assimilate Giottesque ideals of composition and figure-painting as interpreted by the late Trecento (for example, *Agony in the Garden*; Galleria dell' Accademia, Florence).

After 1400 both the plasticity of his figures and the gracefulness of his compositions increase, in a fashion that suggests renewed contacts with Sienese art and the possibility that he had learned about the late Gothic International style from Ghiberti. His works begin to show a greater sense of linear design and calligraphic beauty (seen in his *Annunciation*,

Galleria dell'Accademia, Florence). His *Coronation of the Virgin* (1413; Uffizi, Florence) seems to mark a return to aspects of his early work as forms take on increased volume and density. Late works such as the S. Trinità *Annunciation* (1422–4; Bartolini Chapel, S. Trinità, Florence) embody a more realistic description of figures and space.

Lorenzo's genius lay in his personal vision of a world in which natural and supernatural were convincingly united by calligraphic means, a world at once lyrical, exotic, and strangely compelling (seen in his *Adoration of the Magi*, c1410; Uffizi, Florence). Although he produced many impressive large works, it is perhaps in the small panels of his *predellae* and in his miniatures that his poetic imagination found its most vivid expression. Florence's chief exponent of the International Gothic style, he had many assistants and immediate followers; but his style was not to have long-term influence. The new preoccupations of the early Quattrocento led in other directions.

Lotto Lorenzo c1480–1556

The painter Lorenzo Lotto was born in Venice and presumably had his artistic training there. Bernard Berenson has plausibly suggested Alvise Vivarini (c1446–1503/5) as his primary master, but he was influenced, like all his generation in Venice, by Giovanni Bellini. He was also influenced by Jacopo dei Barbari and by contemporary German work. He was little employed in Venice itself, and the main fields of his activity were Bergamo and the district of Treviso, and such cities of the Marches as Jesi, Recanati, and Ancona. he is recorded as working in Rome in 1509. In 1554 he entered the Holy House at Loreto as an oblate.

Lotto was, after Giorgione, the most sensitive painter of his generation in Venice. Time and again we find passages in his work where the brushwork and the handling of light and color are a sheer delight. Yet in many of his larger paintings and in the impression given by his work as a whole he disappoints; in spite of the advocacy of devoted admirers, he retains the status of a minor master.

The *Madonna and Child with St Peter Martyr* (1503; Museo e Gallerie Nazionali di Capodimonte, Naples) is composed of Bellinesque elements but shows individual sensibility, especially in the landscape. The

Lorenzo Lotto: Portrait of a Gentleman in a Black Silk Cape; oil on canvas; 94×82cm (37×32in); 1546. New Orleans Museum of Art

Bishop Bernardo de' Rossi (1505; Museo e Gallerie Nazionali di Capodimonte, Naples) reveals at once, in its vivid characterization, Lotto's outstanding qualities as a portrait-painter. The enchanting cover of this work, the *Allegory* and the related *Maiden's Dream* (both 1505; National Gallery of Art, Washington, D.C.) have a magic akin to—though quite distinct from—that of Giorgione's almost contemporary *Tempestà* (Gallerie dell'Accademia, Venice). German influence is clearly to be seen in the *Bernardo de' Rossi* and also in the wooded landscape of the little *St Jerome* (1506; Louvre, Paris). The *Virgin Enthroned with Four Saints* (1506; S. Cristina al Tiverone, Treviso) is a dazzling variation on the theme of Giovanni Bellini's *Madonna Enthroned with Four Saints* (1505; S. Zaccaria, Venice). This period, in which Lotto experiments with the Venetian heritage of the Quattrocento, ends with the splendid polyptych of the *Madonna and Saints* (1508; Pinacoteca Civica, Recanati).

Lotto's visit to Rome in 1509 seems to have thrown him off balance, and the *Deposition* (1512; Museo e Pinacoteca Communali, Jesi, Ancona) is a turgid exercise in the Raphaelesque. Back in north Italy in the middle of the decade, he combines Raphaelesque elements with the Bellinesque tradition in the *Madonna Enthroned with Saints* (1516; S. Bartolomeo, Bergamo), achieving a style close to the contemporary work of Correggio.

The *Christ Taking Leave of His Mother* (1531; Staatliche Museen, Berlin) has a marvelous setting—a dark basilica giving on to a brightly lit garden—painted with a deftness that looks forward to Guardi (18th century). This technical bravura finds its fullest development in the main panel and the *predella* of the St Lucy Altarpiece (1532; Museo e Pinacoteca Communali, Jesi, Ancona), and is still to be seen in his last work, *The Presentation in the Temple* (c1555; Palazzo Apostolico, Loreto). Throughout his career he continued to paint fine portraits.

Morris Louis: Vav; acrylic on canvas; 262×359cm (103×142in); 1960. Tate Gallery, London

Louis Morris 1912–62

The American painter Morris Louis was born Morris Louis Bernst, in Baltimore. After studying at the Maryland Institute of Fine Arts he spent four years in New York (1936–40). He returned in 1940 to Balti-more, exhibiting there regularly until he moved to Washington, D.C. in 1952. In 1953, Louis became friendly with Clement Greenberg, who was to encourage and support his work. Although Louis was to exhibit throughout the 1950s, he was often discouraged by the reception of his pictures and destroyed many canvases.

His mature style, expressed in large-scale works, is Abstract in character and often lyrical in feeling. In the series of "Veil" paintings the color is almost floated on to the canvas in wedges and splashes, creating an effect sometimes reminiscent of silk-screen printing or even of watercolor (seen in *Point of Tranquility*, 1958; Joseph Hirshhorn Museum, Washington, D.C.). In the final phase of his career the colors are separated and applied either in rough parallel groupings across the corners of white canvases, or in vertical stripes and bands straight down the canvas, which is otherwise left plain.

Loutherbourg Philip de
1740–1812

The place of Philip James de Louther-bourg's paintings in the history of English landscape painting is between the classi-cism of Richard Wilson and the naturalism of Turner and Constable. A native of Alsace, he studied under the battle painter Francesco Casanova, and in 1767 was made a member of the French Academy. He was living in London by 1771, and worked as David Garrick's stage and scenery designer until 1785. Although the detailing in his landscapes is derived from Philips Wouwermans (1619–68), Nicolaes Berchem (1620–83), and the Dutch school, his somewhat contrived composi-tions reflect an over-exaggeration of the classical tradition in landscape painting.

Lowry L.S. 1887–1976

The British painter Laurence Stephen

Philip de Loutherbourg: Coalbrookdale by Night; oil on canvas; 68×107cm (27×42in); 1801. Science Museum, London

L.S. Lowry: Flowers in the Window; oil on canvas; 50×60cm (20×24in); 1956. Private collection

Lowry was born in Manchester. He studied painting and drawing at the Manchester Municipal Art College between 1905 and 1915 and also studied at Salford School of Art. It was not until c1916 that he developed an interest in the artistic possibilities of the bleak Northern industrial landscape, which he depicted in a "naive" style outside the general trends of his time. From 1909 until 1948 he lived and worked at Pendlebury; he was hardly known until his first one-man show in London in 1939.

This lateness of recognition rankled long after he had achieved fame and fortune. By the end of his life, Lowry was widely recognized as one of the leading British painters. At his best he went far deeper than the "naive" tone of his work initially suggests (for example, *An Accident*, 1926; City of Manchester Art Gallery). There is a satiric edge to his imagination, an ambiguous fondness for the grotesque, a darkness at the center of his vision (for example, *In a Park*, 1963; Whitworth Art Gallery, University of Manchester).

Further reading. Levy, M. *The Paintings of L.S. Lowry*, London (1975). Mullins, E.

L.S. Lowry, R.A., London (1966). Rothenstein, J. *Modern English Painters* vol. 2, London (1956). Spalding, J. *Lowry*, Oxford (1979).

Lucas van Leyden 1494–1533

The Flemish painter Lucas Hugensz. van Leyden trained under both his father Hugo Jacobsz. and the Leiden artist Cornelis Engelbrechtsz. He remained a member of the guild of painters at Leiden after also registering as a painter at Antwerp in 1522. Unlike many Netherlandish artists of the early 16th century, Lucas never became tied to the conventions of court art; he was one of the most original artists of his age in Northern Europe, despite the hardship of persistent ill-health throughout his life.

His earliest religious paintings, such as the *Adoration of the Kings* altarpiece (c1500–10; Barnes Foundation, Merion, Pa.) are close in style to late-15th-century Flemish works, and especially to the paintings of Geertgen tot Sint Jans. In later, more ambitious works such as *The Healing of the Blind Man of Jericho* (1531; Hermitage Museum, Leningrad), the hor-

izon line is lowered, the figures are more monumental, and the landscape is more spatially convincing, with subtle use of light and shade between the trees. Even where he retains the traditional triptych form, as in the *Last Judgment* of 1526–7 (Stedelijk Museum "De Lakenhal", Leiden), the continuous landscape across the three panels and the bell-shaped top lend the work a fluency of narrative and a spaciousness new to Flemish art.

He is also important for the development of Flemish genre painting. His scenes with half-length figures, such as the *Card Players* (c1514; Wilton House Collection, near Salisbury, Wilts.) are not only new in Flemish art by their size and relation of figures to picture-field, they also take a significant step toward the true genre picture, free of all moral connotations. Such works as these lack only the vital humorous ingredient to prefigure the finest 17th-century Dutch genre painting.

Lucas van Leyden's graphic works were much admired in his lifetime, especially in Italy, where Vasari judged his achievement as equal to Albrecht Dürer's in technique and composition. Certainly his prints had a profound impact on Florentine artists of the generation after the High Renaissance. He is said to have issued his first engravings at the age of nine, but the first securely dated work is the *Mahomet and the Monk Sergius* of 1508. This exemplifies the qualities that Vasari praised, for the skillful fading of distance and softening of tone are

Bernardino Luini: Virgin and Child; oil on panel; 74×53cm (29×21in). Wallace Collection, London

Lucas van Leyden: Card Players; oil on wood; 36×46cm (14×18in); c1514. Wilton House Collection, near Salisbury, Wiltshire

painterly in treatment. The *Ecce Homo* of 1510 is innovatory in its composition. The figure of Christ, hitherto in Northern art placed at the left of the scene in front of the crowd, is here moved to a place right of center and in the background, amid a vast scenario of buildings and landscape. Its format was to influence Rembrandt in his etching of this subject in the following century.

Luini Bernardino 1480/5–1532

The Milanese painter Bernardino Luini was a follower of Leonardo da Vinci. His earliest known works date from c1512 (for example, his *Annunciation*, c1512; Pinacoteca di Brera, Milan), by which time his style was already strongly Leonardesque, although this may have been preceded by an earlier phase influenced by Bramantino. Luini's understanding of Leonardo was to remain superficial. He tended to borrow external mannerisms, such as the famous enigmatic smile, rather than anything essential; but his ability to simplify and popularize Leonardo's style, without unpleasantly distorting it, won him great local success. His talents were much in demand both as a large-scale decorator and as a painter of small devotional panels.

Luks George 1867–1933

The American painter George Benjamin Luks was the most flamboyant and garrulous but technically unsound member of the New York group of The Eight of 1908, the nucleus of the Ash Can School. His style reflected the dark tones and slashing brush stroke that was popular in Munich, Paris, and America at the end of the 19th century. Luks' interest in realism, and his speed of execution, were the products of his work as a graphic journalist on *The Philadelphia Bulletin*, *The Philadelphia Press*, and the New York *World*. He was a member of the group of journalists seeking to become realist painters who gathered around Robert Henri in Philadelphia and later in New York. He was at his best with genre scenes and portraits of slum life in New York, such as *The Spielers* (oil on canvas; 1905; Addison Gallery of American Art, Andover, Mass.) and *The Wrestlers* (oil on canvas; 1905; Museum of Fine Arts, Boston).

Lurçat Jean 1892–1966

The French painter and tapestry designer Jean Lurçat studied painting under V. Prouvé in Nancy until 1912. He then went to Paris, becoming a pupil of B. Naudin at the Académie Colarossi. He belonged to the Paris circle of the poets Vildrac and Elie Faure, and knew artists such as Marcoussis and Picasso. He was in the French armed forces (1914–17), traveled in Spain (1923), North Africa, the Sahara, Greece, and the Near East (1924–9). He settled in Switzerland in 1931, traveling widely from 1936. He lived in Paris from 1955 until his death.

Lurçat is best known for tapestry designs which were first realized in 1939. With Marcel Gromaire, Henri Matisse, Marc Saint-Saens, and others, he revitalized the tapestry workshops at Aubusson. His own work had a brief association with Surrealism, but he found major inspiration from the designs of 14th-century French tapestries as well as Pre-Columbian textiles (seen in *Le Corton*, tapestry; 1947; Peter Stuyvesant Foundation, London).

Lutyens Edwin 1869–1944

The English architect Edwin Landseer Lutyens was born in London. After working briefly with George & Peto he set up his own architectural practice in 1889. He soon established a reputation for distinguished country houses, many of which had gardens laid out by Gertrude Jekyll (for example, Munstead Wood, Surrey, 1896; The Orchards, Godalming, 1899; Deanery Gardens, Sonning, Berkshire, 1901). These houses combined a display of craftsmanship and vernacular materials (such as brick, tile, and woodwork) with a Voysey-like massing of the parts.

Gradually Lutyens moved from this Arts and Crafts manner to a more formal and symmetrical style, adopting details that were Queen Anne (as at Great Maytham, Kent, 1910) or Palladian (as at Heathcote, Ilkley, 1906) in origin. This formality can also be seen in his axial plan for the centerpiece of Hampstead Garden Suburb (1908–10), which included two powerfully composed churches and a neo-Georgian Institute. In his designs for the enormous Viceroy's House at New Delhi (1913 onwards) he created a genuinely imposing effect by his highly competent handling of a fully classical vocabulary, with ranges of columns and a central dome.

The confidence Lutyens derived from his New Delhi work inspired him to undertake a number of monumental schemes: in central London alone these include the Cenotaph (1919), the Midland Bank headquarters (1924), the Britannic House, Finsbury Circus (1924-7). But in many ways his smaller commercial buildings, like the Midland Bank's Piccadilly branch in the style of Wren (1922), are more fitting monuments to Lutyens' skills, to be set beside the achievement of his more famous country houses.

Lydos *fl. c560-540 BC*

Lydos was an Athenian-trained painter of uncertain birthplace. He signed two vases "painted by the Lydian", so was therefore either an immigrant from the East or born in Greece of Lydian parentage. Whatever his origins, he learned his trade in Athens, and took his place in the dazzling generation of black-figure masters headed by Exekias and the Amasis Painter.

Lydos began his career at an awkward moment in the history of 6th-century painting. He and his contemporaries had not yet abandoned their infatuation with the conventional figures and lumbering animal friezes they had learned from their competitors in Corinth. On the other hand, the quest for narrative painting had already been initiated by Sophilos; Kleitias had proclaimed its manifesto on his François Vase, and by the 550s it was the prime concern of almost every painter.

A neck-*amphora* in Florence belonging to Lydos' early days illustrates the confrontation of these two conflicting traditions. The main scene is devoted to *The Judgment of Paris* and on the reverse, to a symposium. Above and below are animal friezes in the time-worn Corinthian style. The figures are painted in a bold, broad style quite unlike the diminutive tribe of Kleitias, and incised with a clean and steady hand unknown to Sophilos.

A signed work belonging to Lydos' prime is the fragmentary *dinos* from the Acropolis, Athens. The upper frieze is dedicated to the *Battle of Gods and Giants*, set in an intricate composition of fierce, overlapping figures. Helmets, thigh-armor, and sword-handles are incised with great care and there are some exceptionally fine shield-devices: a Gorgon head, a great winged bee, and a hairy satyr face in profile relief. In the middle zone, a cow, a sow, and a sheep are led to sacrifice by two robust men with trim red beards and hair. One of them wears a kilt with a case of knives slung over his shoulder and must be the slaughterer. The large somber animals are painted in clean-edged strokes and

incised with patterns to suggest the contrasting textures of sheepskin, pigskin, and cowhide. The rendering of these doomed beasts is exceptional and of a rare sensitivity that anticipates the procession of sacrificial animals along the north and south friezes of the Parthenon. The lower zone contains a frieze of unexpectedly sturdy animals.

Another mature work is his column-*krater* in New York, which is almost as large as the François Vase. But whereas Kleitias had relied upon six narrow friezes (depicting no less than eight mythological subjects and one animal brigade) to cover the *krater* and its foot, Lydos needed only one frieze and this was dedicated exclusively to a monumental rendition of *The Return of Hephaistos*. It is a riotous procession of loose bouncy satyrs and their companions, the maenads. The satyrs are corporeal creatures with knees sagging beneath their body-weight as they plod along. There are incidents of bottom-slapping, tail-pulling, and shoving; one large-headed satyr steals a drink from his friend's wine-skin. On the reverse comes Hephaistos—the *raison d'être* of the procession—riding on his mule and holding a drinking horn, the source of his undoing.

The New York *krater* gives eloquent testimony to the importance of Lydos as a master of large-scale narrative painting. The mouth of the *krater*, however, is decorated in a fine miniaturist style with tidy florals on the side, animals on the top, and a gorgoneion on each handle-plate. It should serve as a reminder of the numerous small vases that have also been attributed to his hand.

Lysippos *4th century BC*

Lysippos was a Greek late Classical and early Hellenistic sculptor from Sicyon who specialized in bronze. His impact on Greek sculpture was comparable to that of Pheidias. He marked the transition from the Classical to the Hellenistic, as his style gradually developed in the direction of greater naturalism.

He was said to acknowledge no masters but Nature and the *Doryphoros* of Polycleitos, whose stance and proportions he altered drastically by adapting the innovations of his predecessors. The heads of his figures he made small and the bodies long and slim so that they looked taller than they were; in this way, the optical distortions of figures placed at an elevation were

reduced. Lysippos also converted the carefully balanced Classical pose to a restless momentary impression, truer to nature.

The sculptor's most famous work (known through Roman copies, now in the Vatican Museums) seems to have been a rather late work, the nude *Apoxyomenos* (*Youth Scraping Oil off his Body with a Strigil*; there is a copy in reverse in the Terme Museum, Rome). The youth stands tense in the process of shifting his weight from one foot to the other; one arm is brought across the body to be scraped by the other hand. This revolutionary protrusion of the arms breaks the frontal plane of the statue and invites the spectator to walk around it, thus realizing its third dimension. The *Apoxyomenos* was later taken to Rome.

Lysippos lived long and was reputed to have produced 1,500 statues. His large repertory looks forward to Hellenistic taste. Besides the traditional gods, heroes, and athletes, he created *colossi*, large groups, animal allegories, chariots, and portraits. His works stood all over the Greek world from southern Italy to Asia Minor. The School of Sicyon flourished until late in the Hellenistic period, developing his innovations.

A new process of making portraits from life masks and another of making copies from casts taken from statues were ascribed to Lysistratos, brother of Lysippos. The continuous spiral torsion of the figure in movement seems to have developed among that group of artists: one of the earliest specimens, a *Dancing Girl* known from fragmentary copies, may derive from Lysippos' *Drunken Flute Player*.

Lysippos was favored by the royal house of Macedon. He produced portraits of Alexander as a boy and as King which combined the fierceness and sensitivity of the subject. He also made a bronze group of Alexander among the 25 of his nobles who fell at Granicus, all on horseback; a portrait of Seleucus; and, in collaboration with Leochares, a bronze group of *Alexander and Craterus Hunting*, dedicated at Delphi by Craterus' son after his death in 321.

Closest to Lysippos' early style comes the marble statue of the athlete *Agias*, part of the Daochus family dedication at Delphi (337-332 BC; Delphi Museum). This seems to be a contemporary copy of his bronze *Agias* in Thessaly. The relief base of his statue of the athlete Pulydamas survives in the Museum at Olympia.

M

Macdonald-Wright Stanton
1890–1973

The American painter Stanton Mac-Donald-Wright was born in Charlottes-ville, Va. He studied at the Los Angeles Art Students' League (1905–6). From 1907 to 1913 he lived in Paris, at first studying color theory with the Canadian painter Percyval Tudor-Hart (1873–1954). He then developed the principles of Synchromism with Morgan Russell. The Synchromist paintings they exhibited together were Abstract and based on the juxtaposition of shapes whose colors came from different parts of the spectrum. After his return to California in 1919 he lost interest in Synchromism; he taught painting until the early 1950s, then took up Abstract painting again, continuing until his death in 1973.

Stanton Macdonald-Wright: Synchromy in Purple; oil on canvas; 91×71cm (36×28in); 1917. Los Angeles County Museum of Art, Los Angeles

Machuca Pedro *fl.* 1520–50

Pedro Machuca was a Spanish painter, architect, and sculptor, born at Toledo. With Alonso Berruguete (1486–1561), Machuca shared the distinctions of being the greatest Spanish representative of Renaissance artistic versatility and contributing to the birth of Florentine Mannerism in painting (with, for example, *Virgin of Suffrage*, 1517; Prado, Madrid).

After studying under Michelangelo, he returned to Spain in 1520 and designed the Palace of Charles V in the Alhambra, Granada: basically a square block with a raised circular courtyard within. Begun in 1527 in an Italianate style recalling Bramante, it was slightly influenced by contemporary Plateresque details. Machuca also contributed stone reliefs in a purely classical style. He died in 1550.

Mack Heinz 1931–

The optical-kinetic artist Otto Heinz Mack was born in Loller, Germany. Between

Pedro Machuca: the Palace of Charles V in the Alhambra, Granada; begun in 1527

C.R. Mackintosh: Preliminary Design for Mural Decoration of the First Floor Room of Miss Cranston's Buchanan Street Tearooms; pencil and watercolor on tracing paper; 36×75cm (14×29in); 1896/7. Mackintosh Collection, Glasgow University

1950 and 1953 he studied at the Academy of Art in Düsseldorf, and in 1956 at the University of Cologne. With Otto Piene he founded the "Zero" group in 1957. In 1960 he began an important series of rotating reliefs and "light dynamos".

Mack's constructions are concerned primarily with movement, light, and dissolution of form. They involve the use of reflecting surfaces (mirror, glass, aluminum), beams of light, and motors, and thus affect the entire environment in which they are placed. Institutions that own his work include the Museum of Modern Art, New York, the Niigata B.S.N. Art Museum, Japan, and the Victoria and Albert Museum, London.

Mackintosh C.R. 1868–1928

The Scottish architect Charles Rennie Mackintosh was born in Glasgow. He attended evening classes at the Glasgow School of Art, and from 1884 to 1889 was articled to a local architect. In 1890 he joined the firm of Honeyman & Keppie (becoming a full partner in 1904), received his first commission, and won a traveling scholarship which enabled him to spend several months sketching buildings in Italy.

While pursuing his architectural career he also took an interest in graphic design and furniture. He was one of a group ("The Four") whose work was shown in a London Arts and Crafts exhibition, illustrated in *The Studio*, and exhibited in Vienna and Turin. Much of The Four's work was marked by an attenuated, almost Art Nouveau stylization, which was considered decadent by the English public and which figured in many of the remarkable decorative schemes Mackintosh designed for a series of Glasgow tearooms for Mrs Cranston.

But in most of his work this element was only a complement to plainer and more rational forms. Thus the emphatic austerity of large studio windows dominates his most famous building, the Glasgow School of Art (1897–9), despite the discreet elegance of the external ironwork. Mackintosh's dependence on vernacular building traditions can be detected in the asymmetrically arranged features around the Art School's entrance. It is to be seen more clearly in his domestic buildings (for example, Windyhill, Kilmacolm, 1899; Hill House, Helensburgh, 1902; and his entry for the German "House of an Art-Lover" competition, 1901), though these buildings are outstanding for their freedom from historical detail.

The impression of solidity given by large areas of plain masonry in Mackintosh's later buildings is often counteracted by expansive spatial effects, such as the dramatically glazed stair towers of Scotland Street School, Glasgow (1904). In his designs for the 1907-9 extension to the Glasgow School of Art, the forbidding castle-like exterior, with its tall oriel windows, conceals the rich and exciting space of the library, based on a robust but ingenious wooden framework.

The Art School extension was Mackintosh's last major architectural work. His relations with colleagues and clients were not easy, and the strain of his fastidious working methods eventually began to tell. He resigned from Honeyman & Keppie in 1913, moved to Suffolk in 1914, and thence to London. His alterations to No. 78 Derngate, Northampton (1916), show that his imaginative flair did not diminish, but he was unable to reestablish an architectural practice and in 1923 moved to the south of France. There he produced a number of powerful landscape paintings before illness overcame him and forced his return to London, where he died in 1928.

McWilliam F.E. 1909–1989

The British sculptor Frederick Edward McWilliam was born in Northern Ireland. From 1928 to 1931 he studied painting and drawing at the Slade School of Fine Art, London. His sculptural imagination was fired by a visit to Brancusi's studio in Paris in 1931. This made him receptive to the smooth shapes and human references in Henry Moore's work, and pushed him

F.E. McWilliam: Portrait of Elizabeth Frink; bronze; height 183cm (72in); 1956. Harlow New Town, England

Carlo Maderno: the facade of S. Susanna, Rome; 1603

away from pure abstraction towards Surrealism. He joined the British Surrealist Group in 1938. In his first one-man exhibition at the London Gallery in 1939, his series of carvings called *The Complete Fragment* clearly showed his debt to Picasso, Arp, and Magritte: they represented parts of the head that the observer was invited to complete (for example *Eye, Nose, and Cheek*, 1939; Tate Gallery, London). McWilliam's postwar sculptures are mainly cast in bronze; in style and temperament they reflect the move away from Surrealism towards Existentialism, as championed by Alberto Giacometti, Lynn Chadwick, and Kenneth Armitage.

Maderno Carlo 1556–1629

The Italian architect Carlo Maderno was the most important practitioner of the early Baroque style in Rome in the early 17th century. Born at Capolago, he was in Rome by 1588 where he was a pupil of his uncle, Domenico Fontana. In 1603 he was made architect of St Peter's, and from 1607 to 1612 he added the nave and facade to the existing centralized structure by Michelangelo. His other important works in Rome include the facade of S. Susanna (1603), the dome of S. Andrea della Valle (1622), and the Palazzo Barberini (from 1621, later completed by Bernini).

Further reading. Donati, U. *Carlo Maderno, Architetto Ticinese a Roma*, Lugano (1957). Hibbard, H. *Carlo Maderno and Roman Architecture 1580–1630*, London (1971).

Maes Nicolaes 1634–93

A Dutch painter originally from Dordrecht, Nicolaes Maes studied under Rembrandt from c1650 to 1654. His earliest works have much of the rich, warm, reddish colors of Rembrandt's paintings from the 1640s, and also something of their subtle light and shade effects. Some of them are biblical pictures, but Maes' forte

was household interiors with large figures (particularly old women praying, sleeping, or engaged in household tasks), and intimate anecdotal genre scenes (for example, *Saying Grace*, 1648; Louvre, Paris). These, showing the domestic life of women and children, occasionally have the tenderness of the drawings of such themes made by Rembrandt in the 1640s.

Maes' subject matter and style changed after his return *c*1665–7 from Antwerp, which he visited in order to see pictures by Rubens, van Dyck, and Jordaens. He subsequently became a fashionable portraitist, producing large numbers of small, brightly colored pictures of elegantly dressed sitters (for example, *Portrait of a Man*, *c*1675; Niedersächsische Landesgalerie und Städtische Galerie, Hannover). These paintings are mostly from after 1673—the date of Maes' move to Amsterdam. They have a much lighter tonality than the Rembrandtesque early works.

Maffei Francesco *c*1620?–60

The Vicentine painter Francesco Maffei was also active in Venice, Brescia, Rovigo, and Padua. Despite the provincial character of his origins and career, Maffei is one of the most impressive artists of the Venetian 17th century. He derived from his study of the great masters of the previous century a freshness and vigor absent from the academic Mannerism of his metropolitan contemporaries. He was also influenced by the works of earlier visitors to Venice, such as Johann Liss and Bernardo Strozzi, though he preserved a very personal taste for loose brushwork and dissonant color schemes, creating effects that often verge on the fantastic.

Magnasco Alessandro 1667–1749

Born in Genoa, the painter Alessandro Magnasco moved to Milan between 1680 and 1688. In the early 18th century he visited Florence and in 1735 returned to Genoa. He specialized in small figures in wild landscapes, influenced by Salvator Rosa (1615–73) and by the elongated figure style of the late Mannerist etchings of Jacques Callot (1592–1635). Magnasco's fragmented and rapid brush strokes

Alessandro Magnasco: A Scene of the Inquisition; oil on canvas; 44×83cm (17×33cm); *c*1710–20. Kunsthistorisches Museum, Vienna

Francesco Maffei: The Israelites Gathering Manna; oil on canvas; *c*1658–60. S. Giustina, Padua

Nicolaes Maes: Portrait of a Woman; oil on canvas; 90×72cm (35×28in); 1667. Musée d'Arras

René Magritte: Memory; gouache and watercolor on paper; 35×26cm (14×10in); c1942. Private collection

and ghostly, bizarre figures are frantic and psychologically disturbing. He chose strange subjects—witches and magic, obscure religious sects, quack doctors, scenes of trial and torture, saints and monks in ecstasy. Whether these are intended to be satire or farce, or whether they are the outpourings of a religious fanatic, remains unclear.

Magritte René 1898–1967

The Belgian Surrealist painter René Magritte was born in Lessines, Hainaut. He studied at the Académie des Beaux-Arts, Brussels (1916–18). His work from 1920 to 1924—in its treatment of themes of modern life, its bright color, and its exploration of the relationship of three-dimensional form to flat picture plane—shows the combined influence of Cubism,

Orphism, Futurism, and Purism. But in 1925, Magritte was profoundly moved by reproductions of the Metaphysical paintings of de Chirico and abandoned his earlier manner. In such works as *The Robe of Adventure* (1926; private collection), which owe much to de Chirico and to Ernst's work of 1921 to 1924, he expressed his sense of the mystery of the world by means of abrupt, irrational juxtapositions of objects and the evocation of a silent, trance-like atmosphere.

An active member of the Surrealist group in Brussels from 1925, Magritte remained unaffected by the emphasis on automatism in the Parisian group during the mid 1920s. In September 1927, he moved to the Parisian suburb Le Perreux-sur-Marne, where he lived for three years; his example contributed to the resurgence of illusionism in Surrealist painting in the late 1920s.

Unlike Dali, Magritte does not use painting to express his private obsessions or fantasies: wit, irony, and a spirit of intelligent debate rather than self-revelation characterize his work. Thus, in the word-paintings of 1928 to 1930 he explores the ambiguous relationship between words and images and the objects they denote. In such works as *The Human Condition I* (1933; private collection) where a canvas on an easel exactly reproduces the "real" landscape beyond the window, he probes the relationship of art to nature. There is a studied objectivity—Magritte liked to pose as the average bourgeois. But the frequent repetition of themes of suffocation, and the sense of claustrophobia induced by the extreme shallowness of the pictorial space, seem to correspond to some personal anxiety. These themes have been interpreted as reflecting Magritte's unconscious memory of his mother's suicide by drowning when he was 14.

In many paintings, Magritte questions our assumptions about the world—for instance, he disturbs normal scale or defies the laws of gravity—and implies that nothing is sure, everything is mysterious. The force of the image always depends upon the impersonality of the style, which resembles that of a sign-painter and forbids disbelief. It was a style that remained virtually unchanged throughout Magritte's mature work, except during the 1940s. From 1943 to 1946 he adopted an Impressionist brushwork and palette, apparently in order to alleviate the gloom of the war years. In the winter of 1947 to 1948—his so-called "Fauve" or "Vache" period—he painted a series of works remarkable for their violent color and grotesque imagery. The critical response to these experiments was generally hostile, and Magritte reverted to his accustomed manner. In his later work, despite a number of masterpieces, he was too often content to repeat successful themes or images; inevitably, a certain blandness entered his work.

Magritte's influence on Pop art was significant; the cerebral quality of his work also makes it relevant to other recent avant-garde developments.

Further reading. Calvocoressi, R. *Magritte*, Oxford (1979). Gablik, S. *Magritte*, London (1970). *Rétrospective Magritte*, Brussels (1978) and Paris (1979). Sylvester, D. *Magritte*, New York (1969). Waldberg, P. *René Magritte*, Brussels (1965).

Mahmud Muzahhib *fl. c1538–c60*

The Persian illuminator Mahmud Muzah-hib came from Herat but worked at Bukhara from *c*1538 to *c*1560. He is said to have been a pupil of Shaykh Zadeh, a Safavid master who may himself have gone to Bukhara. Mahmud Muzahhib preserved the style of Herat of the 1490s, especially in manuscript illustration, a particular feature of his work being a preference for illuminated double-page openings (seen for example in the *Bustan* of Sa'di, *c*1548; Gulbenkian Foundation, Lisbon). He also painted single figures or pairs of figures.

Maillol Aristide 1861–1944

The French sculptor, painter, and graphic artist Aristide Joseph Bonaventure Maillol was born in the southern town of Banyuls-sur-Mer. In 1893 he established a tapestry workshop, and his early paintings reflect in their flatness and formalization both tap-estry design and the influence of Gauguin. He began making sculpture in 1895, but only in 1900, after a temporary blindness, did he fully devote himself to it. His austere bronzes of the female nude, compactly designed and lacking in surface appeal, were in strong contrast to the fluid Impressionism of Rodin. Although they corresponded to a movement towards classicism and against anecdote among younger French sculptors, the robust female types owe more to local beauty than to the Greek ideal. His late sculptures such as the *Seated Figure* (1930) or *The River* (1939–43; both in the Museum of Modern Art, New York) avoid monumentality in favor of a dynamic relationship between figure and base.

Maitani Lorenzo *c1275–1330*

Lorenzo Maitani was a Sienese architect and sculptor. From 1310 until his death in 1330, Maitani was "Capomaestro" of the cathedral at Orvieto. Although documents reveal Lorenzo's supervision of every aspect of the cathedral fabric, the assumption that he was the creator of any of the facade sculptures rests on a single document of 1330. This refers to bronze supplied to Maitani for the casting of *The Eagle of St John*, one of the *Four Symbols of the Evangelists* on the cornice that runs across the facade just above the three main doors. Over the center door is a freestanding bronze group of the *Madonna and Child with Angels*, and there are stylistic similarities between these bronzes and the reliefs on the facade.

The four piers that divide the three doorways are covered with carved reliefs up to the level of the cornice. From the left they contain *The Creation and the Fall*, *The Tree of Jesse* and *Prophecies of Christ's Coming*, *The Life of Christ*, and *The Last Judgment*. Apart from its extraordinary

Aristide Maillol: Profile of a Young Girl; oil on canvas; 74×103cm (29×41in); c1895–6. Musée Hyacinthe Rigaud, Perpignan

quality, often seeming to possess a French Gothic lyricism, this extensive series contains fascinating evidence about the collaborative methods of a large 14th-century workshop. The sculptures are in varying stages of completion, and from these it can be seen that a sequence of operations was carried out by different workmen over the whole surface of the reliefs. This operation would have been done to the design of Maitani who might be assumed to have intervened at any time, especially on the final stage. While Maitani's workshop can be regarded as responsible for the majority of the reliefs, those in the lower part of the two central piers were done by someone else altogether.

If Maitani's precise role as sculptor is a matter of some guesswork, his role as architect of the cathedral facade as a whole is less open to dispute. There survive two designs for the facade, in pen on parchment. The later of these, much closer to the facade as it appears today, is probably that by Maitani referred to in an inventory of 1356. Comparison with the earlier, anonymous design reveals a change to a broader, less vertical effect; but the salient features of a triple, gabled portal, a rose window, and mosaic and sculptural decoration are retained. The first of the designs, which shows knowledge of French Gothic architecture, probably reflects the influence of

Lorenzo Maitani: detail of The Last Judgment; marble; c1310–30. Orvieto Cathedral

the transept ends of Notre Dame in Paris. This is combined with a regard for decorative and pictorial elements, especially evident in the siting of the mosaic *Coronation of the Virgin* in the main gable. Maitani's changes towards a broader, more spreadout effect emphasize this rather Italian element in the design, and the result is a profusion of architecture, sculpture (in bronze and stone), and mosaic that forms a splendid whole.

Malevich Kasimir 1878–1935

The Russian painter Kasimir Malevich was born in Kiev; he came to Moscow in 1902 to study art. In the 1900s he painted Impressionist-influenced landscape and figure scenes. In 1907 he met Michail Larionoff, and over the next few years shared a strong primitive manner employing popular art conventions, particularly the depiction of uncompromisingly frontal figures. However, Malevich's paintings are far more intense in color, the technique of gouache on paper lending itself to a broad treatment; they reflect the influence of Matisse, whose work he saw in the private collection of Sergei Shchukin.

In 1912 Malevich showed his paintings of peasant subjects at the "Donkey's Tail" exhibition in Moscow. The most recent of these *Taking in the Rye* (1912; Stedelijk Museum, Amsterdam) showed a turning away from the crudely graphic manner that had linked him to Larionoff, towards massive, tubular forms owing something to Picasso's paintings of 1908–9.

Malevich's paintings showed an increasing absorption of Western avant-garde influences, so placing him in strong opposition to the anti-European bias of Larionoff. *The Knife Grinder* (1912; Yale University Art Gallery, New Haven) combines Cubist fragmentation and Futurist multiplication of the image. The Cubist *Head of a Peasant* (1912; Stedelijk Museum, Amsterdam) is arbitrary in its relation to the subject, compared with the classic paintings of Picasso and Braque.

After breaking with Larionoff, Malevich came into contact with a new intellectual circle including the writer Kruchenykh and the composer M.V. Matyushin. The group subscribed to the concept of "alogism" which, as its name implies, was an attempt to break free from the bounds of casual connection. An "alogical" painting, such as *An Englishman in Moscow* (1914; Stedelijk Museum, Amsterdam) superim-

poses varied words and images in a way that cannot be resolved in the way most intricate Cubist pictures can; it undermines any kind of representational logic. Malevich's interest in popular art persists in the emblematic representation of everyday objects, reminiscent of sign painting. In *Woman at a Poster Column* (1914; Stedelijk Museum, Amsterdam), simple abstract shapes are as important to the composition as the vestigial references to the outside world in the form of collage and lettering.

The culmination of "alogism" was the production in St Petersburg in December 1913 of the opera *Victory over the Sun* with a libretto by Kruchenykh, music by Matyushin, and designs by Malevich. The title suggests a disturbing reversal of established values. The cancellation of the sun and its imprisonment in a box, achieved by the hero, can be equated with the partially deleted *Mona Lisa* in a painting of 1914. Malevich's designs included a curtain with a black square, which for him symbolized the zero, full of the new potentialities that arose from the passing of the old order.

This square was to acquire the significance of an icon for Malevich. As a painting on a white ground it occupied a central position—hung high up and straddled between two walls—when in December 1915 at the "0.10" exhibition at St Petersburg he showed, for the first time, his "Suprematist" paintings. These were nonfigurative compositions based on compositions of simple geometric forms, generally deriving from the square. By confining himself to such elementary means and a small predefined repertoire of "Suprematist" colors he was able to arrive at an independence from the subject which had evaded earlier Russian avant-garde painters. Occasional titles in the exhibition catalog, such as *Boy with Knapsack* (probably the painting now known as *Supremus no. 56*, in the State Russian Museum, St Petersburg) should be seen as indicating an attempt to represent in geometric terms the interaction of forces and masses, rather than an abstraction of the visible form.

Malevich justified his Suprematism by condemning representational art as a theft from nature, and said that the artist must construct "on the basis of weight, speed, and the direction of movement". In these paintings he conveyed strong impressions of floating or falling by placing shapes against a plain background which permitted no spatial interpretations. How-

Kasimir Malevich: An Englishman in Moscow; oil on canvas; 88×57cm (35×57in); 1914. Stedelijk Museum, Amsterdam

Russia who renounced painting as a speculative activity. Although a supporter of the Revolution and not conventionally religious, Malevich's thinking was of a mystical bent. He was concerned with presenting a new vision which, though not possible outside the context of a scientific and industrial society, was not directly related to the problems of functional design. In *The Non-Objective World* published in Munich in 1927 he stated that the artist would always be in advance of society. This being the case, he could not willingly suppress his own ideas for the sake of socially defined concepts of utility.

Malevich's principal activities during the 1920s seem to have been as a teacher. Invited by Chagall in 1919 to Vitebsk to teach at his school, he formed among his pupils the "Unovis" group (1920) which became a sufficiently powerful force to lead to the resignation of the former artist when the two quarreled. In 1921 the group itself was ousted, and after 1922 was based in St Petersburg (then Petrograd). Under Malevich, who had virtually given up painting, the group made a number of models that attempted an investigation of his theories of "planity" and "arkhitektory" (basic architectural form).

After 1930 Malevich began painting again. He returned to the peasant themes that had occupied him in his early years, employing basic shapes as if trying to establish a new grammar of form in terms of the human body. This partial return to figuration may have been an attempt to come to terms with the newly established official doctrine of "socialist realism", with its demand that art be comprehensible to the masses; but on the basis of the material available in the West, any assessment of Malevich's last phase must be tentative.

Further reading. Anderson, T. *Malevich*, Amsterdam (1970). Gray, C. *The Great Experiment: Russian Art 1863–1922*, London (1962). Karshan, D.H. *Malevich: the Graphic Work*, Jerusalem (1973). Malevich, K. *Essays in Art, 1915–33* (2 vols.), London (1969). Malevich, K. *From Cubism and Futurism to Suprematism*, Moscow and St Petersburg (1915). Milner, J. *Kasimir Malevich and the Art of Geometry*, New Haven (1996). Moholy-Nagy, S. "Constructivism from Kasimir Malevich to Laszlo Moholy-Nagy", *Arts and Architecture*, New York (June 1966). Zhadova, L. *Malevich*, London (1982).

ever, relationships can sometimes be inferred from overlappings, so that while volume is rarely hinted at there is no suggestion of purely two-dimensional pattern.

Most of the early Suprematist paintings take their cue from *Black Square* in the austerity of their conception. Later, superimpositions and the incorporation of irregular quadrilaterals create a more complex image. Malevich faced the dilemma that to develop Abstract images through formal elaboration increased the associative content of the painting, so impeding

its ability to communicate pure sensation. In paintings after 1917 he returned to a simple structure, often basing his paintings on no more than a cross. Elsewhere he worked on the edge of perception by painting in white on white, confounding spatial readings by emphasizing the fact of the pigment. When in 1918 he painted *White Square on a White Background* (Museum of Modern Art, New York) this was a virtual admission that his researches had come to a dead end.

At the same time he was out of sympathy with advanced artists in post-Revolutionary

Mallarmé Stéphane 1842–98

The French poet and art and theater critic Stéphane Mallarmé was a close friend of Manet, and the center of an avant-garde Parisian salon. A devotee of British and American culture, he popularized translations of Edgar Allen Poe and his friend Whistler's *Ten O'Clock Lecture* (1888) in France as well as information about Tennyson, Swinburne, and London art exhibitions. Born in Paris, he earned his living teaching English in *lycées* in Tournon, Besançon, Avignon, and, from 1871, in Paris. He established his famous "Tuesday" *salon* in 1875; here writers such as Huysmans and Verlaine met and mixed with such artists as Manet, Pissarro, Gauguin, and Redon.

His poetic output was small and sporadic but of seminal importance to Symbolist writers and artists. Following a spiritual crisis during the winter of 1864–5, Mallarmé rejected his earlier style—reminiscent of Baudelaire's—to evolve a radically new poetry whose aim was to intimate the Objective Ideal. The Ideal, defined by Mallarmé as the void left vacant by the dethronement of God, could not be defined in concrete, finite language; its existence could only be suggested by the ambiguity of words with multivalent meaning and the random placing of stanzas across a page. This new poetry received its complete expression in his poem, *Le Coup de Dés* (1897).

Malouel Jean *fl.* 1396–1415

The Netherlandish artist Jean Malouel was born in Nijmegen. He became Court Painter and *Valet de Chambre* to the Dukes of Burgundy. He belonged to a family of artists who were active in Nijmegen in Guelders in the late 14th century, and was uncle to the Limburg brothers, whose careers he helped to establish. He is recorded in Paris in 1396, when he was working for the Queen of France; but in 1397 he was called to Dijon by Philip the Bold to become his official painter in Burgundy. The remainder of his life was spent in the service of the Burgundian court.

Although he traveled for the Duke to Conflans, Paris, and Arras, and numerous documents testify to his varied activities in Burgundy, attempts to identify his individual style focus on works commissioned for the Carthusian Monastery on the outskirts of Dijon known as the Chartreuse de Champmol. This foundation of Philip the Bold's was a major center of artistic activity c1400, and there Malouel was associated with Claus Sluter, whose sculptures in the large cloister were painted by him.

The Chartreuse was demolished after the French Revolution and its works of art dispersed. Five large altarpieces for it were commissioned from Malouel in 1398, but the only relevant identifiable work from the Chartreuse is an altarpiece now in the Louvre, Paris, known to have been completed in 1416, after Malouel's death, by his successor Henri Bellechose. Its complex iconography shows the martyrdom and mystic communion of St Denis dominated by the crucified Christ and the other two Persons of the Trinity (to whom the Chartreuse was dedicated). Stylistically it appears to involve two artists. An apparently earlier work in a related style bearing the arms of Burgundy on the reverse (Louvre, Paris) is attributed by most scholars to Malouel and is the key work in his identification. One of the earliest surviving circular paintings, it combines the Trinity with a poignant rendering of mourning over the dead Christ.

Further attributions include a *Pietà* (Musée des Beaux-Arts, Troyes) and a *Madonna with Angels* (Staatliche Museen, Berlin). It is possible that the latter painting (in tempera on cloth) once formed part of a diptych. An 18th-century drawing of John the Fearless (Bibliothèque Nationale, Paris; Coll. Bourgogne xx fol. 308) is thought to be derived from an original portrait by Malouel.

Manessier Alfred 1911–1993

The French artist Alfred Manessier was born in Saint-Ouen. He studied architecture at the École des Beaux-Arts in Amiens, and went to Paris in 1929 to continue architectural studies at the École des Beaux-Arts, with extra classes at the Louvre and various academies in Montparnasse. He met and studied with the painter Roger Bissière in 1935, joining the group around him. From 1936 to 1938 he

Jean Malouel (attrib.): Pietà; panel; diameter 64cm (25in); c1400/10. Louvre, Paris

Alfred Manessier: And I Saw the Glory of the Resurrection; 230×200cm (91×79in); 1961. Private collection

lived in Saint-Ouen, returning to Paris in 1939. After military service from 1939 to 1940, he resumed his studies with Bissière in 1940. In 1943 he spent some time in a Trappist Monastery at Soligny-la-Trappe, Orme—a period important to the development of his work.

Manessier is a member of the School of Paris. Besides painting, he designs stained-glass windows, tapestries, stage-sets, and costumes. His mature works, especially those of the 1950s, consist of abstract symbols in glowing colors, with figurative, often religious titles (for example, *Près d'Harlem*, oil on canvas; 1953; Musée des Beaux-Arts, Dijon).

Manet Édouard 1832–83

Édouard Manet was born in Paris in 1832, and it was at the annual Paris Salon that, for over 20 years, he sought academic and public acceptance for his original, brilliant, and enigmatic canvases. Because of the furore that his works created at the Salons, he became the first major artist in whose career the journalists and the general public played vital roles.

Intended for the law by his father, head of staff at the Ministry of Justice, Manet chose the navy; he voyaged to South America as a naval cadet in 1838. But after twice failing his entrance examinations to naval college (in 1848 and 1849), he was allowed to enroll at the École des Beaux-Arts, in the studio of Thomas Couture, then highly respected for his academic historical compositions. Manet is said to have quarreled frequently with Couture, but nevertheless studied with him for six years and acquired the basis of his later technique.

Manet was 26 when he first submitted to the Salon. His *Absinthe Drinker* (1858–9; Ny Carlsberg Glyptotek, Copenhagen), a cloaked, top-hatted bohemian figure, was rejected in 1859. But in 1861 his large *Spanish Singer* (1860; Metropolitan Museum, New York) was accepted, given

Édouard Manet: Study of a Woman; charcoal on paper; 55×41cm (22×16in); 1881. Rijksmuseum Vincent van Gogh, Amsterdam

an honorable mention, and was widely acclaimed. An admirer said that it stood between Realism and Romanticism. Manet worked throughout 1862 and began 1863 by showing 14 canvases at a dealer's art gallery and sending three major works to the Salon. All three were rejected. But that

Édouard Manet: Races at Longchamp; oil on canvas; 44×85cm (17×33in); 1864. Art Institute of Chicago

Édouard Manet: A Villa at Rueil; oil on canvas; 92×72cm (36×28in); 1882. National Gallery of Victoria, Melbourne

year artists were allowed, by Imperial decree, to show their rejected works separately at a Salon des Refusés. There Manet's large composition *Le Déjeuner sur l'Herbe* (or *Luncheon on the Grass*, originally called *Le Bain* (Bathing) 1863; Musée du Jeu de Paume, Paris) in which women were shown undressed beside clothed men in a wood, created a scandal; it became the object of press ridicule and attracted crowds of sightseers.

From that time, Manet's new canvases were the focus of popular attention. When, in 1865, the Salon did show his *Olympia* (1863; Musée du Jeu de Paume, Paris) an even greater outcry followed. The following year, his *Fifer* (1866; Musée du Jeu de Paume, Paris) was rejected. So in 1867, when he was not invited to exhibit at the Paris World Fair, Manet erected his own pavilion to show 50 works. Later that year the authorities forbade him to exhibit *The Execution of the Emperor Maximilian* because of its topical political relevance. (Several versions of *The Execution of the Emperor Maximilian* survive; the most complete is in the Städtische Kunsthalle Mannheim.)

If, like Chardin before him, Manet had confined himself to still life and small subject pictures, he might have been excused or even accepted. But his canvases of the 1860s were large, challenging comparison with the great art of the past. And Manet was aware of the great masters: he had spent six years copying them. He did not simply paint what he found around him; he painted modern versions of old subjects. *Le Déjeuner sur l'Herbe* was a version of Giorgione's *Fête Champêtre* (c1510; Louvre, Paris), *Olympia* was based on Titian's *Venus of Urbino* (1538; Uffizi, Florence), and almost every canvas of the decade had its precedent in earlier art. But in Manet's variations, traditional motifs became enigmatic, even ambiguous. Giorgione's naked nymphs and Titian's Venus looked frankly indecent in modern settings.

Nor did Manet just set up his models in traditional poses. His vision was itself original. He analyzed and simplified his motifs, eliminating half-tones, using a frontal light that flattened planes and reduced shadows to outlines, and so created bold patterns of colored patches.

In this he was guided by an odd range of earlier examples: the works of Frans Hals and Velazquez, but also Japanese woodcuts. His broad simplifications at last led to the *Fifer* in which the flat heraldic colors of the boy's uniform are set off by an almost blank background.

For almost a decade, Manet challenged the Salon with a sequence of heroic versions of works by artists ranging from Mantegna to Goya. He was controversial, which meant he had his supporters. By 1860, he had been befriended by Baudelaire, and for a time the poet and painter seem to have shared a vision of modern heroism, as Baudelaire described in his essay "The Painter of Modern Life". Manet met Degas in 1862, and soon afterwards Pissarro, Renoir, and the other painters later to become the Impressionists. In 1867, he was championed by the novelist Émile Zola.

With the end of the Franco-Prussian war and the coming of the Third Republic, the tide had turned for Manet. His work was usually, though not always, accepted for the Salon; and in 1873 his *Le Bon Bock* (*Portrait of Émile Bellot*, 1873; Philadelphia Museum of Art), a portrait of a jovial beer drinker, enjoyed a real popular success. But public attention had been diverted to the new artistic scandal: Impressionism.

Although Manet was respected by the

Impressionists, who were sometimes called "la bande à Manet", he never exhibited with them or painted a truly Impressionist work. Nevertheless, his paintings of the early 1870s do seem influenced by Impressionism, or perhaps by Berthe Morisot, who had become his pupil in 1868, was later his model and, in 1874, his sister-in-law. His canvases became smaller, his motifs less monumental, and his touch more broken. There are fewer set pieces, and even the largest of these do not match the scale of his earlier works.

It was in the second half of the decade that Manet developed his latest style. This was a sequence of portraits of contemporary life, which developed hints of his own earliest canvases and of some of Degas' portraits. These paintings showed characteristic types of the period in their settings. They included *The Prune* (1877; Paul Mellon Collection, Upperville, Virginia), a woman drinking alone in a bar; *Nana* (1877; Hamburger Kunsthalle, Hamburg), a prostitute and her client; and compositions based on cafés, concerts, and beer halls (for example, *Waitress* or *La Servante de Bocks*, 1878–9; National Gallery, London). That Manet was following a conscious program is confirmed by his letter of 1879 offering to decorate the new Town Hall with scenes showing the heart of Paris.

In 1881, at the age of 49, Manet had his triumph at the Salon. His portrait of the big-game hunter *Pertuiset* (Museum of Art, Sao Paulo) was awarded a second class medal, and with it the right to exhibit at future Salons without the approval of the jury. Unfortunately he was already suffering from locomotor ataxia. He was in pain, walked with difficulty, and worked more and more with pastel as his condition deteriorated. But he painted a final masterpiece: *The Bar at the Folies-Bergère* (1881–2; Courtauld Institute Galleries, London) which in its motif, a radiant young woman typifying contemporary life, in its monumental composition, and in its new brilliant technique, unifies the various strands of his earlier works. It was a success in the Salon of 1882.

Early in 1883, Manet, already bedfast, had a leg amputated and died soon after the operation, on 30 April, at the age of 51.

Further reading. Cachin, F. *Manet*, New York (1991). Fried, M. *Manet's Modernism*, Chicago (1998). Krell, A. *Manet and the Painters of Contemporary Life*, London (1996). Locke, N. *Manet and the Family Romance*, Princeton, N.J. (2001). Mauner, G. *Manet: the Still Life Paintings*, New York (2001). Wilson-Bareau, J. and Degener, D. *Manet and the Sea*, New Haven, (2003).

Manohar *c1565–c1628*

Manohar was a Hindu painter at the Mughal court. Born in the Imperial household, he was the son of Basawan, and served as his father's apprentice in 1581. He collaborated with Basawan, Mukund, and Anant on the *Akbar-nama* (Victoria and Albert Museum, London), and at an early age was entrusted with illustrating a *Gulistan* (Royal Asiatic Society, London); the manuscript contains a youthful self-portrait. He rose to eminence during the reign of Jahangir (1605–27). The Emperor gave a portrait of him by Manohar to Sir Thomas Roe, the English ambassador at the Mughal court; the original has been lost. He painted a number of Christian subjects and was influenced by European art. The Leningrad Album in the Hermitage Museum, Leningrad, contains several of his works: a coronation scene on which he collaborated with Mansur, two portraits of Jahangir, and European allegorical and religious subjects. He ceased to work *c1628*.

Mansart François *1598–1666*

In many ways the French architect François Mansart followed the French classical style created by Salomon de Brosse (1571–1626). He remained loyal to its traditions and was deeply suspicious of the Baroque style championed by Louis Levau. It is worth comparing the formality, subtlety, and classical integrity of his château of Maisons-Lafitte (1642–6), with Levau's château at Vaux-le-Vicomte (1658–61). It is easy to see in Mansart his development from the conservative if not vernacular style in the château at Berny, through the less complex and more compact manner of Balleroy (*c1626*), to the final classical maturity of his rebuilding of the château of Blois (1635–8) and his schemes of 1664 for the Louvre. Yet he did not entirely turn his back on the Baroque. In the staircase hall at Blois, in the dome of his church of the Visitation, Paris (begun as a centralized plan in 1632), and in his projected staircase for the Louvre, he showed a dramatic use of light and a structural ingenuity worthy of the Baroque.

In many respects Mansart continued the nationalistic classical style evolved in the 1550s. He disliked the Italianate manner eagerly taken up by Levau at Vaux-le-Vicomte. Mansart's refusal to leave France or even stray too far from Paris isolated him and threw him back on his own resources. His lack of success at court heightened this, and his bids for favor with the schemes for the Louvre of 1664 and the Bourbon Mausoleum at St-Denis were unsuccessful.

His influence in France after his death was more apparent than real. The practical, perhaps slipshod, classicism of his nephew J.-H. Mansart would have pleased him little, and it was only with the classical revival of the mid 18th century that he was once again appreciated and understood in France.

Mansart J.-H. *1646–1708*

Great-nephew of the more distinguished architect François Mansart, Jules-Hardouin Mansart was the perfect example of the court architect. His entire career was spent in the service of Louis XIV, beginning with his work with Le Notre at the château for Mme de Montespan at Bosquet des Domes in 1675, and closing with his designs for the chapel at Versailles of 1689, which was completed after his death in 1708 by his pupil Robert de Cotte.

At Versailles, where he was heir to the work of Levau and François d'Orbay, his most dramatic, and at the same time unfortunate, contribution was the filling in of the center of the park facade with the sumptuous Hall of Mirrors (1678–81). He worked there and on the adjoining *Salon de la Guerre* and *Salon de la Paix* in a particularly fruitful partnership with Charles Lebrun. His success repeated what he had undertaken at the château at Clagny in 1676 for Madame de Montespan, and was itself repeated on a more intimate scale for his Grand Trianon (1678) in the park at Versailles.

The Trianon was followed by the now destroyed château of Marly, which developed the pavilion or *trianon* principle, laying out a parallel row of them on either side of the main block of the palace. In this as in some other designs, he showed a Baroque inventiveness which counteracted his rather pompous classicism. The former

J.-H. Mansart: the Hall of Mirrors in the Palace of Versailles; 1678–81

was obvious in the twin stables built at Versailles in 1678 and 1686, which completed a grand forecourt to the palace and echoed the layout and scale of the Roman Piazza del Popolo. Apart from his royal commissions, his most distinguished buildings were the rebuilding of the chapel at the Invalides (1680–91), and the layout of the Parisian Place Vendôme (1698) and Place des Victoires (1685) which did much to set the tone of urban planning in the city. Their influence was felt in the provinces in a scheme such as the Place des États at Dijon of 1686, and ultimately in Gabriel's Place de la Concorde in Paris.

Perhaps one of the most notable aspects of his career was his ability both to delegate and cooperate. At Versailles, his vital association with Lebrun continued that formed by Levau; it stretched to sculptors and stuccoists like Coysevox, Tubi, and Cucci, and more significantly to the gardener Le Notre. He worked with Le Notre at Versailles, Trianon, and at Chantilly.

His method of giving much of his work to assistants, especially to talented ones like L'Assurance and Pierre le Peintre, helped to foster the style of the Rococo.

Mansur *fl.* late 16th–mid 17th century

The Muslim painter Ustad (master) Mansur received from the Emperor Jahangir the title "Nadir-al-Asr" ("Wonder of the Age"). He started work in the Akbar period (1556–1605) painting in the *Akbarnama* (Victoria and Albert Museum, London) and the *Babur-nama* (divided between the British Museum, London, and the National Museum of India, New Delhi). Although famous for natural history subjects he was no mean portraitist, as is evident from *The Vina Player* (c1600; Edward Croft-Murray Collection, London). The St Petersburg Album (Hermitage Museum) contains a fine portrait of Jahangir by Mansur and Manohar.

Mansur was instructed by Jahangir to

paint the flowers of Kashmir; he recorded some 100 specimens. His reputation rests chiefly on his portrayal of exotic and domestic animals, painted with meticulous accuracy and with frozen, stylized grandeur—including a zebra, a turkey cock, a cheer pheasant, and a hornbill.

Mansur: An Abyssinian Zebra; gouache on paper; 18×24cm (7×9in). Victoria and Albert Museum, London

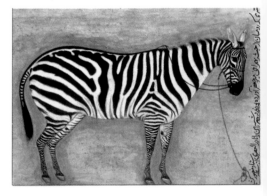

Mantegna Andrea 1431–1506

Andrea Mantegna was an Italian painter and engraver and, according to his contemporaries, also a sculptor. The adopted son and apprentice of a Paduan painter and antiquary, Francesco Squarcione, Mantegna's first big commission was for frescoes of scenes from *The Lives of SS. James and Christopher* (1448–52; Eremitani, Ovetari Chapel, Padua; destroyed in the Second World War). Their success no doubt inspired the commission for the San Zeno Altarpiece (1456–9; S. Zeno, Verona). In 1457 he accepted the invitation of Lodovico Gonzaga, Marquis of Mantua, to be his court painter, and settled by 1460 in that humanistic court.

Documents record the variety of his tasks: portraits, designs for buildings, tapestries, vases and cups, and frescoes both religious and profane. He also created stage designs on canvas (the newly restored *Triumphs of Caesar*, c1486–c94; Hampton Court Palace, London) and painted panels of *Parnassus* and *The Triumph of Virtue* (c1497; both in the Louvre, Paris) for Isabella d'Este's Studiolo, which housed her antiquities. He visited Venice in 1448, and in Ferrara, in 1449, may have met Piero della Francesca whose monumentality probably affected his style. He was in Florence in 1466, and from 1488 to 1490 Marquis Francesco "lent" him to the Pope to fresco a chapel in the Vatican Belvedere.

Florentine art and the antiquarianism of the Paduan *milieu* (his father had visited Greece, and had a large collection of antiquities) were decisive influences on Mantegna's style. He knew the vigorous and sculptural frescoes by Andrea del Castagno in Venice (1442; S. Zaccaria). Another Florentine, Filippo Lippi, had worked in Padua c1434 (in the Capella del Podestà now destroyed), and Mantegna learned through his example the gravity of style and three-dimensionality of Masaccio, whose pupil Filippo may have been. Furthermore, Giotto's frescoes in the Capella dell'Arena in Padua proclaimed essentially similar qualities.

More important to the young man than any of these was the arrival of Donatello and his assistants in 1443 to make an altar for the Basilica of St Anthony (the Santo Altar), and the statue of *Gattamelata* which stands, like Marcus Aurelius reborn, near the Basilica. Uccello came also, and painted monochrome frescoes (now lost) which probably showed his intense involvement with problems of perspective. Echoes of Donatello's art, steeped in antique grandeur, occur throughout Mantegna's career; and his concern with the excitement of perspective is continuous.

Mantegna's importance derives from his evocative antiquarianism, his sculptural figure-style, and his startling illusionism. In *The Martyrdom of St James* (?1554–7; Ovetari Chapel, Padua), we look up at the scene, with its background of Roman ruins and town. A soldier leans over the foreground fence, but that fence is attached to the frame of the fresco at the left, and so the soldier obtrudes into our own space, and the head of the executed saint will soon roll down towards us.

The San Zeno Altarpiece again profits from perspective to draw together into an airy loggia those elements of the *sacra conversazione* that were usually marooned in separate panels. He may have taken the concept from Filippo Lippi's Barbadori Altarpiece (commissioned 1437; Louvre, Paris) or from the original figure arrangement and architectural canopy of Donatello's Santo Altar. Mantegna's loggia resembles an antique shrine, with its columns and pillars with antique friezes, and garlands of fruit and flowers. As is frequently the case, humor tempers and therefore underlines the high seriousness of this monumental work: for the Anatolian carpet below the Virgin's throne hides the upper part of the two putti, while their fellows (brothers to those on the bronze panels of the Santo Altar) concentrate on their singing.

In Mantua, in the Camera degli Sposi (1472–4; Palazzo Ducale), Mantegna created another "loggia" with scenes of court life. Two walls were hung with actual gold-painted leather curtains, and these Mantegna continues on his painted walls, hanging them behind the scene of the Gonzaga court on one wall, and swept back (somewhat twisted over the door) to reveal on the adjacent wall the meeting of the Marquis with his son, Cardinal Francesco Gonzaga. Behind them lies a landscape strewn with evidence of the Romans—a colosseum, pyramid, great statue, mausoleum—and thus evidence, too, of the court's scholarly inclinations. We then look up past spandrels with scenes from Classical mythology, past cofferings wherein putti hold roundels with the heads of Roman emperors, to a central oculus with elaborate balcony, over which people stare down and around which putti edge precariously. Painted ceiling and painted people seem real because they are apparently in our space, and hence we are in their space and share their life. This room deliberately confuses the real with the painted; Correggio, in his work in the Camera di San Paolo (1518–19; S. Paolo, Parma) was later to imitate elements from it. And it is, indeed, from the Camera degli Sposi that the illusionistic ceiling decoration of the Baroque ultimately derives.

Mantegna's figure-style, popular in his day in northern Italy, was too brittle and linear to appeal to the High Renaissance, but his vision of Antiquity continued to hold great fascination. He never copied antiquities exactly, but sought to recreate an antique spirit, as in the nine monumental *Triumphs of Caesar*, painted in tempera on canvas (an early use of this support), which imitate Roman triumphal monuments and sculpture, and parallel Mantuan ceremonial.

Mantegna's influence was wide-ranging. He had begun to engrave c1465, and works by him and an extensive school further popularized his paintings. He was partly responsible for transmitting Florentine ideas to his brother-in-law, Giovanni Bellini, including the idea of the unified altarpiece. His works in Mantua increased Titian's interest in the Antique when he visited the city in 1523. They also impressed Giulio Romano when he settled there in 1524 and built the Palazzo del Tè (which one early commentator claimed was built just to house *The Triumphs of Caesar*). Rubens' period as court painter (1600–8 with interruptions) converted him, so to speak, to the Italian language of painting.

With the impoverishment of Mantua, Charles I bought the *Triumphs*, together with other paintings and Antique sculptures, in 1629; Richelieu eventually bought the paintings from the Studiolo after the Sack of 1630. The Camera degli Sposi remains a reminder of the Mantuan passion for Antiquity in plays, processions, ceremonial, scholarship, and art. Its illusionism might well derive from antique fresco decoration, just as the Palazzo del Tè imitates Roman villa design, and Alberti's churches in Mantua are based on antique temples and triumphal arches.

Further reading. Greenstein, J. *Mantegna and Painting as Historical Narrative*, Chicago (1992). Kristeller, P. *Andrea Mantegna*, London (1901). Levenson, J.A.,

Andrea Mantegna: The Agony in the Garden; panel; 63×80cm (25×32in); c1455. National Gallery, London

Oberhuber, K., and Sheehan, J.L. *Early Italian Engravings from the National Gallery of Art* (sections VIII and IX), Washington, D.C. (1973). Martindale, A. *The Triumphs of Caesar: Mantegna Paintings in the Collection of H.M. The Queen at Hampton Court*, London (1979). Paccagnini, G. *Andrea Mantegna*, Venice (1961). Paccagnini, G. and Mezzetti, A. *Andrea Mantegna*, Venice (1961).

Maratti Carlo 1625–1713

Carlo Maratti was the leading exponent of High Baroque Classicism in later 17th-century Rome. His achievement was based mainly on the production of altarpieces in the grand manner. A pupil of Andrea

protégé, Baciccia, during the 1670s, Maratti's classicizing and somewhat academic style was to dominate Roman painting for the rest of his long life.

Marc Franz 1880–1916

In his mature work the German painter Franz Marc pursued a mystical relationship between form and color using animals as his subjects. Like Kandinsky, with whom he organized the first *Blaue Reiter* exhibition in Munich in 1911, he adopted a spiritual attitude to the color and content of his paintings.

The son of a minor genre and landscape painter, Marc studied theology and then received a full academic training in art in Munich (1900–3), visiting Paris in 1903 and again in 1907. In his early work, most of which he destroyed, animals had already assumed a place of importance. The flat decorative patterns of *Jugendstil* liberated him from a servile study of nature, and his early decorative paintings are enlivened by the light in Impressionist art and the color of Van Gogh, whose paintings had particularly impressed him in Paris.

After his second visit to Paris in 1907, he applied himself to a rigorous study of animal anatomy, and painted in a number of Post-Impressionist styles, including Di-

Carlo Maratti: Self-portrait; red chalk on paper; 37×27cm (15×11in); 1684. British Museum, London

visionism. He developed a rhythmic approach to animals in landscape which he later described as "the anatomization of art". By 1910 he had adopted a theory of symbolic colors, and the flat strong color

Franz Marc: Two Cats: oil on canvas; 74×98cm (29×39in); 1912. Öffentliche Kunstsammlung, Kunstmuseum Basel

Sacchi and a friend of the theorist Pietro Bellori, he shared their admiration of Raphael and Annibale Carracci, and their disapproval of the more radically Baroque styles of Bernini and Pietro da Cortona. After a period of rivalry with Bernini's

of his paintings, reminiscent of Fauvism and the *Brücke*, brought him to the brink of Expressionist abstraction (in, for example, *House in Landscape*, 1910; Museum Folkwang, Essen). These works were intended to convey in symbolic color the rhythms of nature and of animal life.

In February 1911, when he joined the *Neue Künstlervereinigung* with Kandinsky, he wrote: "there are no 'subjects', and no 'colors' in art, only expression'". He later admitted that it was Kandinsky's painting that allowed him to use color to liberate and communicate his emotions. His paintings became more expressive and his color intense, with animals and landscape interlocked in a continuous rhythmic space (for example, *Blue Horses*, 1911; Walker Art Center, Minneapolis).

After participating in the *Blaue Reiter* exhibition and editing the *Blaue Reiter* almanac with Kandinsky, he went to Paris in 1912 with Macke (whom he had met in 1910) and visited Robert Delaunay, whose chromatic series of window-pictures made a strong impression on him. The interpretation of subject and surroundings in Marc's work after 1912 owes something to Delaunay's theories of Orphic "simultaneity", and to his contact with Cubism, which he described as a "mystic-inward construction".

The planar rhythms of Futurist painting also appealed to Marc and pushed him further towards abstraction. By 1913 the animals in his paintings assume a lesser importance and are dominated by swirling geometric forms in brilliant colors (for example, *Tyrol*, 1913–14; Neue Pinakothek, Munich). After participating in Walden's *Erster Deutscher Herbstsalon* in Berlin in 1913, Marc abandoned altogether the use of the subject. From then onwards he occupied himself almost exclusively with Abstract compositions, to which he gave titles such as *Struggling Forms*, *Broken Forms*, and *Cheerful Forms*. After moving to Ried (Upper Bavaria) in 1914, he was called up for military service and was killed at Verdun in 1916.

Further reading. Gerhardus, M. and D. *Expressionism*, Oxford (1979). Kandinsky, W. and Marc, F. *Der Blaue Reiter*, Munich (1965).

Marca-Relli Conrad 1913–

Corrado di Marca-Relli (or Conrad Marca-Relli) was one of the earliest of the second generation of American Abstract Expressionists. Born in Boston, he studied at the Cooper Union in New York (1930). He worked in the Federal Art Project, New York, from 1935 to 1938 and served in the U.S. army from 1941 to 1945. His favored technique is a painted collage with cut-out pieces of canvas laid on the canvas itself. His art in the 1950s owed something to Arshile Gorky, Willem de Kooning, and Robert Motherwell. His compositions ranged from the expressive and classical to the more Expressionist *The Battle* (1956; Metropolitan Museum, New York), a theme that was nonetheless inspired by Uccello's *Rout of San Romano* (c1456; panels in the Uffizi, Florence; National Gallery, London; and Louvre, Paris). Marca-Relli has developed a luminous and lyrical style of Abstract painting.

Marées Hans von 1837–87

The German painter Hans von Marées studied under Carl Steffek in Berlin (1853–5) and Carl Piloty in Munich (1857–64). In the early 1860s he began to work from nature under the influence of the Barbizon School, and painted landscapes in which the figure groups were integrated with their setting. In 1864 Count Schack sent him to Italy to copy Old Master paintings. This led to a more richly painted, but less realistically detailed style: a development strengthened in Paris in 1869, when he probably saw works by Puvis de Chavannes.

From this time onwards, Marées' work became more Symbolist in subject matter (for example *The Golden Age*; 1879–85 version and *Garden of the Hesperides*, 1884–5, both in the Neue Pinakothek, Munich) and more monumental in style (for example *Friends of the Artist in a Pergola*, 1873; part of the fresco done for the Stazione Zoologica, Naples). Influenced by the aesthetic ideas of Konrad Fiedler and Adolf von Hildebrand, Marées attempted to reconcile the tactile feeling for the third dimension with the two-dimensional demands of the picture plane: the constant reworking of his later canvases is evidence of his failure to achieve this goal.

Margaritone d'Arezzo 1216–93

The Tuscan Romanesque painter Mar-

Hans von Marées: Self-portrait with Franz Lenbach; oil on canvas; 54×62cm (21×24in); 1863. Neue Pinakothek, Munich

Margaritone d'Arezzo: The Virgin and Child Enthroned, with Scenes of the Nativity and the Lives of the Saints; panel; 93×183cm (37×72in); c1262? National Gallery, London

garitone d'Arezzo worked in a style similar to that of Coppo di Marcovaldo and Guido da Siena. Our information about this artist comes mostly from Vasari's *Lives*, where he appears to have been given prominence not because of artistic quality, but because he and Vasari shared the same birthplace. Of one of his works, Vasari says that it was executed "with diligence and grace ... the little figures in it are so carefully finished that they resemble the work of an illuminator". This agrees with surviving works, such as his *Virgin and Child Enthroned* (National Gallery, London), where the figures are contained within a delicate mandorla. Again according to Vasari, Margaritone was also a sculptor in wood, an experimenter with canvas as a support, and an architect.

Marin John 1870–1953

An American painter, promoted by Alfred Stieglitz, John Marin developed a style based on a combination of a Futurist shorthand interpretation of New York and a romantic appreciation of the landscape of New England. He trained as an architect, traveled (though was relatively untouched by his European experiences), and had reached a personal expression by 1912 with *Movement: Fifth Avenue* (water-color; Art Institute of Chicago). Later, his fragmented but painterly style was applied to landscape, as in *Maine Islands* (water-color; 1922; The Phillips Collection, Washington, D.C.). As a watercolorist and etcher he was at his best; he achieved a personal vision, developed from Futurist sources, combined with a poetic identification with a particular landscape, and forged by an artistic single-mindedness.

Marinetti Emilio 1876–1944

Emilio Filippo Tommaso Marinetti was an Italian poet and writer, editor of *Poesia* from 1905, and founder of the literary Futurist movement. He became dissatisfied with the "passivity" of literature, and used the political manifesto as an instrument of artistic innovation in the *First Futurist Manifesto* published in the Paris *Figaro* of 20 February 1909. In 1910 the *Technical Manifesto of Futurist Painting*, signed by Carlo Carrà, Giacomo Balla, Umberto Boccioni, Gino Severini, and Luigi Russolo, embodied Marinetti's love of destruction and speed. In 1912 he proposed a poetry of "free words" in which the text is freely disposed on the page; *Zang-tumb tuum* (1914) was his first work in this style. He later became an apologist of Fascism (*Futurisimo e fascismo*, 1924).

Marini Marino 1901–80

The Italian sculptor and painter Marino Marini was born in Pistoia and studied at the Academy of Art in Florence with Domenico Trentacosta. He taught at the School of Art at the Villa Reale in Monza

Marino Marini: Horseman; bronze; 163×155×68cm (65×61×27in); 1947. Tate Gallery, London

(1929–40) and in 1940 he was appointed Professor of Sculpture at the Brera Academy in Milan. In Paris he became acquainted with Kandinsky, Maillol, and Picasso, and in Switzerland (1942–6) he met Fritz Wotruba and Alberto Giacometti. Later he lived and worked in Milan.

Marini's best known works—sculpture, painting, and graphics—deal with portrait heads and the themes of "Pomona" and the "Horse and Rider" (for example, *Horse and Rider*, 1957; Peggy Guggenheim Collection, Venice). After the Second World War the development of the latter theme reflected Marini's ideas on the tragedy of human existence (for example, *Horse and Rider*; bronze; 1947; Tate Gallery, London). He is also famous for his portrait busts (for example *Igor Stravinsky*, 1950; San Francisco Museum of Art).

Further reading. Finn, D. and Hunter, S. *Marino Marini*, New York (1993).

Marinus van Reymerswaele
*c*1493–*c*1567

Marinus Claesz. van Reymerswaele was a Flemish artist, probably born in Roymerswaele, Zeeland, trained at Antwerp. He painted several versions of the *St Jerome in his Study* theme (1521 version; Prado, Madrid), which is loosely derived from a composition by Albrecht Dürer and influenced by the fashion for caricature painting established by the Massys workshop. The usual humanistic portrayal of the Saint is here replaced by strong asceticism. His style became increasingly exaggerated and linear; the elaborate headgear of the *Tax Gatherers* (National Gallery, London) may be a satirical comment on official dress of the period. In 1567 he participated in the destruction of images in Middelburg Cathedral (Zeeland) and was exiled.

Marisol 1930–

Marisol Escobar, who never uses her second name, is an American Pop sculptor. She is a Venezuelan, born in Paris, who studied at the École des Beaux-Arts, Paris, in 1949, and later with Hans Hofmann in New York. Her art is one of Pop assemblage, in a style more refined and whimsical than that of Claes Oldenburg and less savage than that of Edward Kienholz. Marisol creates wooden groups of figures, such as *The Family* (1961; Museum of Modern Art, New York), from carving, assemblage, drawing, and stencil work. Her own face frequently appears in her work, which, despite its sophistication, has a self-conscious naivety that links it with the craft tradition in American art.

Marmion Simon *c*1420–89

Simon Marmion was a French painter active in Flanders at the time when the munificent Philip the Good (Duke of Burgundy 1419–67) afforded such liberal patronage to artists. Marmion was born in Amiens, where he still lived in 1454. He subsequently moved to Valenciennes, where he is recorded from 1458 to 1484. There he worked in the publishing house of the scribe and historian Jean Mansel; the so-called "Mansel Master", a painter in the tradition of the Master of the Duke of Bedford, was his collaborator and may have been his teacher. Some miniatures in the Mansel Master's sumptuous *La Fleur des Histoires* (Bibliothèque Royale Albert I, Brussels; MS. 9231–9232) may be by the young Marmion. More than 50 manuscripts and panel paintings formerly attributed to him are now regarded as the work of several hands; it is not certain which, if any, should be attributed to Marmion himself.

Simon Marmion: St Jerome with a Donor; panel; 65×49cm (26×19in). John G. Johnson Art Collection, Philadelphia Museum of Art

Marisol: The Family; painted wood and other materials in three sections; 210×166cm (83×65in); 1962. Museum of Modern Art, New York

The first work to be hypothetically associated with his name was the fragmentary St Bertin Altarpiece (Staatliche Museen, Berlin, and National Gallery, London). Surviving panels depict scenes from the life of the Saint; the narrative is expertly controlled and exquisitely detailed. The same hand contributed to the *Grandes Chroniques de France* (State Library, St Petersburg), another copy of the *Fleur des Histoires* (Scottenstift, Vienna; MS. 139–140), and a number of devotional books. These show the artist to have been influenced by Jan van Eyck and Rogier van der Weyden, but his ability to tell a story is unprecedented.

Many of the "Marmion" miniatures illustrate historical texts that had no established iconographic tradition: the inventiveness shown in devising appropriate images is unfailing. Various individual hands have been distinguished among these manuscripts, including that of the Louthe Master, named after a book of hours in Louvain (Library of the Catholic University; MS. A. 2), and the Tondal Master, named after the *Vision du Chevalier Tondal*, a moralizing tract in Cambridge, Mass. (Houghton Library, MS. 235H).

The palettes of the "Marmion" painters differ widely, but all the artists share a competence in linear perspective that is suavely manipulated to avoid destroying the essentially flat surface of the manuscript page. Their landscapes are elegant and fanciful, their figures individually characterized, and their subject matter is often original. Their influence can be seen in the work of contemporaries like Loyset Liédet, and their effect on the next generation of illuminators was profound. Although there is no solid evidence to link Marmion himself with any extant paintings, he is extensively documented in legal and fiscal records. He was evidently regarded as the most important of the Valenciennes artists, and was described by a contemporary poet as "prince d'enluminure".

Martin John 1789–1854

John Martin was an English history and landscape painter and engraver. Born in Haydon Bridge, Northumberland, he exhibited his first major history painting, *Joshua Commanding the Sun to Stand Still Upon Gibeon* (Grand Lodge Museum, London), at the Royal Academy in 1816.

John Martin: The Assuaging of the Waters; oil on canvas; 132×203cm (52×80in); 1840. General Assembly of the Church of Scotland, Edinburgh

He specialized in painting catastrophic history subjects in which multitudes of figures were convulsed in turbulent landscapes or dwarfed by elaborate architectural fantasies. *Joshua* was followed by a succession of equally sensational canvases: *Belshazzar's Feast* (1821; Mansion House, Newcastle-upon-Tyne), *The Fall of Nineveh* (1827/8), and trilogies on the themes of the *Deluge* (1826–40) and *Last Judgment* (1851–4).

Martin became a bitter opponent of the London art establishment, by whom he was treated badly, and in the 1820s took to promoting his pictures by publishing his own mezzotint reproductions. His paintings and engravings, and his published illustrations to *Paradise Lost* (1825) and the Old Testament (1831–5) were immensely successful with the public, both in England and France, influencing painters and writers from Thomas Cole to Victor Hugo.

Further reading. Feaver, W. *The Art of John Martin*, London (1975).

Martin Kenneth and Mary
20th century

The British painters and sculptors Kenneth and Mary Martin were married in 1930. Kenneth Martin (1905–) was born in Sheffield, studying at the city's School of Art and at the Royal College of Art in London (1929–32). During the 1930s he painted landscapes but after the mid 1940s turned to Abstract styles. He is best known for his mobiles and sculpture in metal, often small in scale, severe in style, and made, seemingly, with mathematical precision (for example, *Rotary Rings (4th version)*, 1968; Tate Gallery, London).

Mary Martin (1907–69) was born in Folkestone and studied at Goldsmiths' School of Art and at the Royal College of Art. Landscape and still life were her favorite themes, but she also produced constructed Abstract reliefs and was associated with the constructivist group that included Anthony Hill, Victor Pasmore, and her husband.

Martini Arturo 1889–1947

The Italian sculptor Arturo Martini was born in Treviso. He studied under Adolf von Hildebrand in Munich in 1909. Hildebrand's belief that the parts of a sculpture should be instantaneously visible was an influence on the later art of Martini. Therefore he often used high relief evoking an interior space, as did Italian Renaissance sculptors. In 1921 he joined the *Valori Plastici* ("Plastic Values") group which advocated a return to classicism. The geometric treatment of the figures in many of Martini's sculptures recalls the painting of another member of the group, Carlo Carrà. Martini believed that sculpture was an impersonal, universal art. He executed many public commissions in Italy (for example, *Corporate Justice*, 1937; Palace of Justice, Milan), including *Italian Pioneers of America* (1927–8; Worcester, Mass.) in collaboration with Maurice Sterne (1878–1957). His complex, turbulent, and always original work has been influential on subsequent Italian sculpture.

Martins Maria 1900–73

The Brazilian sculptor Maria Martins (also known simply as Maria) was born in Campanha, Brazil, and studied painting at the Academy in Rio de Janeiro and with Catherine Barjanski in Paris, before turning to sculpture in wood in 1926. In the 1930s in Japan she worked in ceramics, then in 1939 studied under the sculptor Oscar Jespers in Brussels. Eventually she turned from wood and stone to work in bronze. She was represented at the "Surrealist International Exhibition" in Paris in 1947. Her work, which refers to her memories of the tropical vegetation of her home country, was inspired by Surrealism and approaches abstraction (for example, *The Impossible III*; bronze; 1946; Museum of Modern Art, New York).

Masaccio: Study of a Student; pen and ink on paper. Uffizi, Florence

Masaccio 1401–28?

The Italian painter Tommaso Cassai is known to us by his nickname. "Masaccio" is a shortened form of "Tommasaccio", today the Italian for something equivalent to "big ugly Tom"; the name Masaccio may have been adopted to distinguish him from his older colleague, Tommaso di Cristoforo Fini, nicknamed "Masolino" (1383–1440/7), "little Thomas", with whom Masaccio worked. Masaccio died at the early age of 26 or 27 but managed to paint a few pictures of such enormous impact as to affect not only the whole future course of Florentine painting but also that of European painting in general.

He was born on 21 December 1401 at Castel San Giovanni, the modern San Giovanni Valdarno. Located in the upper Arno valley, San Giovanni lies some 28 miles (45 km) from Florence and about 18½ miles (30 km) from Arezzo. Masaccio's father was a young notary, his mother, Mona Jacopa di Martinozzo, the daughter of an innkeeper from a nearby town. Masaccio's father died young, but his mother remarried, this time a rich apothecary in San Giovanni. This second husband, Tedesco del Maestro Feo, died in 1417. Masaccio had one brother, the painter Giovanni di Ser Giovanni (1406–?) nicknamed "Lo Scheggia". One of their step-sisters, Caterina, married in 1422 the painter Mariotto di Cristofano.

Beyond what can be gleamed from his paintings, very little is known of Masaccio's life. From documents it is, however, known that on 7 January 1422 he became a member of the Florentine painters' guild, the Arte de' Medici e Speziali, while living in the parish of San Niccolò Oltrarno. In 1424 he joined the Compagnia di San Luca, to which painters often belonged. Eight payments towards an altarpiece painted for the Carmelite church in Pisa attest to the fact that he was in that city during much of 1426, that he knew Donatello, and employed Andrea di Giusto. There is a mention of Masaccio and his brother in the 1426 *Estimo* for San Giovanni Valdarno. In 1427 Masaccio made, in his own handwriting, his tax declaration to the newly instituted *Catasto*: he was then living in what is now the Via dei Servi and had his shop near the Badia. This same source gives us the approximate date of his death: next to his name for the returns of 1429 is written, "Dicesi è morto a Roma", that is: "He is said to have died in Rome".

Nothing is known of Masaccio's training. The apprentice system was such that he was probably learning a trade as early as 1410. This may have begun in a local painter's shop, or else in a family workshop. (Masaccio's paternal grandfather was a maker of *cassoni* or wooden chests; these were often painted.) Or he may have been sent to train in a *bottega* in Arezzo, in Florence, or elsewhere—but there is no evidence to show his early training was necessarily in the painter's craft.

Masaccio's earliest known extant painting, an altarpiece of the *Madonna and Child with Two Angels and Four Saints* (1422; from S. Giovenale di Cascia, near S. Giovanni; now in the Uffizi, Florence) does give us some idea of what his training as a painter must have been. Masaccio was 20 years old when this picture was dated. It shows us that he is already interested in space: not only do the lines in the floor indicate an attempt to grasp the laws of linear perspective, but so does the structure of the throne, with its slanted sides and curved back. The sense of space is heightened both by the apparent modeling of the robes and faces and by the use of alternating light and dark colors. Wherever Masaccio trained, it can hardly have been in the strongly International Gothic atmosphere prevalent in Florentine painting in the first two decades of the 15th century, where a sinuous elegant surface line was more important than depth within the picture. On the contrary an interest in modeling, in flesh tones, in space, and in light is much more characteristic of Marchigian painters. Both Arcangelo di Cola da Camerino (fl. 1416–22) and Gentile da Fabriano (c1370–1427) show particular interest in these things, and both were in Florence, the former c1419–22, the latter first in 1419–20 and then again in 1422–5. It is possible that Masaccio was influenced by one or both of them. There is also one Florentine painter who shows much of Masaccio's interest in modeling and space, Giovanni Toscani, and it is not unlikely that Masaccio was trained by him. Other possible masters to Masaccio were Bicci di Lorenzo and Francesco di Antonio. Masolino, who came from near San Giovanni, and with whom Masaccio worked on at least three commissions, was almost certainly not Masaccio's master. Masolino probably hired Masaccio to help him with important commissions; but it was the much younger painter, Masaccio, who then influenced his senior.

The whole of Masaccio's authenticated extant work, besides the San Giovenale painting, derives from only five other commissions: the so-called "Matterza" *Madonna and Child with St Anne* (c1424; Uffizi Florence), the Pisa Altarpiece (panels now dispersed), a fresco of *The Trinity* in S. Maria Novella, Florence, frescoes in the Brancacci Chapel, S. Maria del Carmine, Florence, and *SS. Jerome and John the Baptist* from an altarpiece originally in S. Maria Maggiore, Rome.

The first of these, the Uffizi *Madonna and Child with St Anne*, was executed with the help of Masolino c1424 for the church of S. Ambrogio in Florence. Masolino painted St Anne, plus all the angels except the middle one on the right; Masaccio did the Virgin, Christ Child, and remaining angel. In spite of the difference between Masolino's more orthodox approach and Masaccio's strong volumes, the picture is remarkably harmonious. Masaccio has placed his Madonna extremely low, emphasizing the light and shade falling on her knees, on the folds in her robes, and on the Infant Christ. As in the S. Giovenale painting, he has painted the Christ Child nude; but here the figure seems so solid and is so Classical in flavor that the painter must have drawn it after an antique statue. There are, in fact, many extant antique statues of babes in just this pose.

The chronology of the other known works is not clear, although they seem all to have been painted between 1425 and the artist's death, probably some time in 1428. It seems possible that Masaccio painted *The Trinity* in S. Maria Novella, Florence, in 1425 or 1426, perhaps for the feast of Corpus Domini in one of those years, although stylistically the painting is so advanced that it may well date after the painter's earliest work in the Brancacci chapel. Masaccio probably helped Masolino to plan the frescoes in the Brancacci Chapel in S. Maria del Carmine during 1425, and then began himself to paint there some time after Masolino's departure for Hungary in September of the same year. Masaccio must have worked at them during 1426, as well perhaps as during 1427. The Pisa Altarpiece is, as mentioned above, documented during much of 1426; while the panel of *SS. Jerome and John the Baptist* (National Gallery, London) from the S. Maria Maggiore altarpiece was probably painted during Masaccio's trip to Rome in 1427/28.

From the tentative converging lines of the San Giovenale triptych, right through all his subsequent works, Masaccio developed two themes that were to remain central to the history of Western painting. The first is the successful portrayal of a natural world within the painting, with convincing space, light, air, and objects. The second is part of this, but at the same time independent of it: the portrayal of a convincing replica of man, who dominates and gives order to that world. This is, of course, a visual version of the more general search for a correct scientific definition of man's place in the natural world, which occupies the Renaissance in all its facets.

Masaccio's *Trinity* terminates the Middle Ages by expressing the essence of medieval Christian belief in Renaissance terms. His *The Tribute Money* in the Brancacci Chapel, on the other hand, stands clearly beyond the threshold, in the light-filled world of the Renaissance.

Nothing could be more traditional to the waning Christian age than Masaccio's *Trinity* theme of a predominant God the Father, supporting his crucified human Son, joined by the white dove of the Holy Spirit: the universal, the human, the spiritual. But nothing could be less traditional in its expression. Vaulted by a magnificent Renaissance triumphal arch, the divine trio appears almost suspended before a pierced wall. This coffered Brunelleschian space seems to be a mortuary chamber, a holy sepulcher from which the Christ is shown resurrected by His Father, Savior to a waiting world, presented by the Virgin and St John; this world is symbolized by the two donors just outside. The worldly spectator is also included in the painting by association with the skeleton under the altar; unlike the human body of Christ, which rose intact, our worldly bodies decay. Above the skeleton are written some words to warn the passerby; "I was that which you are, you will be that which I am". Inside the sepulcher, the space has been constructed according to the laws of linear perspective, so that the eye appears to be looking into the interior of a magnificent Renaissance building.

Masaccio set the background to *The Tribute Money*, in the Brancacci Chapel at S. Maria del Carmine, in a light-filled landscape, dominated (as is the countryside at San Giovanni Valdarno) by high hills. The painter, using newly established laws of perspective, created an infallible illusion of air, light, and space. But whereas in *The Trinity* God is the theme, here it is Man who dominates. Masaccio places in the natural scene classical statuesque figures, also apparently modeled after the Antique, who are above all human and free to move within their own natural world.

The Tribute Money emerges as, historically, the most important single picture in Florence today. Each individual in the painting stands, for the first time, strong and solitary, on a natural and benevolent earth, sustained by real air, bathed in light, master of the world stretching all around. Masaccio threw off the gloom and mystery of earlier times, resurrecting the forms of an ancient pre-Christian world. In the painting Christ stands equal to Man, not dominating him: a human being Himself, giving good advice to His followers. In *The Tribute Money* we already witness a Reformation—clearly evident too in the humanistic work of Donatello and Brunelleschi—in which Man does not cease to believe in Christ, although he may cease to believe the infallibility of the Roman Church. Rather, Man ceases to believe in a triumphal Christ-God and begins to believe in a human Christ-Man.

The frescoes in the Brancacci chapel, of which *The Tribute Money* is one, relate scenes from the life of St Peter. The whole cycle seems to have been begun by Masolino c1425, and then continued by Masaccio. The chapel was not actually finished until much later in the 15th century, by Filippino Lippi. *The Tribute Money* itself alludes in some way to Man's separate duties to the State and to the Church. In it St Peter is instructed by Christ to pay a tax to the civil authority. This must certainly be a reference to the obligations of the Roman Church towards secular authority; it probably also refers to each individual man's obligation to render separately to God and to Caesar that which is due to them.

The other paintings by Masaccio in the chapel seem to confirm this message: St Peter is seen preaching, baptizing, healing, and distributing alms: all corporal works of mercy. What then is the meaning of Masaccio's stupendous fresco of *The Expulsion from Paradise* on the entrance arch to the chapel? Perhaps Masaccio meant simply to point out that the anguish of Man over his loss of paradise can be solaced by the good works of Holy Mother the Church; the Church is the source of grace, through which Man can be saved.

The only two other extant, autograph works by Masaccio have already been

Masaccio: Madonna and Child with Angels, from the Pisa Altarpiece; panel; 136×73cm (54×29in); 1426. National Gallery, London

else, he introduces the greatest innovation of Renaissance painting: light defined as coming from a single source, by the shadows it casts. In this painting too, one is aware of the great sensitivity and delicacy of the painter's brushwork—the angels playing lutes are of such a simplicity and craftsmanship as to make them seem to sing. Two other remarkable paintings from this altarpiece are the small panels of the *Crucifixion* now in Naples (Museo e Gallerie Nazionali di Capodimonte), and the *Nativity* in Berlin (Staatliche Museen). In the former the animal-like figure of the crouched Magdalene gesturing towards the anguish of St John and of the Virgin is of such a simple expressive force as almost to defy analysis. Christ's stark, shadow-struck body, meant to be seen from below, is also intensely expressive. As for the small *Nativity* panel, its lifelike Kings, the animals, the Holy Family—all are bathed in a dawn light, clearly defining the spaces involved, throwing sharp shadows.

The London panel of *SS. Jerome and John the Baptist* was once part of a triptych painted on both sides for the Roman basilica of S. Maria Maggiore. This painting, which represents the founding of that church, flanked by saints, is predominantly by Masolino; for some unknown reason, however, Masaccio executed this one panel. Since Masaccio and Masolino worked together on the Uffizi Madonna, in the Brancacci Chapel, as well as perhaps in other places, it is not so surprising that they collaborated here too.

Masaccio's contribution to the development of Western painting is enormous. During the first two decades of the 15th century, both sculpture (primarily through the work of Jacopo della Quercia and Donatello) and architecture (through that of Brunelleschi) began to be cast in a new Renaissance idiom. In the course of a few years during the 1420s, Masaccio managed to set Western painting on a Renaissance course, similar in essence and language to that taken by those other expressions. Whereas Giotto had created, over a century earlier, an ideal world in which Christian myths were acted out, Masaccio secularized that world by filling it with space, light, and air, and by placing a Classical sort of man within it, surrounded by nature. This idea of man as central to a logical natural world, and master of it, was to remain the principal source of imagery for Western painting until very recent times.

mentioned: the various panels from the Pisa polyptych, and the panel of *SS. Jerome and John the Baptist* from Masolino's S. Maria Maggiore altarpiece. The former group includes the strongly rendered *Madonna and Child with Four Angels*, now in London's National Gallery, the central panel of the original altarpiece. Here, even within the most traditional late medieval *schema*, the painter introduces strong volumes for the Madonna's robes, and space all around the throne. Above all

Further reading. Berenson, B. *The Italian Painters of the Renaissance*, New York (1952, reissued 1980). Berti, L. *Masaccio*, London and University Park, Pa. (1967). Meiss, M. "Masaccio and the Early Renaissance", *Studies in Western Art: Acts of the XXth International Congress* vol. II, Princeton (1963). Procacci, U. *The Complete Paintings of Masaccio*, New York (1962). Spike, J. *Masaccio*, New York (1995).

Masanobu Kano *c1434–c1530*

The Japanese painter Kano Masanobu was the founder of the *Kano* School, whose members were official painters to the government and court for 400 years. His appointment as leader of the academy was a major innovation, since he was of lowly birth and not a Zen devotee (though he learned landscape in the Chinese monochrome style). His few surviving works show the exaggerated contrast between strongly outlined, hatched rocks and trees, and misty washes and patches of color, that became the standard *Kano* style.

Maso di Banco *fl. 1340–50*

The Florentine painter Maso di Banco was a pupil of Giotto. (Vasari identified him with an artist named "Giottino", but modern critics do not accept this and there is some doubt whether Giottino ever existed.) Little is known of Maso di Banco apart from documentary references between 1341 and 1350.

In 1341 his painting equipment was confiscated by Ridolfo dei Bardi, probably because he failed to finish the frescoes in the Chapel of S. Silvestro, S. Croce, Florence, by the stipulated time. These frescoes form the basis for attributing to him two altarpieces, one in S. Spirito, Florence, and the other formerly divided between a private collection and Berlin (the Berlin panels were destroyed in the Second World War). To these works can be added a fragmentary fresco of *The Coronation of the Virgin* (entry to the cloister, S. Croce, Florence) and a small panel in Budapest.

Although the S. Silvestro frescoes have been repainted, they show Maso to be a highly original artist as well as a logical and supremely able follower of Giotto. In *St Sylvester Reviving a Bull* the absence of decorative framing round the scene is part of a general breaking down of the division between real and pictorial space. Over a tomb in the same chapel is a powerful fresco portrait of Ridolfo dei Bardi praying to Christ the Judge while the Last Trump is sounded over a deserted landscape.

Maso's S. Spirito Altarpiece contrasts with the vigor of the S. Silvestro frescoes, and shows a gentle refinement of design and execution. The figures on either side of the Madonna and Child are shown in rather more than half-length, helping to emphasize the effect of each figure turning inwards. Despite the gold background of each compartment, the final impression is of a row of sculptural niches with three-dimensional figures. Typically, his achievement here is founded on a deep knowledge of Giotto's work, together with a sensitivity to the contemporary influence of Sienese art on Florentine painting.

Maso di Banco: St Sylvester Restores to Life Two Sorcerers; fresco; *c*1340. Chapel of S. Silvestro, S. Croce, Florence

Masolino: detail of St Peter raising St Tabitha; fresco; 1424/5. S. Maria del Carmine, Florence

Masolino 1383–c1447

The early work of the Florentine painter, Tommaso di Cristoforo Fini, called Masolino, was rooted in the 14th century, as for example his *Madonna* of 1423 (Kunsthalle Bremen). But while engaged on frescoes in the Brancacci Chapel (S. Maria del Carmine, Florence) during the years 1424 and 1425 he momentarily adopted the grander, weightier figure-style of the young Masaccio, with whom he shared the project. Masolino's later work, such as the fresco cycles in Rome (1427–31?; S. Clemente) and in the Baptistery at Castiglione d'Olona near Milan (1435), show a reversion to the softer, more decorative style associated with International Gothic. This can look incongruous against his occasional virtuoso displays of perspective.

Further reading. Roberts, P. *Masolino da Panicale*, Oxford (1993).

Masson André 1896–1987

André Masson was a French painter who was associated with the Surrealist movement. At first influenced by Cubism (as in *Card Players*, 1923; private collection) he began to frequent the Surrealist group in 1923 and 1924, having attracted André Breton's attention, and produced, in a remarkable series of drawings, some of the earliest essays in pictorial automatism. With his sand-paintings of 1926 onwards, they epitomize the Surrealist doctrine of obedience to chance and the unconscious. He broke with the Surrealists in 1929, but reestablished contact in the late 1930s. From 1941 to 1945 he lived in Connecticut, where his work was a formative influence on Abstract Expressionism.

Masson's work underwent many stylistic changes. Influenced by philosophy and myth, he concentrated on rendering symbolically man's relationship to nature and the urgency of human passion. His work is frequently erotic and violent (for example, *Massacres*, 1932–3; a pen and ink drawing in the Galerie Louise Leiris, Paris) characterized by expressionistic line, color, and brushwork (for example, *Nioke*, 1947; Galerie Louise Leiris, Paris), and agitated composition *(Wave of the Future*, 1976; private collection). He executed sculptures and Surrealist objects, illustrated books (for example, Malraux's *Conquerors*, 1948) and designed sets and costumes for the theater.

Further reading. Clebert, J.-P. *Mythologie de André Masson*, Geneva (1971). Hahn, O. *Masson*, Paris (1965). Leiris, M. and Limbour, G. *André Masson and his Universe*, London (1947). Rubin, W. and Lanchner, C. *André Masson*, New York (1976).

Massys family
15th and 16th centuries

The Massys were a family of Flemish painters, which included Quentin (1465/6–1530), Cornelis (c1508–c60), and Jan (c1510–75). Quentin Massys was born at Louvain in the southern Netherlands. There is no record of his training in any specific workshop. His early style suggests a grounding in the current Flemish idiom of such painters as Hans Memling and Gerard David, with the additional knowledge of current trends in the High Renaissance painting of Italy.

His *The Betrothal of St Catherine* (c1500; National Gallery, London), painted on canvas, shows a three-quarter-length Madonna and Child, flanked by saints in an architectural setting. The format and courtly style of dress parallels other Flemish pictures, but the scale of work is Italian and the soft treatment of the features reminiscent of Leonardo. In 1511 Massys completed a life-size triptych of *The Family of St Anne* for S. Pierre, Louvain (now Musées Royaux des Beaux-Arts de Belgique, Brussels). Again the figures are placed before an architectural screen, which here gives on to landscape. Softness of line and color is accentuated by the diffusion of light so that the forms appear almost shadowless.

The other important triptych of these years, the Lamentation Altar (1507–9; Royal Museum of Fine Arts, Antwerp), reveals a close study of Rogier van der Weyden's *Deposition* (Prado, Madrid), then in Louvain. But it substitutes a landscape background, and suppresses the heightened emotion of the earlier work. The top of the altarpiece when opened is shaped as a double curve, a form that Massys helped introduce to Flemish art.

Later works show a certain sentimentality, as in the entwined gestures of the *Madonna and Child* of c1520 (Staatliche Museen, Berlin). Massys came closest to Leonardo's figure-style in the *Virgin and Child* (National Museum, Poznan) which directly reflects Leonardo's concern with a pyramidal grouping of figures in a land-

André Masson: Battle of the Fishes; mixed media including sand on canvas; 36×73cm (14×29in); 1926. Museum of Modern Art, New York

Quentin Massys: The Banker and his Wife; panel; 74×68cm (29×27in); 1514. Louvre, Paris

scape setting. It is significant that the chief attraction of Italy for Massys was the work of Leonardo and the Lombard school; he seems less interested than other Netherlandish artists in Rome and the Antique. He was always aware of the Flemish 15th-century tradition; works such as *The Banker and his Wife* (1514; Louvre, Paris) are a conscious revival of the techniques and style of dress of the age of Jan van Eyck.

Quentin Massys' influence was profound, not only technically and stylistically but in the creation of new fashions in pictures; he is credited, for example, with the invention of the theme of the "ill-matched couple" that became a popular subject in northern Europe.

Cornelis Massys, the elder son of Quentin, was chiefly a painter of landscape subjects. In *The Arrival of the Holy Family at Bethlehem* (1543; Staatliche Museen, Berlin), the landscape takes precedence over the religious subject.

Jan Massys, the younger son, was banished from Antwerp as a Protestant and worked mainly in France and Italy. His *Flora Meretrix* (1561; National-museum, Stockholm), while close to Quentin Massys in countenance, has the elegance and courtliness of the painting style of the School of Fontainebleau. His choice of religious subjects is often determined by this style, as in *Susanna and the Elders* (1567; Musées Royaux des Beaux-Arts de Belgique, Brussels).

Further reading. Bosque, A. de *Quentin Metsys*, Brussels (1974). Friedländer, M.J. *Early Netherlandish Painting* (vol. 7), Leiden (1971).

Master Bertram c1345–1415

The German painter Master Bertram, apparently a native of Minden, is first recorded in Hamburg in 1367. His name appears in the town accounts in connection with official commissions until 1387. From 1379 to 1383 he painted the great altarpiece for the high altar of St Peter in Hamburg (Hamburger Kunsthalle, Hamburg) known as the Grabower Altarpiece. The realism he exhibits in this work anticipates certain qualities of 15th-century Flemish painting and provides a parallel to contemporary painting in Bohemia. Master Bertram's later activity, and the status of the Buxtehuder and Harvestehuder Altars (Hamburger Kunsthalle, Hamburg) is less certain, though he died in Hamburg having been the most important painter there.

Master of Cabestany
fl. mid–late 12th century

The Master of Cabestany was a sculptor trained either in Tuscany or Roussillon, whose career spanned the years from the middle to the end of the 12th century. His works can be found in two areas: either in churches on both sides of the modern frontier between France and Spain (some fragments from works in this area are to be found in the Fitzwilliam Museum, Cambridge, and in the Cloisters, New York) or else in Tuscany, most notably in the abbey church of S. Antimo. The tympanum of the church at Cabestany near Perpignan (hence the Master's name) is decorated with scenes of the Death and Assumption of the Virgin, whose girdle is held by St Thomas. This may indicate that the Master was of Tuscan origin—Prato in Tuscany was the most famous of several places to claim possession of the Virgin's girdle. But whether the Master was Italian, French, or Catalan it is impossible to say.

His highly charged emotional figures with massive heads are swathed in toga-like garments etched into deep drilled channels. It was probably from a study of late Roman or Early Christian sarcophagus sculpture that he developed a highly idiosyncratic use of the drill. He also liked working in marble.

Master of the Duke of Bedford
fl. 1405–35

The Master of the Duke of Bedford was head of one of the major illuminators' shops in Paris. He was named after his patron, the Regent of France, for whom he produced his two masterpieces: the Bedford Hours (British Library, London; Add. MS. 18850; c1423) and Breviary (Bibliothèque Nationale, Paris; MS. Lat. 17294; c1435). These profusely illustrated books, in which the miniatures are surrounded by smaller scenes set in medallions in the ornamental borders, reveal a sophisticated sense of color. He collaborated with the Boucicaut and Rohan Masters; compared with theirs, this technique is more "painterly". A panel-painting of the *Last Judgment* (Louvre, Paris) has been attributed to him.

Master of the Duke of Bedford: The Building of the Ark, from the Bedford Hours; 41×28cm (16×11in); c1423. British Library, London

Master ES *c1430–67*

The father of true copperplate engraving, the Master ES is named from the signature "E" or "ES" on a group of 18 engravings, some of which are also dated 1466 and 1467. The "S" could possibly stand for Strasbourg since some engravings include Alsatian coats of arms; around them an oeuvre of more than 300 plates has been assembled. The Master ES was responsible for a technical revolution when he developed an intricate repertoire of short flicks of the burin combined with dots and crosshatching to model his forms. His most sophisticated works are the dated plates of 1466 and 1467. Scholars have concluded that he probably died soon after completing them. Examples of his work may be seen in the Graphische Sammlung Albertina, Vienna.

Master of Flémalle *c1375–1444*

The Flemish painter known as the Master of Flémalle takes his name from a group of panel-paintings at Frankfurt which allegedly come from a putative abbey at Flémalle-lez-Liège. This artist is now usually identified with Robert Campin. Although the latter has no surviving documented works, this identification appears secure, because the pictures of artists known to have been Campin's pupils reveal an intimate knowledge of the style of the Master of Flémalle. A significant number of paintings have been attributed to the composite personality Flémalle/Campin, but the general lack of documentation inhibits unanimity of opinion on the precise nature of his oeuvre.

Campin may have been born in Valenciennes. By 1406 he had moved to Tournai, where he remained until his death. He enjoyed various influential posts in the painters' guild and in the city. From 1423 until 1428 the guilds held political power in Tournai, and Campin became a councillor. After the return of the patriciate he was victimized by the authorities, being prosecuted for alleged immorality in 1429 and 1432. In spite of this, he continued to receive municipal commissions, maintained a large workshop, and seems to have remained extremely prosperous. His most famous pupil was Rogier van der Weyden.

Campin's earliest surviving work is probably the *Entombment* triptych in the Home House Collection, London. Although this altarpiece retains the gold

Master of Flémalle: Virgin and Child before a Firescreen; oil on oak panel; 64×49cm (25×19in); c1430. National Gallery, London

ground typical of earlier panel-paintings, the conception of the figures represents a dramatic break with the International Gothic tradition. The voluminous draperies of Campin's weighty figures relate more closely to the sculpture of Claus Sluter than to any previous pictorial models. As the motif of the angel wiping his eyes with the back of his hand appears to derive from Sluter's *Well of Moses* for the center of the great cloister of the Charterhouse of Champmol in Dijon, the possibility of direct contact is all the more

likely. On iconographic grounds the double-faced panel *The Betrothal of the Virgin* (c1420–30; Prado, Madrid) is equally revolutionary: the main composition incorporates Romanesque and Flamboyant Gothic buildings to symbolize the distinction between the Old and the New Testaments, and the reverse side features simulated statues painted in grisaille. Both ideas soon became characteristic of the Early Netherlandish school.

Campin's Dijon *Nativity* (Musée des Beaux-Arts) includes an impressively naturalistic landscape. Although derived from earlier illuminated manuscripts, this represents a substantial improvement upon its models, and appears to be the earliest depiction of such a view in the larger format of panel painting. Paintings such as the Mérode Altarpiece (Cloisters, New York) and the *Virgin and Child before a Firescreen* (National Gallery, London) are among the very first large-scale representations of another theme borrowed from manuscript illumination: the so-called "Bourgeois Interior".

It seems probable that the large Frankfurt panels of the *Virgin and Child, St Veronica*, the *Trinity*, and the fragmentary *Thief on the Cross* (Städelsches Kunstinstitut, Frankfurt am Main), from which Campin acquired his pseudonym, ought to be placed late in his career. They are solemn and monumental conceptions which nevertheless reveal a superb delicacy of touch. The huge dismembered altarpieces of which they once formed a part must have counted among the grandest conceptions of the first generation of Early Netherlandish painting.

As the contemporary of Jan van Eyck and the master of Rogier van der Weyden, the Master of Flémalle/Robert Campin belongs with the pioneers of the new naturalistic style in the Netherlands. He was a fearless innovator, and it is difficult to understate the significance of his art for his generation.

Master Francke *fl.* 1405–25

Master Francke was a German painter who is documented as having worked in Hamburg. He may have trained in France, possibly in Paris, since his style indicates a knowledge of French manuscript illumination.

Although one of the most important German painters of his time, his reputation rests on only a few paintings, of which the St Thomas Altarpiece (Hamburger Kunsthalle, Hamburg) is his major work. It was commissioned in 1424 by the Hamburg merchants who traded with England, for their chapel in St John's church. Although the eight scenes of the wings of the altar are complete, only one fragment of the center panel survives. The two scenes on the outside of the wings represent the Flight and Martyrdom of St Thomas à Becket while the remainder depict scenes from the Life of Christ. Originally the Crucifixion filled the center panel.

Master Francke: The Nativity, a fragment of the St Thomas Altarpiece; 99×89cm (39×35in); 1424. Hamburger Kunsthalle, Hamburg

Francke was a painter in the elegant International Gothic style. His colors are cleverly graded and his details realistically portrayed. He is exceptional in the way he has carefully contrived the composition in each panel. In some, he has successfully achieved an impression of spatial depth by attempting perspective in the architecture and by foreshortening objects. The Flagellation panel in particular combines all these qualities, and the figures also add drama by their contrasting expressions and poses. The men with whips are violent and brutal, the seated Pilate luxuriously robed and shifty eyed, as is his adviser, while the bowed body of Christ is as expressive as his anguished face. The Martyrdom of St Thomas is an equally powerful composition, with the kneeling Saint a horrific blood-bespattered figure. In such pictures, Francke appears to have been influenced by harsh Netherlandish realism as well as by French delicacy.

His other great work is the St Barbara Altarpiece (*c*1410; Amos Anderson Art Museum, Helsinki). It contains eight scenes from the legend of the Saint's life. Again the characteristics of the International Gothic style are displayed. The charming rural scene—in which the ragged shepherds betray the Saint, while their sheep turn into grasshoppers—has been compared to miniatures by the Limburg brothers. This link, and the less adventurous composition of the scenes compared to those in the St Thomas Altarpiece, suggest that it is an early work.

The contrast between Francke's early and late work is well illustrated by two panels depicting the same subject, *The Man of Sorrows*, or Christ displaying his wounds. The first, in the Museum der Bildenden Künste, Leipzig, shows Christ supported by angels in an angular awkward pose holding the instruments of the Passion, which together form a confused tableau on a gold ground. The latter work, in the Kunsthalle in Hamburg, has a more monumental figure of Christ dominating the panel with the five angels placed in subordinate roles. Most striking are the features of Christ's face, which have been softened to have a chiaroscuro effect.

Francke's influence was widespread and can be traced in numerous altarpieces throughout north Germany and the Baltic countries.

Master of the Housebook
*fl. c*1475–90

The German artist known as the Master of the Housebook was formerly called "The Master of the Amsterdam Cabinet", because the collection in the Rijksmuseum Print Room in Amsterdam houses 82 of his 91 known drypoints, and additionally as "The Master of 1480" from the date on one of his engravings. The Master of the Housebook takes his name from a volume of drawings called the *Hausbuch* in Schloss Wolfegg near Antendorf (Lake Constance, Switzerland). He was active as a draftsman and painter, as well as as an engraver, in the central Rhine area and probably around Lake Constance. He may have used pewter plates rather than copper, since most of his surviving drypoints are unique. The velvety quality of his lines and his pictorial technique mark a complete break with the traditions of silver engraving and woodcutting.

Master of the Isaac Frescoes
fl. late 13th century

The Master of the Isaac Frescoes, probably a Roman painter, was active in the last quarter of the 13th century. It is a measure of his enormous originality and power that attempts have been made to identify the Isaac Master with the young Giotto, or to identify him as Giotto's teacher. While he probably did influence Giotto, his work is that of an individual, mature artist. He is named after the frescoes of *Isaac and Esau* and *Isaac and Jacob* in the second bay on the right-hand wall of the Upper Church of St Francis at Assisi. His workshop also painted the *Four Doctors of the Church* in the entrance vault of the nave, and other scenes in the upper register of the first two bays of the nave. The Isaac Master's sense

Master of the Isaac Frescoes: Pietà; fresco; late 13th century; Upper church of S. Francesco, Assisi

of dramatic composition is profoundly like Giotto's, as is his understanding and use of Classical models for his figures. He takes his place with Cimabue, Cavallini, and Giotto as a founder of the new naturalistic style in painting that developed in Italy at the time. He is only less famous because anonymous, and because so little of his work survives.

Master of Liesborn
fl. mid 15th century

The Master of Liesborn takes his name from the now dismembered high altarpiece of the Benedictine Abbey of Liesborn in Westphalia, of which the most important surviving panels are in the National Gallery, London. Nothing is known of the location of the studio of this Westphalian painter and the documentary evidence concerning his activity is minimal. The Liesborn high altar was dedicated by Abbot Heinrich von Kleve in 1465, together with four other altars, and he is recorded as having commissioned the paintings for all five. Since he was enthroned as abbot only in 1464 and did not die until 1490, the year 1465 can be interpreted in the light of

the abbey chronicle written between 1515 and 1520 as the earliest likely date for the Liesborn high altarpiece.

Apart from this celebrated work, which remained in situ until the suppression of the abbey in 1803, there are no other certain autograph works by the Master of Liesborn. The tentative reconstruction of his oeuvre depends upon the variations in quality acceptable to historians, and upon any development that can be postulated. The influence of the 15th-century Cologne school of painters is self-evident. The strongly Netherlandish character of the *Annunciation* from the Liesborn high altarpiece (National Gallery, London), with its unusually detailed interior, may even indicate direct contact with Netherlandish prototypes. Based on the style of the furniture, a case can be made for dating the *Annunciation*, and by implication the whole high altarpiece, to as late as c1480; but it was presumably completed by 1490.

Master of Mary of Burgundy
fl. c1470–90

The Master of Mary of Burgundy was the leading Flemish book-illuminator, work-

ing probably in Ghent in the 1470s and 1480s. Various attempts have been made to identify him, for instance with Sanders Bening. He receives his name from two Books of Hours made for Mary of Burgundy, daughter of Charles the Bold and Margaret of York (1457–82). One is in Berlin (Kupferstichkabinett; MS. 78 B. 12) the other in Vienna (Nationalbibliothek; MS. 1857). Outstanding among the other works attributed to him are the Hours of Engelbert of Nassau (Bodleian Library, Oxford; MS. Douce 219–20) and a book of Hours in Madrid (National Library; MS. Vit. 25–5). A group of manuscripts, some of which were made for Margaret of York, appear to be earlier works that he did in the 1470s (St John's College, Cambridge; H. 13, Breviary, etc).

A master of the depiction of space and light, responsible for "the first example of plein-air painting in Northern art" (Pächt), he also introduces original solutions to the problem of relating the picture to the surface of the page. His scenes appear as though viewed through a window, and his borders are exquisitely painted with *trompe-l'oeil* flowers and insects.

Further reading. Alexander, J.J.G. *The Master of Mary of Burgundy*, London (1970). Schryver, A. de and Unterkircher, F. *Stundenbuch der Maria van Burgund*, Graz (1969).

Master of Moulins *fl. c1480–c1500*

The French painter known as the Master of Moulins takes his name from the triptych in Moulins Cathedral, an altarpiece of the Virgin and Child surrounded by Angels commissioned by the Duke of Bourbon which is datable to c1498. This painting is

Master of Moulins: Nativity, with Cardinal Rolin; panel; 55×73cm (22×29in); c1480–3. Musée des Beaux Arts, Autun

stylistically analogous to a *Nativity* at Autun (Musée des Beaux-Arts) painted for Cardinal Jean Rolin which cannot be later than 1483. Both works indicate a clear debt to Hugo van der Goes, so it seems likely that their author was trained in the Netherlands. A number of other pictures have been attributed to this Master. Some of them, such as the fragment of *Charlemagne and the Meeting at the Golden Gate* (National Gallery, London) include Italianate architectural details which probably derive from the studio of Jean Fouquet. Monumental clarity of form and a delicate but rich use of color distinguish the style of the Master of Moulins. He was the last great French painter of the 15th-century tradition.

Master of Naumburg *fl. c1230–70*

The German sculptor known as the Master of Naumburg takes his name from the superb series of sculptures in the west choir of Naumburg Cathedral. His style as revealed there is so clearly defined that his activity can be traced for some 40 years. Such a distinct artistic personality is most exceptional during the 13th century, and thus the reconstruction of his career must be treated with caution.

The hand of the Master of Naumburg has been detected at Noyon, and he also seems to have worked in Metz (fragments from the Portal of the Virgin, Metz Cathedral). It is much more certain that by c1239 he was active in Mainz, where he was responsible for the figurative sculpture decorating the west rood screen of the cathedral. Dismembered and scattered, the relief of *St Martin and the Beggar* (the so-called *Bassenheim Rider*), now in the parish church of Bassenheim, probably comes from Mainz Cathedral together with the equally expressive *Head with a Bandeau* and fragments of a *Last Judgment* (Bischöfliches Dom- und Diözesanmuseum, Mainz).

The west choir of Naumburg Cathedral was built by Bishop Dietrich from 1249 onwards, and the interior is decorated with life-size figures of princes and princesses of his family, the House of Wettin. Together with the *Bamberg Rider* (Bamberg Cathedral) these dignified figures not only embody the noblest ideals of medieval chivalry, but also portray within closely defined limits their individual personalities. Internal evidence suggests that they were completed a few years before the death of Bishop Dietrich in 1273, and that the highly expressive *Passion* reliefs and figures on the west rood screen date from his last years.

Master of the Playing Cards
fl. c1430–60

Probably active in the Upper Rhineland, and possibly in Basel, the Master of the Playing Cards seems also to have worked as a painter and goldsmith. He takes his name from a series of engraved playing cards. The animals he includes in them are copied from the decorations painted in Mainz in the margins of a group of Bibles dating from the 1450s. His modeling of forms by means of massed strokes and occasional crosshatching is closely based on the technique of pen-and-ink drawings. The importance of the Master of the Playing Cards lies in his growing independence from the techniques of the silversmiths.

Master of Naumburg: Hermann and Reglindis, from the series of sculptures on the west choir of Naumburg Cathedral; c1249–70

Master of St Cecilia: the St Cecilia Altarpiece; panel; 85×181cm (33×71in); before 1304? Uffizi, Florence

Master of the Rohan Hours
fl. c1410–25

The Master of the Rohan Hours was a French miniaturist and painter, to whose workshop some 35 manuscripts can be assigned, mainly Books of Hours. A few of these were made for the use of Troyes, but the majority were for the use of Paris; not all of them have miniatures by the hand of the Master. He is named after the most important of these Books of Hours (Bibliothèque Nationale, Paris; MS. Lat. 9471), which at some later date in the 15th century belonged to a member of the Rohan family, whose coat-of-arms was then added. This manuscript contains the most impressive miniatures by the Master. He knew and made use of a number of compositions and single figures by the Limburgs and by the Boucicaut Master, which helps to date and locate his works.

He is an extraordinary artist, who has rightly been called an "expressionist". He often covers the entire parchment with compositions, leaving no room for the customary borders; he fills the space with a few large figures in profile, with heightened tension between them. He has a strong predilection for macabre subjects: the *Lamentation*, the *Dying Man in Front of Christ*, and the *Last Judgment* are all presented with stark simplicity. By including enlarged figures (such as that of a corpse) which up to then had been displayed only in small size in the borders, he enhances them

and invests them with new intensity.

The Rohan Hours is a late work and his most accomplished and substantial one. The much smaller Giac Hours, now in Toronto (Royal Ontario Museum), is one of his earliest works, but already displays similar tendencies. Another speciality of his studio is long additional series in the margins of the front and back of each page, carrying on their independent story regardless of the main text and of the main illustrations. The *Bible moralisée* is added in this manner to the Rohan Hours, and the *Pèlérinages* of Guillaume de Digueville to the Cambridge Hours.

There is evidence that the Rohan Master worked not only as a miniaturist, but also as a panel-painter. The fragment of an altarpiece in Laon with a donor portrait and apostle figures has been ascribed to his hand; a single parchment sheet with a drawing of *The Miracle of Bethesda* (Herzog Anton Ulrich Museum, Brunswick) is undoubtedly his.

Master of St Cecilia *fl. c1290–1304*

The Italian painter known as the Master of St Cecilia may have come from Florence. He takes his name from the St Cecilia Altarpiece (Uffizi, Florence) painted in the years shortly before 1304. He was one of the major masters who collaborated on *The Legend of St Francis* at Assisi (Upper Church of St Francis) of which he painted

the first and the last three scenes. (All four were painted after the completion of the rest of the cycle.) In addition he painted two altarpieces in S. Margherita a Montici near Florence, and a panel of *St Peter Enthroned* (S. Simone, Florence). All his narrative scenes are characterized by figures with elongated bodies, small heads, and rake-like hands. Apart from these eccentricities, he possessed a remarkable feeling for architecture, often including portraits of appropriate Classical buildings in Rome. His drapery has soft, naturalistic folds. He made a significant contribution to artistic development in Italy at the beginning of the 14th century.

Master of Wittingau *fl. c1380–95*

The Bohemian painter known as the Master of Wittingau was the greatest middle European artist of his time. He is named after the winged altarpiece created for the church of St Giles at the Augustine monastery in Třeboň (formerly Wittingau). This probably consisted of five panels, with a large central Crucifixion scene. Only three panels from the wings remain: *Gethsemane, The Resurrection* and *The Entombment* (c1380–5; National Gallery, Prague). On the reverse of each panel is a group of three apostles or saints. The altarpiece was dismantled during the 18th century, and dispersed to various neighboring churches.

Mateo of Santiago: the Portico of Glory; St James Cathedral, Santiago de Compostela; completed c1188

Mateo of Santiago *fl. c1168–1217*

Mateo of Santiago was a Spanish sculptor whose gigantic main entrance to St James Cathedral, Santiago de Compostela, is signed and dated 1188. The work was started in 1168, and in 1217 Mateo was still employed by the cathedral chapter. The triple entrance, known as the "Portico de la Gloria", is within the narthex. The central doorway, with the Christ in Majesty on a huge tympanum, has a trumeau on which is carved the Tree of Jesse and the figure of St James, patron saint of the cathedral and of Spain. All three doorways have column-figures, a clear indication of the influence from France. There are still traces of polychromy.

Mathieu Georges 1921–

The French painter Georges Mathieu was born in Boulogne-sur-Mer. He studied English, law, and philosophy, and moved to Paris in 1947. There he organized exhibitions of "lyrical abstraction" (his own term), becoming a major publicist for antigeometric painting, including American Abstract Expressionism. In 1953 he founded the *United States Lines Paris Review*.

He created his first Abstract-Surrealist paintings in 1944. Influenced by Wols, in 1947 he began to develop his unique calligraphic style; this relies upon spontaneous improvisation, so that speed minimizes conscious control. His works display open dynamic arabesques in thick lines sitting on the surface of the canvas; lattice-like complexes, layered and blotched, contrast vividly with expansive monochrome grounds.

Further reading. Charpentier, J. *Georges Mathieu*, Paris (1965).

Georges Mathieu: Danâ; oil on canvas; 65×100cm (26×39in); 1958. Museum Ludwig, Cologne

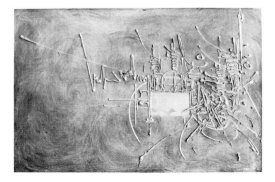

The Wittingau Master was undoubtedly responsible for introducing the so-called "beautiful" style which reached its apotheosis in Bohemia c1400. The source of his singular authority is not easily traceable to Bohemian forerunners. Towards the end of the 14th century the court of Charles IV in Prague provided an international *milieu* for artists, which may partly account for Italian and Franco-Flemish influences in his work. It cannot explain his advanced technique, in which older Gothic conventions are combined with an understanding of chiaroscuro, which was revolutionary in his time. His altarpiece panels display a visionary conception, while an unearthly radiance illuminates the figural focus of the composition.

Some paintings, once attributed to assistants, are now assigned mainly to his own hand. These include the *Crucifixion* from the chapel of St Barbara near Třeboň (c1380–5; National Gallery, Prague) and the *Roudnice Madonna* (c1390–5; National Gallery, Prague). This Madonna compares closely with the St Catherine on the reverse of the *Gethsemane* panel. It is an important work, demonstrating the "beautiful" style at its finest. No contemporary artist developed immediately from the Wittingau Master, and it was some years before his innovatory genius was understood in Bohemia. His influence on the painting of central and western Europe and on manuscript-illumination was profound, and can be traced by c1400.

Matisse Henri 1869–1954

Henri Matisse, born at Le Cateau-Cambrésis (Nord, France), was one of the leaders of avant-garde art before the First World War. He was famous for his brilliant and expressive use of color, and his bold innovations. His artistic identity evolved slowly and with apparent difficulty. Although he was 30 at the beginning of the century, it was not until 1905 that he discovered his own vision. Thereafter he rapidly became notorious as the leader of the group of painters known as the Fauves. He lived to become, in his old age, internationally honored as a master.

At 17, Matisse was set to study law by his father, a corn merchant. It is said that when he was 20 and convalescing from an appendectomy his mother gave him a paintbox and so he began painting. His earliest works, still lifes of 1890, are strikingly assured in a conventional academic manner. He quickly became technically skillful and for several years was able to supplement his meager allowance by making official copies in the Louvre.

He was never officially accepted as a student at the École des Beaux-Arts. In 1891, he was allowed to leave the lawyer's office in St Quentin and go to Paris where he attended the Académie Julian under Bouguereau, but he soon transferred unofficially to Gustave Moreau's classes at the École des Beaux-Arts. Among his fellow students were Marquet, Manguin, and Rouault, all younger than him.

In 1896, Matisse appeared to be on the threshold of his professional career. His painting of a woman reading in a lamplit interior, in the tradition of Henri Fantin-Latour, was shown at the Salon de la Société Nationale des Beaux-Arts, and was bought by the State for Rambouillet; the Société Nationale itself elected him an associate member, and he was introduced to Pissarro and Rodin. The following year, he showed *The Dinner Table* (private collection) at the Salon. This large canvas, depicting a servant arranging flowers on a table sumptuously spread for a large family meal, was painted in brilliant impressionist colors. His first major composition, it was badly hung and harshly criticized.

Mateo of Santiago: St Peter, St Paul, St James and St John, on the Portico of Glory; St James Cathedral, Santiago de Compostela; stone; completed c1188 (see page 435)

"The Swan". Etching from the illustrated book *"Poems of Stéphane Mallarmé"* by Henri Matisse, published in 1932 by Albert Skira. Victoria and Albert Museum, London.

From that time onward, the course of Matisse's career changed radically. For seven years he worked constantly. But his canvases were researches rather than achievements, being either sketches roughly laid in and then abandoned, or labored exercises killed by overworking. He developed no consistent style but conducted a variety of experiments in the use of brilliant color.

In 1898 he married, and the following year bought with money from his wife's dowry a small painting, *Three Bathers*, by Cézanne. Though he never directly imitated Cézanne's style, this painting became a talisman for him which he cherished for many years, until in 1936 he presented it to the Musée d'Art Moderne de la Ville de Paris.

But the years of study and hardship continued. In 1900 Matisse attended evening classes in sculpture, and in later years sculptured many important works in bronze. He painted exhibition decorations for a living, and in 1902 Mme Matisse opened a millinery shop.

In 1904 Matisse worked with Paul Signac at St Tropez, and adopted his own, intuitive version of *pointillisme*. In this technique he painted an idyllic fantasy of women bathing on a beach (1905; private collection). Its title, *Luxe, Calme et Volupté*, he took from Baudelaire's poem "The Invitation to the Voyage", an invitation to a loved one to a dream land where all is harmony and beauty, "luxury, tranquillity and delight". The picture and its title announce Matisse's arrival at his own vision of art.

But his own version of *pointillisme* was too rigid for him. In 1905 at Collioure, where he spent the summer with the much younger Derain, he painted small canvases with an apparent careless abandon he had never dared before. *Open Window, Collioure* (1905; Collection of John Hay Whitney, New York), bold in its calligraphy and indifferent to the original colors of the motif, captures the sparkle of light glancing off the ripples of the harbor alive with bobbing boats. He painted two portraits of Mme Matisse (*Woman with the Hat*, Walter A. Haas Collection, San Francisco; *Madame Matisse: the Green Line*, State Art Museum, Copenhagen) that were no less bold, and he vied with Derain as they painted each other's portraits (*André Derain*, 1905; Tate Gallery, London).

At the Salon d'Automne that year, Matisse's new canvases and works of similar violence by Derain, Vlaminck, Marquet, and others, were hung together in one room. The public was appalled by such crude daubs and the painters were called "Fauves"—wild beasts. The *Woman with the Hat* (1905; Walter A. Haas Collection, San Francisco) caused a particular sensation.

But this new style had admirers too, and a wealthy American brother and sister living in Paris, Leo and Gertrude Stein, met Matisse and bought this work. The following year, at the Salon des Indépendants, Matisse showed an ambitious composition, *Joy of Life* (1906; Barnes Foundation, Merion, Pennsylvania). It was an Arcadian scene with naked nymphs and shepherds, drawn with a new calligraphic boldness and with the clear coloring of an Oriental rug. Leo Stein bought it immediately.

Leo remained Matisse's friend, admirer, and patron (Gertrude favored Picasso) and soon other collectors began to vie for Matisse's new works. From 1906 his patrons included the Cone sisters of Baltimore, after 1908 the Russian merchant Sergei Shchukin, and from 1912 another Russian, Morosov. In 1909, Shchukin commissioned two important works, *Dance* (study, 1909, Museum of Modern Art, New York; oil, 1910, Hermitage Museum, St Petersburg) and *Music* (1910; Hermitage Museum, St Petersburg). Between them the Russians bought almost 50 works; these were acquired by the Russian state in 1923.

With this patronage, Matisse was able to visit Algeria in 1906. In later years he traveled widely, to Italy, Spain, Germany, Russia, and the U.S.A.; but his most significant visits were to North Africa in 1906, 1911, and 1912, and to Tahiti in 1930.

In 1908 Matisse was encouraged to open a small school, the Atelier Matisse, where he taught for a short time. In that same year he published his first theoretical essay "Notes of a Painter", in *La Grande Revue* (25 December 1908).

He was rejected for military service in 1914; he spent the War years painting, at Issy, Paris, and Nice. For the rest of his life he was to spend much of his time either in Paris or Nice.

With the return of peace, Matisse became more and more widely recognized as the master of the École de Paris and of modern painting. In 1925, he was made a Chevalier of the Legion of Honor. He worked in a growing variety of media. In addition to painting and sculpture, he designed for the ballet and designed illustrated editions: of Mallarmé's poems for Skira (1932), Joyce's *Ulysses* (1935),

Baudelaire's *Fleurs du Mal* (1943), and the *Florilège des Amours de Ronsard* (1941). His most important book was *Jazz* (1947) which combined his colored designs and a poetic essay on art in his own script.

In 1931 the great American collector, Dr Albert C. Barnes commissioned murals for the hall of the Barnes Foundation, Merion, Pa. When Matisse had completed the panels in his Paris studio they were found to be to wrong measurements, so he painted completely new versions which were successfully installed.

Matisse's last commission, despite his earlier lack of religious conviction, was the small Chapel of the Rosary of the Dominican nuns, Vence, begun in 1948 and consecrated in 1951.

After 1941, the aging Matisse suffered increasing ill health and often worked in bed. He died on 3 November 1954 at Nice, shortly before his 85th birthday.

Matisse first wrote about his art in 1908, in "Notes of a Painter", and 44 years later, when he was 82, he insisted that in spirit he had remained unchanged, because "all this time I have sought the same ends, which perhaps I have achieved in different ways". His end was always expression. Expression was a strenuous, paradoxical

achievement, the result of the artist's intuitive pictorial response to his experience of the object. Thus he painted in many different ways that at first sight show little consistency, modeling forms heavily in one canvas and painting with the flat simplicity of a child in another. He avoided any system of representation that depended on applied skills, but sought the pure spontaneous expression of each unique experience. Nevertheless, the metamorphoses of his style may be seen to follow a broad sequence of development.

Immediately after the sophisticated abstractions of *The Joy of Life*, he painted a number of canvases (notably *Le Luxe I*, 1907, Musée National d'Art Moderne, Paris; and *Le Luxe II*, 1907, State Art Museum, Copenhagen) in which he developed a childlike or primitive simplicity of line. (Matisse was among the first to collect Negro art.) This search for uncompromisingly "pure" form and color culminated in the Hermitage Museum's *Dance* and *Music* (1909–10). Drawn with a stark primitive outline and painted in the three basic colors of blue sky, green earth, and scarlet flesh, they are as theoretical as any later canvases by Kandinsky or Mondrian, but remain representational. The other single work with a similar doctrinaire spirit is a still life of 1914 entitled *Lemons: Still Life of Lemons the forms of which correspond to that of a drawing of a black vase on the wall* (Museum of Art, Rhode Island School of Design, Providence, Rhode Island).

The austere abstractions of *Dance* and *Music* were followed shortly afterwards by the fruits of his first visit to North Africa, a series of large scenes of Islamic life glowing with sensuous color. They appear effortlessly spontaneous, and their simple outlines could be mistaken as genuinely naive. These were followed by a further advance towards abstraction in *Open Window, Collioure* (1914; private collection) in which vertical bands of green, gray, and pale blue that are the window shutters frame a plain black rectangle, an entirely opaque night sky. *Composition: Yellow Curtain* (1915; private collection) is too big to be its pendant, yet is, formally, its daytime equivalent.

About the beginning of the War, Matisse showed the influence of Cubism. In *Mlle Yvonne Landsberg* (1914; Philadelphia Museum of Art) the negroid mask and expanding arcs scratched in the paint appear unconvincing. But *Moroccans*

Henri Matisse:
Seated Nude;
woodcut; 58×46cm
(23×18in); 1906.
Scottish National
Gallery of Modern
Art, Edinburgh

(1916; Museum of Modern Art, New York), though undoubtedly reflecting post-Cubist abstraction, is one of the most mysterious and powerful of his images. Its boldly silhouetted shapes anticipate the qualities of his own cut paper compositions of 20 years later.

As the War continued, Matisse in the isolation of his Paris studio painted a number of large canvases: somber, noble images of the studio, with Paris glimpsed through the window; they recall in their scale and spatial quality some of the great canvases of Manet.

In a hotel room in Nice in 1919, Matisse painted a totally different kind of *Artist and his Model* (Collection of Dr and Mrs Harry Bakwin, New York). The artist, by the quality of his line and the tentative washes of color, might be an elderly amateur faced with his first nude model. But ironically this naive gentleman is included in the picture; and the picture itself, despite its sketchy brushmarks, is taut and delicately precise in its spatial relationships. For another ten years, Matisse painted a sequence of such small genre scenes of the hedonism of sunlit Mediterranean hotels, in which the qualities of Impressionism or the intimate vision of his friend Bonnard were matched with an enigmatic simplicity.

In contrast, the Barnes murals were perhaps the most mannered inventions of Matisse's career. The flat shapes of the dancers, anticipating his later use of cut paper, leap into and out of the lunettes with a brittle vitality. Nevertheless, they point towards the painter's return to a more monumental imagery.

Over the last 20 years of his long life, Matisse perfected his last, most consistent, mode of represen-tation. He worked with thin, fluid paint, washing off unacceptable essays and starting afresh on the cleaned canvas, so pre-serving the vital quality of spontaneity. He drew with broad gestures, avoiding fore-shortenings, and filling the canvas with grand arabesques which he charged with dazzling combinations of glowing color. Though many of these canvases are small they have a monumental quality.

After the Second World War, Matisse began to work increasingly in cut paper. He had immense sheets of paper washed over with gouache colors and then cut out his shapes and stuck them together (for example, *The Snail*, 1953; Tate Gallery, London). He said: "Cutting into living

Roberto Matta: Eros Precipitate (LeVertiged'Eros); oil on canvas; 196×251cm (77×99in); 1944. Museum of Modern Art, New York

color reminds me of the sculptor's direct carving." Though he cut often trite vegetable shapes, he composed them into splendid harmonies that are a fitting climax to his career.

His last masterpiece was the Dominican chapel of Notre-Dame du Rosaire (1947–51) at Vence, a small spare space made large and noble by the subtle balance of simple elements: the deliberately schematic black outline drawings on the white tiled walls, illuminated by the abstract colors flooding exultantly through the windows.

Further reading. Elderfield, J. *Henri Matisse: a Retrospective*, London (1992). Escholier, R. *Matisse: a Portrait of the Artist and the Man*, London and New York (1960). Flam, J. D. *Matisse on Art*, London (1973). Gowing, L. *Matisse*, London (1979). Percheron, R. and Brouder, C. *Matisse: From Color to Architecture*, New York (2004). Schneider, P. *Matisse*, New York (2002). Spurling, H. *Matisse the Master: A Life of Henri Matisse, The Conquest of Color 1909–1954*, New York (2005). Wright, A. *Matisse and the Subject of Modernism*, Princeteon, N.J. (2004).

Matta Roberto 1912–2002

The Chilean painter Roberto Echaurren Matta enrolled in 1934 to study architecture in Le Corbusier's Paris office. He joined the Surrealists in 1937 and began to paint in 1938. In 1939 he emigrated to

New York where his friends Duchamp, Ernst, Tanguy, and André Breton exerted an enormous influence on his work. He traveled to Mexico In 1941, and after 1949 paid long visits to Italy, England, and France.

Matta's personal brand of Surrealism dealt in its early years with the morphology of shapes in an ever-changing dream world. By the mid 1940s there appeared the tortured humanoid creatures that dominated his work thereafter, seen, for example, in *Eros Precipitate* (or *Le Vertige d'Eros*; oil on canvas; 1944; Museum of Modern Art, New York).

Matteo di Giovanni c1430?–95

The Italian painter Matteo di Giovanni was also known as Matteo da Siena. He was Siena's dominant painter during the second half of the 15th century. He was trained by Vecchietta, from whom he inherited interests in naturalism and in rigid sculptural forms, and was subsequently influenced by Antonio Pollaiuolo. From 1475 onwards his work saw an increasing assimilation of Antiquity with his naturalistic tendencies. About 1490 he reverted to a less innovative style, and thereafter placed emphasis on decorative effects of flat pattern. Representative works by Matteo include *Assumption of the Virgin* (c1470/5; National Gallery, London), *Massacre of the Innocents* (1482; S. Agostino, Siena), and *Madonna*

Matteo di Giovanni: Assumption of the Virgin;
panel; 332×174cm (131×69in); c1470/5.
National Gallery, London

*and Child with SS. John the Baptist and
Michael (c1490; Barber Institute of Fine
Arts, Birmingham, England).*

Matyushin Mikhail 1861–1934

The Russian artist Mikhail Vasil'evich
Matyushin was originally a musician. His
artistic training, begun in 1898, included
studying with Leon Bakst and Mstislav
Dobuzhinsky. He was a cofounder of the
Union of Youth group (1909) and in 1913
wrote the music for the opera *Victory over
the Sun* (prologue by Khlebnikov, libretto
by Kruchenykh, decor by Malevich). As
head of the Organic Culture department at
the Institute of Artistic Culture in Leningrad (c1920–6), he elaborated his concept
of *Zorved* ("see-know"), devising exercises
in cognitive (intuitive) and physical vision
towards a perception of the fourth dimension. His theoretical and practical work on
color was published in 1933, and his color
investigation tablets (Stedelijk Museum,
Amsterdam) were until recently attributed
to Malevich.

Maulbertsch F.A. 1724–96

Franz Anton Maulbertsch (or Maul-
pertsch) was the outstanding monumental
painter active in the Hapsburg territories
during the second half of the 18th century.
He was born at Langenargen on the
Bodensee. He was first trained by his
father, the painter Anton Maulbertsch,
and may have been subsequently in contact
with F.J. Spielgler. In 1739, under the
patronage of Count Ernst von Montfort,
he was sent to study in Vienna under Peter
van Roy; he also came into contact with
the Vienna Academy.

In 1745 Maulbertsch became a master in
Vienna and his early style reveals the
impact of Paul Troger. Although primarily
a fresco painter, he also executed altarpieces and smaller special commissions,
and the superb quality of his oil sketches
for these has always been recognized. The
chronology of Maulbertsch's work is
based on the long series of documented
frescoes, but study of the oil paintings is
greatly complicated by the large number of
his pupils and imitators.

Major commissions came early. The
swirling clouds and figures in the vaults of

F.A. Maulbertsch: Self-portrait; oil on canvas; 119×93cm (47×37in); c1970. Österreichische Galerie, Vienna

the Piaristenkirche, Vienna (1752–3), are a prelude to the brilliant series of frescoes in the abbey church of Heiligenkreuz-Gutenbrunn (Lower Austria, 1757), the parish church of Sümeg (Hungary, 1757–8), and the Feudal Hall of the Residence of Kroměříž (Moravia, 1759). During the 1760s Maulbertsch began to move away from this exuberance. The frescoes in Schloss Halbturn (Burgenland, 1765) reveal a growing clarity of lighting and the use of sculptural forms; these were to lead inexorably to the classicism of the frescoes at Strahov (Prague, 1794).

Ma Yuan 1190–1224

Ma Yuan, the great-grandson of the famous bird painter Ma Fen, was a member of a scholarly family that produced many painters. Ma Yuan himself was an Academy painter of the late Sung Court who was noted for his lyrical use of the brush strokes of Li T'ang, and the exaggerated "one corner" composition developed in the Sung Court style. He often chose to paint on silk and used soft colors.

Although he used the same vocabulary of brush strokes as Hsia Kuei, Ma Yuan seems to have softened the effect, partly by the use of silk as a base and partly by his own characteristic elegance of brush. The two painters' treatment of subject matter is also contrasting, for Ma Yuan's figures set

the atmosphere of the scene and indeed are often courtly people. This is evident in the small painting of the poet in the garden with his servant. This gentleman seems to be a forerunner of Shen Chou's scholar walking in his landscape and speaking through his poem to the viewer.

Ma Yuan's son, Ma Lin, was a painter and has left a tiny masterpiece in a fan painting (now in the National Palace Museum, Taipei) *Waiting for Guests by Candlelight*.

The school that has linked Hsia Kuei and Ma Yuan is one of elegant decorative painting in which both brushwork and composition are of refined sophistication. There have been a number of fine exponents of this style, which has also been regarded as the progenitor of decorative bird and flower painting.

Mazerolles Philippe de c1420–79

Philippe de Mazerolles was an illuminator working in Paris (1454) and Bruges (from 1467), where he was court painter to the Dukes of Burgundy. He is credited with the introduction of a new kind of manuscript illumination in which the figures are smaller than before, landscapes more extensive, and the importance of the decorative borders is reasserted. Calligraphic flourishes in the margins are particularly distinctive, as in the prayer book of Charles the Bold (Nationalbibliothek, Vienna). Recent scholarship has attributed his extant oeuvre to an artist from Ghent named Liévin van Lathem, who worked in Bruges from 1468 and also in Antwerp. He too is documented as having made a prayer book for Charles (Durrieu Collection, Larivière). Whatever the actual identity of the artist of the works associated with the name of de Mazerolles, he was a major figure in the history of Flemish illumination.

Meckenem Israhel van, the Younger *fl.* 1450–1503

A pupil of Master ES, Israhel van Meckenem the Younger was a goldsmith and prolific engraver active in Bocholt and Cleve in Westphalia. More than 600 plates bear his initials or signature, and as the first of the large-scale producers of prints he appears to have used factory methods. As might be expected, he did not hesitate to copy designs from a wide range of sources, including the productions of other

Ma Yuan: Egrets on a Snowy Bank; ink and light color on silk scroll; 95×38cm (37×15in). National Palace Museum, Taipei

printmakers, and he reworked at least 41 plates by Master ES.

Further plates were copied from the Master of the Berlin Passion (Israhel van Meckenem the Elder), the Master of the Housebook, and Hans Holbein the Elder, among others; but most of his compositions are original, if uninspired. Clearly he must have employed many assistants, including possibly his wife Ida, and many of the editions were sufficiently large to require reworking of the copper plates.

The artist's late plates, such as *The Madonna on the Crescent Moon Surrounded by Six Angels*, dated 1502, are in their technique highly competent; but the stereotyped facial expressions and drapery patterns, and the lack of energy, belong to the final phase of late Gothic engraving.

Meidias Painter *fl.* c420–400 BC

The Meidias Painter was a Greek vase-painter who worked in Athens. His name is short for "the painter of the vase in London with the potter-signature of Meidias". Vase-painting in the second half of the 5th century BC owed much to the freer art of panel and wall painting. From

Israhel van Meckenem the Younger: The Artist and his Wife Ida; copperplate engraving; 12×17cm (5×7in); c1490. Staatliche Museen, Berlin

these sources come the Meidias Painter's use of different levels within his pictures, three-quarter views with quite successful foreshortenings, and personified abstractions.

He was a follower of the Eretria Painter. The stately figures of the previous generation, however, have now become more effeminate, the drapery more luxurious, and the drawing more mannered. His style also reflects contemporary sculpture, especially the Nike Balustrade, but utterly lacks its dignity. The Meidias Painter's world is full of scented bowers, clinging drapery, pouting lips, and soulful glances: a gilded world of love and daydreams. His favorite subjects are from the realms of Aphrodite and Dionysos. Such themes were perhaps an attempt to escape the agonies of a Greece wracked by the Peloponnesian War.

Two *hydriae* found in the same tomb in Populonia show the Meidias Painter at the height of his rich mannerism. Both depict figures from Aphrodite's exploits: on one is Adonis; on the other, preserved intact, is Phaon. Phaon was an aged boatman to whom Aphrodite gave youth and external beauty. Here he plays the lyre to Demonassa under a gilded laurel canopy (Museo Archeologico, Florence; 81947). On the left two nymphs watch longingly, but on the right Leto has eyes only for her son Apollo. Above, Aphrodite circles in a chariot drawn by Desire and Longing, while other symbolic figures look on— Health, Happiness, All-Night Feasting, and Spring Time. Wavy incised lines, as usual in this painter's works, give an impression of the rocks on which some of the characters sit.

The Meidias Painter had much influence on the painters of small vases, both during his own period and later.

Meier Richard 1934–

The American architect Richard Meier was born in Newark, New Jersey. After graduating from Cornell University in 1957, he worked with top firms such as Skidmore, Owings and Merrill (1959–60) and Marcel Breuer and Associates (1960–3).

By the late 1960s Meier became known as part of the "New York Five," a group of architects dedicated to modernist principles. He applied these ideals—clean, geometric lines and crisp whiteness inspired by Le Corbusier—to a series of private residences in the late 1960s and early '70s. He went on to apply this vision to large-scale public and private institutions, including the Athenaeum (1975–9) in New Harmony, Indiana. Meier's most famous work is the J. Paul Getty Arts Center (1984–97) in Los Angeles, California, a commission that called for a series of separate, but related, buildings. The center's visual unity, clean lines, and flowing spaces represent the apotheosis of Meier's aesthetic.

Meissonier J.-L.-E. 1815–91

Jean-Louis-Ernest Meissonier was a French genre and military painter. He worked as an illustrator early in his career, and showed his first Salon painting in 1834. He specialized in genre scenes on a very small scale, depicting such figures as painters, cardplayers, and Flemish burghers, using carefully documented historical settings. These works of Dutch inspiration acquired immense popularity. In 1859 he joined Napoleon III's staff on the Italian campaign, which inspired a group of larger works based on the Napoleonic epic (for example, *The Emperor at Solferino*, 1863; Louvre, Paris). His scrupulous craftsmanship and anecdotal qualities made him highly popular among his contemporaries.

Meissonnier Juste-Aurèle 1695–1750

Although little of the work of the French goldsmith and architect Juste-Aurèle Meissonnier survives, he was highly influential in creating the Rococo style in Paris and, through engravings after his designs, in its spread throughout Europe. Meissonnier was born in Turin and was much indebted to the work of the late Baroque artist Filippo Juvara. He was in Paris by c1720,

J.-L.-E. Meissonnier: The Emperor Napoleon III at Solferino (24 June 1859); oil on wood panel; 44×76cm (17×30in); 1863. Louvre, Paris

and in 1725 or 1726 he was given an influential court appointment where his responsibilities ranged from silver designs to firework displays. In the mid 1720s he put forward a plan for the facade of St-Sulpice, Paris, but it was never built.

Meit Conrad c1480–c1550

Conrad Meit was a German sculptor. Originally from Worms, he worked for Frederick the Wise at Wittenberg and for Margaret of Austria at Malines before ending his career at Antwerp. A colleague of Lucas Cranach and Jan Gossaert, he also met Jacopo de' Barbari and Albrecht Dürer. While the tombs at Brou reveal his skill at large-scale work, Meit is best known for his small sculpture. His most famous piece is the exquisite little alabaster

Judith in the Bayerisches National-museum, Munich. Other statuettes indicate that he was equally expert in the handling of boxwood and bronze.

Meit's work is outstanding both for its plasticity and for its luscious surface finish. A pioneering figure in German Renaissance sculpture, his long career spans the period between the break up of the late Gothic and the consolidation of Northern Mannerism.

Melozzo da Forlì 1438–94

Melozzo da Forlì was an Italian painter from Forlì in the Marches. His most important works were executed in Rome for Pope Sixtus IV (1471–84). His fresco in the Vatican Museums, showing the ceremonial appointment of Platina as Vatican Librarian (1477), originally decorated the main wall of Sixtus' library. The scene takes place within a Classically-inspired and marble-faced room; and the figures, which are probably all portraits, have a solemn monumentality clearly inspired by Piero della Francesca, who may have been Melozzo's master.

Contemporaries such as Giovanni Santi (and later Vasari) acclaimed Melozzo for his skill in perspective; but his most ambitious schemes, in vaults and domes of churches in Rome, Loreto, and Forlì (where he spent his last years), are now largely destroyed. The frescoes in the dome of the Capella del Tesoro in the Sacristy of St Mark, Loreto (1480s), use a sophisticated *trompe-l'oeil* technique. They show angels floating in front of each of the eight compartments of the dome behind which the sky is visible, while eight prophets sit below on the cornice of the dome.

Melozzo da Forlì: An Angel Musician; fresco; c1480. Vatican Museums, Rome

Probably the most influential of Melozzo's schemes was the fresco of the Ascension in the choir apse of SS. Apostoli in Rome (by 1480). The surviving fragments (the figure of Christ in the Palazzo del Quirinale; musical angels and heads of Apostles in the Vatican Museums) show clearly how Melozzo's scientific interest was combined with a love of decorative detail, to create an understandably popular idiom.

Memling Hans c1440–94

Although the painter Hans Memling was born at Seligenstadt near Frankfurt am Main, his style is Flemish rather than German. Active in Bruges, he may have been trained in the workshop of Rogier van der Weyden, although the influence of Dieric Bouts is also apparent in his work. Memling enjoyed a wide circle of patronage and several of his most important pictures were produced for foreign clients. The finest collection of his work is in the Memling Museum (Hôpital St-Jean) in Bruges. His numerous altarpieces and portraits are painted in a highly accomplished but rather bland and conservative manner.

Memmi da Siena c1285–c1361

Lippo Memmi da Siena, also known as Filippo di Memmo, was a Sienese painter of religious panels and frescoes, son of the painter Memmo di Filippencio. In 1317, he signed the *Maestà* in the Palazzo Nuovo del Podestà in San Gimignano. This work is in the manner of Simone Martini, and particularly of his *Maestà* of 1315: the two men were, in fact, brothers-in-law, and there is some argument as to how to apportion their works. Obviously a painter of quality, Memmi is documented as having collaborated with his relative on the *Annunciation* now in the Uffizi, Florence (1333); they certainly both signed it. But the extent of his involvement is hotly debated. His other works are devotional pictures which, reflecting the manner of Simone, become increasingly elegant and decorative. He may have accompanied his brother-in-law to Avignon, but was certainly back in Italy by 1361, when he worked on the Sala del Consiglio in the Palazzo Pubblico in Siena.

Hans Memling: The Presentation in the Temple; detail; oil on panel; full size 60×48cm (24×19in); c1463. Kress Collection, Washington, D.C.

Mena Pedro de 1628–88

The Spanish sculptor Pedro de Mena was born in Granada, the son of the sculptor Alonso de Mena. At his father's death in 1646, Mena, aged only 18, became the master of the workshop. When Alonso Cano arrived in Granada in 1652 Mena became his pupil and principal assistant; he collaborated with him on a number of important works until 1656, when Cano left for Madrid. His statue of St Francis in Toledo Cathedral, probably to a design by Cano, gained him the appointment as sculptor to the cathedral in 1653, although he remained working in Granada.

In 1658 Mena moved to Malaga, where he settled for the rest of his career, producing there his most original work on the 40 high-relief figures for the choir of the cathedral. A brief visit to Madrid in 1662–3 brought him under the influence of the great Castilian sculptor Gregorio Fernandez. A fruit of this visit is the famous statue of St Mary Magdalene (National Museum of Sculpture, Valladolid) carved at Malaga in 1664 for the Jesuit Congregation of St Philip Neri at Madrid.

Mena was a wood-carver of outstanding subtlety and technical virtuosity. His art displays an unidealized naturalism, and an emotionalism that is firmly restrained. It is to be seen at its best in the half-lengths of the quietly sorrowing Virgin, of which the finest, carved in 1673, is in the Descalzas Reales in Madrid.

Anton Mengs: Self-portrait; oil on canvas; 98×73cm (39×29in); 1774. Uffizi, Florence

Mendelsohn Erich 1887–1953

The German architect Erich Mendelsohn was associated with Expressionism, and with the use of new building techniques and materials (such as concrete and steel) to produce curvilinear buildings with an expressive organic quality. The dramatic curves of the Einstein Tower, Potsdam (1917–21), were preserved in his later, more functionally determined International style designs for the Schocken stores at Stuttgart (1926) and Chemnitz (1928). In 1933 he moved to England and in partnership with Serge Chermayeff (1900–) designed the De La Warr Pavilion, Bexhill (1934). He went to Israel in 1934 and designed several hospitals there (including one at Haifa, 1937). In 1941 he moved to America where he designed the Maimonides Hospital, San Francisco (1946).

Mengs Anton 1728–79

Anton Raphael Mengs, the purest exponent and theorist of Neoclassical painting, was named by his father, the Dresden court painter, after Antonio Correggio and Raphael. Mengs studied the work of Michelangelo and Raphael in Rome during the 1740s, and on his return to Dresden in 1751 was appointed chief court painter. By 1775 he had met J.J. Winckelmann, in Rome, who praised him and influenced his work.

His finest fresco in Rome was the ceiling of S. Eusebio (1757–8), which is painted in the Baroque style. However, by 1761 he had completed the *Parnassus* fresco on the ceiling of the Villa Albani, Rome, which in contrast shows a careful study of the antiquities at Herculaneum. *Parnassus* rejects the Baroque illusionism of the past and follows the convention of a low relief derived from the Antique.

After this he went to Spain, where he was appointed court painter to Charles III, returning to Rome in 1769. In Spain he painted three mythological cycles on ceilings in the Royal Palace, the last of which was completed on a second visit in 1775. He was elected Principal of the Academy of St Luke in Rome in 1770. In 1772 he worked for Pope Clement XIV on the decorations in the Camera dei Papiri at the Vatican, the program of which is a historical allegory on the function of the Camera.

Mengs' most accomplished work was as a portrait painter; his influential style prefigures much of the Neoclassicism of Jacques-Louis David.

Adolf von Menzel: Studies of a Worker Eating; pencil on paper; 27×37cm (11×15in); c1870-5. Staatliche Museen, Berlin

delicately executed and intimate depictions of domestic middle-class life, and a few market scenes. *Mother and Sick Child* (c1660; Rijksmuseum, Amsterdam) shows him at his best: it is a carefully balanced composition revealing an awareness of Pieter de Hooch and Vermeer, though with added sentiment. Materials and textures are carefully imitated in Metsu's genre pictures, and also in the portraits painted after his move to Amsterdam sometime between 1655 and 1657. In the latter, Metsu sacrificed study of character and psychological relationships to the painstaking transcription of the silks, tapestries, rich carpets, and heavy furniture of the ostentatiously prosperous Dutch bourgeoisie of the 1660s.

Menzel Adolf von 1815–1905

Adolf Friedrich Erdmann von Menzel was a German Realist painter and draftsman. Largely self-taught in his father's lithographic workshop in Berlin (1830–3), Menzel adopted the graphic style of local Biedermeier artists. His woodcut series illustrating the life of Frederick the Great (1839–42) inaugurated an atmospheric style akin to etching.

As a self-taught painter, Menzel was influenced by the painterly techniques of John Constable (whose works were exhibited in Berlin in 1839) and K. Blechen. The works he painted in the 1840s are very advanced, both in their freely handled use of pure color and in their documentation of contemporary reality (for example, *The Berlin–Potsdam Railway*, 1847; Neue Nationalgalerie, Berlin). But Menzel never exhibited them. His contemporary fame rested on his paintings of Frederick the Great.

Metsu Gabriel 1629–67

Gabriel Metsu was a Dutch painter from Leiden who spent most of his working life in Amsterdam. He produced religious, mythological, and allegorical pictures in his youth, but is principally known for

Gabriel Metsu: A Man and Woman Seated by a Virginal; oil on oak panel; 38×32cm (15×13in); c1658–60. National Gallery, London

Meunier Constantin 1831–1905

The Belgian artist Constantin Émile Meunier first trained to become a sculptor, but abandoned this in 1851 and turned to painting. At the Atelier Navez in 1854 he met Charles de Groux, whose Social Realism was later to influence him. Between 1857 and 1875 Meunier painted mainly religious subjects, but in 1878 his discovery of Belgium's industrial area turned his attention to the life of modern working man. He took up sculpture again in 1884, and glorified (in heroic poses) figures symbolizing trades such as *The Porter* (c1900, Kunsthistorisches Museum, Vienna) or *The Longshoreman* (1905; Royal Museum of Fine Arts, Antwerp). Meunier's unfinished *Monument au Travail* (1893–1905; Musée Constantin Meunier, Brussels) borders on Symbolism in its attempt at universal synthesis.

Michael Astrapas and Eutychios
fl. 1295–c1325

Michael Astrapas and Eutychios were Byzantine painters active in Macedonia and Serbia. Their autographed work is in the Peribleptos church at Ohrid (1295), Bogorodica Ieviška at Prizren (1306), St George at Staro Nagoričino (1313–18), and Sveti Nikita at Čučer. Their style exhibits two phases—a provincial and a metropolitan.

The style of the Peribleptos and of several icons at Ohrid, notably St Matthew, is often called "cubist" because of its multiple perspective and fractured surfaces. The compositions are crowded with agitated figures and heavy architecture. The figures are bulky with drooping shoulders, and enveloped by voluminous, angular drapery. Faces are broken into jagged planes. The intense colors are highlighted so as to create sharp edges.

The second phase of work is seen in their other churches, as well as the Joachim and Anna church at Studenica (1314), and the Protaton of Mt Athos, attributed to them by scholars on stylistic grounds. Under influences from Constantinople, there is a trend towards elongated figures, softer modeling, and a more subdued palette.

Michaux Henri 1899–1984

The Belgian-French painter and author Henri Michaux was born in Namur, Belgium. It was in writing that Michaux first expressed himself artistically, in Brussels in 1922. In 1924 he moved to Paris, where the shock of seeing the nonnaturalistic, semiautomatic approach of Klee and Ernst awakened his interest in painting. He began intermittently to draw and paint signs and personal ideograms from 1925, because he felt writing could not express all he had to say. From 1937 onwards both activities were complementary, and he occasionally published books containing both writing and paintings.

Michaux always sought to tap the unconscious mind by allowing his fantasy to develop random blots and squiggles. In the late 1950s he even experimented with hallucinogenic drugs, in an attempt to free his mind from conscious control and facilitate his search for a personal language capable of expressing more directly the movement of his inner being.

Michelangelo 1475–1564

The Italian painter, sculptor, and architect Michelangelo Buonarroti was born at Caprese near Arezzo, the son of a minor official. As a child he was taken to Florence, where he was apprenticed to the painter Ghirlandaio; he seems to have found his master's somewhat bland style uncongenial, preferring the more austere and monumental art of Giotto and Masaccio. He appears to have taken up sculpture almost immediately. Among his earliest works is a relief of the *Battle of Lapiths and Centaurs* (c1492; Casa Buonarroti, Florence), which is clearly inspired by Classical sarcophagi and also reflects the antiquarian interests of the sculptor Bertoldo di Giovanni. The latter was closely associated with Lorenzo de' Medici ("Il Magnifico"), then the virtual ruler of Florence; Lorenzo seems to have allowed the young Michelangelo free access to his collection.

After a brief sojourn in Bologna, in 1496 Michelangelo was in Rome, where he was able to study far finer examples of Classical art than he could have found in Florence. His first work there, a life-sized *Bacchus* (c1496–7; Museo Nazionale, Florence), is an entirely convincing imitation of an antique statue. Its success led to the commission for the *Pietà* (1498–9; St Peter's, Rome). This at once established his reputation as the foremost living sculptor, both because of the exceptional beauty and pathos of its composition, and because of the amazing virtuosity of its technique.

Shortly afterwards Michelangelo returned to Florence, where he began work on a colossal statue of *David* (1501–4; Galleria dell'Accademia, Florence). This was the largest marble statue to be carved in Italy since the end of the Roman Empire and the first to bear comparison, in its mastery of human anatomy, with the finest achievements of Antiquity. However, the tension of the figure—and the mood of suppressed energy—is wholly un-Classical.

While he was in Florence Michelangelo also produced four devotional works for private patrons, namely the *Bruges Madonna* (1501–6; Notre Dame, Bruges), a freestanding group; the *Pitti Tondo* (c1503–5; Museo Nazionale, Florence) and the *Taddei Tondo* (c1504–5; Royal Academy of Arts, London), both unfinished marble reliefs; and also the *Doni Tondo* (c1504–6; Uffizi, Florence), his only known completed oil painting. This last work is wholly sculptural in feeling. The principal group, the Holy Family, is shown as if carved from a single block, with hard, absolutely clear contours and bright unrealistic colors; the poses are deliberately complex, with an exaggerated use of contrapposto, suggesting that Michelangelo's interest lay almost exclusively in the exploration of formal problems, rather than in the content.

These preoccupations are equally apparent in his last major work of this period, a cartoon for a fresco of *The Battle of Cascina*, commissioned for the Great Council chamber of Florence in 1504. The cartoon, known only through copies (a copy by Bastiano da Sangallo is in Holkham Hall, Norfolk), constituted the central section of a much larger composition and showed a group of soliders surprised by the enemy while bathing. Michelangelo seems to have regarded the subject merely as a pretext for showing the heroic male nude in a great variety of poses of outstanding beauty and originality, which were to provide a constant source of inspiration for later Florentine artists.

In 1505 he was summoned to Rome to make a gigantic tomb for Pope Julius II in St Peter's; the project was to obsess him for more than three decades, as successive powerful patrons demanded his services for other commissions. In the next year, for example, he was forced to make a colossal bronze statue of Julius in Bologna, which was destroyed soon afterwards. Then in 1508 the Pope ordered him to paint the vault of the Sistine Chapel in the

Michelangelo: The Creation of Man, a detail of the ceiling of the Sistine Chapel, the Vatican, Rome; 1508–12

Vatican: the result was the most influential single work in the history of European art.

The original project consisted simply of frescoes of the 12 Apostles, but Michelangelo soon replaced this with a much more elaborate scheme. In the center of the vault there are nine scenes taken from Genesis, flanked by pairs of naked youths (the *Ignudi*), who are in fact angels. Towards the sides of the ceiling there are 12 large seated Prophets and Sibyls, and then, lower still, the Ancestors of Christ. The various separate elements are arranged within an elaborate painted architectural framework. As Michelangelo proceeded his draftsmanship became even more assured, the poses increasingly varied and bold, and the figures endowed

with ever-greater energy and nobility. His frescoes are the most perfect visual embodiment of the then-current Neoplatonic belief, to which he was deeply committed, that physical beauty, and especially that of the human figure, is a reflection of the Divine.

After completing the ceiling in 1512 Michelangelo was able to resume his work on the tomb. The initial plan had involved a freestanding two-story monument with more than 40 large sculptured figures. He now decided on a three-sided structure projecting from a wall, but the quantity of sculpture required was not substantially reduced. Michelangelo was only able to carve two figures of *Slaves* (*c*1513; Louvre, Paris) and the seated *Moses* (1515–16; San

Pietro in Vincoli, Rome). Then in 1516 Julius' successor, Leo X, a member of the Medici family, ordered him to return to Florence (now once again under Medici rule), in order to design a new facade for the church of S. Lorenzo. This commission, like the ceiling and the tomb, involved an elaborate combination of figures and architecture, and it was conceived on an equally ambitious scale. For much of the next three years Michelangelo remained in the mountains near Carrara, making arrangements for the quarrying and transportation of the enormous blocks of marble required for the facade. But in 1519 Leo lost interest in the commission, which was canceled in the next year, and instead ordered Michelangelo to begin

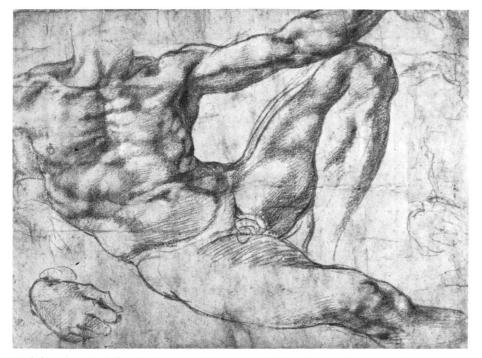

Michelangelo: a Study for The Creation of Adam on the Sistine Chapel ceiling; red chalk on paper; 19×26cm (7½×10in); 1510/11. British Museum, London

namely the four unfinished *Slaves* (1519–34; Galleria dell'Accademia, Florence) and the *Victory* group (*c*1532–4; Palazzo Vecchio, Florence). The *Slaves* very clearly illustrate his conception of sculpture as a process of revealing the underlying form concealed within the block of marble; but it would be unjustified to infer, as many critics have done, that he left so many of his works unfinished by choice, as a way of demonstrating this idea.

In 1534 Michelangelo moved to Rome, where he remained for the rest of his life. His first work there, commissioned by Pope Paul III, was the gigantic fresco of the *Last Judgment* on the altar wall of the Sistine Chapel, which was painted between 1536 and 1541. By now the optimistic Neoplatonism of his earlier years had been replaced by a more austere piety typical of the new climate of the Counter-Reformation, and in this fresco the figures have none of the ideal beauty of those on the ceiling. Instead, the anatomy is often grossly exaggerated, with deliberately inelegant, distorted poses and violent foreshortening. Deviations from the Classical norm of an equally extreme kind are to be found in the work of many of Michelangelo's contemporaries, whose style would now be described as Mannerist; but no other artist was capable of matching the intense expressive power of his composition, the

work on a mausoleum for the Medici family to be built at the other end of the church.

The mausoleum, usually known as the New Sacristy, is a square structure surmounted by a cupola; one wall is broken by a deep niche containing an altar. As usual with his major projects, Michelangelo only gradually reached his final solution, which in the event was never carried out in its entirety. Opposite the altar there was to have been a double tomb for Lorenzo il Magnifico and his brother Giuliano; but the only tombs actually built were those on the side walls, for two of Lorenzo's sons. Each consists of a highly idealized seated effigy of the deceased in a narrow niche, framed by an elaborate architectural setting, in front of which there is a huge sarcophagus surmounted by a pair of reclining figures symbolizing the times of day. The precise meaning of the scheme is not entirely clear, but it seems to have some kind of Neoplatonic theme, with the oppressively crowded lower zone of the building symbolizing the material world, and the more brilliantly illuminated and simpler architecture of the cupola representing the ideal world of the spirit. Even in its present uncompleted form, the Sacristy conveys an unparalleled impression of solemnity; it exists as a complete and consistent environment, in which the normal boundary between reality and the work of art is dissolved.

While he was in Florence Michelangelo also undertook one other project for the Medici, the construction of the Laurentian

Library in the monastery of San Lorenzo, begun in 1524. The most remarkable feature of the design is the small vestibule, in which the conventional language of Renaissance architecture is distorted in a seemingly almost perverse way for expressive effect. During this period, and especially from 1527 to 1529 when the Medici family temporarily lost control of the city, he was also able to work on additional figures for the tomb of Julius II,

Michelangelo: Joel, a detail of the Sistine Chapel ceiling, the Vatican, Rome; 1508–12

quality defined so succinctly by his friend and biographer Vasari as "terribilità".

Soon after finishing the *Last Judgment* Michelangelo began two much smaller frescoes in the Pauline Chapel, also in the Vatican: these were *The Crucifixion of St Peter* (1542–5) and *The Conversion of St Paul* (1545–50). In the total elimination of any suggestion of physical beauty, and in the extreme simplicity of pose and gesture, they represent the final development of his figure-style. The only concession to conventional aesthetic standards is in the treatment of color, which has an unexpected delicacy and luminosity.

The austerity of these paintings is matched in the late sculpture. In 1542 the "tragedy of the tomb", as Michelangelo himself described the fiasco of the Julius monument, was finally ended by an agreement with the Pope's heirs. They were now prepared to accept an extremely modest structure in S. Pietro in Vincoli, containing only the *Moses* and some other statues executed by pupils. The only major sculptures of Michelangelo's old age are two *Pietà* groups, one intended for his own tomb and then abandoned (c1550–61; Florence Cathedral), and the other, the *Ronadanini Pietà* (1560s; Castello Sforzesco, Milan), also produced for his own satisfaction and still unfinished at his death. Both bear eloquent witness to his inability to give concrete physical expression to his by now virtually abstract conceptions.

Michelangelo's growing disillusionment with the figurative arts was matched by an increasing interest in architecture, especially after he was put in charge of the reconstruction of St Peter's in 1546. He totally rejected the proposals of his predecessor Antonio da Sangallo the Younger, which involved a consistent system of proportion and an accumulation of individual elements. He favored a much more unified and simple scheme, relying for its effect on an undulating exterior wall articulated by a few massive pilasters, which created a strong upward emphasis and led the eye directly to the huge cupola. The style is dynamic and overtly dramatic, and anticipates the Baroque.

His other late Roman projects—notably the reconstruction of the Capitol (probably designed in 1538), the completion of the Palazzo Farnese (late 1540s) and the Porta Pia (1561–5)—are equally subjective, and no less radical in their rejection of Renaissance and Classical norms.

In his own lifetime Michelangelo enjoyed greater fame and prestige than any artist before him, thanks in part to the efforts of his contemporary biographers Condivi and Vasari. The scale of his projects, the difficulties he encountered, his total single-mindedness, and his solitary and austere personality established the concept of the creative genius that has become a fundamental element of the European consciousness. Works such as the Sistine Chapel ceiling, the *Moses*, and the New Sacristy provided standards that later artists might reject, but which they could not disregard. Thus it was almost entirely through Michelangelo's efforts that for three centuries the heroic male nude should have been considered the major challenge open to painters and sculptors, the one indispensable characteristic of great art.

Further reading. Beck, J., Paolucci, A., and Santi, B. *Michelangelo: The Medici Chapel*, London (1994). Hibbard, H. *Michelangelo*, 2nd ed., New York (1985, reissued 1998). Wallace, W. *Michelangelo: The Complete Sculpture, Painting, Architecture*, Washington, D.C. (1998).

Michelozzo di Bartolomeo: a Virtue, part of the tomb of Cardinal Brancacci in S. Angelo a Nilo, Naples; c1426–30

Michelozzo di Bartolomeo
1396–1472

The Florentine architect and sculptor Michelozzo di Bartolomeo was the son of an immigrant Burgundian tailor. He appears as a die-caster at the Florentine mint in 1410. From 1419 to 1424 he assisted Ghiberti, presumably as a bronzecaster and chaser. Thereafter he worked in partnership with Donatello for a decade, carving the Madonna and Child and the figures of the Virtues for the Coscia monument in Florence Baptistery (c1424–7), most of the marble figures for the tomb of Cardinal Brancacci in S. Angelo a Nilo in Naples (c1426–30), and substantial parts of the outdoor pulpit at Prato Cathedral (c1428–38). The Aragazzi monument in Montepulciano Cathedral (c1430–8) is entirely his own work. During the years 1430–3 he and Donatello worked in Rome.

As early as the period from 1420 to 1427 Michelozzo was already working as an architect, on the little church of S. Francesco al Bosco in the Mugello near Florence. After his return from Rome he turned increasingly towards architecture.

In the 1430s, he redesigned the church of S. Marco in Florence, one of the earliest of the many commissions he received from the Medici. He began the rebuilding of SS. Annunziata in Florence in 1444 for the Marquis of Mantua. This daring design incorporated an east rotunda closely based upon the temple of Minerva Medica which caused a storm of controversy in architectural circles. The church was still incomplete when Michelozzo withdrew from the project in 1455, and it was subsequently finished under the supervision of Alberti. Michelozzo's most important architectural commission was the Palazzo Medici, begun in 1444. With its boldly rusticated ground story and its massive raking cornice, this building became a model of Renaissance *palazzo* design. He received many other commissions for buildings in and around Florence and as far afield as Venice, Milan, and Dubrovnik.

Michelozzo's reputation has suffered as the result of comparison with his more illustrious contemporaries Brunelleschi and Donatello. While he had a less inquiring mind than either, he was second only to Brunelleschi as an architect. He was also a very distinguished sculptor who played a crucial role in the development of the Quattrocento wall tomb.

Mies van der Rohe Ludwig
1886–1969

The German architect Ludwig Mies van der Rohe was born in Aachen. He was apprenticed as a stone-cutter between 1900 and 1902, a training that probably influenced his lifelong attention to detailing in his buildings. In 1907 he traveled to Italy and was impressed with the work of Brunelleschi (1377–1446) and Palladio (1508–80), in particular the manner in which they articulated their buildings while confining themselves to few means.

Mies entered the office of Behrens in 1908 (Gropius and Le Corbusier also spent a period working with Behrens) and was introduced by him to the German classical tradition of K.F. Schinkel, whose Altes Museum in Berlin Mies particularly admired—from which, he was later to state, one could learn everything in architecture. Behrens placed him in charge of the building of the German Embassy in St Petersburg (1909). The German publishing house, Wasmuth, introduced the work of Frank Lloyd Wright to European architects in 1910, an event that was to clarify Mies' thinking. He left Behrens in 1911 and set up his own practice. In 1912 he was engaged on a project for Madame H.E.L.J. Kröller for the Kröller-Müller house at the Hague.

His first major postwar undertakings were the projects for Berlin's Friedrichstrasse (c1921) and a skyscraper (c1922), both of which were to be glass-walled, a revolutionary idea on this scale. Expressionist in ambition and concept, these may possibly have been influenced by the writing of Scheerbart and the architecture of Bruno Taut—for instance Taut's use of glass in the Glass Pavilion, in the Cologne *Werkbund* Exhibition, 1914. The chief determinants for Mies were the provision of sufficient illumination of interiors, the play of reflections, and the revealing of structure. In 1921 he became Director of Architectural Exhibitions for the *Novembergruppe* in Berlin, a group loosely Expressionist, sympathetic to socialism, whose aim was to exploit the possibilities for cooperation between art and society.

Mies' 1922 project for a concrete office block still shows some Expressionist qualities, for example the tapering outward of floors towards the top; but compared with his glass tower projects, the emphasis is now more horizontal. The weight is carried by an internal post and slab system, allowing alternating continuous bands of windows around the building. His work became increasingly Elementarist and less Expressionist in nature, the emphasis being placed upon the skeletal structure. His move towards an Elementarist position is manifested in his 1923 brick-villa project (where there are elements reminiscent of some *De Stijl* work and of El Lissitzky) and in his membership of "G" (*Gestaltung*, creative force) a group of Abstract artists. In 1925 he joined the *Ring*, a loose association of Berlin architects, Expressionists, and Elementarists, including Gropius, Mendelsohn, and the Tauts; and by the late 1920s he was among the leading architects in the city.

The *Deutscher Werkbund*, the official German Design authority, invited Mies to take charge of overall planning for a big architectural exhibition of modern residential buildings to be held in 1927, at the Weissenhof Siedlung (housing estate) in Stuttgart. Although modified by practical constraints, his planning of the site, and the relationship of buildings to the landscape, was striking. Mies, who was responsible for an apartment block, did not confine participation to German architects; J.J.D. Oud, Mart Stam, and Le Corbusier took part.

Another official undertaking, the German Pavilion at the Barcelona International Exhibition of 1928–9, was the occasion for one of his most famous and contentious buildings. Rich in the materials used—marble, onyx, tinted glass, chromium glazing bars, steel and leather chairs—the design is spare and in the Elementarist manner, with echoes of Frank Lloyd Wright (the emphatic roof line) and possibly Adolf Loos (rich materials combined with severe design). The Pavilion had no doors. Each room was only partially enclosed by three partitions on three sides, made from large tinted glass sheets, with some walls faced with marble or onyx. These walls reached to the roof but it was, in fact, supported by regularly placed freestanding columns. Two large pools were set into the extensive marble floor. Critics were divided: within its rationalist tradition it did not seem functional.

Towards the end of the decade and into the 1930s Mies was engaged on a number of projects which were to prefigure clearly his later buildings in America. In 1928 he planned the remodeling of the Alexanderplatz in Berlin. Here the structural regularity of the steel skeleton determines the strict rectangular shapes; metal framing and glass curtain walls emphasize the effect. In 1928–30 the "Tugendhat" house was built in Brno, Czechoslovakia. The 1933 Reichsbank project, more horizontal in its emphasis, also uses the curtain wall. Between these dates he became involved with the Bauhaus. As a result of political pressures, the Marxist Hannes Meyer, a Swiss architect, was removed from his post as Principal of the Bauhaus in 1930 and Mies was appointed in his place. Under Nazi pressure Mies finally moved the Bauhaus from Dessau to Berlin, being forced to close it in 1933 because of its alleged "Kultural Bolshevismus". He received a number of offers from America. In 1938 he became Director of Architecture at the Illinois Institute of Technology, a position he held until 1958, when he resigned in order to give more time to his practice.

His American work shows the development of ideas already implicit in his work of the 1920s and 1930s, for example his apartment blocks at Lake Shore Drive, Chicago (1948–51), through to Lafayette Towers, Detroit (1955–63). However, the works that have probably claimed most attention are the Farnsworth house (1945–50), a simply designed steel-and-glass residence, slightly raised above the ground, suspended on steel beams, isolated and open to nature on all sides; his Seagram building (1954–8), with its attention to detailing, its facade of bronze sections and glass tinted to match; and his work for the Illinois Institute of Technology (started 1940, completed 1962). Among his European work of the later period is his Gallery of the Twentieth Century, Berlin (1962–8).

Central to an understanding of Mies' development and work are arguments concerning functionalism, rationalism, and idealism as determinants on his style. He himself claimed an indifference to style. According to him there is an unfolding of the great form in each epoch: this is not invented by a particular architect but is contributed to by the individual. His emphasis was on structural architecture, as he felt this was based on reason, an architecture for a technological society, an architecture that anybody could practice.

Further reading. Blaser, W. *Mies van der Rohe: the Art of Structure*, London and New York, rev. ed. (1972). Carter, P. *Mies van der Rohe at Work*, Chicago (1972). Schulze, F. *Mies van der Rohe: A Critical Biography*, Chicago (1995).

Mignard Pierre 1612–95

The French painter, Pierre Mignard trained at Bourges and in Paris under Simon Vouet. From 1636 to 1657 he worked in Italy, where he was influenced by Poussin and by Bolognese classicism. He was to be more a practicing classicist than his rival Charles Lebrun, whom he was to succeed in all respects in 1690. In Paris he painted a number of decorations for private houses and churches. But he is best remembered as a portraitist in a rather stiff Italian manner, reviving the 16th-century allegorical/mythological type.

His brother, Nicolas (1606–68), worked mainly as a religious painter at Avignon, in a dry manner derived from Vouet, Poussin, and the Roman Seicento.

Mikon fl. early 5th century BC

Mikon was an Athenian painter of the early 5th century BC. He suffered in Antiquity by comparison with his greater contemporary and part-time collaborator Polygnotus. His most famous works were in Athens: battles against the Amazons were in the Stoa Poikile (the Painted Stoa, which gave its name to the Stoic school of philosophy) and probably also in the sanctuary of Theseus, where he certainly painted exploits of the Athenian hero; and the expedition of the Argonauts was in the Anakeion.

Millais J.E. 1829–96

The English painter John Everett Millais was born in Southampton. His family, having lived for some time in Jersey and northern France, moved in 1838 to London, where Millais' precocious talent could be properly developed; between the ages of 11 and 17 he attended the Royal Academy Schools. His first exhibited oil was the conventional romantic *Pizarro Seizing the Inca of Peru* (1846; Victoria and Albert Museum, London).

He was one of the young and dissatisfied artists who banded together in 1848 as the Pre-Raphaelite Brotherhood. Exhibited the following year, his *Lorenzo and Isabella* (Walker Art Gallery, Liverpool) shows the minute detailing, the pristine color, the symbolism, and the use of friends as models seen in contemporary works by Holman Hunt and Rossetti. *Christ in the House of His Parents* (1850; Tate Gallery, London) applied the same principles to religious subject matter. It was attacked for its unidealized depiction of the Holy Family, while its stylized, almost ritualistic quality associated it disastrously with the dreaded encroachment of the Roman Church and "popish" asceticism. The paintings he exhibited in 1851 were also badly received.

J.E. Millais: A Dream of the Past, Sir Isumbras at the Ford; oil on canvas; 124×170cm (49×67in); 1856–7. Lady Lever Art Gallery, Port Sunlight

A Huguenot (1851–2; private collection) won great popularity, however, and its pathetic theme of lovers parted by historical circumstances recurred in *The Proscribed Royalist* (1852–3; private collection), *The Black Brunswicker* (1860; Lady Lever Art Gallery, Port Sunlight), and others. The two-figure formula removed the need for more complex compositions, which Millais seems to have found difficult. His best-known picture, *Ophelia* (1851–2; Tate Gallery, London), illustrates his working method at this period, the setting painted painstakingly from nature in summer and the figure added from a model in the studio during the winter, ready for the Academy exhibition in May.

While painting John Ruskin's portrait, staged on a Scottish waterfall (1853–4; private collection), Millais fell in love with his sitter's wife, Effie. Soon after her divorce from Ruskin they married, and the first of eight children was born in 1856. Family commitments inevitably made Millais conscious of the need to sell his work, which he did with mounting success, earning by the 1880s some £30,000 a year.

In the later 1850s he produced a series of pictures whose power lay in the evocation of a general mood rather than the description of a particular situation. The most atmospheric is *Autumn Leaves* (1855–6; City of Manchester Art Gallery), in which the budding youth of some girls is set against the cyclical decay of natural things: dead leaves burning at dusk. The conjunction was calculated to induce, he claimed, "the deepest religious reflection". Landscape and figures interact similarly in other works, including *The Blind Girl* (1854–6; City of Birmingham Museums and Art Gallery), in which the beauty of the scenery intensifies the subject's pathos, and *The Vale of Rest* (1858–9; Tate Gallery, London), a strange image of nuns digging a grave in the gathering gloom of evening.

Millais had always shown himself a gifted draftsman and his many finished pen-and-ink drawings of the earlier 1850s, for example *The Race-Meeting* (1853; Ashmolean Museum, Oxford), a scene reminiscent of contemporary novels, led naturally on to his illustrative work, which begins with the edition of Tennyson's poems published by Moxon in 1857. Throughout the 1860s he was a prolific illustrator, both for magazines, notably *Once a Week*, and for novels, especially those of Trollope.

His painting technique, already losing its Pre-Raphaelite meticulousness, became increasingly broad from now on, enabling him to work more quickly and on larger canvases. He admired English 18th-century portraitists and the Old Masters, calling his presentation picture as an Academician *Souvenir of Velazquez* (1867–8; Royal Academy of Arts, London).

First in a line of studies of single children—often his own—was *My First Sermon* (1862–3; Guildhall Art Gallery, London), depicting a little girl in a pew. The Reynolds-like *Cherry Ripe* (1879; private collection), the much more painterly manner of which exemplifies the evolution of Millais' style, was published as a color reproduction, selling 600,000 copies. He also dealt in historical child-subjects such as *The Boyhood of Raleigh* (1870; Tate Gallery, London). Another category was the young lady in 18th-century costume; *Clarissa* for instance (1887; private collection), modeled by his daughter Sophie, imitates Gainsborough's portrait *The Honourable Mrs Graham* (c1777; National Gallery of Scotland, Edinburgh).

His first major pure landscape was *Chill October* (1870; private collection). Autumn and winter visits to Scotland, during which he did much hunting and shooting as well as landscape-painting, came to provide a welcome escape from the increasing pressures of his London portrait practice. His depictions of often rather bleak scenes were intended to suggest human sentiments, especially loneliness and a sense of the impassivity of Nature. They show technical subtlety in rendering effects of wind, dew, and mist, and sensitivity in capturing the mood of a certain season or time of day, as for example in *Lingering Autumn* (1890; Lady Lever Art Gallery, Port Sunlight).

Hearts are Trumps (1872; Tate Gallery, London), showing three ladies around a card-table, is an early example of his society portraiture. Such luxuriously dressed female sitters exercised Millais' now bold and rich handling of paint. With male subjects he concentrated on the delineation of strong character in the features: in the two portraits of Gladstone, for example (1879, National Portrait Gallery, London; 1884–5, Christ Church, Oxford). Outline is a particularly telling aspect of his work, seen to effect in *Mrs Jopling* (1879; Collection of L.M. Jopling, on loan to the Ashmolean Museum, Oxford). With its three-quarter-length figure depicted

against a plain background, this compares in simplicity of statement with contemporary work by Manet.

Of several studies of old age, the patriotic *North-West Passage* (1874; Tate Gallery, London), which shows a retired sea-dog, is the most attractive, especially in its coloring. *The Ruling Passion* (1885; Glasgow Art Gallery and Museum), depicting a bedridden ornithologist, typifies Millais' later preference for dark tones and an overall impression of brownness. This is also seen in the late religious paintings, for instance *St Stephen* (1895; Tate Gallery, London).

Created a baronet in 1885, and elected President of the Royal Academy in 1896, Millais commanded the highest personal popularity and professional esteem.

Further reading. Bennett, M. *P.R.B. Millais P.R.A.* (London 1967). Gaunt, W. *The Restless Century*, London (1972). Lutyens, M. *Millais and the Ruskins*, London (1967). Millais, J.G. *Life and Letters of Sir John Everett Millais* (2 vols.), London (1899).

Milles Carl 1875–1955

The Swedish sculptor Carl Milles was renowned for his fountains. Born near Uppsala and trained in Stockholm, he settled in Paris in 1897. He made his debut at the Salon of 1899 and met Rodin in 1900. After living in Munich and Rome, he returned to Sweden in 1908 to work on monumental commissions. His studio at Lidings eventually became the Millesgarden (Milles Museum) famous for its terraces and waterfalls. His early works in the style of Rodin and Maillol brought him international acclaim at the 1914 Malmö Baltic Exhibition. Around 1917 he came under the influence of the German sculptor and theorist, Adolf Hildebrand, and his style changed dramatically. *The Meeting of the Waters* (1940; Aloo Plaza, St Louis, Missouri) illustrates Milles' new-found belief that sculpture can be monumental and architectural without being contained within an architectural framework; the freestanding figures are grouped into a balanced composition and movement is provided by the play of the water. Milles moved to the United States in 1931. Major works include *Man and Nature* (1940; wood; Rockefeller Center, New York) and *The Hand of God* (1954, Eskèltsuna, Sweden).

Jean-François Millet: The Gleaners; oil on canvas; 84×111cm (33×44in); 1857. Louvre, Paris

Millet Jean-François 1814–75

A leading painter of the Barbizon School, Jean-François Millet was noted for his portrayal of peasant themes. He was born into a Norman farming family, and received his earliest artistic instruction in Cherbourg. In 1837 he went to Paris, where he studied under Paul Delaroche. His first Salon exhibit, a portrait, was shown in 1840. After years of penury in Paris, he moved in 1849 to Barbizon, where the peasant stream of his art developed, and where he remained for the rest of his life.

His earliest surviving works are portraits, for example that of his first wife, *Pauline Ono* (1841–2; Musée Thomas Henry, Cherbourg). In the early 1840s he painted in a Rococo manner, producing erotic nudes and *scènes galantes* reminiscent of Diaz de la Pena (for example, *Reclining Nude*, 1844–5; Louvre, Paris). A more forceful style emerged c1847 as can be seen in *The Quarrymen* (1846–7; Toledo Museum of Art, Toledo, Ohio). The dynamic poses of the workers reflect Michelangelo and Daumier, but the style is still related to earlier works.

Millet turned to peasant subjects as he became aware of the changes brought about by urbanization and the industrial revolution. The immediate stimulus was the Revolution of 1848, which brought social questions to the fore. Millet exhibited a peasant subject, *The Winnower* (1848; private collection) in the Salon of 1848, and *The Sower* (1850; Provident National Bank, Philadelphia), a monumental figure of rustic labor, in 1850.

The stark portrayal of the peasant, on a large scale and without an element of humor or anecdote, was new in France; it was not considered a worthy pictorial motif. In the sensitive political climate of the day, such works were also seen as revolutionary statements. However, Millet seems to have intended to express only his fatalistic conception that man was doomed to unremitting labor. *The Gleaners* (1857; Louvre, Paris), and *The Man with the Hoe* (1860–2; private collection) aroused much criticism over their supposed political content.

Although seen as a revolutionary, Millet shows continuity with traditional Western art in some themes and compositions. *The Harvester Meal* (1851–3; Museum of Fine Arts, Boston) refers to the biblical story of Ruth and Boaz, and reflects some compositions of Poussin. His *Peasant Grafting a Tree* (1855; private collection) evokes Virgil. He uses a somber palette to depict the rough faces and ungainly figures of his peasant subjects (for example, *Woman Grazing her Cow*, 1858; Musée de l'Ain, Bourg-en-Bresse). His melancholy, idealized settings often exploit the diffused light of dawn or dusk (for example, *The Angelus*, 1855–7; Louvre, Paris). After 1863, under the influence of Rousseau, he painted more pure landscapes (such as *L'Hiver aux Corbeaux*, 1862; Kunsthistorisches Museum, Vienna).

Millet produced many drawings and pastels, which are among his most attractive works, being simple depictions of ordinary life and everyday tasks (for example, *Shepherdess Resting*, 1849; Fitzwilliam Museum, Cambridge.)

Milow Keith 1945–

The English artist Keith Milow was born in London. He studied at the Camberwell School of Art (1962–7) and at the Royal College of Art (1967–8). He was appointed Gregory Fellow at Leeds University (1970) and subsequently awarded a Harkness Fellowship to the United States.

Working in series, each one characterized by strikingly different materials and approaches, Milow's works are always based on images of real objects which are manipulated by the creative process. Since the late 1960s he has produced reliefs that explore the nature of both painting and sculpture.

Earlier works, for example *Improved Reproductions* (1970; Tate Gallery, London) were in resin, based on photographs. The *Split Definitives* in the mid 1970s were painted on panels set at right angles to the walls, as were the *Cenotaphs* (1979), based on the famous London monument. Since 1974 Milow has produced over a hundred *Crosses* in various materials and sizes. In them he explores the form of the cross through variations in an attempt both to acknowledge and deny its powerful symbolism.

Mincho Kichisan 1352–1431

The Japanese painter Kichisan Mincho was also known as Cho Densu. A priest of the Tofukuji Temple in Kyoto, he was the major artist in the change from brilliantly colored figure-painting of *rakan* (saints) and famous priests, with mixed ink and color landscape backgrounds, to pure ink paintings of mythical figures and almost unpeopled landscapes. His skill in the former style is seen in the *tour-de-force* of the *Five Hundred Rakan* (Nezu Museum of Art, Tokyo). This was painted in the Takuma figure-style, of which he was the last great exponent. His painting in pure ink is more tentative, like the attributed *Hut by a Mountain Stream* of 1413 (Nanzenji Temple, Kyoto); but it has great historical importance.

Mino da Fiesole 1429–84

Mino da Fiesole was an Italian sculptor. He is said by Vasari to have been trained by his near-contemporary Desiderio da Settignano, though there is little sign of it in his early work. He was a less gifted carver of marble than Desiderio or Antonio Rossellino, though he was strongly influenced by their style. His earliest dated work is a portrait bust of Piero de' Medici of 1453 and he carved six other good busts. He produced several large tombs and tabernacles in and around Florence, and also worked extensively at Rome in the 1460s and 1470s. He may be identical with a sculptor active there and in Naples who signed himself Mino del Reame.

Mino da Fiesole: Portrait of Astorgio Manfredi; marble; 52×54×28cm (20×21×11in); c1456. National Gallery of Art, Washington, D.C.

Mino's cutting of drapery is slick and linear, his faces are bland stereotypes, and his compositions naive. While superficially attractive, his sculpture is devoid of emotional involvement and degenerates into sentimentality.

Mirak Naqqash late 15th century

The Persian painter Mirak Naqqash was a Sayyid of Herat. A versatile artist, he was

Joan Miró: Women and Bird in the Moonlight; oil on canvas; 81×66cm (32×26in); 1949. Tate Gallery, London

in turn calligrapher, illuminator, and painter. He became head of the library of Sultan Husayn Bayqara (1469–1507). He is said to have designed inscriptions for all the principal buildings of Herat, no doubt in tile mosaic. He was the painting master of Bihzad. Six miniatures in a *Khamsa* of Nizami (British Library London; MS. Or. 6810), datable to 1494–5 but old-fashioned for that date, have been plausibly attributed to him. He also gained a reputation as an athlete and pugilist. He died in 1507. He should not be confused with Aqa Mirak, an early Safavid court painter.

Mir Musavvir *fl.* 1520–60

The Persian painter Mir Musavvir of Badakhshan contributed three miniatures to the royal Safavid *Shah-nama* of Tahmasp (one dated 1527/8; private col-

lection) and one dated 1540 to the *Khamsa* of Nizami in the British Library, London. About 1540 he succeeded Sultan Muhammad as head of the Library of Shah Tahmasp in Qazwin. He excelled in figure drawing. His son, Mir Sayyid Ali, was a founder of the Mughal court school under Humayun (c1549), who offered to buy him from the Shah; shortly afterwards, Humayun retook Delhi (1555) and founded the Mughal School of Indian painting. Mir Sayyid's father joined him in India and died there.

Miró Joan 1893–1983

Joan Miró was a Spanish painter, ceramist, and sculptor, and a leading member of the Surrealist movement. Born in Barcelona, he at first hesitated between art and business studies, but in 1912, after a serious breakdown, he enrolled in Francesco Galí's School of Art in Barcelona, where he was introduced to avant-garde French art. His paintings of 1914 show a highly original amalgam of Post-Impressionist, Fauve, and Cubist influences. Several landscapes painted in 1918 are reminiscent of Persian miniatures in their precision of line, decorative treatment of flat areas of color, and patterning of forms.

On his first visit to Paris in 1919, Miró sought out his countryman, Picasso, with whom he developed an enduring and mutually stimulating friendship. In 1920 he took a studio in Paris, and through André Masson—a neighbor—he met the Dada and Surrealist poets. Henceforward he divided his time between Paris and Spain.

Although still anchored in the "real" world, Miró's paintings of 1918 to 1923 became increasingly strange, due to an almost manic attention to detail, a hallucinatory vision of ordinary objects, and an expressive intensity. In works such as *The Tilled Field* (1923–4; Solomon R. Guggenheim Museum, New York), the element of fantasy and irrationality is pronounced. In 1924 he joined the Surrealists, who encouraged him to rely on imagination and dreams for his imagery (as in *The Harlequin's Carnival*, 1924–5; Albright-Knox Art Gallery, Buffalo). During the years 1925 to 1927, responding to Surrealist theories of automatism, Miró produced a large number of spontaneously and rapidly executed "dream" paintings, which border on abstraction. In these he began to develop the sign-language—cosmic and sexual in its subject matter—characteristic of much of his later work.

In 1928, Miró reverted to his detailed manner in the *Dutch Interiors*, which were based on Old Master paintings. From that time until his death his work alternated between freedom and precision, the two extremes occasionally being combined in the same work. During the 1930s, his distress at the political situation in Europe was reflected in the savage subject matter and mood of such paintings as *Seated Woman* (1932; private collection).

In 1940 and 1941 Miró painted his *Constellations*—a series of gouaches which demonstrates his dazzling command of overall pictorial design and linear rhythm. He made his first ceramics in 1944, in collaboration with Llorens Artigas, abandoning painting from 1955 to 1959 in order to explore this new medium with characteristically radical inventiveness. In the 1960s, he devoted much time to huge sculptures based on the biomorphic personages in his paintings, and to sculptures created from found objects.

Miró's paintings after 1960 were large, simple, bold abstractions, employing his personal sign-language with great expressive inventiveness. He enjoyed experimenting with a wide variety of unconventional techniques such as tearing and burning. His influence on postwar painting—especially Abstract Expressionism—was considerable.

Further reading. Dupin, J. *Joan Miró: Life and Work*, London (1962). Dupin, J. *Miró Engravings Vol. III 1973–1975*, New York (1989). Gimferrer, P. *The Roots of Miró*, New York (1993).

Mir Sayyid Ali *fl. c1530–80*

Mir Sayyid Ali was a Persian painter born in Tabriz. As the son of the painter Mir Musavvir he worked at the Safavid court from early youth, contributing one miniature to the *Nizami* of Tahmasp (1539–43), and probably also to his *Shah-nama* (78 of its 258 illustrations are in the Metropolitan Museum, New York). He joined the Mughal emperor in exile in Kabul (1545), and went with him to India. There he painted for him a large imaginary group portrait of his ancestors reaching back to Timur, at a picnic in a garden (British Museum, London). The painting is in pure Safavid style, but on cloth 45 in (114 cm) square. With Abd al-Samad he founded the Mughal School of Indian painting.

Mitsunobu Tosa *c1430–c1521*

Tosa Mitsunobu was a Japanese *Yamatoe*-style painter, the greatest of the family who dominated the Kyoto *edokoro* (painting office). Later he became an official painter to the Shogun's government. This, and the marriage of his daughter to Kano Motonobu, began the 16th-century union of the Japanese and Chinese styles.

In Kyoto temples, many sets of screens of figure-subjects against gold backgrounds are attributed to Mitsunobu. His major certified works are the sets of handscrolls *Kitano Tenjin Engi* (1502; Kitano Shrine) and *Kiyomizudera Engi* (1517; Tokyo National Museum). In both these works, the traditional narrative style is given power and cohesion by an extremely forceful personality.

Mochi Francesco *1580–1654*

The Italian artist Francesco Mochi was the most idiosyncratic of the great sculptors of the Roman Baroque. His *St Veronica* (1629–40; St Peter's, Rome) displays his violent dramatic power through an abstract play of near-geometric forms and taut linear rhythms. His monuments in Piacenza to Ranuccio (1612–22) and Alessandro Farnese (completed 1625) are the most forceful and inspired equestrian statues of the 17th century, while the scenes on their bases (completed 1629) perfect the pictorial low-relief style originated by Giovanni da Bologna in Mochi's native Tuscany. The psychological intensity of Mochi's vision, and the increasingly unrealistic forms in which he embodied it, found little favor in 17th-century Rome.

Modersohn-Becker Paula *1876–1907*

After studying in London and Berlin, the German artist Paula Becker moved in 1898 to the artists' colony of Worpswede in northern Germany, where she met and married the painter Otto Modersohn. Increasingly dissatisfied with the naturalism and sentimentality of the Worpswede painters, she visited Paris several times, where she discovered the works of Van Gogh, Cézanne, and Gauguin (she was one of the very first German artists to respond to Post-Impressionism). Painting mostly women, children and herself, she used bold colors and flat, simplified forms, with leaves and flowers as recurrent motifs. The themes of nature, motherhood and female identity play a major role in her work. She met with little understanding or success, even at Worpswede, though she was encouraged by the poet Rainer Maria Rilke, whose portrait she painted. A characteristic work from her maturity is her nude *Self-Portrait with Amber Necklace* (1906; Roselius Collection, Bremen). In her use of form and color she was an important precursor of Expressionism.

Further reading. Perry, G. *Paula Modersohn-Becker*, New York (1979).

Modigliani Amedeo *1884–1920*

The Italian painter and sculptor Amedeo Modigliani was born at Livorno. He was encouraged in his early talent by his mother, before studying at the Academies of Rome, Florence, and Venice. During his

Francesco Mochi:
equestrian monument to
Alessandro Farnese; cast
bronze; completed
1625. Piazza Cavalli,
Piacenza

stay in Venice from 1903 to 1906, the
Biennale introduced him to the current Art
Nouveau and Impressionist trends; he
traveled to Paris in 1906.

He quickly joined the artists in Montmartre and showed seven works at the
1907 Salon d'Automne, a remarkable success for a recently arrived young man. The
Cézanne retrospective was mounted in the
same exhibition. Modigliani's work, however, was nearer to Lautrec or early Picasso
in style, with an elegance of line that
betrays his Art Nouveau tendencies.

He turned to sculpture in 1910. While
continuing to paint, he became fascinated
by primitive sculpture, probably under the
influence of Brancusi and Matisse. He
carved heads directly in stone; some have
rudimentary features that respect the original block to such an extent that they have
been called unfinished. Others are elegant,
mannered versions of ethnographic types,
extravagantly elongated, with stylized features (for example, *Head*, 1911–12; Tate
Gallery, London).

After 1910, these features began to show
themselves in his paintings, from now on
almost exclusively figures and portraits.
He seems to have worked out the formal
aspects of this style in his imaginative work
first, developing a series of *Caryatids*;
these began quite close to their ethnographic models in 1911 but their style
became increasingly arabesque by 1913.

In 1914 or 1915 he made the ac-
quaintance of the English poet Beatrice
Hastings, who lived with him until 1916
and looked after him irregularly as his
health deteriorated. In this short period he
produced his most powerful paintings,
including portraits of *Juan Gris* (1915;
Metropolitan Museum, New York), *Beatrice Hastings* (1915; Art Gallery of Ontario, Toronto), *Picasso* (1915; private collection), *Jean Cocteau* (1916; Pearlman
Foundation, New York), *Paul Guillaume*
(1916; Galleria d'Arte Moderna, Milan),
and *Chaim Soutine* (1916–17; National
Gallery of Art, Washington, D.C.). When
confronted by a sitter he modified his
stereotype and produced extraordinarily
perceptive studies; his portrait of *Picasso*
(1915; George Moos Collection, Geneva),
seems to have been taken over by the vitality of the subject.

**Amedeo Modigliani: Head of a Woman
Wearing a Hat; watercolor; 35×27cm
(14×11in); 1907. Collection of William Young
and Co., Boston, Mass.**

After Modigliani had taken part in a successful group exhibition in 1916, the dealer Leopold Zborowski furnished him with models and a studio. However, he continued his irregular mode of life, shared after 1917 by Jeanne Hébuterne, who bore him a child in 1918. Increasingly his figures, particularly his nudes, take on a lassitude that is both voluptuous and melancholic. The day after he died of tuberculosis Jeanne Hébuterne, who was seven months pregnant, killed herself.

Further reading. Fifield, W. *Modigliani, a Biography*, London (1978). Hall, D. *Modigliani*, Oxford (1979). Lanthemann, J. *Modigliani: Catalogue Raisonné*, Barcelona (1970). Soby, J.T. *Modigliani*, New York (1954).

Laszlo Moholy-Nagy: Light-Space Modulator; reflecting metals and transparent plastics; height 151cm (59in); 1923–30. Busch-Reisinger Museum, Cambridge, Mass.

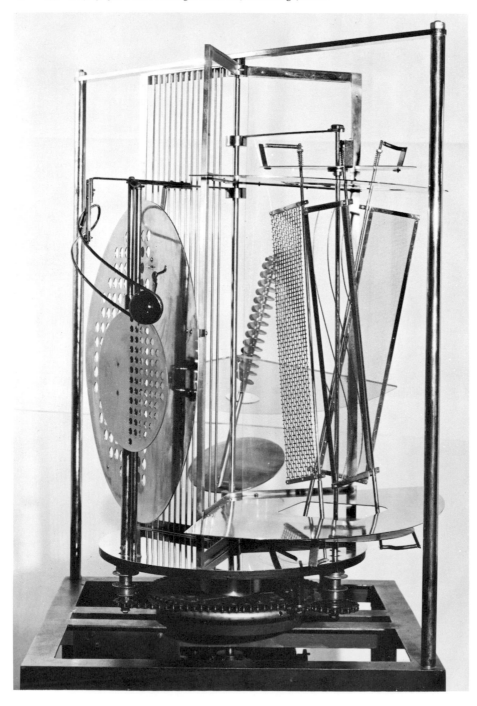

Moholy-Nagy Laszlo 1895–1946

Laszlo Moholy-Nagy was a Hungarian painter, theorist, and maker of constructions. He first studied law, but by the end of the First World War he had begun to paint, influenced by the contemporary Hungarian painters Janos Uitz and Jozsef Nemes-Lamperth, both associates of the politically engaged MA circle. In 1921 he moved to Berlin, and in the same year was a signatory to the short manifesto "A Call for Elementarist Art", published in *De Stijl*. Essentially Moholy-Nagy opposed individualism in style—on which he made common cause with Theo van Doesburg and El Lissitzky.

Moholy-Nagy's early painting uses Suprematist elements of circle, cross, and square. In 1924 he exhibited at the Sturm Gallery, Berlin, three factory-made works of identical composition but varying sizes; painted on porcelain enamel these were made by the factory supervisor from his instructions. By this time he was interesting himself in modern materials, for instance transparent plastics, which allowed him to experiment with light, and in photography.

He was appointed to the Bauhaus in 1923, when the emphasis there shifted from Expressionism to Constructivism, and was put in charge of both the metalwork shop and the preliminary course. His Constructivist ideas were also to change the direction of typography and its layout, towards greater order and clarity. With Gropius he coedited a series of Bauhaus books, and was also responsible for the layout and design of some of them. These set out the ideas of leading artists and architects, including Klee, Mondrian, and Malevich. *Von Material zu Architektur*, his own contribution, dealt with various artists and photography, with kinetic sculpture, and with illuminated advertising. An important part of his theory was concerned with the creation of "virtual" volume by light: to realize this he created his "Light-Space Modulators". He resigned from the Bauhaus in 1928, after a policy change.

In 1934 he left Germany for Holland, then lived in London from 1935 to 1937, before emigrating to America. In 1937 the New Bauhaus was established in Chicago (it became the Institute of Design in 1958) with Moholy-Nagy as its head until his death. He was a prolific writer and theorist and in 1946 published *A New Vision and Abstract of an Artist*.

Further reading. Fawkes, C. *Moholy-Nagy and the Bauhaus*, London (1973). Kostelanetz, R. *Moholy-Nagy*, New York (1970). Moholy-Nagy, L. *Painting, Photography, Film*, London (1969). Moholy-Nagy, S. *Moholy-Nagy: Experiment in Totality*, Cambridge, Mass. (1972).

Mokubei Aoki 1767–1833

Aoki Mokubei was a Japanese painter and potter of the *Bunjinga* School. He was born in Kyoto, where he acquired a taste for things Chinese. He became a maker of Chinese-style pottery and porcelain, especially for the *sencha* form of tea ceremony favored by the literary, and opened kilns in Kyoto, Wakayama, and Kaga. His painting consists mostly of landscapes in a superficially *Bunjinga* style, but with a light delicacy of touch and a predominantly pink and blue palette which are all his own. Sometimes of real Japanese scenes, they have a quality of dreamy fantasy, as in his *Sunny Morning at Uji* (Tokyo National Museum).

Mola Pier 1612–66

The Italian painter Pier Francesco Mola was a native of Coldrerio, near Como; by 1616 his family had moved to Rome. From 1633 to 1640 and again from 1641 to 1647 he worked in Venice and northern Italy, studying for two years (1645–7) with Albani in Bologna. His earliest known works are frescoes at Coldrerio. In these years he was deeply influenced by Venetian art and by Guercino (1591–1666). A group of small-scale landscapes show the development of an intensely romantic style; his palette is dark and his chiaroscuro rich and warm.

Under the influence of Albani, Mola's landscapes became more classical. In 1647 he returned to Rome, where he painted frescoes and altarpieces that continue the traditions of Bolognese classicism. In his major official commission, *Joseph and his Brethren* (1636–7; Palazzo del Quirinale, Rome) he moves towards the grandeur of the High Renaissance and the vivid colors of Pietro da Cortona. In 1658 he began frescoes in the Palazzo Pamphili at Valmontone, but a dispute with his patron led to their destruction.

Mola remained a romantic, most successful in the exotic *Barbary Pirate* (1650; Louvre, Paris) and in a beautiful series of hermits in Venetian landscapes. After 1660

Pier Mola: Joseph and his Brethren; fresco; 475×475cm (187×187in); 1656–7. Palazzo del Quirinale, Rome

he again sought inspiration in 16th-century Venetian art. His highly dramatic paintings of anchorite saints—*St Bruno* (1665, Jannetti Collection, Rome) and *St Jerome* (Buscot Park, Faringdon, Oxfordshire)—and his tender and idyllic treatment of poetic subjects—*Bacchus and Ariadne* (Wilton House, Salisbury, Wiltshire) and *Erminia tending the wounded Tancred* (M.H. de Young Memorial Museum, San Francisco)—are perhaps his most personal and attractive contributions to the Baroque.

Momper Joos de 1564–1635

Joos de Momper was a Flemish painter from Antwerp. Taught by his father, Bartholomeus de Momper, he also trained his sons Phillips and Gaspard. Although he spent most of his life in his native Antwerp, Momper visited Italy in 1581 and 1591. In 1594 he worked beside Cornelis Floris on the decorations for the triumphal entry of Archduke Ernest.

Momper's fanciful mountain panoramas (examples in many European public galleries) earned him great success during his lifetime. Strictly a landscape specialist, he developed Pieter Bruegel the Elder's investigations of this genre to their ultimate degree. The figures in his paintings were generally executed by other painters, notably Jan Bruegel. His work occupies an important place in the development from the Flemish Mannerist landscape to the more naturalistic style of the 17th century.

Mondrian Piet 1872–1944

Pieter Cornelisz. Mondriaan, the eldest child of a schoolmaster in Amersfoort, Holland, is ranked among the greatest pioneers of Abstract art. His austere compositions of horizontal and vertical lines and primary colors, taken with his theoretical writings, have had a profound influence on 20th-century art and aesthetics.

Intended by his Calvinist father to become a schoolteacher, Mondriaan completed his training and was 20 before he determined to enrol at the Amsterdam Academy of Fine Arts, in 1892.

For the following 15 years, though he worked assiduously, he had little success. He taught, and did portraits, copies, and technical drawings, in order to continue his own work. He became a landscape painter in the manner of such Dutch contemporaries as Jozef Israels and Maris. The early work of Van Gogh inspired him to live at Uden, in Brabant, throughout 1904.

Piet Mondrian: Composition with Yellow; oil on canvas; 46×47cm (18×19in); 1930.
Kunstsammlung Nordrhein-Westfalen, Düsseldorf

Returning to Amsterdam in 1905, he began to respond to Modernist ideas. He met the painter Jan Toorop in 1908 on the island of Walcheren. From this time he began to paint a succession of series—studies of a lighthouse, a windmill, a church tower, of sea and dunes, and especially of an apple tree—in which he experimented with the innovations of the Divisionists and the Fauves.

In 1909 came two significant events. In January, at the Stedelijk Museum, Amsterdam, with Jan Sluters and Cornelis Spoor, he exhibited work that conservative critics attacked as being unbalanced. And he joined the Theosophical Society of Holland. Theosophy became an alternative to Calvinism and gave him a metaphysical theory out of which he later developed his theory of art. In the following two years his reputation grew. In 1911, he became a Director of Amsterdam's *Moderne Kunstring*, and at the Society's October exhibition his canvases were hung beside works by the Fauves, the Cubists, and

Cézanne. It was then that he began to sign his name "Mondrian".

In December 1911 he settled in Paris, where he remained, apart from the years of the First World War, until 1938. Although Paris was one of the centers of early modernism, Mondrian lived alone, seldom mixing with other painters. His work, however, showed the influence of Cubism. His exhibits at the Salon des Indépendants of 1913 were noticed favorably by Apollinaire. By 1914, his representations of trees, building facades, and still life had become patterns of staccato verticals and horizontals with occasional arcs, tinted in pale pastel colors. Nevertheless, like other Cubist works, they remained essentially based on individual motifs.

Mondrian returned to Holland in 1914 to attend his father's deathbed. The outbreak of war compelled him to stay in Holland for five crucial years. He returned to painting the sea, and his sequence of studies *Pier and Ocean* confirmed for him the need to abandon the individual motif for a more

universal expression. At the same time, he discovered three friends and a patron, Salomon Slijper.

His first friend was a younger painter, Bart van der Leck, who was also exploring abstraction. Together, they developed a system restricted to rectangular shapes. The second friendship was with M.H.J. Schoenmaekers, a philosopher, whose book *New Image of the World*, almost the only volume Mondrian owned, profoundly influenced his theory of art. The third friendship was with C.E.M. Kupper (also known as I.K. Bonset among Dadaists). As "Theo van Doesberg" Kupper founded with Mondrian the movement and the periodical *De Stijl*, in 1917. *De Stijl* stood for abstraction, the unification of the arts, and the creation of new values for humanity.

In *De Stijl* Mondrian began to publish his theory of art. In 1919 he wrote: "the truly modern artist is aware of abstraction in an emotion of beauty; he is conscious of the fact that the emotion of beauty is cosmic, universal". Therefore, he argues, modern art will ignore "natural form and color. On the contrary, it should find its expression in the abstraction of form and color, that is to say, in the straight line and clearly defined primary color".

He justified his extreme abstraction, saying "we find that in nature all relations are dominated by a single primordial relation which is defined by the opposition of two extremes". In painting, this primordial relation should be represented by horizontals and verticals "which form the right angle. This positional relation is the most balanced of all … and contains all other relations". He believed that his austere system did contain all other relations and express universal harmony. So when, in 1925, van Doesberg based his compositions on diagonals, Mondrian denounced them and left *De Stijl*.

Theory preceded his mature practice. In 1919, when he returned to Paris, he did adopt a severe rectilinear form. But it was not until 1921 that he settled for the ultimate primordial relationship of intersecting horizontal and vertical bands of black on white—spare grids to which he added occasional rectangles of primary red, yellow, or blue. In these severely restricted forms he found a theme capable of infinite variations, which he developed with austere integrity for another 20 years.

In 1925 (the year of his break with *De Stijl*) his essay on "Neo-plasticism", originally published in French in 1920, was translated into German and published by the Bauhaus in Weimar. Mondrian was thus established as one of the leaders of modernism. More practical recognition came the following year when the American collector, Katherine S. Dreier, bought one of his works. From that time, Mondrian acquired the patronage of a few Americans and Germans that sustained him for the rest of his life.

Mondrian's final years were among the most eventful. In September 1938, disturbed by the prospect of war, he left Paris for London, where he was befriended by the circle of Abstract artists around Ben Nicholson and Barbara Hepworth. In 1940, a bomb falling close to his London studio drove him to New York. There he established another bare, cell-like studio, identical in its essentials to those he had abandoned in Paris and London.

The experience of New York was stimulating. The skyscrapers were like the realization of his art. This, and the jazz music he had loved for years, led him to a transformation of his art so extreme as to verge on the rejection of his own tenets. It produced some of his most brilliant compositions, including *Broadway Boogie Woogie* (1942–3; Museum of Modern Art, New York) and *Victory Boogie Woogie* (1943–4; Tremaine Collection, Meridien, Connecticut), *Trafalgar Square* (1939–43; Museum of Modern Art, New York), and *New York City I* (1942; Sidney Janis Gallery, New York). In January 1942 he had his first one-man show at the Valentin Dudensing Gallery, New York.

On 1 February 1944 he died of pneumonia at Murray Hill hospital, New York, a month before his 72nd birthday.

Further reading. Faucchereau, S. *Mondrian*, New York (1994). Milner, J. *Mondrian*, London (1992, reissued 1994). Mondrian, P. (ed. Holzman, H.) *The New Art; the New Life; the Collected Writings of Piet Mondrian*, New York (1972). Mondrian, P. (trans. Welsh, R.P.) *Two Mondrian Sketchbooks: 1912–14*, Amsterdam (1969). Welsh, R. and Joosten, J. *Piet Mondrian: Catalogue Raisonné* (3 vols. in 2), New York (1998).

Monet Claude 1840–1926

The French Impressionist painter Claude Oscar Monet was born in Paris but spent his childhood on the Channel Coast at Le Havre. In his teens, he won a local reputation as a caricaturist; but he was converted to the art of landscape painting by Eugène Boudin, who was then living locally, and whom he met in c1856. On Boudin's advice, Monet visited Paris in 1859 and 1860, and there met Camille Pissarro. After a spell of military service in Algeria, he returned to the Le Havre area, where in 1862 he met the Dutch landscapist Johan Barthold Jongkind. Boudin and Jongkind were to have a strong influence on his early artistic development. From 1862 to 1864, Monet studied in Paris in the studio of Charles Gleyre, where he met Pierre-Auguste Renoir, Frédéric Bazille, and Alfred Sisley; Renoir and Bazille became particularly close friends.

Monet made his public debut at the Salon exhibition of 1865; he showed two large seascapes (including *La Pointe de la Hève*, Kimbell Art Museum, Fort Worth, Texas), whose fluent yet concise brushwork shows a debt to Jongkind. Inspired by the success of these pictures, he undertook a vast project in the summer of 1865, an outdoor picnic scene measuring about 15 ft by 20 ft (approximately 6 m by 8 m). In this *Déjeuner sur l'Herbe* he aimed to reinterpret the theme of Manet's notorious *Le Déjeuner sur l'Herbe* (Musée du Jeu de Paume, Paris) of 1863, by treating the figures more naturally than Manet had, and by putting them into a more convincing outdoor setting and lighting. He was unable to complete this huge canvas (oil sketch, 1865; State Pushkin Museum of Fine Arts, Moscow) but realized a similar aim in *Women in the Garden* (1866–7; Musée du Jeu de Paume, Paris), a painting 8 ft 5 in by 6 ft 10 in (2.56 by 2.08 m) much of which was actually painted in the open air. *Women in the Garden* was rejected at the 1867 Salon, and Monet never again painted on such a scale out of doors.

At the same time, he was making important experiments on smaller canvases. In *Terrace at Sainte-Adresse* (1867; Metropolitan Museum, New York) and in three views of Paris, all of 1867, he adopted a high viewpoint; he avoided a single central focus in his compositions in order to suggest the animation and multiplicity characteristic of the way we see the scenes around us. Monet's subject matter at this period sets him firmly among the painters who were focusing on city life and fashionable figures, in their attempt to become painters of modern life. The detached mood of Monet's scenes allies them with the ideas of Baudelaire's essay "Le Peintre de la Vie Moderne" ("The Painter of Modern Life"; published in 1863); while the crisp individual strokes of paint that he used to define forms show his debt to Manet. In *Terrace at Sainte-Adresse*, the structured grid-like composition is an early example of the impact of Japanese color prints, which had such a wide influence on younger painters from the 1860s onwards.

In the late 1860s, Monet was also pursuing his observation of light and color, seeking ways of translating natural effects quickly and directly on to the canvas. His studies of La Grenouillère of 1869, though he did not at the time regard them as finished paintings, show how freely he could use paint and color. During the Franco-Prussian War of 1870–1 Monet lived in London, and there he first saw the art of Joseph Mallord William Turner. However, his paintings from immediately after his return to France in 1871 show no clear sign of Turner's influence; rather, they continue one facet of his work of the late 1860s—his concern with variations of weather and lighting. In this respect, the La Grenouillère paintings of 1869 anticipate the ensuing developments in his art.

Monet concentrated on smaller-scale landscapes during the 1870s. Many of them showed scenes around Argenteuil, a village on the Seine a few miles downstream of Paris, where he lived between 1872 and 1878. The handling and coloring of these paintings varies greatly in response to the varied natural scenes he had in front of him. By 1873, his technique had become a type of representational shorthand, so adaptable that he could convey the most diverse effects of weather and light. One example of these preoccupations is the rapidly executed *Impression: Sunrise* (Musée Marmottan, Paris), whose title gave the Impressionists their name when it was included in their first group exhibition in 1874. However, canvases as summary as this were not the principal focus of Monet's work at the time. Alongside this painting, which he titled *Impression* to indicate that it was only a sketch, Monet also exhibited more highly finished pictures, such as *Boulevard des Capucines* (State Pushkin Museum of Fine Arts, Moscow).

He kept to the same pattern in the group exhibitions later in the 1870s, including the occasional rapid notation of nature, but only side by side with more fully worked canvases. He wanted his audience

Claude Monet: The Seine at Lavacourt; oil on canvas; 98×149cm (39×59in); 1880. Dallas Museum of Fine Arts

to witness the directness of his response to nature, but also to see how he transformed this into more complete works of art. He even continued to punctuate his exhibits with large pictures of a type suitable for the Salon exhibitions, such as *La Japonaise* of 1876 (Museum of Fine Arts, Boston). Though sketches such as *Impression: Sunrise* gave Impressionism its public reputation, and Monet was prepared to sell his less-finished paintings when short of money, his art in the 1870s can only be fully understood when these are seen beside his more fully completed statements.

During the 1870s, Monet's fluent and varied brushwork was accompanied by an increasingly bold use of color. In his sunlit scenes of the 1860s, such as *Terrace at Sainte-Adresse*, he had begun to introduce color into areas of shadow—generally soft blues; the lessons of Eugène Delacroix's coloration were important for this development. In the following decade, he came to use nuances of color with increasing subtlety to suggest light effects. In some sunlit scenes, such as *Autumn at Argenteuil* (1873; Courtauld Institute Galleries, London), the contrast between dark and light tones is almost entirely abandoned in

favor of a rich play of varied high-key colors which suggest the forms in the picture. Even in overcast scenes that retain strong tonal contrasts, such as *Men Unloading Coal* (c1875; private collection), he used soft touches of varied color to convey atmosphere. This development—towards the suggestion of forms by the use of variations and contrasts of color rather than by tonal modeling—was at the center of the Impressionists' ideas on color.

Monet's subject matter remained essentially modern and man-made throughout the 1870s. Sometimes, as in *Men Unloading Coal* and in his paintings of the Gare

Claude Monet: The Port of Zaandam; oil on canvas; 47×74cm (19×29in); 1871. Private collection

Saint-Lazare of 1877, his subjects overtly reflected industry and mechanization. More often, they showed life at Argenteuil: originally a country village, Argenteuil was becoming industrialized at the time, and was also a center for sailing and rowing, fashionable pastimes of the day.

The pattern of Monet's life, and his choice of subject matter, changed in the 1880s. He moved away from the Paris area, further down the Seine Valley, finally settling in 1883 at Giverny where he spent the rest of his life. At the same time, he took less part in the Impressionists' group exhibitions, apparently feeling that their

notoriety had harmed his commercial prospects. From 1881 onwards he had, for the first time, a regular if not wholly secure source of income from sales to dealers—at first mainly to Paul Durand-Ruel.

Monet traveled widely in the 1880s seeking dramatic natural subjects and extreme effects of weather and light. He painted the cliffs of Normandy, the Atlantic storms on the island of Belle-Isle off Brittany, the rocky hills of the Massif Central, and the luminous atmosphere of the Mediterranean coast. Instead of the horizontality that dominates his pictures of the Seine Valley, he often adopted high viewpoints, and chose subjects with dramatic contrasts of scale and jumps in space. In paintings such as *Varengeville Church* (1882; Barber Institute of Fine Arts, Birmingham, England) the off-center composition and silhouetted trees have close parallels in Japanese color prints, of which Monet was an avid collector. However, their influence on him was not a matter of direct imitation: their example helped him to select viewpoints for his landscapes which revealed the full drama of his subjects.

Varengeville Church also shows a richer and more elaborate color scheme than his previous work. Even the shadows are rich in color, and the whole painting is based on an opposition of oranges and pinks against greens and blues. His later experience of working beside the Mediterranean in 1884 and 1888 showed him further

possibilities of using color harmonies as a means of expressing light and atmosphere; in the South, he favored high-key contrasts of rose and blue, as seen in *The Corniche de Monaco* of 1884 (Stedelijk Museum, Amsterdam).

Equally, in the 1880s his brushwork became more elaborate. In the 1870s it had varied greatly from part to part of the same picture; but in the 1880s he came to link whole paintings together by recurrent rhythms, as in *Storm on Belle-Isle* (1886; Musée du Jeu de Paume, Paris) in which sweeping brush strokes convey the violence of the storm and at the same time create a rich surface pattern in the picture.

During this period, Monet came increasingly to rework his paintings in the studio. In part, this was for practical reasons. As his eye became more and more sensitive to minute changes in natural effects, he could spend less time on a picture before the effect he was painting was compromised by changes in the lighting; so he was forced to paint in the studio in order to finish any work at all. However, he came to see a more positive value in studio work, realizing that he could better judge his paintings away from their subject. He could thus more easily add those final touches that recreated nature's effects in pictorial terms—not by direct imitation of individual forms, but by emphasizing unifying effects of color and pattern on the picture surface.

Studio work became still more important after 1890, when he embarked on a succession of series of paintings of single subjects in different lightings. The first of these was the group of 15 paintings of haystacks exhibited in 1891 (three in the Art Institute of Chicago; two in the Museum of Fine Arts, Boston; one each in the Musée du Jeu de Paume, Paris, National Gallery of Scotland, Edinburgh, Metropolitan Museum, New York). In their rich color harmonies, these continue his work of the 1880s, but in two ways they are very different: in their subjects, and in the way they were exhibited. In place of his dramatic scenes of the 1880s, the *Haystacks* are a wholly unpicturesque subject, seen near his home; the prime focus is on their atmospheric effects. They were exhibited together as a unit, gaining, Monet said, "their full value only by the comparison and the succession of the whole series". Previously, Monet had deliberately included diverse paintings in his exhibitions, to show the range of his work.

In later series, such as that of *Rouen Cathedral* (1892–4; five in the Musée du Jeu de Paume, Paris), Monet's color schemes became still more elaborate, and only distantly related to the initial effect of light on the cathedral's stone facade. The encrusted colored surfaces of these paintings, no longer animated by the dynamic brushwork that Monet had used during the 1880s, evoke the harmonizing effect of sunlight, but also bear witness to long periods of work in the studio.

After 1900, Monet focused on a new subject, one that bridged the gap between art and nature—the elaborate water garden, with trees and water lilies, that he had built near his house at Giverny. He painted it first in series of individual canvases, and then, after 1914, embarked on a long-held plan to make the pond the subject for a continuous decoration to run around a room. This project was finally realized in the two oval rooms of Water Lily decorations, installed after Monet's death in the Orangerie in Paris according to his precise instructions. The large canvases which make them up, over 6 ft high (approximately 2 m), were painted in a studio, but developed from outdoor studies. They form a continuous frieze of water, without horizon, and cut by occasional trees. The water surfaces are punctuated by lily pads and by the reflections of trees and sky beyond. To suit their scale, Monet enlarged his brush stroke.

The lilies are conveyed by bold calligraphic strokes which, seen from close to, float freely across the picture surface. From a distance, though, all become part of the continuous effect of light and atmosphere, which is enhanced by their unified color scheme, dominantly in soft greens and blues. Other versions of his Water-Lily paintings and many canvases may be seen in the Musée Marmottan in Paris. More *Water Lilies* are in the National Gallery, London.

Even at the end of his life, Monet's basic aim remained, as he described it in 1926, to "render my impressions in front of the most fleeting effects"—a phrase he could equally have used 50 years earlier. His development as an artist lay in his evolving ways of realizing this aim—from his direct sketches of nature of the 1870s, through a gradual process of elaboration and interpretation, to the rich color harmonies and densely worked surfaces of his later paintings. In these, he found a way of going beyond his immediate experience of nature, of recreating visual experience in purely pictorial terms.

Further reading. Forge, A. *Monet* (the Art Institute of Chicago Artists in Focus Series), New York (1995). Lochnan, K. and Warrell, I. *Turner, Whistler, Monet: Impressionist Visions*, London (2004). Pissarro, J. *Monet and the Mediterranean*, New York (1997). Russell, V. *Monet's Landscapes* London (2005). Spate, V. *Claude Monet, Life and Work*, New York (1992). Sproccati, S. *Monet*, New York (2000). Tucker, P. H. *Monet in the 20th Century*, New Haven (1998). Wildenstein, D. *Monet's Years at Giverny*, New York (1995).

Montañés Juan 1568–1649

The Spanish sculptor Juan Martínez Montañés was born at Alcalá la Real (Jaen). At the age of 14 he went to Seville, where he was to be based for the rest of his life, becoming the head of the school of sculpture at Seville. Probably initially a pupil of Juan-Bautista Vázquez the Elder, he worked for a short time (1598–1602) in Granada with Pablo de Rojas, whose pupil he claimed to be. Returning to Seville, he set up his own workshop, which soon became the busiest and most important in Andalusia. It is only from 1603, when he was aged 35, that his own distinct artistic personality began to emerge. Known in his day as the "God of Woodcarving", Montañés enjoyed a reputation that has never been eclipsed in Spain.

To the powerful realism of Andalusian sculpture he united a classical sense of composition. His sculpture, always in wood, was in many cases painted by the erudite painter Francisco Pacheco, the master of Velázquez. In 1635 Montañés was invited to Court by Velázquez to model the bust of Philip IV for the great bronze equestrian statue to be cast in Italy by Tacca. Veláquez' portrait of him (Prado, Madrid) dates from this time. His output, some of which was exported to Spanish America, was vast. His major works are in and around Seville; they include his great masterpiece, the high altar in S. Isidoro del Campo, Santiponce.

Monticelli Adolphe 1824–96

Adolphe Joseph Thomas Monticelli was a French painter. Born in Marseilles, he is sometimes classed with Cézanne and Daumier as a purveyor of a Provençal style. He worked in Paris between 1856 and 1870, when he achieved some recognition for subjects drawn from Boccaccio and from the 18th-century French tradition of *fêtes galantes*, as seen in the works of Watteau. Monticelli's versions were painted in a strongly handled, often violent, occasionally highcolored manner, partly influenced by Delacroix and Diaz. He also produced portraits and still lifes in the same style. He died, allegedly, of alcoholism. Van Gogh greatly admired his paintings, often producing works as a gesture of homage to Mont-icelli.

Moore Albert 1841–93

Albert Joseph Moore was an English painter of decorative color harmonies, born at York. He first painted biblical works (for example, *Elijah's Sacrifice*, 1863; Art Gallery and Museum, Bury) and architectural decorative schemes. In the mid 1860s he began to merge the decorative aesthetic into his easel paintings, using classically-draped women in various postures as the basis of his compositions. Without ostensible subject-matter they were used simply to portray elaborately worked-out color schemes (for example, *Apricots*, 1866; Public Library, Fulham, London). Much admired by the Aesthetic Movement, this type of draped female figure scarcely

Albert Moore: Portrait of a Girl; oil on canvas; 25×25cm (10×10in). Private collection

changed during Moore's remaining career, featuring both in major compositions (such as *Reading Aloud*, 1884; Art Gallery and Museum, Glasgow), and in simpler works (for example, *Birds*, 1878; City of Birmingham Museums and Art Gallery).

Moore Henry 1898–1986

Henry Moore, long considered England's greatest sculptor, was largely responsible for the gradual emergence of British art from provincialism into the mainstream of modern art. Ironically it was during the 1930s, when Moore's work was so violently attacked in the press, that he and his contemporaries Ben Nicholson and Barbara Hepworth were laying the foundations of modern art in England. By 1946, with his first major retrospective exhibition at the Museum of Modern Art, New York, the art of sculpture in England was fully established, and Moore had become one of the most admired and influential sculptors in the world.

Born in Castleford, Yorkshire, the seventh child of a miner, Henry Moore by the age of 10 or 11 had decided that he wanted to become a sculptor. He received

his first lessons in drawing at the Castleford Grammar School from the art mistress, Alice Gostick, whose support and encouragement meant a great deal to him. After serving two years in the Army, Moore was awarded an ex-serviceman's grant to the Leeds School of Art, and enrolled in the two-year course in September 1919. He was joined there in 1920 by Barbara Hepworth, who became a friend and close associate during the next 20 years. While at Leeds he met Sir Michael Sadler, whose remarkable collection included paintings by Cézanne, Gauguin, and Matisse, the first examples of modern art that Moore saw. At the time he read Roger Fry's *Vision and Design* and was particularly influenced by the chapters on "Ancient American Art" and "Negro Sculpture".

In 1921 Moore began the three-year diploma course at the Royal College of Art in London. A conflict soon developed between the academic course-work and his desire to follow his own direction in sculpture, based on knowledge gained from numerous visits to the British Museum. There he studied sculpture of many periods: prehistoric, Egyptian, Assyrian,

Sumerian, Archaic Greek, African, and Oceanic; but he was most attracted to Mexican art, which was to become the major influence on his work during the 1920s. He managed a compromise, drawing and modeling from life during term time, with evenings and holidays free to pursue his own interests.

In 1922, on the first of many trips to Paris, he saw the Pellerin Collection, which included Cézanne's *Grandes Baigneuses* (now in the Philadelphia Museum of Art). He has written: "Seeing that picture, for me, was like seeing Chartres Cathedral. It was one of the big impacts." In 1924 he was awarded a traveling scholarship, and was also appointed instructor in sculpture at the Royal College of Art for a period of seven years. He left for France and Italy in January 1925. He greatly admired the monumentality of the Masaccio frescoes in the Brancacci Chapel, S. Maria del Carmine, Florence.

On his return to London in the summer of 1925 he completed the Hornton stone *Mother and Child* of 1924–5 (City of Manchester Art Gallery). Almost all his sculptures between 1921 and 1939 were carvings. Like Modigliani, Gaudier-Brzeska, Brancusi, Epstein, and Hepworth, Moore was interested in direct carving; he believed in the doctrine of truth to materials, of understanding and being in sympathy with the qualities of wood or stone. In the Manchester carving, the forms have not been freed from the material, and remain somewhat buried in the blockiness of the stone. The carving is, like the kind of sculpture Moore most admires, "not perfectly symmetrical, it is static and it is strong and vital, giving off something of the energy and power of great mountains." Unlike Hepworth, for example, Moore is not concerned with an ideal, classical beauty and purity. He aims at the power of expression, giving his sculpture a pent-up energy, a life of its own.

Moore's first one-man exhibition was held at Warren Gallery, London, in 1928. That same year he received his first public commission, a relief entitled *North Wind* for the new London Passenger Transport Board headquarters.

Reclining Figure of 1929 (Leeds City Art Gallery), undoubtedly Moore's most important sculpture of the 1920s, was the first work to reflect the tremendous influence of the Mexican Chac Mool reclining figure. Although the Leeds carving has the same massiveness and weight that he admired in the Mexican prototype and the alert, mask-like head turned at right angles to the body, the reclining pose is quite different. The figure rests on its side, with the left arm raised behind the head, and the left leg looming above the right one. In the reclining figure Moore had found a subject that allowed him to experiment with new formal ideas, to explore infinite variations on a single theme. By the late 1920s the mother-and-child theme and the reclining figure had become the two principal obsessions in Moore's work.

In 1929 Moore married Irina Radetsky, a student at the Royal College of Art School of Painting. They moved to Parkhill Road, Hampstead, London, where they lived until 1940. The first of two country cottages in Kent, for use during vacations, was bought in 1931.

The enigmatic carved *Composition* of 1931 marked a radical new departure that allied Moore's work to the biomorphic abstractions current in the work of Arp, Miró, Tanguy, and above all Picasso. The sculpture and drawings Picasso created during the late 1920s exerted a direct influence on Moore's sculpture and drawings of the early 1930s. Like Hepworth and Nicholson, Moore visited the Paris studios of Picasso, Braque, and Brancusi. *Composition* illustrates how quickly and intuitively Moore had assimilated the visual imagery of Picasso's work.

In 1932 he established the Department of Sculpture at the Chelsea School of Art. The following year he was elected a member of "Unit One". The first of his two-, three-, and four-piece compositions appeared in 1934 and are related to the work of Arp and Giacometti. He often used the Surrealist idiom of the found object, and made several carvings using ironstone pebbles. In 1932, he did a series of drawings of bones and shells, transforming shapes in nature into human forms. In the multipart sculptures of 1934 the human body was divided into fragments and reassembled. It was not until the late 1950s and 1960s that he returned to the two- and three-piece figure theme.

Moore's square-form carvings of 1935 and 1937, among his most abstract works, reflect the influence of Ben Nicholson's reliefs of the period. During these years, when he was living in Hampstead near Hepworth, Nicholson, and the critic Herbert Read, there was a fruitful exchange of ideas among these artists with broadly similar aims. Moore's work never became

totally Abstract; there is always some reference to human or organic forms. He participated in the "International Surrealist Exhibition" in London in 1936, and in the following year contributed to *Circle: International Survey of Constructive Art*.

The idea of the reclining female figure as a metaphor for landscape first appeared in the *Reclining Figure* of 1929 (City Art Gallery, Leeds) and then in the *Reclining Woman* of 1930 (National Gallery of Canada, Ottawa). The landscape idiom, in which breast and knees are like hills or mountains, and holes like caves in a hillside, is beautifully resolved in *Recumbent Figure* of 1938 (Tate Gallery, London). The gently rising and falling rhythms echo the Sussex Downs, where the sculpture was originally sited.

From 1937 to 1939 Moore executed a series of stringed figure-drawings and sculptures, a brief interlude in his work. His first "helmet sculpture" appeared in 1939–40.

Between 1921 and the mid 1950s the genesis for almost all Moore's sculptures is to be found in the sketchbooks and larger drawings. The drawings for sculpture were a means of generating ideas for sculpture, of recording the overflow of ideas too numerous to explore directly in wood or stone.

In September 1940 Moore began work on his shelter drawings, scenes of Londoners sheltering from the Blitz in the London Underground stations. The following month his Hampstead studio was badly damaged by a bomb, and the Moores moved to a 17th-century farmhouse at Much Hadham, 30 miles north of London. As a war artist, he spent the next year working on the shelter drawings. He visited the shelters once or twice a week, and did the drawings from memory on his return home. In 1942 he did a series of drawings of miners at work at the coalface.

The *Madonna and Child* of 1943–4, commissioned for the Church of St Matthew, Northampton, reflects the influence of the shelter drawings in the use of drapery and in the humanist emphasis. The Mediterranean tradition, which on his Italian trip in 1925 had been in conflict with his interest in primitive art, had come once more to the surface.

In 1946, the year of his first retrospective at the Museum of Modern Art, New York, his daughter Mary was born. Two years later he won the International Sculpture Prize at the 24th Venice Biennale. His first

retrospective at the Tate Gallery was held in 1951. Moore's worldwide reputation was now firmly established.

During the 1950s the two most important commissions were for a screen for the facade and the bronze *Draped Reclining Figure* (1952–3) for the new Time-Life Building in London, and the large Roman travertine marble *Reclining Figure* (1957–8) for UNESCO headquarters in Paris.

Although Moore's interest in carving continued throughout his life, many of his best-known postwar sculptures—such as *Family Group* (1948–9; Museum of Modern Art, New York), *King and Queen* (1952–3; Joseph Hirshhorn Museum and Sculpture Garden, Smithsonian Institution, Washington, D.C.), *Warrior with Shield* (1953–4; Art Gallery of Ontario, Toronto), *Reclining Figure* (1963–5; Lincoln Center, New York), and *Nuclear Energy* (1964–6; University of Chicago)—were made in plaster and cast in bronze. A fine collection of the plasters can be seen in the Art Gallery of Ontario, Toronto.

Among the most impressive sculptures of the past two decades are the two- and three-piece reclining figures of 1959–62 (examples can be seen in the Albright-Knox Art Gallery, Buffalo; the Museum of Modern Art, New York; etc). The landscape metaphor, a source of Moore's inspiration since the late 1920s, is reversed: the sculptures are more landscape than human. Fragmentary elements of a rugged landscape of rocks, cliffs, and caves become the female figure.

By the mid 1950s, as his sculpture was becoming more three-dimensional, having an organic completeness from every point of view, drawing no longer served as a way of developing ideas for sculpture. The point of departure for most of his subsequent sculpture has been the bones, shells, and flint stones that abound in the maquette studio at Much Hadham.

After 1968 Moore showed a renewed interest in drawing as an activity independent of sculpture, and in printmaking, and produced more than 260 lithographs and etchings, including the *Elephant Skull, Auden, Stonehenge*, and *Sheep* portfolios.

The major retrospective at the Tate Gallery in 1968 was followed in 1972 by the magnificent exhibition at the Forte di Belvedere in Florence. Many large bronzes and fiberglass casts were placed on the terraces; the architecture of Florence and the hills beyond made this one of the most splendid sites in the world to exhibit

Henry Moore: Reclining Figure; plaster; 105×227×89cm (42×90×35in); 1951. Tate Gallery, London

sculpture on the enormous scale of Moore's late work. October 1974 saw the opening of the Henry Moore Sculpture Center in Toronto; the Center houses Moore's gift to the Art Gallery of Ontario of more than 500 original plasters, bronzes, drawings, and prints.

Moore continued to work for most of the year in Much Hadham, and spent a month or two each summer in Italy, carving at the Querceta marble works of Messrs Henraux. From his small house nearby at Forte dei Marmi he could see the Carrara Mountains where Michelangelo is said to have selected large blocks of marble for his carvings.

The essential humanism of Moore's art has been nourished by sources as disparate as Paleolithic sculpture and the work of Picasso. With the human figure as the central subject of his work, he used elements of landscape, the shapes of bones, shells, and pebbles to enlarge the three-dimensional language of sculpture. Henry Moore takes his rightful place among the greatest sculptors in Western art, having built on and extended the tradition to which his work belongs.

Further reading. Bowness, A. (ed.) *Henry Moore, Sculpture and Drawings 1949–1954*, London (1965). Bowness, A. (ed.) *Henry Moore, Sculpture 1955–1964*, London (1965). Clark, K. *Henry Moore, Drawings*, London (1964). Cramer, G., Grant, A., and Mitchinson, D. *Henry Moore, the Graphic Work 1931–1972*, Geneva (1973). Cramer, G., Grant, A., and Mitchinson, D. *Henry Moore, the Graphic Work 1973–1975*, Geneva (1976). Hall, D. *Henry Moore, the Life and Work of a Great Sculptor*, London (1966). Hedgecoe, J. (ed.) *Henry Moore*, London (1968). James, P. (ed.) *Henry Moore on Sculpture*, London (1966). Melville, R. *Henry Moore, Sculpture and Drawings 1921–1969*, London (1970). Read, H. *Henry Moore*, London (1965). Read, H. *Henry Moore Sculptor*, London (1934). Russell, J. *Henry Moore*, London (1968). Seldis, H. *Henry Moore in America*, New York (1973). Sweeney, J.J. *Henry Moore*, New York (1946). Sylvester, D. *Henry Moore*, London (1968). Sylvester, D. (ed.) *Henry Moore, Sculpture and Drawings 1921–1948*, London (1957). Wilkinson, A.G. *The Henry Moore Sculpture Centre*, Toronto (1974).

Mor van Dashorst Anthonis
*c*1517–76/7

Born at Utrecht, the Netherlandish painter Anthonis Mor van Dashorst was probably a pupil of Jan van Scorel. He joined the Antwerp guild in 1547, but worked mainly as a portrait-painter at several European courts, and visited Rome from 1550 to 1551. His portraits combine the elegance of the three-quarter length form, influenced by Italian art, with the minute description of surface texture common to Northern painting. This is best seen in his portraits of *The Duke of Alba* (1549; Hispanic Society, New York) and of *Mary Tudor* (1554; Prado, Madrid); the latter was painted on the occasion of the English Queen's marriage to Philip of Spain.

Morales Luis de c1520–86

The Spanish painter Luis de Morales was probably born at Badajoz. It is not known with certainty whether he ever traveled outside his native region of Extremadura, but Morales undoubtedly absorbed a strong influence from Flemish painting, particularly from the work of Quentin Massys, and also from Leonardo da Vinci, perhaps via Flanders.

Often known as *El Divino* because of the predominance of religious subjects in his work, Morales frequently painted Passion scenes, especially *Ecce Homo, Pietà*, and *Christ at the Column*. He also painted many Madonnas (for example, *Virgin and Child*, National Gallery, London) in a highly finished, smooth style, with little variation or development throughout his career. Among Church patrons in Extremadura and neighboring Portugal, his success was considerable.

Morandi Giorgio 1890–1964

Giorgio Morandi was an Italian painter and etcher. His paintings of 1918 to 1920 were influenced by the metaphysical painting of Carlo Carrà. They depict precisely delineated groups of objects, their metaphysical element arising out of an extreme formalization combined with visual paradox. His career after 1920 was marked by the intensity he applied to the still life. He achieved an extraordinary monumentality within a small scale, by means of the idealization of simple objects, using light to make an abstraction of their shapes without recourse to distortion. The unswerving path followed by Morandi reflects his isolation from the contemporary art world. He spent all his life near Bologna, travelling seldom, and never leaving his native Italy.

Moreau Gustave 1826–98

Born the son of an architect in Paris, Gustave Moreau became an eminently successful painter. He was an influential figure in the move away from Realist attitudes that occurred in the 1880s, and showed himself sympathetic to originality, as a teacher at the École des Beaux-Arts in Paris. He had studied there himself as a young man under Picot; Théodore Chassé-

Anthonis Mor van Dashorst: Mary Tudor; detail; oil on canvas; full size 109×84cm (43×33in); 1554. Prado, Madrid

Giorgio Morandi: Still Life; oil on canvas; 30×35cm (12×14in); 1942. Private collection

Gustave Moreau: The Unicorns; oil on canvas; 115×90cm (45×35in); c1885. Musée Gustave Moreau, Paris

riau, with whom Moreau became friendly, and Eugène Delacroix, were also important formative influences upon him, as the painterliness of his mature style suggests. His exhibits at the Salons of 1852 and 1853 reflected his respect for the imaginative force of their work.

No hint of Courbet's Realist school is evident in Moreau. He returns in contrast to erudite antique themes, rich in narrative and emotional expression, echoing and even quoting directly from the Italian Renaissance painters he admired. Moreau studied in Rome between 1857 and 1859, painting landscapes and copying works by

Carpaccio, Mantegna, and Michelangelo. Subsequently many of his paintings were to reveal in addition a debt to Leonardo da Vinci. His circle of friends in Rome included Puvis de Chavannes, Élie Delaunay, and Degas.

Success at the Paris Salon followed, with a sequence of sumptuous paintings on mythological themes. *Oedipus and the Sphinx* (Metropolitan Museum, New York), strongly reminiscent of Ingres' treatment of the subject, was shown at the Salon in 1864. Its success was consolidated in the following year when Moreau exhibited *Jason* (Louvre, Paris). In 1866, Moreau's *Orpheus* (Louvre, Paris) was purchased by the State. He returned to the Salon in the 1870s, reestablishing his reputation as an erudite, original, and talented painter with *Hercules and the Hydra* (1876; Art Institute of Chicago), paintings of *Salomé* and *The Apparition* (one example *c*1876; William Hayes Fogg Art Museum, Cambridge, Mass.), and a tempera painting of *St Sebastian* (1876; William Hayes Fogg Art Museum, Cambridge, Mass.). He exhibited further at the *Exposition Universelle* in Paris in 1878 and for the last time at the Salon in 1880 with *Helen* and *Galatea* (Collection of Robert Lebel, Paris).

As a man of private means, Moreau did not need to court financial success, yet recognition had come through the Salon and had established his reputation. His independence did mean, however, that he could give free rein to his imagination. He was absolved from a need to be either explicit or popular. The densely worked, scratched, glazed, and impasto surfaces of his paintings, their lavish textures and otherworldly subjects, gave vent to an extraordinary imagination, as if his canvases were illumined by a light that was beyond the here and now.

It is curious to consider Moreau's success at the Salon of 1876 in contrast with the emergence of Impressionist painting, particularly in view of his friendship with Degas. Indeed, when the Symbolist movement evolved during the mid 1880s, it was the obsessive, emotive, and suggestive qualities of Moreau's paintings that attracted and excited Symbolist painters and writers. The novelist and critic Joris-Karl Huysmans in *À Rebours*, published in 1884, had described Moreau's shimmering and supernatural *Apparition* among the possessions of Des Esseintes, the central figure of his novel. Together with Redon

Moretto: Portrait of Count Sciarra Martinengo-Cesaresco; oil on canvas; 114×94cm (45×37in); c1516–18. National Gallery, London

and the poet Mallarmé, Moreau was emulated by Symbolists as a precursor of their demands for an art of imagination and ideas, and also as an honorary member of the multifarious Symbolist groups. In 1886, the year that Jean Moréas published his *Symbolist Manifesto*, Gustave Moreau gave his last public exhibition: 65 illustrations to the *Fables* of La Fontaine shown at the Goupil Gallery, Paris.

Moreau had attracted many younger admirers. In the face of growing interest in the depiction of the daily world, he had asserted the effectiveness of erudition in subject matter and of suggestive handling of his paint as vehicles for emotional and imaginative expression. His individuality itself provided an influential and an encouraging example. When Moreau's friend Élie Delaunay died in 1891, Moreau assumed his teaching atelier at the École des Beaux-Arts, Paris (1892–8). His influence upon the individual development of younger painters extended to many later

associated with the Fauves: Matisse, Manguin, Marquet, and Rouault were all pupils at the Beaux-Arts under Moreau. Rouault became the Keeper of the Musée Gustave Moreau in Paris where Moreau's studio and many of his works are still preserved. The studio became in due course a place for pilgrimage for the Surrealists, as it had been earlier for Symbolists.

Further reading. *French Symbolist Painters, Moreau, Puvis de Chavannes, Redon and their Followers*, London (1972). Mathieu, P.-L. *Gustave Moreau*, Oxford (1977). Paladilhe, J. *Gustave Moreau*, Paris (1971).

Moretto *c*1498–1554

Alessandro Bonvicino, known as Moretto, was a Brescian painter whose style, more eclectic than that of his slightly older contemporary Romanino, shows evident

Central Italian influences, particularly from Raphael; these reached him through the engravings of Marc Antonio Raimondi and others. His elevated, monumental style has hard outlines and clear sharp forms, which give to his figures some of the qualities of sculpture. Although, on occasion, he uses deep chiaroscuro and painterly effects of texture, his works are always more conceptualized than those of Romanino or the Venetians, and further away from visual experience. He lacks entirely the earthy realism of Romanino, and the factual detail always characteristic of Brescian painters sometimes sits rather oddly on his idealized forms.

Moretto's most individual quality is a personal range of low, muted color, often dominated by a gray-violet, which more than anything else sets the key of contemplative melancholy typical of his work. His art shows considerable development. A first phase may be seen in the varied canvases he painted alongside Romanino for the Chapel of the Sacrament in S. Giovanni Evangelista, Brescia. Roman, Venetian, Flemish, and Brescian elements mingle and contrast in the different subjects, while in the *Coronation of the Virgin* from SS. Nazaro e Celso, one of his numerous altarpieces for Brescian churches, he combines a more specifically Romanist vein with Correggesque sentiment and silvery color.

In Moretto's work the coldness of the color, while emphasizing the still detachment of his figures, often seems at variance with the sentimental ardor of their expressions. This tension is not really resolved even when, as in many of his later works, he adopted a more Venetian chiaroscuro. To this later period belongs his elegaic *Crucified Christ with a Mourning Angel* in the Pinacoteca Civica "Tosio Martinengo", Brescia, which shows him at his most painterly.

Moretto also practiced as a portrait-painter. His lovesick member of the Martinengo-Cesaresco family in the National Gallery, London, is in a sense, halfway between Titian and Holbein. The generalized poetic mood, characteristic of so many Giorgionesque portraits of young men, is given an emotional context as specific as the veristically painted details of costume and accoutrements. Also in the National Gallery is a swagger, full-length portrait of a Brescian nobleman, which is dated 1526 and is therefore the first full-length portrait known to have been

Berthe Morisot: In the Dining Room; oil on canvas; 62×50cm (24×20in); 1886. National Gallery of Art, Washington, D.C.

painted in Italy. The full-length portrait seems to have originated in Germany, and the type may have reached Moretto from the north. Certainly his portraiture shows a fusion between Italian idealization and Northern verism, typical of Brescian painting as a whole.

Morikage Kuzumi *fl. c1680*

The Japanese painter Kuzumi Morikage was the most independent of the pupils of Kano Tan'yu. He is said to have been expelled from Tan'yu's studio for lack of orthodoxy. Little of his life is known, but many of his works are concentrated in the Kanazawa area where he probably worked for the Maeda family. He was mainly an ink painter, though he used pale color washes with great charm, specializing in powerful, economical sketches of people, animals, and birds and in larger-scale misty landscapes peopled with real farmers and peasants. Of these, his masterpieces are the sixfold screens of agricultural scenes in the Ishikawa Prefectural Art Museum, Kanazawa.

Morisot Berthe 1841–95

The French painter Berthe Marie Pauline Morisot was taught by Corot in the early

George Morland: Ferreting; oil on canvas; 29×38cm (11×15in); 1792. Private collection

1860s. She met Édouard Manet c1868, and married his brother Eugène in 1874. After exhibiting at the Salon in the 1860s, she showed at most of the Impressionists' group exhibitions between 1874 and 1886. From the later 1880s onwards, she gave regular dinners, bringing together painters such as Monet, Renoir, Degas, and Puvis de Chavannes with Mallarmé and other poets and writers. Her painting owes much to Manet in its free, delicate brushwork, and in the 1870s she adopted the light and varied color of Impressionism. Her favorite subjects were garden scenes with figures.

Morland George 1763–1804

George Charles Morland was an English genre painter, the son of a minor artist and art dealer, to whom he was apprenticed before entering the Royal Academy schools in 1784. He set up as a portrait-painter in London in 1785, but soon discovered a more lucrative practice in painting sentimental fancy pictures of the type popularized by Francis Wheatley. About 1790 his interests shifted to rustic and picturesque themes. His best compositions date to the early 1790s and include a variety of farmyard and hunt scenes, coastal views with smugglers, and gypsy en-campments, to which he was apparently no stranger during the course of his dissolute life. His debt to the 17th-century Dutch landscapists is most evident in his winter landscapes, which are often rich in texture and masterly in design. Morland's promising development was halted by the rapid decline of his health and powers after 1800.

Morone Domenico c1442–c1517

Domenico Morone was a Veronese painter. Many of his works, including fresco cycles, have not survived. The influence of Gentile Bellini is apparent in three of his earliest extant paintings: two *cassone* panels decorated with tournament scenes (*c*1490; National Gallery, London) and *The Fight between the Gonzagas and Buonaccolsi* (1494; Palazzo Ducale, Mantua). Between *c*1498 and 1503 he was engaged on frescoes in S. Bernardino, Verona (Chapel of S. Antonio and Old Library) which are Mantegnesque in style. Domenico was a leading figure in Veronese art of the later Quattrocento. His son Francesco (*c*1471–1529) was also a painter.

Moroni Giambattista *c*1525–78

Moroni was an Italian painter, trained by Moretto, who worked both in Brescia and in his native city of Bergamo. While he painted numerous monumental altarpieces in the manner of his master, he is most individual and important as a portrait-painter. Although he was influenced by Lotto as well as Moretto, his portraits are less romantic than theirs: his approach to character is more detached, and his treatment of costume and accoutrements dryly realistic.

The elegance of his portraits (particularly the emphasis on the silhouette) allies him to central Italian Mannerist court portrait-ure, for example to Bronzino. But the low-keyed color and the precise detail are typically Brescian, evoking a sense of reality, objectively observed and coolly apprehended, that at its best anticipates Velázquez.

Moroni's portraits cover an unusually wide social range for the period, and some of the best of them, for example *The Tailor* (National Gallery, London) are of plebeian or middle-class sitters.

Domenico Morone: detail of the frescoes in the Old Library, S. Bernardino, Verona, Lionello Sagramoso Presented to the Virgin by St Francis; *c*1498–1503

Moronobu Hishikawa *c*1625–*c*94

The Japanese artist Hishikawa Moronobu stabilized the *Ukiyoe* School. He was born near Edo (Tokyo), was the son of a textile-designer, and his work always showed an interest in fashion and fabrics. Some of his over 100 printed books are in fact pattern-books, but in others he established the picture-book of the gay world of Edo as an important genre. These, like his sheet prints, were in ink monochrome, brilliantly exploiting the lustrous Japanese ink and

Left: Hishikawa Moronobu: A Riverboat Party; color woodblock print; 19×17cm (7½×6½in); 1683. British Museum, London

Giambattista Moroni: Portrait of a Man ("The Tailor"); oil on canvas; 97×74cm (39×30in); *c*1571. National Gallery, London

receptive paper. He was also a fine painter, giving the Edo *Ukiyoe* movement a distinctive style of restrained modishness. His best works are the handscroll of Yoshiwara scenes (Tokyo National Museum), and his sixfold screens of Edo life (Freer Gallery of Art, Washington, D.C.).

Morris Robert 1931–

The American sculptor Robert Morris was born in Kansas City. He first studied engineering at the University of Kansas City, and then art at Kansas City Art Institute (1948–50), California School of Fine Arts (1951), and Reed College, Oregon (1953–5). He later studied art history at Hunter College, New York (1962–3).

Morris was initially a painter. From his first sculptures in 1961, the great variety of his sculptural modes allies him closely with Conceptual art. From 1964 to 1966 he made simple, minimal geometric structures in wood, fiberglass, and metal, devoid of formal expressive qualities. These were followed by randomly placed felt wall and floor sculptures, mixed media "scatter" pieces, and process works involving natural phenomena, such as growth and steam. In 1970 he began to make environmental sculptures in timber and concrete, and earthworks. His concern for active involvement with art-making is manifested in his choreography, performances, films, participation pieces, and writings.

Morris William 1834–96

The English artist William Morris was born in Walthamstow into a wealthy family; he enjoyed a private income from the time he came of age. As a child, riding in Epping Forest, he began to develop his lifelong love of the English countryside, together with the habit of imagining what it was like in the Middle Ages. In 1853 he went up to Oxford intending to enter the Church, but he found himself increasingly attracted to the architecture, literature, and life of the medieval past. At Oxford he met Edward Jones (later Sir Edward Burne-Jones) and together they studied illuminated manuscripts, Dürer prints, and brass rubbings, and read ancient and modern authors such as Chaucer, Malory, Scott, La Motte-Fouqué, Carlyle, Kingsley, and Ruskin.

In 1855, on his second visit to the cathedrals of northern France, Morris de-

cided to become an architect and for a short time worked in the office of G.E. Street. But early in 1856 he met the Pre-Raphaelites' leader D.G. Rossetti, and was persuaded to become a painter. Rossetti was in turn impressed by Morris' poems and stories, which appeared throughout 1856 in the *Oxford and Cambridge Magazine*. These works and the poems published in his first book *The Defence of Guenevere* (1858), dedicated to Rossetti, strongly convey Morris' intense awareness of the vitality, landscape, pattern, and color of the Middle Ages but also his awareness of the period's brutality.

Rossetti involved Morris in painting the Oxford Union in 1857, and partly through this work Morris realized that his genius lay in pattern design. His fondness for the Middle Ages and his hatred of industrialization led him to recreate the spirit of the past. In 1856 he had massive medieval furniture built for his rooms in London. Four years later, after his marriage to Jane Burden, he moved into Red House, Bexleyheath, designed for him by his friend Philip Webb. This was a simple red brick house, Gothic in style; Morris furnished it with furniture painted by himself and his friends, embroidered hangings, stained glass, and wall paintings, so that it became a richly colored medieval palace of art.

Morris' experience at Red House led him and his friends to set up the firm Morris, Marshall, Faulkner and Company in 1861. With Rossetti, Madox Brown, Jones, Arthur Hughes, and other painters working for it, this firm showed how the rift between the "fine arts" and the "minor arts" could be healed. At the International Exhibition in 1862 they showed painted furniture and stained glass. Stained glass was to provide much of the firm's income and Morris himself was responsible for a few complete cartoons (in the early days), the foliage backgrounds to many figures drawn by the other artists, and always for the coloring.

He also designed wallpapers, at first (c1862–4) simple, naively naturalistic ones such as *Daisy*; and then, from the early 1870s, papers such as *Jasmine*, full of growth, controlled depth, and a suggestion of mysterious abundance. In deliberate opposition to the theories of the South Kensington School of Design, Morris wanted his designs to provide a substitute for nature, with familiar plants and believable patterns of growth. He also designed chintzes (from 1873), carpets (from 1878),

tapestries (from 1879), and embroideries, always taking great care to use natural processes and often reviving forgotten methods such as dyeing with vegetable dyes. Because of the time and skill needed to execute his designs the firm's work was always expensive, but in the 1870s and early 1880s it was taken up by the Aesthetic Movement and sold well.

Morris continued to write poetry, publishing *The Life and Death of Jason* (1867), *The Earthly Paradise* (1868–70), and *Sigurd the Volsung* (1876), perhaps his finest poem. With the help of E. Magnusson, whom he met in 1868, he translated Icelandic sagas and in 1871 and 1873 made visits to Iceland, which impressed him deeply. He had in 1871 leased Kelmscott Manor on the Upper Thames; from about this time, vernacular buildings made from local materials by local craftsmen began to interest him as much as, if not more than, the famous monuments. In 1877 he was instrumental in founding the "Society for the Protection of Ancient Buildings": an attempt to prevent the overzealous restoration of historic buildings that often destroyed their surface, and with it, the hand of the original craftsman.

At the same time, and with the growing realization that art and society were indivisible, Morris began to play an active role in politics and the tackling of social problems. Ruskin's belief (expressed in the chapter "The Nature of Gothic" in *The Stones of Venice*), that the division of labor in industry prevented the workers from using their imagination and enjoying their work, formed the keystone of Morris' thinking. With its "profit mongering", the capitalist system had killed the practice and appreciation of art except for the privileged few. Morris, like Ruskin, believed that "Art is Man's Expression of his Joy in Labour".

In January 1883 Morris joined the Social Democratic Federation, and in the following year formed his own Socialist League. He continued to play an active part in this until 1890, editing and financing its paper *The Commonweal*, and lecturing up and down the country to foment discontent among the lower classes, and encourage an educated, directed revolution.

William Morris: Queen Guinevere; oil on canvas; 71×51cm (28×20in); 1858. Tate Gallery, London

Shortly before anarchist domination of the League forced him to withdraw and establish the Hammersmith Socialist Society, Morris published his utopian socialist novel *News from Nowhere* in *The Commonweal* (1890). Here he clearly expresses his hope for the future, when the English population would have left the large towns for small holdings in the revivified countryside; men and women would develop freely in beautiful surroundings, enjoying varied manual and intellectual work, and producing unconsciously, in everything they did, beautiful works of art. From 1890 until his death in 1896, Morris put his theories into practice, in the production of fine books at the Kelmscott Press and in his presidency of the Arts and Crafts Exhibition Society. His influence was immense and cannot be overestimated. Followers concerned about the crafts and their place in society included Walter Crane, Arthur Mackmurdo, Ernest Gimson, C.R. Ashbee, Henri van de Velde, and, for a short time, Walter Gropius; while poets like W.B. Yeats and socialists like Clement Attlee also acknowledged their debt to him.

Further reading. Briggs, A. (ed.) *William Morris: Selected Writings and Designs*, London (1962) and New York (1964). Gaunt, W. *The Restless Century*, London (1972). Henderson, P. *William Morris*, New York (1967). Thompson, E.P. *The Work of William Morris*, London (1967).

Moser Lukas *fl. c*1431

The German painter Lukas Moser is known only from the pioneer Magdalene Altar in the parish church of Tiefenbronn near Pforzheim, which he signed and dated in 1431. He is one of the key artists in Germany in the move away from the International Gothic towards a more realistic style. The figures of *Mary Magdalene* and *St Lazarus* on the inside of the wings, represented against patterned gold grounds, display a new monumentality, while the scenes on the outside are represented in naturalistic settings with a wealth of closely observed details. The spatial relationships, nevertheless, remain tentative and unconvincing when compared to the work of the Master of Flémalle (Robert Campin).

Motherwell Robert 1915–91

Robert Burns Motherwell was the youngest of the group of Abstract Expressionist painters in New York in the early 1940s. A student of philosophy and art history, he was a link between the exiled Surrealists in New York and modern American painters. His art, however, fits neither into the expressionist category of Jackson Pollock and Willem de Kooning nor into that of the Color field paintings of Mark Rothko and Barnett Newman. Motherwell's works consist of series of powerful images, often derived from semiautomatic doodlings but subsequently highly controlled, such as *Pancho Villa, Dead and Alive* (gouache and oil with collage on cardboard, 1943; Museum of Modern Art, New York) and his series of *Elegies for the Spanish Republic* (begun in 1947; for example, *Elegy for the Spanish Republic XXIV*, 1953–4; Albright-Knox Art Gallery, Buffalo). His themes and symbols seem to be endlessly expanded, contracted, and juxtaposed until they finally appropriate the entire picture plane.

Further reading. Carmeau, E.A. Jr *The Collages of Robert Motherwell*, Houston,

Robert Motherwell: Je t'aime; oil on canvas; 183×137cm (72×54in); 1955. Sidney Janis Gallery, New York

Tex. (1972). Greenberg, C. "Art", *The Nation* vol. 159, New York (1948). Krauss, R. "Robert Motherwell's New Paintings", *Artforum*, New York (May 1969). Motherwell, R. *Collages 1943–1949*, New York (1949). Raynor, V. "A Talk with Robert Motherwell", *Art News*, New York (April 1974).

Motonobu Kano 1476–1559

The Japanese painter Kano Motonobu was the second master of the *Kano* School, succeeding his father Masanobu as official government artist. He married the daughter of Tosa Mitsunobu, leader of the court painters, and thus started over a century of close cooperation between the schools and mutual influence between their styles. Motonobu studied Zen, but like his father he was a lay adherent of the more popular Amidist Buddhism. He became a freelance decorator-painter, specializing in large-scale compositions over sliding doors and panels in palaces and temples. His vast output has assured the survival of a fair body of his work.

Motonobu's achievement was to devise a genuinely Japanese style suitable for decorative sets of doors while retaining some of the elevated seriousness of the 15th-century monochrome tradition. In his magnificent set of doors from the Daisen'in of the Daitokuji Temple, Kyoto, foreground elements are given great prominence—a huge twisted tree-trunk, a highly stylized waterfall that owes much to *Tosa* style, carefully selected and placed birds. The line is so thick, firm, and varied that it is in itself decorative rather than expressive. Color is used selectively on plants, animals, and birds—not symbolically as in Chinese painting, but solely for visual impact. A landscape background is retained, misty and deep and rather undefined. This series was done before 1513, and is a little lacking in movement, but it remains one of the peaks of Japanese screen painting. His series for the Reiun'in in the same temple, done some 20 years later, is more fluid and assured, especially in its handling of rocks, water, and mist.

Mu Ch'i c1200–70

Little is known of the identity of the painter Mu Ch'i. Although he worked in China, it is sometimes claimed that he was in fact Japanese. However it is known that he was an abbot (sometimes called Fa-

Kano Motonobu: Pheasants and Paeonies. Daisen'in, Daitokuji Temple, Kyoto

ch'ang) who was influential in the revitalized monasteries of the Hangchow area in the early 13th century. Here he practiced painting which, despite a pronounced Ch'an (Zen) outlook, shows an elegant and disciplined brushwork indicative of a Chinese academic training. As a Ch'an Buddhist painter Mu Ch'i's choice of subject is unorthodox, and many of his finest paintings have been preserved in Japan. His characteristically daring composition and ink tone is seen at its best in the *Six Persimmons* where color is evoked by tone.

The triptych now in the Daitokuji Temple, Kyoto, Japan, presents some of the most elegant and moving painting by this artist. The goddess Kuan Yin (seated on a rock by a stream) is flanked by a scroll of gibbons and one of a walking crane; they may not have been intended to hang together but now complement each other. Here the portrayal of the figure of the white-robed Kuan Yin seems to reach unusual expressiveness in the context of Chinese Buddhist iconographic painting. The use of fluent brushwork, well within the style of the period, is most imaginative and inventive. A comparison between this painting and the work of the contemporary artist Ma Yuan is instructive in assessing their related styles. (*See* overleaf.)

Mu Ch'i (attrib.): A Wild Goose; ink on paper (hanging scroll); 87×34cm (34×13in). Staatliche Museen, East Berlin

Muhammadi *fl.* late 16th century

Muhammadi, *ustad* (master) of Herat, was a leading Persian painter during the 1570s. He was reputedly a son of Sultan Muhammad, who died *c*1540. Muhammadi probably trained in Qazwin in the 1550s. After the death of Shah Isma'il II in 1576, he returned to Herat and worked for Ali Quli Khan Shamlu who was Governor from 1576 to 1587. His masterpiece is the sensitive *Pastoral* (or *Country*) *Scene* dated 1578 (Louvre, Paris). He made other tinted drawings, of dervishes dancing (Public Library, Leningrad; Freer Gallery of Art, Washington, D.C.) and elegant figure-paintings including a self-portrait (Museum of Fine Arts, Boston). Both of these types were later copied and imitated in Isfahan.

Muhammad Nadir 17th century

The Indian painter Muhammad Nadir came from Samarkand. Working at the Mughal court, he continued to paint in the style of the Jahangir period (1605–27) during the period of Shah Jahan (1628–58). One of the finest painters of the era, he was specially known for his animal painting. The falcon attributed to him recalls the work of Chinese artists in its finesse. There are six portraits attributed to Nadir in the British Museum, London. These show restraint and economy, strong drawing, and the use of a new idiom, *siyahi qalam*. With Muhammad Murad, he was the last foreign painter to work at the Mughal court.

Muhammad Zaman
fl. late 17th century

Muhammad Zaman was the son of Hajji Yusuf of Isfahan. A painter in the European style, he was active in the court of Shah Sulayman from *c*1671 to 1695. For Shah Sulayman he added two miniatures each to the *Khamsa* of Nizami of 1539–43 (British Library, London; Or. 2265) and to the *Shah-nama* of Shah Abbas I of *c*1590 in the Chester Beatty Library, Dublin. He also contributed to a *Nizami* dated 1675/6 in the Pierpont Morgan Library, New York (M. 469). These and album paintings in the Hermitage Museum, Leningrad, are based on the work of Hendrick Goltzius and other northern artists of the school of Caravaggio. His identification with a student sent to Rome by Abbas II and converted there to Christianity is incorrect. His son Muhammad Ali was also a painter, active from 1700 to 1722 at the court of Sultan Husayn Safavi.

Mu'in Musavvir *c*1617–*c*1700

The Persian painter Mu'in Musavvir was a pupil of Riza Abbasi. A prolific draftsman and miniaturist he was active in the city of Isfahan from 1635. He worked for the Shah Sulayman, probably designing the figured tile panels—including a confronted pair of peacock-bearing angels—over the gate in the Hasht Bihisht palace (1677). He also painted many miniatures in a life of Shah Isma'il I. His style is easily recognized by the dashing calligraphic line, and is usually signed. When full color is added in his work it is strong but harmonious, and always free from Western influence.

Müller Otto 1874–1930

Born in Liebau (Saxony), the German painter Otto Müller studied in Dresden (1894–6) and Munich (1898–9). He destroyed his own early work which had been influenced by Arnold Böcklin, and the *Jugendstil*. His mature style was formed by 1908, when he moved to Berlin; there he painted a series of nudes in landscapes which were influenced by Matisse, primitive art, and Egyptian painting. His work was rejected by the Berlin Secession in 1910. He joined the *Brücke* group, whose members were attracted by his use of flat distemper colors. After he had worked with Ernst Kirchner, Müller's nudes became more angular and geometric (for example, *Three Nudes*, *c*1912; Neue Pinakothek, Munich). From 1920 onwards he mostly painted gypsy subjects.

Multscher Hans *c*1400–67

The German sculptor and painter Hans Multscher was the most important late Gothic sculptor in Swabia. He ran a large and influential workshop at Ulm. In common with workshops in other prosperous south German towns, Multscher's undertook a wide variety of commissions including stone tomb monuments, single limewood figures, and large elaborate altar retables. The latter involved both painting and sculpture and Multscher made at least two of them.

He was born *c*1400 in Allgäu but became a citizen of Ulm in 1427. Documentation and authenticated works survive for only two periods of his life, the 1430s and 1450s. Some time between 1427 and 1433 he carved a number of stone figures for the principal window of Ulm Town Hall (now in the Ulmer Museum) representing the Emperor and various princes with their pages. Two works in Ulm Minster also date from this time, a statue of the *Man of Sorrows* (1429) on the west portal, and inside, a stone altar (largely destroyed) produced for the Karg family, dated 1433. For a tomb (projected but never carried out) for Duke Ludwig the Beardless of Bavaria, he made a model of the lid (Bayerisches Nationalmuseum, Munich) showing the Duke dressed as a knight kneeling before the Trinity. However, the major work of this period was probably the so-called "Wurzach" Altar, signed and dated 1437, from which remain the painted wings (Staatliche Museen, Berlin). They consist of four scenes from the Pas-

Otto Müller: Two Female Nudes in the Open Air; canvas; 175×110cm (69×43in); 1915. Städtische Kunsthalle, Mannheim

Sterzing (now Vipiteno) in the South Tyrol. He supervised its erection from 1458 to 1459. Now dismembered, it originally consisted of a central shrine containing limewood sculptures of the Madonna and Child and four saints. The painted wings and decorated finials were the work of assistants. Flanking the altarpiece were two freestanding figures of Saints George and Florian.

Munch Edvard 1863–1944

Edvard Munch was the most internationally important Scandinavian artist of the early modern movement. Born of a doctor's family in Løten, Norway, he grew up in Oslo (known as Kristiania until 1924) where he received his initial art training. Early in the 1880s he became influenced by two older compatriots, Christian Krohg and Frits Thaulow, who were then enlivening the conservative Norwegian art scene with paintings based on French naturalism. In 1886, after a brief first visit to Paris, he discovered his own direction with *The Sick Child* (1885–6; National Gallery, Oslo). With impressionistic simplification, he fused an observed experience with recollections of the earlier death of a sister from tuberculosis, creating a haunting tragedy of doomed youth.

From 1889 to 1892 State scholarships enabled him to live mainly in France, although he established the habit of returning to Norway for the summers. In Paris he explored the new French painting, while formulating his intention to replace naturalism with an art symbolizing man's deepest emotions. His new works, based mostly on variations of French Impressionist technique, were included in his large exhibitions in Oslo and Berlin during the autumn of 1892. In both cities they were disliked, but in Berlin they provoked a scandal which caused the exhibition's closure after a week, and split the host organization, the Berlin Artists' Association. However, this notoriety earned Munch further exhibitions in Germany and he decided to base himself there. The *Portrait of the Artist's Sister Inger* (1892; National Gallery, Oslo) marks a decisive turning point in his career.

In Berlin he developed a series of subjects linked by the sequence of love, suffering, and death—the *Frieze of Life*, which dominated his work for many years. He publicly initiated this cycle in 1893 by exhibiting the six related paintings of the

sion and four depicting the life of the Virgin. It is likely that they once enclosed a central compartment containing sculpture.

A gap of more than a decade follows before Multscher's next surviving works in the 1450s. Among these are a bronze monument to Countess Mechthild of the Palatinate (Stiftskirche, Tübingen) and some wood carvings including a Palmesel (Dominikanerinnenkloster, Wettenhausen) of 1456. Palmesel sculptures depict Christ riding an ass; they were led in procession through the streets of south German towns on Palm Sunday.

In 1456 Multscher contracted to supply an altarpiece to the Stadtpfarrkirche at

Edvard Munch: Self-portrait in Blue Suit; oil on canvas; 100×110cm (39×43in); 1909. Bergen Art Gallery

Love series, including those today entitled *The Kiss* (1892), *Madonna* (c1893), and *The Scream* (1893; all in the National Gallery, Oslo). Factual experiences were still synthesized into an expression of emotional forces, but impressionistic treatment was now replaced by a dramatic yet decorative symbolism, recalling Gauguin or Van Gogh. Munch's tortured self-portraits reveal that the feeling of uncontrollable life forces which grip his figures arises from personal emotional insecurity. These works found appreciation among the Berlin avant-garde, writers like Strindberg, Przybyszewski, and Dehmel, who were equally intensely preoccupied with man's psychic condition.

It was during his years in Berlin that Munch started to make prints. Etching, lithographs, and woodcuts became as important to him as painting. He spent 1896 and 1897 in Paris where he developed color printing, working with the master printers Lemercier and Clot (who printed for Bonnard and Vuillard). He saw woodcuts by Gauguin and the Japanese: woodcuts were to become his own most consis-tently original graphic achievements. His boldly cut images, often with complex color combinations and wood-grain over-printing, were to have a strong influence on German Expressionist printmaking. In Paris Munch moved in literary Symbolist circles, portraying Mallarmé, and design-ing programs for productions of Ibsen (whose plays fascinated him) at the *Théâtre de l'Oeuvre*. He exhibited at Bing's Art Nouveau gallery and the Indépendants.

During the next few years Munch lived more in Norway, expanding the *Frieze of Life* in paintings and prints, his ambition for large-scale projects stimulated by visits to Italy. Several new subjects, such as *Mother and Daughter* (c1897; National Gallery, Oslo), *Girls on the Jetty* (c1899–1901; National Gallery, Oslo), and the impressive portraits he executed (for example, *The Four Sons of Dr Max Linde*, 1903; Behnhaus-Museum, Lübeck), imply a less pessimistic philosophy; while some magnificent Oslo Fjord landscapes (for example, *View of Oslo Fjord from Nord-strand*, c1900; Städtische Kunsthalle, Mannheim)—always Munch's favorite scenery—and paintings such as *Winter* (1899; National Gallery, Oslo) and *The Dance on the Shore* (1900–2; National Gallery, Prague) demonstrate a renewed interest in the external forces of nature.

The year 1902 proved to be a crisis year. The violent end of a protracted love affair and subsequent quarrels with Norwegian artists aggravated Munch's insecurity, convincing him of persecution at home and causing him to live increasingly in Germany. There, recognition was grow-ing. A major selection from the *Frieze of Life* was well received at the 1902 exhibition of the Berlin Secession, and frequent exhibitions followed in Germany and central Europe. Wealthy patrons were forth-coming, art dealers offered contracts, and commissions for stage designs and decorations came from Max Reinhardt's Berlin theater. Munch now started changing his painting style from the somber tonalities and swirling patterns of the 1890s (which he felt might become mannered) to staccato brush strokes of brilliant, high-keyed colors, appropriate to his new, more frequently extrovert subjects.

In 1908 Munch's nervous condition finally reached complete breakdown and he retired to a Danish nursing home. There he took stock of himself and his art and the following spring he felt able to settle again in Norway, where his art was now increasingly appreciated.

From then until 1916 Munch's major works were the murals for the Great Hall of Oslo University. As if symbolizing his recovery, their theme was human life as part of nature's continuity ("the great external forces" as Munch expressed it), and it was to complement the *Frieze of Life* ("the suffering and joys of the individual as seen from close at hand"). Many of the motifs were developed from the more optimistic paintings he had created from the late 1890s onward. The brightly col-ored figures in their Oslo Fjord setting seem, as Munch intended, both typically Norwegian yet universal, and opposite to the Hall's Neoclassical architecture.

Despite increasing fame, Munch con-tinued to live quietly outside Oslo, work-ing hard. Motifs included landscapes, figure compositions, and subjects from the past, often reworked in his new color range. He also painted decorative murals for a factory canteen, and among the new prints he made at this time were subjects from Ibsen. The quality of his late works is less even than before, but to the end he could still paint new masterpieces like the remarkable *Self-portrait Between the Clock and the Bed* (1940–2; Munch Museum, Oslo).

Munch's most obvious importance lies in his uniquely powerful synthesis of northern *fin-de-siècle* ideas with French Post-Impressionist styles; his famous paintings of the 1890s link Gauguin and Van Gogh with modern German Expressionism. The best work of his later years, although no longer avant-garde, can contribute equally personal images that enlarge his total artistic personality.

Further reading. Benesch, O. *Edvard Munch*, London (1960). Boulton-Smith, J. *Munch*, New York and Oxford (1977). Deknatel, F.B. *Edvard Munch*, New York (1950). Heller, R. *Edvard Munch: The Scream*, London (1973). Langaard, J.H. and Revold, R. *A Year by Year Record of Edvard Munch's Life*, Oslo (1961). Stang, R. *Edvard Munch: the Man and the Artist*, London (1979). Timm, W. *The Graphic Art of Edvard Munch*, London (1969).

Münter Gabriele 1877–1962

The German artist Gabriele Münter was one of the leading figures in the development of German Expressionism. After studying briefly at the Women Artists' Association in Munich, she moved (1902) to the progressive Phalanx Art School, where she met Wassily Kandinsky. Living together from 1903 to 1914, they first traveled widely and then settled in Murnau, becoming the leading figures in the New Artists' Association and *Der Blaue Reiter* (The Blue Rider) group. Despite their closeness, Münter developed an independent style, drawing inspiration from Van Gogh, Jawlensky and Bavarian folk art (in the form of religious images painted on glass). She painted mainly landscapes and still lifes, her colors bold, expressive and often somber, her simplified forms bounded by strong, flowing outlines. Her works include *Man Listening (Portrait of Jawlensky)* and *Still Life with Chair* (both 1909; both Städtische Galerie im Lenbachhaus, Munich). She did little work after her relationship with Kandinsky ended in 1917.

Further reading. Hoberg, A. *Wassily Kandinsky and Gabriele Münter*, New York (1994). Lohnstein, P. *Gabriele Münter*, New York (1971).

Murillo Bartolomé 1617–82

The Spanish painter Bartolomé Esteban Murillo was born and died in Seville. Probably apprenticed there to Juan del Castillo, he produced a large number of religious compositions in Seville for churches and monasteries. These were painted in a graceful and colorful late Baroque style, full of movement, his handling steadily becoming freer and his outlines more diffused. His command of tonal values and of light exceeded from the beginning anything that his master could have taught him.

Although they were only a small part of his large output, his portraits in simple but effective full- or half-length poses reached a high level of technical accomplishment.

They may have owed something indirectly to Velázquez (whom Murillo could not have met before visiting Madrid in the late 1650s). His scenes of everyday life, particularly those of beggar-boys (a fine example, undated, is in the Louvre, Paris) have always been among his most popular works (see also *Grape and Melon Eaters*, Alte Pinakothek, Munich).

Murillo's first large commission was a series of 11 compositions of Franciscan subjects (including the *Miracle of S. Diego of Alcalá* or *Angel's Kitchen*, Louvre, Paris). Painted in 1645 and 1646 for the Franciscan monastery in Seville, these are now widely dispersed in Europe and America. Though less impressive than Zurbarán's earlier Hieronymite series at

Bartolomé Murillo: The Beggar-boy; oil on canvas; 137×115cm (54×45in). Louvre, Paris

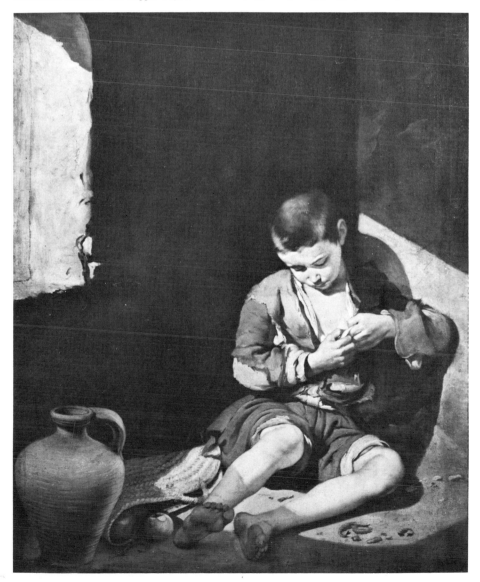

Guadalupe, and equally lacking in movement, these compositions immediately
gained him fame; thereafter, Murillo's
popularity began to overtake Zurbarán's.

From this period also date the earliest
representations of the *Virgin and Child,* at
Pollok House, Glasgow, and the Palazzo
Pitti, Florence. Many others date from the
1650s, as do his depictions of such popular
subjects as the *Adoration of the Shepherds,*
the *Holy Family,* and the *Annunciation*
(Prado, Madrid).

In 1656 Murillo painted one of his largest
works, *The Vision of St Anthony of Padua*
(Seville Cathedral). This skillfully contrasts
the supernatural light of the celestial vision
above with the sunlight seen through the
doorway below, while on the saint's table
a glass jar of lilies demonstrates the
painter's mastery of still life details.

Although he never painted landscapes
without figures, Murillo was a fine landscapist, as in the freely handled backgrounds of the large series of canvases of
the *Story of Jacob* of the late 1660s
(Cleveland Museum of Art; Meadows
Museum and Sculpture Court, Texas; and
the Hermitage Museum, St Petersburg).

The half-length *Self-portrait* (c1672; National Gallery, London) is of superb quality. So is the slightly earlier *Flower-Girl*
(Dulwich College Picture Gallery, London)
which is notable for its crisp handling and
toneful color scheme. Murillo's best-
known works are the series of enormous
biblical subjects painted during the years
1667 to 1674 for the Charity Hospital,
Seville (some still *in situ*); and the many
versions of the Immaculate Conception, in
widely varying poses, that he painted from
1652 onward. Like some of his Virgins
and compositions of the youthful St John
the Baptist, a few of these verge on the
sentimental: they have thus contributed to
the decline of Murillo's popularity in the
20th century, unduly obscuring the brilliant painterly qualities of most of his
work.

Murillo's pupils and collaborators included the landscape specialist Ignacio
Iriarte and the genre-painter Pedro Núñez
de Villavicencio.

Further reading. Abbad Rios, F. *Las In-
maculadas de Murillo: Estudio Critico,*
Barcelona (1948). Angulo Íñiquez, D.
Murillo (3 vols.), Madrid (1981). Brown,
J. *Murillo and his Drawings,* Princeton
(1977).

Myron 5th century BC

Myron was a Greek bronze sculptor from Eleutherae, a border town between Boeotia and Attica. He was a reputed pupil of Ageladas and an older contemporary of Pheidias and Polycleitos. The most interesting part of his career falls within the early Classical phase, as he experimented in the rendering of motion, aiming at a higher degree of naturalism than his successors. The ancient critics noticed that he employed a greater stock of positions than Polycleitos and was also more consistent in his use of the rule of proportions.

The high point of Myron's career is the statue of the *Discobolus* (*Discus-thrower*), described in detail by Lucian (2nd century AD) and identified in copies (the best in the Terme Museum, Rome). It represents the moment of back-swing, the athlete looking back at the hand holding the discus. In a second he will lunge forward, pivoting on his right leg. Myron captures the dynamic moment of suspended action. His statue is composed in a system of triangles around the central sweeping S-curve of the body; it depends entirely on its animated outline to express movement, because the anatomy does not respond to the action. It is conceived as a figure in relief and probably owes its inspiration to contemporary painting. Its artificiality had impressed the Romans who saw it as "distorted and elaborate".

Myron's naturalistic tendencies were demonstrated in his bronze *Cow* on the Acropolis, which a calf was said to have mistaken for its mother. He worked mostly in Athens and may have been involved in the Parthenon; his style is recognized on some of the metopes of the south side. A type of quiet standing *Herakles* copied in statuettes is thought to derive from his colossal group of *Herakles, Zeus, and Athena* on Samos. His group of *Athena and Marsyas* has been reconstructed, not without controversy, on the evidence of vases and coins.

Mytens Daniel c1590–1647

Before the arrival of Anthony van Dyck in England in 1632, the work of the Dutch painter, Daniel Mytens, exerted an important foreign influence on English portrai-

Myron: Discobolus (Discus-thrower); height 125cm (49in); a Roman copy after an original of the 5th century BC. Terme Museum, Rome

Daniel Mytens: Portrait of the Duke of Hamilton; oil on canvas; 216×135cm (85×53in); 1629. Scottish National Portrait Gallery, Edinburgh (on loan from the Duke of Hamilton)

ture. Mytens was trained in The Hague, and came to London c1618. He became a royal portraitist on the accession of Charles I. His portraits show a marked break with the Jacobean convention of spectacular patterning and rich detail, and instead concentrate on the sitter's personality. Mytens' realism, an aspect of his work inherited from the art of the Low Countries, gradually became more ambitious and assured. In his late work he produced some of the most elegant and powerful full-length portraits of the 17th century.

N

Nadelman Elie 1882–1946

Elie Nadelman was a Polish sculptor who emigrated to America in 1914. He had already achieved great success in Paris (especially through his famous one-man show at the Galerie Druet, 1909) and had exhibited in London, Barcelona, and Berlin. Helena Rubinstein was an early admirer and supported him by buying much of his work. He went to New York (where his work was included in the 1913 Armory Show) and his almost clinical search for the basic structures of plastic form led him to a style of curvilinear Abstract sculpture which was well received in avant-garde and fashionable circles.

Elie Nadelman: Relief; 1912–13.

Later he also **produced** painted terracotta figures and miniature doll-like carvings. Nadelman's style, primarily transmitted through the early patronage of Helena Rubinstein, was one of the formative ingredients of the style of design later known as Art Deco.

Nainsukh c1725–c90

Nainsukh was a Hindu Pahari artist, the second son of the Brahman *pundit* Seu Raina, and brother of the painter Manaku. A native of Guler, he was responsible for introducing the Mughal style in the Pahari courts, either through being trained by an immigrant Mughal artist, or being trained at the Mughal court. His portraits and animal paintings show the influence of the Muhammad Shah style. Much has been discovered about Nainsukh and his family through recent important researches into temple records at the pilgrim site of Hardwar. There are a number of signed paintings by him of his first patron, Balwant Singh. There is also a self-portrait. After the death of Balwant Singh in 1763, he entered the service of Amrit Pal of Basohli (1757–76). This was a crucial period, when through the influence of Nainsukh a new graceful naturalism entered Basohli painting. His works show a flair for capturing movement and depicting people in action.

Nanni di Banco c1375–1421

The Italian sculptor Giovanni di Antonio di Banco was known as Nanni di Banco. He was born in Florence, the son of a stonemason. Together with Jacopo della Quercia and Lorenzo Ghiberti, he belongs to the first generation of artists who determined the style of the early Renaissance. Though his works are small in number, they excel by their typical interweaving of Gothic reminiscences and neo-antique Classicism, thus showing the transitional period at the beginning of the 15th century.

Two large commissions dominated Nanni's life: the decoration of the Porta della Mandorla, one of the side entrances of Florence Cathedral, and the sculptural adornment of the niches at Orsanmichele, the Florentine guilds' church. He started his career in the first decade of the 15th century by carving the reliefs of the inner arch of the Porta della Mandorla. About 1413, the Chapter of the cathedral as-

signed to Nanni, Donatello, and two lesser known sculptors the execution of the seated marble figures of the Evangelists, destined for the cathedral's facade. Nanni di Banco's *St Luke* (Museo dell'Opera del Duomo, Florence) not only reveals close study of Roman Antiquity, but also shows a new monumental style, which compares with Donatello's early sculptures.

For the niches at Orsanmichele he executed the almost antique statue of *St Philip* (c1412), the important group of Four Crowned Saints called *Quattro Coronati* (c1414), and *St Eligius* (c1417–18), who strongly recalls late Gothic tradition. The four monumental statues of the *Quattro Coronati*, the first attempt to combine several freestanding figures within the architectonic frame of a niche, decisively influenced later generations. His most important work is the relief of the Virgin in the tympanum of the Porta della Mandorla. The dynamic, unique conception is only formally related to Andrea Orcagna's relief of the Virgin in Orsanmichele (1359). Moreover, it shows Nanni's comprehension of the vocabulary of Roman Antiquity.

Nardo di Cione fl. 1343–65/6

The Florentine painter Nardo di Cione was the brother of Orcagna. While Orcagna painted the altarpiece in the Strozzi Chapel in S. Maria Novella, Florence (dated 1357), Nardo painted the fresco decora-

Nardo di Cione: Christ, a detail from the fresco of Heaven in the Strozzi Chapel, S. Maria Novella, Florence; c1354–7

tion on the walls: the *Last Judgment*, *Heaven*, and *Hell*. These probably date from the same period as the altarpiece, (*c*1354–7). It seems likely that Nardo was Orcagna's usual assistant and collaborator, and although he was the lesser artist, his own style can be identified as a less rigorous version of his brother's. The higher quality of the figures of Christ and the Virgin in Heaven, for example, supports the probability that Orcagna was actually responsible for the design and some of the painting of these frescoes.

Nash John 1752–1835

John Nash was the leading architect of the English Regency period. He trained under Sir Robert Taylor. His early career, spent mainly in Wales, was undistinguished, and included a bankruptcy in 1783. In 1796 he formed a highly profitable partnership with the landscape gardener Humphry Repton. Their association ended in 1802, but not before it had established Nash's reputation as a fashionable country house architect.

Talented, self-confident, and enormously ambitious, Nash was assisted by more than a measure of good fortune. The premature death of James Wyatt, in 1813, removed his only serious rival as a country house architect, while his marriage to a mistress of the future George IV introduced him to court circles, enabling him to benefit from the vast expansion of royal patronage that took place in the second and third decades of the 19th century. It was as a result of his close friendship with the Regent that he was awarded two of his most important commissions: Buckingham Palace, London (1825–30) and the Royal Pavilion, Brighton (1815–21).

His success owed little to stylistic integrity. He was prepared, when occasion demanded, to submit designs for classical, castellated, Gothic, or even "Hindoo" buildings, while his notorious indifference to detail forced him to rely heavily on the skill of assistants, including J.A. Repton and A.C. Pugin. His strength was in composition. The partnership with Repton had instilled an appreciation of the Picturesque, and it was Nash, more than any other early-19th-century architect, whose buildings exemplified the Picturesque

Nanni di Banco: Four Crowned Saints with workshop scenes below; stone; c1414. Orsanmichele, Florence

ideal—whether it was in the ragged skyline of Ravensworth Castle, County Durham (1808), the daring asymmetry of Cronkhill, Shropshire (1802), or the interaction of landscape, villas, and terrace facades of The Regent's Park (1821–30).

Further reading. Mansbridge, M. *John Nash: A Complete Catalogue*, New York (1991). Summerson, J.N. *John Nash, Architect to King George IV*, London (1949).

Nash Paul 1889–1946

The English painter Paul Nash was born in London. After initial training in illustration, he studied at the London County Council School (1908–10) and at the Slade School of Fine Art, London (1910–11). Unsuccessful in figure-drawing, he turned increasingly to landscape to express personal feelings. The breakthrough came when as an Official War Artist he painted *We Are Making a New World* (1918; Imperial War Museum, London), which conveyed a sense of desolate outrage by color and form alone. From 1919 to 1925 Nash continued this development in his Cubist-influenced Dymchurch landscapes.

The impact of Surrealism from 1928 onward made his art more openly Symbolic, and led him to use ancient landscape features (such as megaliths) to express the spirit of place and the continuity of history. Both aspects are important to the English landscape tradition, and make Nash one of its central 20th-century figures.

Further reading. Bertram, A. *Paul Nash: the Portrait of an Artist*, London (1955). Causey, A. *Paul Nash*, Oxford (1980). Eates, M. *Paul Nash: the Master of the Image, 1889–1946*, London (1973). Postan, A. *The Complete Graphic Works of Paul Nash*, London (1973). Rothenstein, J. *Paul Nash 1889–1946*, London (1967).

Nattier Jean-Marc 1685–1766

The French painter Jean-Marc Nattier was the son of parents who were themselves both painters. He began life as an engraver, with his father and brother, of Rubens' *Marie de Medici* cycle (the paintings are now in the Louvre, Paris). He then turned to historical portraiture, and finally became a favorite painter of the women at the Court of Louis XV. Those ladies he presented in flights of Rococo splendor as,

for example, his *Duchesse d'Orléans as Hebe* (1745; Nationalmuseum, Stockholm), where the conceit is that the Duchess is a goddess, floating on powder-puff clouds in no earthly paradise. A critic underlined the painting's artificiality by wondering how many women in France actually tamed eagles by feeding them white wine. Nattier's works have charm and delicacy, as well as being likenesses; but, as the criticism intimates, they failed to please the severe demand of nascent Neoclassicism.

Neel Alice 1900–84

The American portrait painter Alice Neel studied at the Philadelphia School of Design for Women, and lived briefly in Cuba before settling in New York. Following a period in a psychiatric hospital in her 20s, she developed an intense, stark form of portraiture reminiscent of German Expressionism: typically her contours are tense and the sitters' features strongly emphasized, while large areas of the canvas are left lightly sketched in. Neel lived in Greenwich Village and then for 25 years in Spanish Harlem, her portraits of friends and neighbors expressing an unsentimental compassion for the physical and psychological effects of poverty—she described herself as a "collector of souls". Uninfluenced by the many avant-garde developments in American 20th-century art, she remained neglected until the late 1960s.

Characteristically frank and incisive portraits include *Andy Warhol* (1970; Whitney Museum of American Art, New York) and her nude *Self-portrait* (1980; Robert Miller Gallery, New York), painted when she was 80.

Further reading. Tempkin, A. and Flood, R. *Alice Neel*, New York (2000).

Neer Aert van der 1603–77

The Dutch landscape painter Aert van der Neer settled in 1630 in Amsterdam, where he specialized in nocturnal and winter scenes. The nocturnal landscapes (usually imaginative interpretations of the countryside around Amsterdam) are sometimes lit by flames from burning buildings, but more usually by the pale, transparent beams of a full moon. These create a melancholy mood as they fall on water, ice, and land, and reflect back on to cloudy

skies. The poetic content of these pictures was admired by 19th-century German Romantic painters. Van der Neer's spacious, multifigured winter landscapes are in the manner of Avercamp's skating scenes. Through the subtle coloristic and tonal modulation of a limited palette of whites, silvery-grays, and pale blues, they brilliantly convey the crisp, cold atmosphere of a winter's day. Van der Neer achieved little success as a painter. A venture into tavern-keeping was also unsuccessful, and the artist was declared bankrupt in 1662.

Nervi Pier Luigi 1891–1979

Pier Luigi Nervi, a structural engineer and architect born in Lombardy, is considered the modern master of concrete construction. His success at vaulting large areas with reinforced concrete, as in his various aircraft hangars of the 1930s, was greatly admired, and led to important cooperative projects after the Second World War. Among these were the UNESCO Building in Paris (1953–6), the Palazzetto dello Sport in Rome (1957), and the Pirelli Skyscraper in Milan (1955–8), where Nervi's structural answer to the problem of the skyscraper block was dazzlingly demonstrated. Nervi is one of the many engineer "heroes" of modern architecture.

Neumann Balthasar 1687–1753

Balthasar Neumann was one of the two leading German architects of the 18th century, the other being J.M. Fischer. Neumann was a native of Eger, and was originally trained as a cannon- and bell-founder. Throughout his career he retained an intensely practical approach to problems, and was a superb technician. In 1714 he enlisted in the Würzburg palace guards as a lieutenant of artillery; he served as an engineer in the Belgrade campaign of 1717, visiting Milan and Vienna in 1718. On his return to Würzburg in 1720, he and Johann Dientzenhofer were appointed by the Prince Bishop, Philip Franz von Schönborn, to be joint surveyors of a vast new palace that was planned. Most of his major architectural commissions were to be closely connected with the Schönborn family.

Aert van der Neer: A Landscape with a River at Evening; oil on canvas; 79×65cm (31×26in); c1650–3. National Gallery, London

Work on the Würzburg Residenz began in earnest under Friedrich Carl von Schönborn (who reigned from 1729 to 1746) and the final designs were influenced by Robert de Cotte and Gabriel-Germain Boffrand as well as by Lucas von Hildebrandt. In the dynamic composition of the Hofkirche in the south wing the architecture is by Neumann (1730); the decoration was designed by Hildebrandt, and much of the strength of the Bohemian-inspired vaulting is dissipated. The design for the staircase was finally approved in 1735; together with the Weissersaal and Kaisersaal which lead from it, it was completed during the 1750s.

Hildebrandt also advised Neumann in the building of the Prince Bishop's summer residence, Schloss Werneck in Schweinfurt (1734–45). Neumann's personal style is best seen there in the dynamic design of the chapel, a type of composition first worked out by him in the Schönborn Chapel attached to Würzburg Cathedral, where he revised the plans of M. von Welsch (1723–36). Unfortunately his great abbey church of Münsterschwarzach (1727–42) was demolished during the 19th century. In it Neumann developed his complex vaults, supported by pillars set obliquely, which break down the traditional spatial divisions of his church interiors, and lead to the almost willful complexity of Vierzehnheiligen.

For other members of the Schönborn family, Neumann was active further west. From 1733 he worked for Franz Georg, Archbishop Elector of Trier, reconstructing the abbey church of St Paulinus there (begun 1734). For Damian Hugo, Bishop of Speyer, he began work on Schloss Bruchsal in 1728. The twin ascending flights of the staircase (1731–2), enfolding the central oval area that links the state rooms, was one of his greatest triumphs. The building was later partially destroyed.

During his later years Neumann's greatest successes lay in his church designs—his projects for vast palaces remained unexecuted. In the pilgrimage church of Vierzehnheiligen, interpenetrating vaults are exploited to the full, in order to focus attention on to the shrine in the nave. In Neumann's last important church, at Neresheim (1747–92), calm reigns again and the interior is dominated by the central rotunda.

Further reading. Freeden, M.H. von *Balthasar Neumann: Leben und Werk*, Munich (1953). Knapp, F. *Balthasar Neumann*, Berlin (1937).

Barnett Newman: Covenant; oil on canvas; 122×152cm (48×60in); 1949. Joseph Hirshhorn Museum, Washington, D.C.

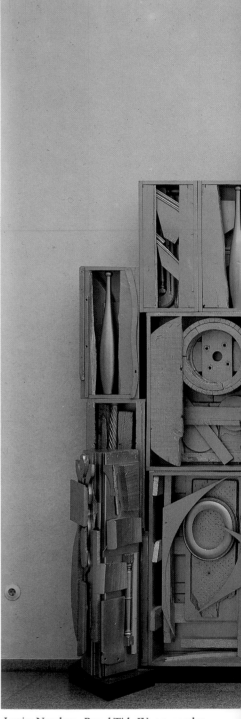

Louise Nevelson: Royal Tide IV; 35 wooden chests painted gold; 335×427cm (131×166in); 1959–60. Wallraf-Richartz-Museum, Cologne

Neutra Richard 1892–1970

The Austrian architect Richard Neutra was a Viennese, and a pupil of Adolf Loos before the First World War. He then worked in Switzerland, and in 1922 in Germany with Eric Mendelsohn, before emigrating to the U.S.A. In 1926 he joined his compatriot Rudolf Schindler in Los Angeles. Both architects were inspired by, and worked with, Frank Lloyd Wright.

Neutra's first work of note, the Lovell

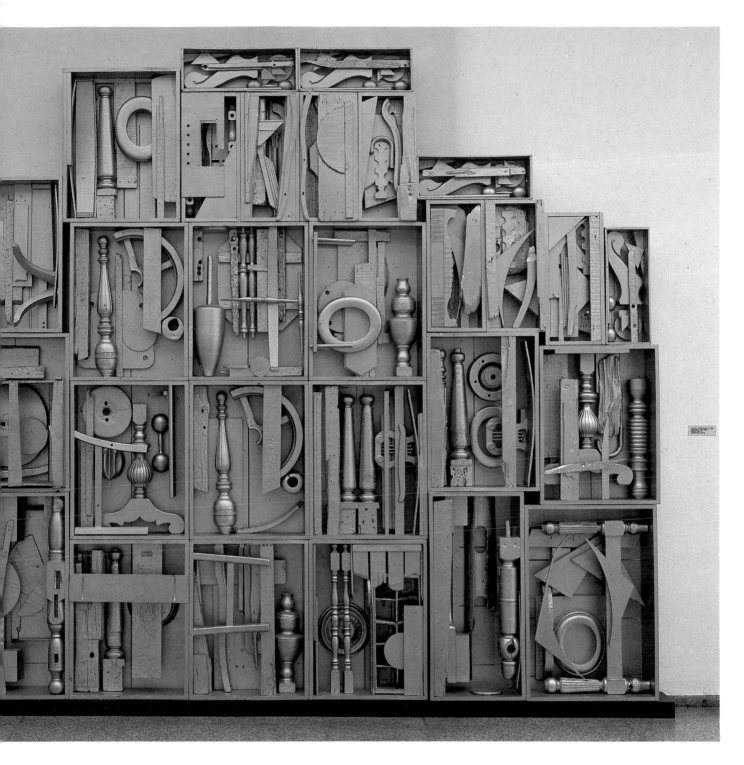

house, Los Angeles (1927–9), is usually seen as the first building in an American "International style". He continued designing in this manner, attaining ever greater heights of elegance and finish, throughout the 1930s and 1940s. The Kaufmann Desert house, Palm Springs (1946–7), is remarkable, like all of Neutra's houses, for its dramatic siting.

Nevelson Louise 1899–1988

Louise Nevelson was an American sculptor born Louise Beliawsky in Kiev, Russia. Her family emigrated to Rockland, Maine, in 1905. She studied painting and drawing in New York, first with Theresa Bernstein and William Meyerowitz (1920), and then at The Art Students League, with Kenneth Hayes Miller and Kimon Nicolaides (1929–30). She also worked briefly with Hans Hofmann in Munich (1931), and assisted Diego Rivera on a mural for the New Workers' School, New York (1932). Her first one-woman show came in 1941 (Nierendorf Gallery, New York).

Nevelson's work has been influenced by a wide variety of sources such as Futurism, Cubism, and the work of Brancusi. Her most characteristic works have come to be "sculptural walls": a series of wooden boxes or "pigeon holes" filled with forms which are usually abstract but which have overtones of ordinary objects.

Further reading. Lisle, L. *Louise Nevelson: a Passionate Life*, New York (2001).

Newman Barnett 1905–70

The American painter Barnett Newman was, with Mark Rothko, one of the leading New York painters of the 1950s. He moved away from the free brushwork of Abstract Expressionism towards a cerebral, restrained yet lyrical Color-field painting. In 1944 and 1945 Newman was working in Abstract Surrealist "automatic" style. By 1948, as in *Onement I* (oil on canvas; 1948; private collection), the Surrealist symbols were eradicated, to be replaced by a flat rectangularly divided picture-plane, the ingredient for all his later work. Vast areas of color are meticulously applied and, perfectly articulated, move horizontally across his canvases, as in *Vir Heroicus Sublimis* (oil on canvas; 1950–1; Museum of Modern Art, New York). Such paintings are early and seminal examples of hard-edge Minimal art.

Further reading. Hess, T. *Barnett Newman*, New York (1971). Newman, B. "Studio 35" in Motherwell, R. and Reinhardt, A. (eds.) *Modern Artists in America*, New York (1952). Restany, P. "Barnett Newman: a Value of Civilization", *Domus*, Milan (Feb. 1973). Rosenberg, H. "Barnett Newman and Meaning in Abstract Art", *Art International*, Lugano (1972).

Niccolò *fl. c1120–c50*

Niccolò was a Romanesque sculptor whose first signed work is the Zodiac Portal of the Abbey of Sagra di S. Michele in Piedmont (1122–30). Subsequently, he carved the south portal of Piacenza Cathedral (*c*1130) and the west portals of Ferrara Cathedral (*c*1135), of S. Zeno's church at Verona (*c*1138), and of Verona Cathedral (*post* 1139). In contrast to the expressive and powerful style of his predecessor Wiligelmo, his reliefs are delicate, almost lyrical, and are carved with great attention to detail.

Niccolò played an important role in the development of portal design. His portals consist of numerous recessed orders of colonnettes (small decorative columns) and arches, a large tympanum (hitherto rare in Italy), and a projecting porch resting on columns carried on the backs of lions or griffins. At Ferrara and the cathedral at Verona, there are in addition figures attached to the jambs, thus providing a design similar to that used at the abbey of St-Denis, which revolutionized portal design for many centuries to come by the use of column-figures. At S. Zeno in Verona, flanking the main portal, are reliefs with scenes from Genesis (south side) and the life of Christ (north side), thus extending the sculptural decoration well

Niccolò: Six Scenes from Genesis, a detail of the south side of the main portal of S. Zeno, Verona; c1138

beyond the portal.

It is often claimed that Niccolò must have known sculpture in France, especially in Languedoc; this is quite feasible, for some elements in his style could have originated there. His influence on the development of sculpture in Italy was profound, but has been little studied. True column-figures in a style similar to that of Niccolò were employed in Ravenna, Ancona, and elsewhere in Italy—and it is tempting to think that Niccolò invented this device in a monument now destroyed. If that were indeed the case, then the column-figures at St-Denis would have been of Italian inspiration.

Niccolò Alunno *c1430–1502*

The Italian painter Niccolò Alunno was also known as Niccolò di Liberatore and

as Niccolò da Foligno. He began as a pupil and imitator of Benozzo Gozzoli: his *Madonna dei Consoli* (signed and dated 1457/8; Pinacoteca Comunale, Deruta) is close to the master's fresco style in S. Francesco at Montefalco, Umbria (finished 1452). Later he moved away from the manner of Gozzoli to that of Alvise Vivarini and Carlo Crivelli, as in the *Coronation of the Virgin, with Saints* (1466; Vatican Museums, Rome) and the *Virgin and Child Enthroned* (1482; Pinacoteca Nazionale, Bologna). His color becomes brighter, his design harder, and he makes great use of expressive gestures.

Towards the end of the 15th century, in *The Nativity* (1492; central panel of a polyptych, Pinacoteca Comunale, Foligno), heroism is coupled with an assured handling of perspective and natural details clearly located in space. The expressive use of drapery contrasts the vigor of the St Joseph with the pious gentleness of the Virgin as she worships the Child.

Niccolò's style was popular in the Marches, where he was active from c1466. Vasari praises his work as "natural", saying that "all his heads were portraits and seemed alive".

Nicholas of Verdun *fl.* 1181–c1205

Nicholas of Verdun is not the earliest medieval artist who can be established historically, either by signed surviving work or documents; but he is the first whose development as an artistic personality can be traced through early, mature, and late work.

He is first established by the great enameled pulpit he made for Klosterneuburg near Vienna, which is signed by him and was completed in 1181. A later addition to the inscription records that after a fire in 1330, the pulpit was reconstructed in 1331 by the addition of six enameled figure-scenes, and painted scenes on the back, to create the present altar retable.

Nicholas' pulpit, originally part of the choir screen of the church, was decorated with 45 large champlevé enameled panels. These were arranged in three horizontal rows, with scenes from the life of Christ in the center; above and below each scene are Old Testament prefigurations from before and after the Law of Moses. Each scene is surrounded by texts, and set under a triple arch carried on paired columns, with half-length angels in the spandrels. Although the whole is clearly the work of one hand, it is possible to see a development within it, ranging from a softer, more static style, with the scene arranged in parallel to the surface in the earlier scenes on the left leaf of the retable, to much more vividly drawn and composed scenes in the center and on the right wing—such as the Sacrifice of Isaac, with strong compositional diagonals, rich use of massed lines of drapery, and expressive heads.

After the pulpit, Nicholas undoubtedly worked on the Shrine of Three Kings in Cologne, although his presence is not recorded by documents. The great silver-gilt figures of Prophets and Apostles are perfect translations of the late expressive style of Klosterneuburg into a powerful three-dimensional presence. A late work, documented by inscriptions, is the Shrine

Ben Nicholson: November 11, 1947 (Mousehole); oil and pencil on canvas mounted on wood; 46×58cm (18×23in); 1947. Collection of the British Council

of Our Lady at Tournai, completed in 1205. Although it has suffered much from later restorations, enough survives to see Nicholas' late style—much less classical in proportion, more fluid in form, flatter, more linear, but of almost visionary intensity.

Both in technique and in iconography—especially at Klosterneuburg—his art is derived from a Mosan background (from the art of the Meuse River Valley area of the 11th and 12th centuries). But his originality as a creative artist is exceptional, and his work marks a new phase in the history of art called the "Transitional style". Nicholas clearly knew both antique and, more especially, contemporary Byzantine works of art; there is more than a suspicion in his work that he was among the first artists working c1200 to seek to imitate nature. However that may be, he certainly made use of his many and varied sources in a personal way, not simply by imitating them, but by studying them, and by absorbing them into a self-conscious creation of an individual style.

Nicholson Ben 1894–1982

Ben Nicholson, who has done more than any other artist to introduce and nurture nonfigurative art in England, was the son of the painter William Nicholson. He studied briefly at the Slade School of Fine Art (1910–11), but was largely self-taught;

very little of his early work remains. After the war, stimulated by early Italian painting and by Cézanne and Cubism, Nicholson began to examine methodically—without preconception of what a picture ought to look like—ways of representing his feeling for space and light. This brought him close to abstraction by 1924. In the later 1920s, living chiefly in Cumberland, he painted simplified, carefully crafted landscapes and still lifes, which became more conceptual after his discovery of the Cornish primitive painter Alfred Wallis in 1928.

From 1931 to 1939 Nicholson lived in Hampstead, as part of the group of avant-garde artists who committed themselves wholeheartedly to links with Paris. With Barbara Hepworth, whom he married as his second wife, Nicholson visited the studios of many Paris artists; he profited from meeting Picasso and Braque and, among the nonfigurative painters, Piet Mondrian. The more abstract Surrealists, such as Miró, helped a new range of cursive forms to emerge in his art. A series of paintings of 1932 allude to France and Nicholson's interest in Cubism, and display his visual humor and sense of enigma at their most developed. From these Nicholson progressed quickly to his first Abstract reliefs (1933) and to the first all-white paintings (1934). His introduction of primary colors shortly afterwards can be taken as a tribute to Mondrian; but a feeling for tonal relationships and a taste for muted color, which Nicholson inherited from his father's generation, were deeply rooted, and he never succumbed to the more extreme severities of Mondrian's art.

Nicholson was a member of the Parisian nonfigurative artists' group *Abstraction-Création* from 1933 to 1935. He showed with the avant-garde Unit One group in London in 1934; and in 1935 he led the Seven and Five Society (of which he had been a member since 1924 and chairman since 1926) to exhibit nonfigurative work only. He was coeditor in 1937 of the publication *Circle*, which acted as a manifesto for the Abstract group in England.

In 1939 Nicholson and Hepworth settled in Cornwall. There, living in the country for the first time since the 1920s, he partly reverted to figurative themes and his colors became closer to nature even in his abstractions. The underlying strength his work had gained in the 1930s made it possible to endure the relative isolation. When research into abstraction in England was reopened towards 1950, Nicholson's experience was of immeasurable value to younger artists—he provided them with the example he had himself lacked after the First World War.

Nicholson won several international prizes in the 1950s, and had major retrospective exhibitions in the United States (1952-3), in Europe (1955), and at the Tate Gallery (1955 and 1969). The lyrical abstractions he made in the 1950s were among the most impressive achievements of his career. After his third marriage, Nicholson lived in Switzerland from 1958 to 1971. He later lived near Cambridge and in Hampstead, London, and continued to paint and exhibit regularly.

Further reading. Harrison, C. *Ben Nicholson*, London (1969). Nicholson, B. *Paintings, Reliefs, and Drawings* (2 vols.), London (1955 and 1956). Read, H. *Ben Nicholson*, London (1956). Sausmarez, M. de *Ben Nicholson*, London (1969). Summerson, J. *Ben Nicholson*, Harmondsworth (1948).

Nicholson William 1872-1949

The English artist William Newzam Prior Nicholson was a painter in oil of portraits, still lifes, and landscapes; he also worked as both graphic artist and stage designer. Born at Newark-upon-Trent, he studied at Bushey School of Art under (Sir) Hubert von Herkomer, and in Paris at the Académie Julian (1889-90). In 1893 he married Mabel Pryde, sister of the painter James Pryde. He collaborated with James Pryde under the name J. and W. Beggarstaff on a revolutionary series of poster designs. It is for these that he remains most famous, but his later works include many other paintings in oil. He was a sensitive portraitist. He visited the U.S.A., India, and South Africa, and also traveled widely in Europe. He was knighted in 1936.

Niemeyer Oscar 1907-

The leading Brazilian architect Oscar Niemeyer Soares Filho began his career in 1936 when, under the direction of Lucio Costa, he worked with Le Corbusier on the design for the Ministry of Health and Education, Rio de Janeiro (1936-43). Le Corbusier was a powerful influence on Niemeyer; but the latter's own qualities of expressiveness are unique and almost unmatched in 20th-century architecture.

A repertory of exciting forms in reinforced concrete and expansive spaces characterizes Niemeyer's dramatic architecture. The buildings he designed at Pampulha (1942-3) were his first important commission. Many others followed, but Niemeyer is best known for his spectacular work at Brasilia, the new capital planned by Lucio Costa (for example the Parliament Buildings, 1957-60).

Further reading. Niemeyer, O. *The Work of Oscar Niemeyer*, New York (1950). Underwood, D. *Oscar Niemeyer and the Architecture of Brazil*, New York (1994).

Nikias fl. c340-300 BC

Nikias was an Athenian painter. Descriptions of his works, which are all lost, suggest a sober Classical style in which the figures are clearly delineated and stand out from their backgrounds in a sculptural manner. He advocated massive composi-

William Nicholson: The Hill above Harlech; oil on canvas; 53×59cm (21×23in); c1917. Tate Gallery, London

tions, in which this technique would have been essential. He also collaborated with the sculptor Praxiteles, painting his statues. He had a special reputation for his depiction of women. Of his works, the *Perseus with Andromeda* and the *Io* were perhaps the inspiration for versions that have been preserved in Roman wall painting.

Ni Tsan 1301–74

The Chinese painter Ni Tsan was the son of a wealthy merchant family. He showed his cultivated tastes early, making collections. of painting and books. He was a fastidious man who, it is related, had an obsession with cleanliness. He was a young friend of Huang Kung-wang in Chiang-nan, but at the time of the troubles in that region he dispersed his property among his family and took to a wandering life with his wife. Ni Tsan was a limited painter of lake landscapes and bamboo, with a strangely haunting and ascetic style. He built up his landscapes of interlocking spurs and spaces of water to create a deserted, still picture into which no human being ever steps, although there is often an empty pavilion. These repetitive compositions, painted with a dry pale ink and sparing brushwork, have fascinated many painters; however, no follower has ever recaptured the special quality of his work.

The fine example in the C.C. Wang Collection, New York (*Trees in the Valley of the River at Yu-chan*, 1371) is typical of this very personal style. The "stretched" surface composition is delicately bound together and tied to the picture frame, while the recession is expressed by daring spaces of calm water defined with slips of land and a distant hill. The use of ink is such as to create a sense of illumination by soft sunlight.

Noguchi Isamu 1904–88

Isamu Noguchi was an American sculptor born in Los Angeles of mixed Japanese and American parentage. He spent 12 years in Japan (1906–18) before returning to the U.S.A. to finish school in Indiana. After two years of medical school at Columbia University he studied sculpture at the Leonardo da Vinci Art School and at the East Side Art School—both in New York (1924–6). He went to Paris on a Guggenheim Fellowship and spent the years 1927 to 1929 in Brancusi's studio. Be-

Isamu Noguchi: Sign of Peace, engraved on the fountain of the Japanese garden, UNESCO, Paris; 1962

tween 1929 and 1939 he returned to the U.S.A. and then traveled to China and Japan, England and Mexico, studying brush drawing (with Chi Pai Shi in Peking) and pottery (with Uno Junnatsu in Kyoto).

Noguchi's concern was to integrate sculpture with man and his environment. This led him to design dance and theater sets: he began a collaboration with Martha Graham in 1935 which led to more than 20 sets. He also designed playgrounds, gardens, and fountains. Works of his are owned by the Metropolitan and Whitney Museums and the Museum of Modern Art, New York.

Further reading. Fuller, R. B., Noguchi, I. and Rychlak, B. *Isamu Noguchi: a Sculptor's World*, Göttingen, Ger. (2004).

Nolan Sidney 1917–1992

The Australian painter Sidney Robert Nolan was born in Melbourne, where he studied art (c1934–6). He took up painting full-time c1938. His first phase was Abstract, but he turned to representational painting at the beginning of the 1940s. He served in the Australian Army from 1942 to 1945, and first visited Europe in 1951, the year of his first London exhibition.

Sidney Nolan: Glenrowan, from the additional paintings for the second Ned Kelly series; acrylic on board; 91×122cm (36×48in); 1956–7. Tate Gallery, London

Kenneth Noland: Gift; acrylic on canvas; 183×183cm (72×72in); 1961–2. Tate Gallery, London

Nolan became well-known through the two series of paintings inspired by the career of the late-19th-century Australian outlaw, Ned Kelly. The first series (1945–7) was painted in Melbourne; the second (1954–5) in Europe, with a few additional canvases dating from 1956–7 (for example *Glenrowan*, 1956–7; Tate Gallery, London). The Ned Kelly pictures, his finest achievement to date, are characterized by a strong sense of atmosphere interacting with a cunning use of Abstract and quasi-Abstract forms. Nolan is a good landscape painter, with a powerful feeling for the heat and emptiness of the Australian scene.

Since Ned Kelly, Nolan has turned to other themes, such as the legend of Leda and the Swan, and the image of Shakespeare. He has traveled a great deal, visiting Greece, Italy, Africa, Mexico, and Japan.

Further reading. Bonythan, K. (ed.) *Modern Australian Painting and Sculpture 1950–1960*, Adelaide (1960). Lynn, E. *Sidney Nolan: Myth and Imagery*, London (1967). Neville, R. *Ned Kelly: Twenty-Seven Paintings by Sidney Nolan*, London (1964); U.S. edn *The Legend of Ned Kelly, Australia's Outlaw Hero*, New York (1964). Reed, J.R. *Australian Landscape*

Painting, Melbourne (1965).

Noland Kenneth 1924–

Kenneth Noland is one of the best known contemporary American Minimalist painters. He works within a range of 1960s styles collectively named "post-painterly abstraction" by Clement Greenberg. The aim is purely optical, and the practice avoids any drawing, line, value, or depth; the painting is therefore reduced to the "hue" on the surface of the canvas.

Born in Asheville, North Carolina, Noland studied in 1946 at Black Mountain

College in North Carolina. In 1948 and 1949 he worked with Ossip Zadkine in Paris, and in the early 1950s met Morris Louis in Washington. In 1953 Clement Greenberg introduced both artists to the work of Helen Frankenthaler, whose "soak-stain" technique, using thin washes of paint, made a great impression on them. Louis and Noland worked closely together for the rest of the decade, using diluted acrylic paints and bright colors in fluent lyrical shapes on unprimed, unsized canvases.

Noland's preoccupation with the relationship of the image to the containing edge of the picture led him in 1958 away from the freedom of Louis, to a series of studies of concentric rings, or bull's-eyes, using unlikely color combinations. Since 1962 he has, like Frank Stella, pioneered the "shaped" canvas, initially with a series of symmetrical and asymmetrical diamonds or chevrons. In these paintings the edges of the canvas become as structurally important as the center.

In 1964 Noland occupied half the American pavilion at the Venice Biennale, and in 1965 his work was exhibited at the Washington Gallery of Modern Art. In the same year he had a major exhibition at the Jewish Museum in New York. He has remained among the best-known internationally of contemporary American painters. His "shaped" canvases are highly irregular and asymmetrical, resulting in increasingly complex structures of great control and integrity.

Nolde Emil 1867–1956

Born Emil Hansen, the painter Emil Nolde took his name from his birthplace in Schleswig, northern Germany. He first worked as an apprentice wood carver and furniture draftsman. After studying in Munich, Karlsruhe, and Paris, he developed an Impressionist style of painting. He continued in this style until 1904, when his work began to reflect the brilliant flat colors and spontaneous brushwork of Gauguin and Van Gogh. This brought him to the attention of the *Brücke* group which he joined in 1906; he was thus alerted to their interest in primitive art, an influence reflected in his woodcuts.

After 1908, his figure-paintings combine the simplified areas of strong color of his *Brücke* colleagues with the intensity of Ensor, whom he visited in 1911. This influence is apparent in his mask and religious paintings after 1909 (for example, *Last Supper*, 1909; Stiftung Seebüll Ada und Emil Nolde, Seebüll). One of these was rejected by the Berlin Secession in 1910, thus provoking Nolde's attack on the Secession and the foundation of the New Secession. In 1912 he participated in the second *Blaue Reiter* exhibition in Munich, and the *Sonderbund* exhibition in Cologne. Controversies over his work encouraged his isolation, but his interest in primitive art did not wane.

After an extended visit to Asia and the South Seas in 1913 and 1914, he returned to northern Germany, eventually settling at Seebüll in 1926. His late works in watercolor, particularly the "Unpainted Pictures" after 1941 when he was forbidden to paint by the Nazis, were done from memory and are remarkable for their luminous, gently floating colors (Stiftung Seebüll Ada und Emil Nolde, Seebüll).

Nollekens Joseph 1737–1823

The English sculptor Joseph Nollekens was the son of a Flemish painter working in London. He was apprenticed in 1750 to the sculptor Peter Scheemaeckers. A brilliant student, he won three prizes at the Society of Arts. In 1760 he went to Rome, where he practiced very successfully for ten years, making busts and restoring and copying Classical sculptures. On his return to London he established a large and prosperous practice in portraiture and monumental sculpture. Nollekens was a hard-headed businessman, and amassed a great fortune from his work; but he was also a sensitive and highly intelligent artist. Among his own works he preferred his ideal statues, but these were in fact his weakest point, and he is remembered chiefly today as an outstandingly fine portrait sculptor.

Nötke Bernt c1440–1509

Bernt Nötke was a German sculptor and painter. Born in Lassan in Pomerania (Poland), he was the greatest sculptor of his day in the Baltic area. For much of his life he lived in Lübeck, where the majority of his works may now be seen in the St Annen-Museum. In 1467 it is recorded that he was exempted from the Guild regulations, indicating the elevated status he enjoyed over contemporary German artists. In 1477 he carved a magnificent cross in polychromed wood for Lübeck Cathedral.

Nötke did not work only in Germany. He was one of several Lübeck artists of the period who went to Scandinavia, where some of his greatest works survive. For Aarhus Cathedral, Denmark, he produced the altar triptych between 1478 and 1482. The precise authorship of the several parts of the work is not certain, but it seems likely that Nötke was responsible for the paintings and his assistants for the sculpture. In 1483 he painted the triptych for the high altar at Reval Cathedral, Sweden; and then in 1484 he traveled to Stockholm, where he remained for the greater part of the next 13 years. During that time he carved in wood his best-known work, the great 10 ft (4 m) high polychrome statue of *St George and the Dragon*, for the church of St Nicholas in Stockholm. It was an important work, commissioned by the Swedish Chancellor to commemorate victory over the Danes on St George's day, 1471.

Stylistically, a number of other works in Scandinavia have been attributed to Nötke and his pupil Henning von der Heide, among them the *St John the Evangelist* in Roskilde Cathedral, Denmark. However, he had returned to Lübeck by c1500. He then produced his great panel painting, the only one firmly attributed to him, of *The Mass of St Gregory*, for the Marienkirche (it was destroyed in 1942). About 1508 he began his last known work, the incised bronze tomb slab in memory of Herman Hutterock, also in the Marienkirche.

At a time when other artists had lapsed into depicting the detailed trivialities so characteristic of the High Gothic style, Nötke never lost sight of the underlying spiritual content in the subject matter of his works. They also display an easy elegance and a fastidious eye for realism, not least in his use of materials. These qualities are most striking in the *St George and the Dragon*. The tableau has an overall bristling Gothic appearance, but through it emerges the divinity of St George and the demonism of the dragon. In his quest for realism, Nötke gave the saint's horse real horsehair, while the dragon boasts elk horns. *The Mass of St Gregory* is equally skilled. The picture displays an awareness of the ritualistic meaning of the scene, which is witnessed by several realistically portrayed faces. Behind them a rugged landscape appears through the window. Nötke's colors, though strong, were nevertheless applied with restraint.

O

Oderisi da Gubbio 1240–99

The Italian painter Oderisi da Gubbio was mentioned by Dante as an artist whose reputation rests on his skill as an illuminator. In Dante's famous comparison of how Giotto was now considered better than Cimabue, the poet said that Oderisi was in his turn outshone by Franco Bolognese. No one has identified any of his work with certainty, but manuscripts at Modena (a Gradual in the Este Library; 'R.I.6) and Turin (the *Informatium of Justinian*, Biblioteca Nazionale; E.I.8.) are often connected with either Oderisi or Franco. Dante's comparison is telling: for the Bolognese school of illumination, and the manuscripts mentioned, show a developing classicism; this can be paralleled by the art of Giotto, whose style finds ready acceptance in Bologna in the 14th century.

O'Keeffe Georgia 1887–1986

The American painter Georgia O'Keeffe was born in Wisconsin. After 1949 she lived in Abiquiu, New Mexico. Distinctive features of her work are the ambivalence of its imagery, and the breadth of its artistic language; this ranges from abstraction to representation, but always has its origins in nature. O'Keeffe studied at the Art Institute of Chicago (1905–6) and the Art Students League, New York (1907–8). She worked for four years as a commercial artist before returning to painting. At this period she was inspired by the ideas of Arthur Dow, with whom she later studied at Columbia University (1914–15). From 1912 to 1918 she taught art. In 1915 O'Keeffe made her first self-consciously original works. These were shown to Alfred Stieglitz, who gave her a solo exhibition in 1917 at the 291 gallery. She gave up teaching in 1918 and moved to New York.

Until 1924, when she married Stieglitz, O'Keeffe's drawings and paintings in watercolor and oil were predominantly Abstract. Works such as *Blue and Green Music* (1919; Art Institute of Chicago) were unique in form, expressive power, and chromatic range. O'Keeffe is probably best known for her large, close-up views of flowers, such as *Black Iris* (1926; Metropolitan Museum, New York) with their sexual associations—she never painted the human figure as such. After the 1920s she often painted in series, such as the six versions of *Jack-in-a-Pulpit* (1930). In 1929 she made her first visit to New Mexico; thereafter she visited the State every year, buying a house in Abiquiu in 1945, the year before Stieglitz's death.

In the 1930s and 1940s she added new imagery to her range—animal bones, the New Mexico landscape, her adobe house. A surrealist feeling emerges in some of the bone pictures. For example, a skull hovers above a desert landscape in *From the Faraway Nearby* (1937; Metropolitan Museum, New York). In 1953 she visited Europe for the first time and began to travel widely. Flying introduced more new imagery—skyscrapers with clouds, views of the land from above. O'Keeffe won numerous awards, and exhibited often in the United States.

Further reading. Buhler Lynes, B. et al. *O'Keeffe's O'Keeffes: the Artist's Collection*, London (2001). Drohojowska-Philp, H. *Full Bloom: the Art and Life of Georgia O'Keeffe*, New York (2004).

Hassrick, P. H. *Georgia O'Keeffe Museum*, New York (1997). Messinger, L. M. *Georgia O'Keeffe*, New York (2001). Robinson, R. and O'Keeffe, G. *Georgia O'Keeffe: a Life*, Hanover (1999).

Okyo Maruyama 1733–95

The Japanese painter Maruyama Okyo was the founder of the *Maruyama* School, and has been a major influence on Japanese painting since. His original synthesis of native brushwork with Chinese and Western elements created a manner that came to dominate over others and that formed the basis for the modern *Nihonga* style.

He was born of farming stock near Kameoka, not far from Kyoto. The accident of birthplace was important in his work. He retained throughout his life an affection for the gentle agricultural landscapes of his home area, for the more dramatic Hozu Gorge through which he would have passed on the way to Kyoto, and for farming people and the ordinary townspeople of Kyoto, among whom he lived as a boy when working there in the toy industry.

Okyo was little educated in an age of increasing prestige for scholarship and his calligraphy was never more than barely competent; as a result his genius was purely visual. His painting was unpretentious, done joyously for its own sake, and these features he passed on to his School.

At 16 Okyo went to study with the *Kano* artist Ishida Yutei. The *Kano* School had by then reached a low point of academic dullness and resistance to innovation, and Okyo was soon looking for more vigorous attitudes. His grounding in *Kano* monochrome brushwork remained with him and he always stayed half a *Kano* artist, but he was so much more talented than his orthodox contemporaries that his style appears completely new.

By the time he reached his mid thirties he had studied Western perspective, through designing copperplate prints for the recently imported *camera oscura*. He had also studied the works of the Japanese and Chinese old masters in the Kyoto collection, and the contemporary decorative Chinese painting practiced in Nagasaki, and from all of these he fashioned a new style.

Okyo's most important innovation was his insistence on painting from nature, exemplified in his detailed sketchbooks of insects in the Tokyo National Museum. It

Georgia O'Keeffe: White Canadian Barn no. 2; oil on canvas; 30×76cm (12×30in); 1932. Metropolitan Museum, New York.

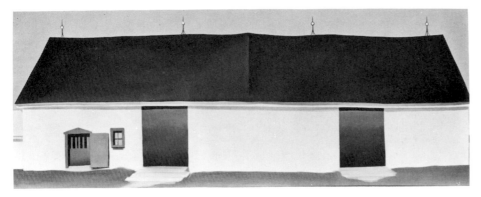

was this above all that breathed new life into Japanese art. From this time he became the most celebrated artist of his day.

Okyo pioneered or revived a number of painting styles which were taken up by his followers. They include the following six types: dramatic decorative screens influenced by Western perspective and sense of space (*Hozu Rapids*, Nishiyama Collection; *Snowy Pines*, Mitsui Collection); studies of nature in free, relaxed brushwork (*Wisteria Screens*, Nezu Museum of Art, Tokyo); unidealized genre paintings (*Seven Happinesses and Seven Misfortunes*, handscrolls, Eman'in, Otsu); formal portraits of Chinese beauties and bird-and-flower paintings in the Chinese style (*Peacocks and Paeonies*, Eman'in, Otsu); displays of ink monochrome of extraordinary virtuosity (*Dragon Screens*, Tokyo National Museum); and soft and misty landscape (screens of *Spring* and *Summer*, Yamato Bunkakan, Nara). Okyo's direct pupils included Matsumura Goshun, Nagasawa Rosetsu, Komai Genki, Watanbe Nangaku, Yamaguchi Soken, and Mori Tessan.

Olbrich Josef Maria 1867–1908

The career of the Austrian architect and designer Josef Olbrich was brief but full of inspiration. He worked as chief draftsman for Otto Wagner and contributed designs for the Vienna Stadtbahn project. One of the cofounders of the Vienna Secession, he designed its exhibition building in 1898. His brilliant *Jugendstil* graphics for *Ver Sacrum*, the magazine of the Secession, were extremely influential; more than anyone else involved, Olbrich's work came to be identified with a Secession style.

In 1899 Olbrich left Vienna for Darmstadt. There he built a large part of the Duke of Hesse's new colony for artists, including his own house (1901) and the transitional and prophetic Hochzeitsturm (1908).

Oldenburg Claes 1929–

Claes Oldenburg is a Swedish-born sculptor and environmentalist. The son of a diplomat, he traveled a great deal during his childhood. After graduating from Yale University, and working as a reporter, he studied at the Chicago Art Institute with Paul Weighardt (1952–4). After moving to New York he worked for a while as a

Claes Oldenburg: Proposed Monument for Thames River, Thames Ball; crayon, ink, watercolor on postcard; 9×14cm (3½×5½in); 1967. Private collection

painter. With a group of New York artists that included Jim Dine, he became involved in a new kind of participatory art known as the "happening". He then turned to painted plaster replicas of food (*Two Cheeseburgers, with Everything*, 1962; Museum of Modern Art, New York). Oldenburg's involvement with popular products (including ice creams, pies, baked potatoes) was an important aspect of the first phase of Pop art.

Further reading. Baro, G. *Claes Oldenburg: Drawings and Prints*, London and New York (1969). Kramer, H. *The Age of the Avant-Garde*, London (1974). Oldenburg, C. *Notes in Hand: Miniatures of my Notebook Pages*, New York (1971). Oldenburg, C. *Claes Oldenburg and Coosje van Bruggen: Large-Scale Projects*, London (1994).

Olitski Jules 1922–

The American painter and sculptor Jules Olitski was born in Snovsk, Russia. He studied in New York at the National Academy of Design, the Beaux-Arts Institute, and New York University (1940–2), and at the Zadkine School of Sculpture, Paris (1949), before teaching at Post College, Conn. and Bennington College, Vt. until 1967. In the 1960s Olitski made large Abstract stained paintings. In 1965 he began his distinctive spray paintings, in which he emphasized the edges and colored surface with hand-painted features.

During the 1970s he came to rely upon thick gestural paint surfaces. Since 1968, when he made his first painted steel sculptures, Olitski has worked with equal critical acclaim in both media. He represented the U.S.A. in the 1966 Venice Biennale.

Jules Olitski: Thigh Smoke; acrylic on canvas; 424×235cm (167×93in); 1966. Collection of the First National Bank, Seattle

Further reading. Olitski, J. *The Prints of Jules Olitski, Catalogue Raisonné 1954–1989*, New York (1989). Olitski, J. *With Love and Disregard: New Paintings by Jules Olitski, an Eightieth Birthday Celebration*, New York (2002).

Oliver Isaac, the Elder
fl. 1568–1617

The English miniaturist Isaac Oliver was born in Rouen of Huguenot parents. He lived in London from 1568, and was apprenticed to Nicolas Hilliard *c*1580. Although he was influenced by Hilliard, Oliver showed a strong preference for Flemish masters and the Italian Mannerists, whose works he copied in Italy in 1596. By 1595 Oliver had become a rival to Hilliard, and in 1604 was appointed limner to Queen Anne of Denmark. Unlike the work of Hilliard, Oliver's limning often resembles a reduction of full-scale portraiture, and his dramatic lighting and shadows in the Flemish manner show a taste for composition on an ambitious scale.

Opicinus de Canistris
1296–*c*1350

The Italian author and draftsman Opicinus de Canistris produced a remarkable series of visionary drawings after a mental breakdown. He was born near Pavia and trained for the priesthood, but poverty forced him to work as a teacher and, from 1315, as a professional illuminator of manuscripts; he also studied medicine. In 1329 he was appointed to the Papal Chancery at Avignon in recognition of his activities as a political writer. His breakdown in 1334 left his right hand paralyzed. This ended his Chancery work, but he was still able to draw—though he claimed that the pictures were not produced by any normal human means.

Certainly, these works (preserved in two manuscripts in the Vatican) are unlike anything else in medieval art. Although his style is typically Lombard and unremarkable, and although the drawings are made up of conventional features derived from cartography, medical illustrations, and schemata, these elements are combined to create grotesque images which are both fantastic and didactic—and also uniquely personal for a Trecento artist.

The biography of Opicinus is known from a pictorial composition consisting of

Isaac Oliver the Elder: Frances Howard, Countess of Somerset and Essex; watercolor on vellum; diameter 13cm (5in); *c*1595. Victoria and Albert Museum, London

40 concentric circles, one for each year of his life, divided into 365 segments; on this "calendar" Opicinus inscribed important events in the appropriate place. He surrounded the whole with busts of the evangelists and four self-portraits, each showing him at a different age.

Many of this artist's drawings are based on the map of Europe, reflecting recent developments in cartography; but the land-masses and seas are, with the addition of a few extra lines, transformed into deformed human figures. Copious inscriptions explain the symbolism of these pictures. Other drawings employ familiar Christian motifs—the Crucifixion, the Virgin and Child—but the scale of the figures varies enormously, creating a hallucinatory effect: tiny bodies are superimposed on gigantic ones, suggesting contemporary medical illustrations of the foetus in the womb. Indeed, a marked sexual ele-

ment pervades Opicinus' work; this, with his mental history, has made him of special interest to students of psychotic art.

Orcagna 1308?–*c*68

Andrea di Cione, known as Orcagna, was a Florentine painter, sculptor, and architect. His signature on his magnificent sculptured *Tabernacle* (1359) in the church of Orsanmichele, Florence, suggests that he thought of himself primarily as a painter. But owing to the loss of many of his frescoes, such as those in the Florentine churches of S. Croce and S. Maria Novella (fragments of which survive), his chief fame in this respect rests on his signed and dated Strozzi Altarpiece (1357) in the Strozzi Chapel, S. Maria Novella, Florence. Our knowledge of his position as "capomaestro" in both Orsanmichele (by 1356) and Orvieto Cathedral (1358–*c*62) as well as his advice on Florence Cathedral (1366), means that, paradoxically, there is more evidence of his work as sculptor, architect, even as mosaicist (at Orvieto), than as a painter.

The Strozzi Altarpiece, however, is enough to show that Orcagna is the most important Florentine painter of his time. It acted not only as chapel altarpiece but also as a focus for the fresco decoration on the chapel walls, which consists of the *Last Judgment, Heaven* and *Hell*, painted by Orcagna's brother, Nardo di Cione.

The theme of the Last Judgment, which also formed the subject of Orcagna's frescoes in S. Croce, can be seen as typical of the age, and probably reflects the experience of the 1348 Black Death. While the first half of the 14th century is marked by an increasing humanity and tenderness in the painting of sacred subjects in Tuscany, the period of Orcagna's activity sees this replaced by an emphasis on the supernatural, hieratic relationship of God to Man, more typical of the previous century. The change in attitude is embodied in a change in style. The creation of three-dimensional realistic space, so characteristic of Giotto and his followers, is not the dominating concern of Orcagna. Instead he contrasts the realistic painting of bodies and drapery with an equivocal space, and stresses the surface pattern formed by severe silhouettes and an unforeshortened ground.

In the centre of the Strozzi Altarpiece is the figure of Christ the Judge surrounded by seraphim, with two pairs of saints at either side. The gold background has vestigial columns incised upon it which connect the back of the ground ("behind" the figures) and the pendentives of the frame ("in front of" the figures). The result is a highly sophisticated spatial tension. This is only clearly resolved in the powerful figure of Christ who, in contrast with the other figures of the altarpiece, is seen in a starkly uncompromising frontal pose.

As well as Nardo di Cione, Orcagna had another brother, Jacopo, who also worked with him. Under Orcagna's leadership, the three together formed the most influential Florentine workshop of the period.

Ordóñez Bartolomé *fl.* 1517–20

The Spanish sculptor Bartolomé Ordóñez was born in Burgos. He was the first of the so-called "Four Eagles" of Spanish Renaissance sculpture. First documented at

Naples in 1517 (where he worked on the Carraciolo Altar in S. Giovanni a Carbonara), he was in Barcelona in 1518 (where he worked on the *trascoro*—the front part on the choir screen—in the cathedral). While in Barcelona, in 1519, he was given the commissions for the tombs of Philip the Handsome and Joan the Mad (Royal Chapel, Granada) and of Cardinal Cisneros (Magistral Church, Alcalá do Henares) by Charles V. The commissions had originally been given to Domenico Fancelli, who died in 1519 and who may have been Ordóñez's master. In order to carry out these commissions Ordóñez moved his workshop to Carrara, where he died in December 1520. One of his last works was the tomb of Bishop Fonseca, in Coca (1520).

Orley Bernaert van 1491/2–1542

The Flemish painter Bernaert van Orley worked mainly at the court of the Regent of the Netherlands, Margaret of Austria, at Brussels. Unlike many of his Flemish contemporaries, who simply incorporated Italian motifs into painting, van Orley had a profound knowledge of the principles of Italian High Renaissance design. The Altarpiece of the Visions of Job (1521; Musées Royaux des Beaux-Arts de Belgique, Brussels) is indebted to Raphael, whose compositions he knew both through engravings and through the original cartoons for the Sistine tapestries, then in the Netherlands. Van Orley himself was highly successful as a designer of tapestry and stained glass. His portraits (for example *Dr Zelle*, 1519; Musées Royaux des Beaux-Arts de Belgique, Brussels) are more schematic, less individually characterized than those of his contemporary, Gossaert.

Orozco José 1883–1949

The Mexican mural painter José Clemente Orozco was one of the three major Mexican muralists of the 20th century, the other two being Diego Rivera and Siqueiros. Born in Ciudad Guzman, Jalisco, Orozco first trained as an agronomist (1895–9), then from 1908 to 1914 he studied art sporadically at the Academia San Carlos in Mexico City. During the Mexican Revolution he worked as a political caricaturist and propagandist (1911–17). From 1923 he painted in public buildings large murals whose thematic content is derived from his Mexican Revolution and Civil War experi-

Bernaert van Orley: Portrait of Emperor Charles V; panel; 72×52cm (28×20in); c1516. Museum of Fine Arts, Budapest

ences (for example, *Prometheus*, 1950; Pomona College, Claremont, California). He spent the years 1930 to 1934 in the U.S.A. and Europe. In his work Orozco angrily criticizes the futile struggles in which people are needlessly sacrificed. His use of color is sober and austere, his forms often tormented (*Man in Flames*; fresco; 1938–9, Hospicio Cabañas, Guadalajara), **and he treated his subjects with a blend of unsentimental social criticism and compassion.**

Further reading. Charlot, J. *An Artist on Art: Collected Essays of Jean Charlot*, Honolulu (1972). Helm, M. *Man of Fire: José Clemente Orozco*, New York (1953). Orozco, J.C. *An Autobiography*, Austin, Tex. (1962). Orozco, J.C. *The Artist in New York: Letters to Jean Charlot and Unpublished Writings 1925–1929*, Austin Tex. and London (1974). Reed, A. *J.C. Orozco*, New York (1956). Reed, A. *The Mexican Muralists*, New York (1960).

Ostade Adriaen van 1610–84

Adriaen Jansz. van Ostade was a Dutch painter and etcher from Haarlem who specialized in low-life genre scenes. He was probably a pupil of Frans Hals about the same time as Adriaen Brouwer, a painter whose pictures influenced his subject matter, style, and content. Ostade's pictures from the 1630s are painted in subdued brown tones with little local color, and generally depict boisterous tavern or

Adriaen van Ostade: The Alchemist; detail; oil on wood panel; full size 34×45cm (14×18in); 1661. National Gallery, London

hovel scenes of drunken, dancing, or brawling peasants. The treatment of such themes is good-humored and without satire.

In the 1640s Ostade's work acquired deepening contrasts of light and shadow and a greater sense of atmosphere. After *c*1650 his peasants became less rowdy and more respectable, his colors richer, his tonality lighter, and his technique more refined (for example, *The Alchemist*, 1661; National Gallery, London). The lessening of vulgarity (which is accompanied by a certain loss of vitality) may be related to changes in the artist's clientele, his financial success, and his marriage to a woman from a higher social class than himself.

Isaack van Ostade (1621–49) was the brother and a pupil of Adriaen. His early pictures are similar to his brother's low-life scenes but he later inclined towards landscape, notably atmospheric silvery-gray winter scenes with many figures.

Oud J.J.P. 1890–1963

The Dutch architect Jacobus Johannes Pieter Oud was born at Purmerend, near Amsterdam. He completed his studies at the Technical University, Delft. In 1917 he was a cofounder of the *De Stijl* movement. His early projects (terrace houses at Scheveningen and a factory at Purmerend) were inspired in part by *De Stijl* principles. After he was appointed City Architect of Rotterdam in 1918 he designed standardized workers' dwellings for the city's Spangen settlement. Oud left *De Stijl* in 1921 but continued partly to apply its principles, emphasizing social context, in designing large housing developments at the Hook of Holland (1924), Kiefhoek, and Rotterdam (1925). His book, *Dutch Architecture*, was published in 1926 by the Bauhaus, where he had lectured in 1922. He built a terrace of small houses at the International Exhibition, Stuttgart, in 1927. Throughout his long career Oud completed many important architectural projects.

Oudry Jean-Baptiste 1686–1755

Jean-Baptiste Oudry was a French painter of hunting and still-life subjects. The pupil first of his father, then of Michel Serre, and especially of Nicolas de Largillière, he continued the tradition of still life and animal painting already well established by Desportes. The type and style of these pictures derive from painters of the Rubens school, such as Frans Snyders and Jan Fyt, or the Dutch Jan Weenix; but Oudry's art is more decorative and Rococo in form and color than the earthier art of Desportes.

A member of the Académie in 1719, he began as a history painter, and also painted portraits. His favorite subjects were of the hunt, and his chief patron Louis XV. For the King, he designed a celebrated series of large tapestries, *The Hunts of Louis XV* (1733–46; cartoons at Fontainebleau), to be executed at the Gobelins works. These skillfully reconcile the older stylized perspectives of decorative tapestries with a more acute sense of realism. Oudry made many studies in the royal forests of Compiègne and Fontainebleau.

In 1726 Oudry became a designer at the Beauvais tapestry works, rising to Director in 1734. Here he employed the young François Boucher, and completely reorganized the works. He introduced more intimate, simple and natural forms, styles, and colors into tapestry design. In 1736, he was made Superintendent of the Gobelins works. As in the case of Boucher, working on tapestry designs had a profound effect on the decorative aspects of Oudry's painting. He also worked for the courts of Denmark, Sweden, and especially Mecklenburg-Schwerin. Oudry's interest in realism is also seen in his very fine landscape drawings, and he seems to have encouraged other artists in this.

Ouwater Albert van *fl. c*1445–*c*80

Albert van Ouwater was a Dutch painter, apparently based in Haarlem. Apart from a solitary documentary reference of 1467, we are entirely dependent upon Carel van Mander's *Schilderboek* of 1604 for information about him. This states that Geertgen tot Sint Jans was his pupil and that he excelled in the painting of landscape. It also describes what is today his only surviving identified work, *The Raising of Lazarus* in the Staatliche Museen, Berlin. This painting implies a degree of association with Bouts and a knowledge of

Jean-Baptiste Oudry: The Farm; oil on canvas; 130×212cm (51×83in); 1750. Louvre, Paris

southern Netherlandish art. *The Raising of Lazarus* is iconographically unprecedented in that it depicts this scene within an interior, rather than out of doors. Ouwater was the dominant artistic personality active in the northern Netherlands in the middle of the 15th century. He is doubly important as the master of Geertgen tot Sint Jans.

Overbeck Johann 1789–1869

Johann Friedrich Overbeck was a German painter and draftsman born in Lübeck. He studied at the Vienna Academy (1806–9), but preferred to frequent the circle around Eberhard Wächter. His friendship with Franz Pforr led to the formation in 1809 of the St Luke Brotherhood (also known as the Nazarenes), one of whose aims was the revival of Christian art. Overbeck was particularly dedicated to this ideal, which he sought to realize by painting religious subjects in the style of Raphael and Perugino (for example, *The Entry into Jerusalem*, 1809–24; formerly Marienkirche, Lübeck, destroyed 1942). Besides the sweetness of expression thereby achieved, the strict use of local colors and the emphasis on line and contour give these works the clarity and flatness of frescoes.

Overbeck's move to Rome in 1810 allowed him to study the Vatican frescoes of Pintoricchio and Raphael and greatly increased the Italianate influence in his work. He acknowledged this debt in the painting *Italia and Germania* (1811–23; Neue Pinakothek, Munich), which expresses not only his own love of Italian art but Germany's constant yearning for the South. Pforr's death in 1812 precipitated a spiritual crisis in Overbeck's life, which he surmounted by becoming a Catholic in 1813. It was probably Overbeck who suggested the religious subject of *Joseph in Egypt* for the frescoes painted in the house of the Prussian Consul in Rome, Salomon Bartholdi (1815–16; now in the Nationalgalerie, East Berlin). His own contributions to the decorations are remarkable for the degree to which he created a personal idiom out of his Italian models. The balance he achieved between a lyrical expression of nature and a humane view of man is truly Romantic in spirit.

These same qualities are evident in the work he did for the Casino Massimo frescoes (1818–27; Casino Massimo, Rome). Typically, Overbeck chose to treat the subject, Tasso's *Gerusalemme Liberata*, undramatically, emphasizing the Christian rather than the heroic aspects of the epic. In 1829 he painted the highly persuasive fresco *The Miracle of the Roses* (Portiuncula Chapel, S. Maria degli Angeli, Assisi). In this painting religious fervor is tempered by a simple, warm humanity; but

his later works, like *The Triumph of Religion in the Arts* (1840; Städelsches Kunstinstitut, Frankfurt am Main) are marred by a dogmatic Catholicism. His line hardened and his color often became cold and enamel-like.

Overbeck became celebrated in his later years. He only returned twice to Germany, but was visited in Rome by statesmen and artists alike. He was particularly influential in England on artists such as W. Dyce and Ford Madox Brown. His frescoes were cited as a model for the decorations of the Houses of Parliament.

Ozenfant Amédée 1886–1966

The French painter Amédée Ozenfant was born at Saint-Quentin. He published the magazine *L'Élan* (1915–17) and, with Charles-Édouard Jeanneret (later called le Corbusier), *L'Esprit Nouveau* (1920–5) and *Aprés le Cubisme* (1919). These expounded the ideas of Purism embodied in his paintings: the removal of the romantic element from Cubism and the use of classically calm, architectonic principles of composition. His mural designs of the 1920s and 1930s culminated in an enormous composition called *Life* (1931–8; Musée National d'Art Moderne, Paris). His theoretical writings include *Art* (1928) and a diary of the period 1931–4. He lived in New York from 1939 to his death.

P

Pacher Michael c1435–98

The greatest sculptor and painter of the late Gothic in Austria, Michael Pacher is documented as a citizen of Brunico (Bruneck) in the Val Pusteria (Pustertal) from 1467 until 1496. He then transferred his center of activity to Salzburg.

A now lost altarpiece is recorded as having been signed and dated 1465, and the contract for the altarpiece in the old parish church of Gríes (Gries) outside Bolzano (Bozen) is dated 27 May 1471. In it Pacher was instructed to follow the pattern of the high altarpiece of the parish church of Bolzano (by Hans von Judenburg, 1422–3), and the composition is accordingly conservative.

On 13 December 1471 Pacher signed the contract for the large-scale altarpiece in the pilgrimage church of St Wolfgang in the Salzkammergut, which he signed and dated 1481, and presumably work on the Gríes Altarpiece continued well after 1471. Similarly, although the documentary evidence suggests that the altarpiece for the parish church of S. Lorenzo in Pusteria (St Lorenzen) was donated in 1462–3, the actual execution of that altarpiece, of which only the carved *Madonna Enthroned* survives (in situ), stretched over many years.

The painted panels depicting scenes of *The Life of St Lawrence* (Alte Pinakothek, Munich, and Österreichische Galerie, Vienna) probably formed part of the S. Lorenzo Altarpiece, but they reveal contacts with Italian 15th-century painting, especially the works of Mantegna, not detectable in the carved figures.

This contrast is even more apparent in Pacher's masterpiece, the St Wolfgang Altarpiece. His tentative attempts, in the Grées Altarpiece, to give a greater illusion of depth by adding painted angels behind are replaced in the St Wolfgang Altarpiece by a fully three-dimensional composition. Again depicting *The Coronation of the Virgin*, the figures and the architecture are completely integrated: the principal

Michael Pacher: altarpiece of The Fathers of the Church; center panel 216×196cm (85×77in), wing paintings 206×93cm (81×37in); c1483. Alte Pinakothek, Munich

protagonists of the *tableau vivant* grow out of the dark, mysterious recesses of the shrine, and the intricate web of pierced canopies is extended up into the elaborate cresting of figures and pinnacles. In this carved and gilt complex there are no echoes of the Italian Renaissance; the evolution of Pacher as a sculptor reveals instead contact with the sculptural traditions of the Upper Rhine, and possibly with Nikolaus Gerhaert van Leyden at Constance, as well as with the engravings of the Master ES.

On the other hand the style of Pacher as a painter, in the wings of the St Wolfgang Altarpiece, shows such a depth of understanding for rationally constructed spaces that direct experience of Italian Renais-

sance painting, probably in Padua, must be postulated. These opposing developments are brought together in the altarpiece of *The Fathers of the Church* from Novacella (Neustift), now in the Alte Pinakothek, Munich, which dates from *c*1483. Pacher was active in Salzburg in 1484, and for longer periods during the years 1496 to 1498. The last payment to him for the destroyed altarpiece formerly in the Franziskanerkirche is dated 7 July, 1498. By 24 August 1498 Pacher was dead.

Further reading. Hempel, E. *Michael Pacher*, Vienna (1931). Rasmo, N. *Michael Pacher*, London (1971) and Milan (1969).

Padarath *c*1550–*c*1650

Padarath was a Mughal painter in the reigns of Akbar (1556–1605) and Jahangir (1605–27). Very little is known about him. One of his most remarkable works is *The Mountain Sheep* from the Royal Albums in the Chester Beatty Library, Dublin. The drawing is subtle, the colors are restrained yet richly glowing with a dominant dark red. It rivals some of the finest animal paintings of Mansur and Abul Hasan. In the Chester Beatty *Akbarnama* album, *Himu Brought Before Akbar* is by Padarath. Another of his works is in the *Anwar-i-Suhayli* (British Library, London).

Paik Nam June 1932–

The South Korean video artist and performance artist Nam June Paik was born in Seoul. He studied music at the University of Tokyo (1952–6) and then moved to West Germany, where he came into contact with John Cage and other members of the Fluxus group.

Paik became involved with the group's irrational "Happenings," which often combined music and live performance. In 1963 he staged *Exposition of Music— Electronic Television*, a performance piece featuring 12 television sets, all electronically modified to create unique effects; this has generally been credited as the first example of "Video art." After creating similar video projects, in 1964 Paik moved to New York, where he began a long-term professional partnership with the cellist Charlotte Moorman.

Throughout the 1970s, '80s, and '90s, Paik continued to create videos, video

Nam June Paik: High Tech Allergy; video installation; 1995. Kunstmuseum, Wolfsburg

sculptures, and multimedia installations. Generally speaking, his video work is characterized by a dreamlike quality in which technologically manipulated visual forms and sound flow together into an overwhelming sensory experience. These works also sometimes contain Post-Modern social commentary on the effects of television and technology; for example, in *TV Buddha* (1974), a Buddha sits transfixed in front of his own image on a television screen. As he became interested in the issue of globalism in the late 20th century, Paik sent live satellite broadcasts to locales throughout the world.

Palladio Andrea 1508–80

Andrea Palladio was perhaps the most distinguished architect working in northern Italy during the 16th century. Certainly to contemporary eyes he was the most famous. Although he was also a builder of churches and palaces, it is his villas that have attracted greatest attention. The villas provided much of the inspiration for the style called Palladianism which rapidly gained currency in England and the United States during the 17th and 18th centuries. The understanding of the work of Inigo Jones, Lord Burlington, or Thomas Jeffer-

Andrea Palladio: the Villa Rotunda, near Vicenza; built 1566–7

son is impossible without an appreciation of Palladio and his book *I Quattro Libri dell'Architettura* ("The Four Books of Architecture").

The life of Palladio is well documented. He was born as Andrea di Pietro in Padua in 1508. His family had moved to Vicenza—not very far away—by 1521, and there Palladio continued his apprenticeship as a mason. He remained in Vicenza and later Venice until his death in 1580. By the accident of birth, he was therefore two things that are of considerable importance in understanding his career and later reputation: he was northern and provincial. Because he chose to remain as such, visiting only briefly the artistic magnet of Rome, success was the greater struggle and fame had perforce to be captured rather than sought.

Palladio was lucky. His translation from di Pietro to Palladio in 1540 marked the real start of his architectural career, and simultaneously his encounter with what may be termed the Vicentine Enlightenment, particularly with Gian Giorgio Trissino. In his work at Trissino's villa at Cricoli in 1538 he was a mason rather than designer, but his latent talents were sufficiently displayed to impress his patron. Trissino took him to Rome the following year and introduced him in 1542 to the important Thiene family. He was involved with their Vicentine palace, and on the death of the designer Giulio Romano in 1546 he took over as architect. He revisited Rome in 1547, and in 1549 won the important commission in Vicenza for the rebuilding of the basilica.

The basilica was a 15th-century building whose surrounding loggias had partially collapsed in 1446; to rebuild them was Palladio's commission. His solution was an outrageously modern one for Vicenza, redolent of Classical ideas, and closely inspired by his visits to Rome. He built a system of what were really small triumphal arches, loosely based on the arch at Aquino, and derived in scale from a structure such as the Theater of Marcellus in Rome. In more contemporary terms it showed a familiarity with Sansovino's Library at S. Marco, Venice (begun in 1537), and a more than diligent reading of Serlio's *Architettura*. This harmonious blending of antique and modern was totally successful, both in visual terms and—of more importance for Palladio's career—with his scholarly patrons in the Vicentine Council.

Close on the heels of his basilica commission followed three villas: the Villa Pisani (now Placco) in Montagnana (1552), the Villa Cornaro at Piombino Dese (c1560–5), and the Villa Chiericati (1554). Of the three, the Villa Chiericati at Vancimuglio near Vicenza was perhaps the most notable, because of its large freestanding portico of the Ionic order. This appeared here for the first time in Palladio's work and cast a long shadow over his later villas, and indeed the whole Palladian school. It was built for Giovanni Chiericati, the brother of Girolamo (for whom Palladio designed the Palazzo Chiericati in Vicenza;

1551–4) and one of his supporters in the basilican scheme.

In 1554 Palladio again visited Rome, this time in the company of another Vicentine oligarch, Daniele Barbaro. One important result of the visit was the publication in Venice in 1556 of Barbaro's edition of Vitruvius's *De Architectura* which was strongly influenced by Palladio in more than just the illustrations. This collaboration was more solidly expressed in the building of the Villa Barbaro at Maser, before 1558, for Daniele and his brother Marc' Antonio. While the villa—with its cruciform hall similar to that of the Villa Pisani, and its flanking ranges of farm buildings—was typical of Palladio, the extraordinary mannered form of the *nymphaeum* in the rear of the villa, and the windows and balconies of the first floor, were quite untypical. It was possibly a cooperative venture between Barbaro and Palladio, strongly influenced by the Roman architecture of Michelangelo. It was certainly at variance with the other villas of the period: Repeta (c1566), Badoer (1566), and the incomplete Thiene at Cicogna. These villas possibly fix the high watermark of Palladio's reputation in Vicenza, and it is significant for Palladio's growing fame that the builders of both the Villa Pisani and the Villa Cornaro were Venetians.

Palladio's reputation had spread. During the 1560s his most notable work was in Venice, where he built the facade of S. Francesco della Vigna (1562), and began work in 1565 at S. Giorgio Maggiore. At the former his design, with its application of the giant order and incidental theme of smaller columns, was considered sufficiently novel to supersede the earlier scheme of Sansovino. It was repeated by Palladio at S. Giorgio—more obviously in the exterior, more subtly in the nave, where the columns on pedestals and the pilasters in the ground make a decisive unity. His plan was a longitudinal one, with a dome at the crossing, typical of Tridentine church architecture, but with the more startling innovation of the choir ending in a screen through which the church extended into the presbytery. Moreover it synthesized the conflicting forms of the Greek Cross, as at Bramante's

Andrea Palladio: the facade of S. Giorgio Maggiore, Venice; begun in 1565

St Peter's, and the longitudinal plan favored by the Catholic reformists. At the same time, the visual extension of the nave into the presbytery gave an axial drive to the church from the very moment it was entered.

In the secular sphere at this time, Palladio designed two contrasting villa types. The Villa Emo at Fanzolo, begun c1562, followed the Villa Barbaro in the use of the flanking farm buildings to make the villa visually more impressive, and to provide a foil to the style of the main building. The latter was typical of what was to become the villa motif: a pedimented portico—in this case, three bays set flush with the walls rather than projecting—with a window bay on either side. As a facade it was a simpler and more successful version of the one Palladio had used some six years earlier at the Villa Badoer, and this spartan quality well became its role as little more than a farmhouse.

Its companion of 1566–7, the famous Rotunda, was a villa of a very different sort. It was foremost a suburban building on a hillside site just outside Vicenza, where the landscape was to be admired rather than farmed. The building, with its central dome and hall and four projecting porticos, was a reworking of his drawings of the ruined temple of Fortune at Palestrina. (The temple's inspiration is again obvious in the grandiose project for the Villa Trissino of c1566.) The Villa Rotunda existed on its own terms as the sophisticated setting for the social life of a retired clergyman. In this way, it belonged with similar but grander Roman villas such as the Madama (which Palladio had seen and drawn) and the Villa Giulia.

The last decade of Palladio's career was dominated by public commissions. With the death of his Venetian rival, Jacopo Sansovino, in 1570, Palladio ruled Venice as he had done Vicenza. In 1571, he built the Loggia del Capitaniato in Vicenza as a public commission from the City Council. Its function as a sort of secular Benediction Loggia dictated its design. His composition for the facade facing the piazza was three bays of the giant order with balconies in between which served to emphasize the center. It was an impressive design, but one achieved at the expense of classical orthodoxy. For the Venetians, he worked at the Doges' Palace in San Marco, and more spectacularly in 1577 at the church of the Redentore.

The Redentore followed roughly the plan of S. Giorgio except that the emphasis on the longitudinal was substantially increased, and the perforated screen walls at the east end became all the more dramatic. The main facade was a fuller and more sophisticated rendering of the temple front found at S. Giorgio. It was composed according to the formula of the Pantheon: portico against abutment, abutment against dome. Although this was a flatter design, it was amazingly successful as a piece of sculpture when seen from the Piazza of San Marco across the lagoon. It had been conceived as a monument to the terrible plague of 1575–6, and as such this scenographic effect was wholly appropriate.

One of the last of Palladio's works was the eye-catching Teatro Olimpico in Vicenza, begun in 1580. It was completed by Scamozzi in 1583. Its semicircular auditorium was based on the antique amphitheater (of which Verona contained a good example), with a permanent scene front in the form of a triumphal arch decorated with statues of the richer and more distinguished members of the Olympic Academy. This was derived appropriately enough from his own illustration in Barbaro's edition of Vitruvius's *De Architectura*.

Palladio died in August 1580. His memorial was the buildings he had built in and around Vicenza and Venice, and more durably his book, *I Quattro Libri dell'Architettura* of 1570. In Books II and III of this he gave a vivid kaleidoscope of his architectural achievements, made the more catching and influential by the series of woodcut plans, elevations, and sections that accompanied and explained most of his schemes. Of the two other parts, Book I was devoted to the Classical orders and Book IV to antique temples. Palladio, like Serlio, intended to continue with further installments, but none was ever published. It was left to Lord Burlington in 1730 to pick up where he had left off, and to publish his drawings of the Roman baths as *Fabriche Antiche disegnate di Andrea Palladio Vicentino* ("Antique Buildings drawn by Andrea Palladio of Vicenza").

By his contemporary, Vasari, Palladio was extolled as "a man of singular judgment and brain", a summary of whose buildings would make "too long a study to seek to recount the many particulars of the strange and lively inventions and fantasies that are in them". To the succeeding centuries, Palladio's claim was much the same: an architect who balanced classicism and imagination, the grand and the utilitarian, and who appealed widely at a variety of levels. It was the extraordinary range of his talents that made him perennially popular, so much so that even the arch-Romantic Goethe wrote in 1795: "The more one studies Palladio, the more incredible one finds the man's genius, mastery, richness, versatility, and grace."

Further reading. Ackerman, J. S. *Palladio*, Harmondsworth (1966). *Andrea Palladio 1508–1580*, London (1975). Puppi, L. *Andrea Palladio*, London (1975).

Palma Vecchio 1480?–1528

The Venetian painter Jocopo d'Antonio Negretti adopted the name of Palma. He is known as Palma Vecchio, "Old Palma", to distinguish him from his great-nephew, Palma Giovine, "Young Palma" (1544–1628). He came from the Province of Bergamo but was settled in Venice by 1510. We know nothing of his training. If Vasari is right in saying he died aged 48, he will probably have been a little younger than Giorgione and a little older than Titian, and we can see his free and rather luscious style as a parallel development to that of those painters from the later style of Giovanni Bellini.

Palma painted religious pictures and straightforward portraits, but his speciality was pictures of blond women of somewhat ample charms, such as the *Portrait of a Lady* (c1520; Museo Poldi Pezzoli, Milan). Good examples of this are the *Girl with a Lute* in the collection of the Duke of Northumberland at Alnwick Castle, Northumberland, and the *Three Sisters*, or *Three Graces* in the Gemäldegalerie Alte Meister, Dresden, an intimate group in which the Bellinesque formula of an oblong picture of the Madonna flanked by two saints is ingeniously adapted to a secular role (unless these in fact represent the Cardinal Virtues). There is also the splendid *Venus and Cupid* in the Fitzwilliam Museum, Cambridge, with its lovely landscape of blue, green, and gold.

His finest religious painting is the *St Barbara* in S. Maria Formosa, Venice. The beautiful *Holy Family with Saints* in the Gallerie dell'Accademia, Venice, was completed by Titian, who defeated Palma in the year of his death in the competition for the altarpiece of *The Death of St Peter Martyr* in SS. Giovanni e Paolo, Venice.

Palma Vecchio: Portrait of a Gentleman; oil on panel transferred to canvas; 70×56cm (27×22in). Philadelphia Museum of Art

Further reading. Mariacher, G. *Palma il Vecchio*, Milan (1968). Rylands, P. *Palma Vecchio*, Cambridge, England (1992).

Palmer Samuel 1805–81

The English painter and printmaker Samuel Palmer was born in London, where he received his first training with a topographical painter of mean talent. His earliest landscapes, which he began exhibiting at the Royal Academy in 1819, show an admiration for Turner and a studied appreciation of the leading watercolor painters of the period. About 1822 he met his future father-in-law, the landscape and portrait painter John Linnell (1792–1882), who encouraged him to study the engravings of Northern Renaissance artists and to approach painting with attention to nature's minute details.

The immediate impact of Linnell's tuition is apparent in Palmer's 1824 sketchbook (British Museum, London, and Victoria and Albert Museum, London). His development of a more unorthodox landscape style was greatly facilitated by his introduction to William Blake in the same year. Devoutly religious, with a keen poetic sense, Palmer enthusiastically embraced Blake's visionary conception of nature; he was especially wrought up by the "mystic and dreamy glimmer" of Blake's woodcut designs for Thornton's *Virgil*. Some of his finest extant drawings, the six sepia landscapes of 1825 (Ashmolean Museum, Oxford), were the first fruits of this intoxicating friendship. These tightly compacted drawings present a completely private view of a nature that is

numinous in its rich details.

Between 1826 and 1832 Palmer lived at Shoreham, where he adopted a rustic lifestyle and entertained a small group of like-minded Blake devotees who called themselves "The Ancients". The almost artless style of his earlier drawings gave way to a more fluid treatment of landscape, and towards the end of this intensively productive period he began to introduce more conventional pastoral imagery.

The Reform Bill of 1833 brought turmoil to Palmer's sheltered retreat, and by 1836 he was permanently resettled in London. The following year he married Hannah Linnell, and in the company of George Richmond left for Italy where he studied the old masters and the landscape terrain that had inspired Claude. In 1839 he returned to London. Concerned with developing a market for his pictures, he began exhibiting regularly with the Society of Painters in Watercolors from 1843; he became a full member of that society in 1854.

Palmer's finished watercolors during the 1840s and 1850s consisted of topographical views in Italy and England, episodes of English history, and literary illustrations, with Milton providing a recurrent inspiration. Calculated to appeal to a public

rapidly becoming accustomed to the scientific naturalism and bright colors of Pre-Raphaelite painting, these exhibition pictures lack the elemental simplicity and spirituality of his earlier works; however, they can be very impressive technically, especially in their light effects, and they have their own unique poetic charm. During this period he also learned etching, a medium he found most congenial to lyric expression.

In the early 1860s Palmer left London for Reigate. From 1864 he worked on illustrations, some of which he etched, for Milton's *Minor Poems*; he left unfinished at his death his illustrated translation of Virgil's *Eclogues*. The diverse and often conflicting aims that plagued Palmer's art throughout his later career are resolved in the twilight reveries and tranquillity of these last designs.

Further reading. Grigson, G. *Samuel Palmer's Valley of Vision*, London (1960). Grigson, G. *Samuel Palmer: the Visionary Years*, London (1947). Melville, R. *Samuel Palmer*, London (1956).

Panini Giovanni 1691–1765

Giovanni Paolo Panini, an Italian painter of ruins, public festivals, and historic

Samuel Palmer: Ruth Returned from Gleaning; pen and ink wash heightened with white chalk on paper; 29×39cm (11×15in); 1828. Victoria and Albert Museum, London

Giovanni Panini: Imaginary Gallery of Ancient Roman Art; oil on canvas; 171×231cm (67×91in); 1757. Metropolitan Museum, New York

events, was born in Piacenza. By 1711 he was in Rome, where he trained with scenographic architects and landscape painters. He became both an architect and a painter of large-scale illusionistic designs (in, for example, the Palazzo Albani, 1720, and the Palazzo Quirinale, 1722, both in Rome). Popular with French patrons, he participated in decorations for the *Fête* held in Rome in 1729 to commemorate the birth of the Dauphin. From *c*1725 Panini painted numerous views both of the modern city and of the ruins of Rome, which were often bought by foreign tourists.

Paolozzi Eduardo 1924–

The Scottish sculptor and printmaker Eduardo Paolozzi was born in Edinburgh of Italian parents. He studied at Edinburgh College of Art (1943–4) and at the Slade School of Fine Art (1944–7). From 1947 to 1949 he lived in Paris, returning to London to teach at the Central School until 1955 and at St Martin's School of Art (1955–8). He was visiting professor at Hamburg School of Art (1960–2) and at the University of California, Berkeley (1968). Since 1967 he has been a lecturer in ceramics at the Royal College of Art, London.

Throughout his career, Paolozzi has been inspired by modern technology and has explored its relationship to art and society in many prints and sculptures. Paolozzi's early contact with Surrealism in Paris has influenced all aspects of his work, mainly through collage techniques. Giacometti is reflected in the open, linear wire and bronze sculptures made between 1947 and 1955. Later he made Pop-related fantastic figures and heads, cast from junk, with richly detailed surfaces. These led to anthropomorphic painted aluminum pieces cast from stock machine parts. Until the early 1970s he made a group of Abstract "futuristic" organic and extremely reductive sculptures in chromed steel and aluminum.

In the 1970s Paolozzi worked mainly in relief both in wood and cast materials. Though such works are Abstract, they are built up of a multiplicity of often repeated elements which are based on one central idea or image. Among his many commissions are the Four Doors for the Hunterian Art Gallery, Glasgow (1979).

Paolozzi has an equally great reputation as a printmaker. His major contribution was to the development of silkscreen and photolithography as fine art media with his Pop art prints, for example *As is When* (1964–5).

Eduardo Paolozzi: Jason; bronze; height 168cm (66in), base 37×29cm (15×11in); 1956. Museum of Modern Art, New York

Paris Matthew   c1200–59

Matthew Paris was an English historian and illuminator. One of the few named medieval artists to whom a substantial body of work can be attributed with some certainty, Paris spent his career at St Albans, England. In 1217 he made his profession as a monk, and c1235 succeeded Roger of Wendover as the Abbey's historian. His interests were wide, including cartography, heraldry, and cosmography, but his main achievement consists of the chronicles and lives of the saints which he both wrote and illustrated. He was probably also involved in practical administrative duties, in connection with which he visited Norway from 1248 to 1249.

Although a monk, Paris had close contact with the lay nobility, including the court at Westminster. Richard Earl of Cornwall (brother of Henry III, whom he also knew) was an important source of information about events described in the chronicles. The inferred format of his saints' lives, with continuous bands of illustration placed above the Anglo-Norman French texts, indicates that they were intended for nobility like the Cornwalls. A note in the *Life of St Alban* (Trinity College Library, Dublin) refers to another saint's life "which I translated and illustrated and which the lady countess of Cornwall may keep till Whitsuntide".

Most of his illustrations are tinted drawings—a technique often favored by English medieval artists—and Paris was possibly familiar with Anglo-Saxon illustration in this medium. Although his work is accomplished, it is not especially advanced in style. The weight and the firm outlines of the figures in the *Life of St Alban* (c1240), probably his earliest surviving work, indicate a considerable debt to the transitional style of c1200. In the scene of Aracle's conversion, however, the agile poses of the soldier's attackers and the slender proportions of the saint are characteristic of early Gothic art. The grotesque faces reveal Paris' interest in striking characterization.

A similar concern with dramatic incident is found in the many marginal drawings of the *Chronica Maiora* (1241–51; Corpus Christi College Library, Cambridge) where unusual, often contemporary subjects are depicted in witty and sharply observed compositions. These freshly executed scenes are frequently new inventions. Typical in its lively, anecdotal quality is the battle between William Mareschall and Baldwin of Guisnes, in which Baldwin

Matthew Paris: An Elephant and its Keeper, an illustration in the "Chronica Maiora"; 14×18cm (5½×7in); c1240–50. Corpus Christi College Library, Cambridge

tumbles from his mount, casually watched by a passing figure leading two horses.

A drawing of the Virgin and Child from the *Historia Anglorum* (British Library, London), with the artist himself at the Virgin's feet, is probably among his last works (1250–5). The delicate faces and the tender relationship between mother and child are characteristic of the developed Gothic style. Although the seated figure still has considerable weight, her rippling drapery has an elegance commonly found in the art of the mid 13th century.

Several manuscripts with illustrations in the St Albans style, though not by Paris himself, show his influence, while the pictures in a copy of his *Life of St Edward* (c1255; University Library, Cambridge), in the style of the Westminster Court School, were probably based on his original.

Parler family   14th and 15th centuries

The most celebrated of the numerous medieval mason families, the Parler family worked chiefly in an area that is now south Germany and Czechoslovakia. About 12 members of the family have been identified as masons or sculptors, or both, in the 14th and early 15th centuries; but attributions have to be treated with caution, since the word *Parlier* is German for foreman-mason and can be confused with the Parlers.

Heinrich I is one of the most distinguished of the Parlers. From being a *Parlier* at Cologne he went to Schwäbisch-Gmünd in 1351, and built the Heiligenkreuzkirche, an early example of the south German hall church. It has a nave and aisles of similar height, giving the interior an unusually spacious appearance flooded with light. The hall church design is one of the most important German contributions to Gothic architecture. Schwäbisch-Gmünd is also notable for the way in which its circular columns rise uninterrupted to join the rib system of the vault, which is a complex pattern described as the *Sondergotik* style. It was probably the same Heinrich who planned the chancel of Ulm Minster *c*1377.

His son Peter was the greatest of the Parlers. In 1356, aged only 23, he went to Prague to continue building the cathedral for the Emperor. It had been started in 1344 by the French mason, Mathias of Arras, and Peter completed the choir from the triforium level. It is a strange synthesis of the French rayonnant style and English early-14th-century features. The latter include a massive triforium level balustrade, like the one at Exeter Cathedral, diagonal arches across the lower part of the clerestory, as at Wells Cathedral choir, and a net vault on the English West Country pattern, as are also the skeleton vaults of Prague's sacristy and south porch. The stellate pattern of the choir vault became usual for churches in Bohemia, for example at St Barbara, Kuttenburg, which may have been built by Peter Parler after 1388.

Like his father, Peter was a sculptor as well as a stonemason. At Prague, his workshop produced the royal tombs and the 21 portrait busts in the choir triforium, including one representing Peter himself together with an inscription that lists his works. These busts are notable for their realism; the style was influential throughout the area of south Germany and environs, where several members of the Parler family are recorded as sculptors.

Another branch of the Parlers may have been based at Freiburg. Johann was master mason there from 1359 and was probably responsible for rebuilding the Minster's choir with its elaborate *Sondergotik* vaults. It was a Michael Parler of Freiburg who drew an elevation, which survives, for Strasbourg Cathedral's west front in the 1380s. He intended to create a huge rose window with a single central tower and spire rising above it in the German manner. The same Michael also worked on the southwest tower of Cologne Cathedral.

Two other Parlers, Heinrich of Gmünd and Hans of Freiburg, were both advisors at Milan Cathedral in the 1390s—although, like other invited foreign masons, they failed to persuade the Italians to accept their plans.

Parmigianino 1503–40

The real name of the artist known as Parmigianino was Girolamo Francesco Maria Mazzola or Mazzuoli. He was an Italian painter and etcher whose canons of suave beauty played a key role in the formation of Mannerist style throughout Europe. His reputation as the artist who developed artificial elegance to a bizarre extreme does less than justice to the emotional complexity of his art, and the increasingly unsettled brilliance of his mind. Gifted with incredible facility and prodigious inventive powers, he was hailed at the age of 21 as Raphael reincarnated, only to end his career in acrimony, imprisonment, flight, and disgrace.

The young man's talent was carefully nurtured in Parma by his painter-uncles. (His father, also a painter, had died when Francesco was two years old.) His *Marriage of St Catherine* (S. Maria, Bardi), probably painted as early as 1521, is remarkably accomplished for a painter still in his teens. His precosity was such that he was asked to decorate a chapel in Parma Cathedral before he was 20; probably at about the same time, he embarked upon frescoes in S. Giovanni Evangelista. Strongly influenced by Correggio (1490–1534), Parmigianino's sophisticated skill was ideally suited to the courtly decoration of a room in the fortress of Fontanellato for Gian Galeazzo Sanvitale, whose portrait he painted in 1524 (Museo e Gallerie Nazionali di Capodimonte, Naples). The vault is envisaged as an airy trellis; winged cherubs look down on the story of Diana and Acteon, which is displayed with fluent elegance and velvety color, belying the violence of the narrative.

In 1524 he arrived in Rome, accompanied by an uncle and some sample pictures, including a meltingly beautiful *Holy Family* (Prado, Madrid) and a consciously clever *Self-portrait in a Convex Mirror* (Kunsthistorisches Museum, Vienna). These paintings exude a confident air of sparkling intelligence and wit. In Rome his drawings, some of which were engraved, show the growing complexity of his figure draftsmanship. Of the few paintings from this period, *The Marriage of St Catherine* (c1526; National Gallery, London) demonstrates his ability to create

Parmigianino: The Vision of St Jerome; panel; 343×149cm (135×59in); 1527. National Gallery, London

intimate delicacy on a small scale, while *The Vision of St Jerome* (1527; National Gallery, London) makes a haunting emotional impact in a large, unusually lofty altarpiece. In front of the diminutive, sleeping figure of St Jerome, the hypnotically staring St John kneels and pivots, directing our attention to a radiant Madonna and Child inspired by Raphael.

After the sack of Rome in 1527, Parmigianino found employment in Bologna and entered upon the most productive phase of his career. The mannered grace of his figures was increasingly combined with a highly charged atmosphere of transcendental spirituality. The contrast between the ethereal saint and the sober donor in his *St Roch* (c1527–8; S. Petronio, Bologna) reveals his aspiration to evoke the otherness of divine power by creating an attenuated beauty remote from natural proportions.

In 1530 he completed an elaborate and influential *Allegorical Portrait of Charles V* (now lost) and probably also the *Madonna della Rosa* (Gemäldegalerie Alte Meister, Dresden), which represents the extreme point in his identification of sensual with spiritual beauty.

Returning to Parma in 1531, he received the important commission to paint the apse of S. Maria della Steccata. The sad story of the Confraternity's slowly exhausted patience with the dilatory artist can be traced through surviving documents. Between 1532 and 1534 Parmigianino seems to have ceased work. A new contract was drawn up in 1535. A further extension was granted in 1538, but the following year he was imprisoned for nonreturn of advances. After his release he took refuge in Casalmaggiore; finally, in 1539, he was irrevocably dismissed. The only section of the painting to be completed was that on the underside of the crossing arch, where two groups of three graceful maidens, carrying vases and the oil lamps of the wise and foolish virgins, glide across the cornice.

During this period, his reported obsession with the mystical science of alchemy appears to have devoured much of his time. The drawings for the Steccata suggest an additional reason for his delays, namely that his boundless ability to design apparently effortless alternatives for each figure resulted in paralyzing indecision.

His progress on the *Madonna del Collo Lungo* ("Madonna of the Long Neck", Uffizi, Florence), commissioned in 1534, was rather better; but this too remained

incomplete. The remarkably slender proportions of the unfinished portico in the background are shared by the sinuous Virgin and seductively pretty angels, who rival the sensuous appeal of his earlier *Cupid* (c1531; Kunsthistorisches Museum, Vienna). The jar of oil held by the nearest angel prefigures Christ's anointment after death, while the Child lies ominously in deathly sleep.

In exile he completed the *Madonna with Saints Stephen and John the Baptist* (1539–40; Gemäldegalerie Alte Meister, Dresden). In this painting his exaggerated system of proportion, already less apparent in the Steccata maidens, has been superseded by monumental forms circumscribed by grand curves, and heavy shadows are used as a foil for the divine radiance of the Madonna and Child. The spaniel-like devotion of the donor suggests a transformation in the painter's own attitude towards spiritual expression, but his early death prevented further development of this more soberly devotional manner.

His European influence was substantially due to his own etchings and the prints after his works by others. His own productions, most notably *The Entombment* (c1528), translate the feathery touch of his sketches into prints of unrivaled evocativeness, in which etching received its first full liberation from the imitation of engraving. The chiaroscuro (3 or 4 tone) woodcuts after his work, particularly those by Antonio da Trento, go far towards capturing the vitality of his brilliant drawings. These have themselves survived in sufficient numbers to have exercised a considerable influence in their own right.

Further reading. Freedberg, S. J. *Parmigianino: his Works in Painting*, Cambridge, Mass. (1950). Popham, A. E. *Catalogue of the Drawings of Parmigianino* (3 vols.), London and New Haven (1971). Quintavale, A. O. *Il Parmigianino*, Milan (1948).

Parrhasios *fl.* late 5th century BC

The Greek painter Parrhasios came from Ephesus and worked in Athens. He prepared drawings that were used by the engraver Mys on the shield of Pheidias' bronze statue of *Athena Promachos* on the Acropolis. His painting was notable for the subtlety of its contour, and for the successful depiction of features and bodies in violent action or under the stress of emotion—for example Odysseus pretending madness, and a characterization of the fickle people (*demos*) of Athens. Parrhasios acquired a reputation for arrogance and extravagance. Xenophon has him discuss with Socrates the possibility of rendering emotion and character in painting.

Pasiteles 1st century BC

Pasiteles was a Greek sculptor and silversmith from south Italy. He became a Roman citizen *c*90 BC. He was involved in the invention of mechanical means for copying the sculptures of earlier periods for Roman clients. The antiquarianism of Pasiteles was manifested in his book on the masterpieces of the ancient world. He was known to have made an ivory statue of Jupiter for the temple of Metellus in Rome, and to have drawn a lion from life for use in a relief. Statues and groups in the manner of the early and late Classical periods signed by members of his school survive in Rome.

Pasmore Victor 1908–98

The British painter Victor Pasmore was born in Chelsham, Surrey. Until 1938 he was able to study art only part time. He first exhibited in 1930, at the Zwemmer Gallery, and had his first one-man show in 1933. He joined the London Group in 1934 and was a founder-member of the Euston Road Group, which consciously rebelled against the "escapism" of the School of Paris. Pasmore's work of this period is representational in character, and serious in tone.

In the mid 1940s, he concentrated on landscape. His sense of atmosphere derives from a deep study of late Turner and, to a lesser extent, Whistler; but already Pasmore has begun to concentrate on certain objects and shapes within the picture that he evidently valued for their abstract qualities. Note the pattern of branches, for example, in the 1944 *Chiswick Reach* (National Gallery of Canada, Ottawa).

By 1946 the abstract emphasis is even stronger, as in *Chiswick: Sun Shining Through Mist* (1946/7; National Gallery of Victoria, Melbourne), with its strong horizontal elements and areas of pointillist technique. In 1947, Pasmore turned to a fully-fledged Abstract style. From 1947 to 1950 he concentrated on a mixture of oils and collage. From 1949 to 1951 he experimented in oil studies of spiral motifs. From the mid 1950s onwards he painted far less and began working on three-dimensional reliefs of great austerity.

Further reading. Bowness, A. *Victor Pasmore*, London (1980).

Patenier Joachim *c*1480–*c*1525

The Flemish painter Joachim Patenier may originally have worked at Bruges before registering as a master at Antwerp in 1515. Only a handful of works by this artist survive, but he had a profound impact on the development of landscape painting in 16th-century northern Europe.

Patenier specialized in scenes where the figure subject is dominated by a vast surrounding landscape. In these his sense of perspective remained empirical; in most of his works, mountains seen from below are placed on a ground plane seen from above. However, his application of color—from brownish foregrounds to green in the middle distance and blue in the background—gives an impression of atmosphere that was innovatory.

In paintings such as the *Landscape with St Jerome* (National Gallery, London) the crags and precipices of the artist's imagination take on a life of their own, and dwarf the true subject of the picture. The *Charon Crossing the Stygian Lake* (Prado, Madrid) restates, with Patenier's more poetic sense of landscape, the juxtaposition of paradise and hell found in the paintings of Hieronymus Bosch. Patenier sometimes painted the backgrounds of figure subjects by his Flemish contemporaries; *The Temptation of St Anthony* (Prado, Madrid) is a joint work with Quentin Massys.

His compositions were reproduced by Herri met de Bles, the chief copyist of his style. Historically Patenier's chief influence was on the painting of Pieter Bruegel the Elder (1525-69), whose vision of landscape, especially in his early years, is particularly indebted to this artist.

Pater Jean-Baptiste 1695–1736

The French painter and draftsman Jean-Baptiste Pater was a pupil of Antoine Watteau for a short time *c*1713, and again in 1721. Pater continued Watteauesque military subjects and *fêtes galantes* into the 1730s, along with artists such as Lancret (for example, *Women Bathing c*1735; Musée de Peinture et de Sculpture, Grenoble). His works are rather poor and eclectic imitations of his master's, and less richly

Victor Pasmore: The Thames at Chiswick: Sun Shining through Mist; oil on canvas; 76×100cm (30×39in); 1946-7. National Gallery of Victoria, Melbourne

Joachim Patenier: Landscape with St Jerome; panel; 36×34cm (14×13½in); c1520. National Gallery, London

to stone or wood. Some of his subjects were remembered for their special effects, for example a frontal view of an ox painted black and making no use of shading or highlights, and a figure of Drunkenness (Methe) with her face appearing through the glass cup. His florals were especially admired and may have inspired the distinctive floral patterns on later mosaic floors in Macedonian palaces and on Italian vases.

Paxton Joseph 1801–65

The English gardener and architect Sir Joseph Paxton was born at Milton Bryant, Bedfordshire. His rise from garden-boy to knighthood was a paradigm of 19th-century self-improvement. As superintendent of the gardens at Chatsworth, Derbyshire, Paxton laid out the estate village (Edensor, c1839). He designed several horticultural buildings, including the Great Conservatory (1836–40) whose "ridge and furrow" glazing system, with light structural supports, was the basis of his successful scheme for the Crystal Palace, London (1851). Prefabrication of the glass and iron elements enabled this, the largest building in the world, to be erected in nine months, bringing world fame to its designer.

colored. Towards the end of his life his art took the more incisive turn first suggested by his engraved illustrations to Paul Scarron's *Roman Comique* (1729–36; published in Potsdam), but he died too young to realize fully the implications of this. Some of his landscapes, with pretty little figures, anticipate the art of François Boucher. His largest and most individual work is *The Fair at Bezons* (c1735, Metropolitan Museum, New York).

Pausias mid 4th century BC

The Greek painter Pausias came from Sicyon and was a leading artist of the influential Sicyonian school of painting. He was said to have introduced the practice of painting panels for ceilings, and he was an early exponent of the "encaustic" technique, using heated wax to bind colors

Jean-Baptiste Pater: Fête Champêtre; oil on canvas; 75×93cm (30×37in); c1730. National Gallery of Art, Washington, D.C.

Peale Charles 1741–1827

The American painter Charles Wilson Peale was born in Maryland, Pa. He was originally apprenticed to a saddler, and briefly entered that trade. At the age of 21 he took lessons in painting, and left for London to study under Benjamin West. He returned to America in 1769 to travel the East Coast, painting portraits. He fought in the War of Independence and painted portraits of many of its prominent figures, including a number of George Washington. Having settled in Philadelphia he opened first a picture gallery in 1782, and then the Peale Museum, containing scientific exhibits and portraits of the leading figures of American history. He was Founder of the Academy of Fine Arts, and became a regular exhibitor. Important collections of his paintings can be seen in Philadelphia, in Independence Hall and at the Historical Society of Pennsylvania. Peale married three times and fathered 17 children, all of whom became artists.

Pearlstein Philip 1924–

The American artist Philip Pearlstein was one of the leading figures in the return to figurative painting in the 1960s. He studied at the Carnegie Institute of Technology. In the 1950s Pearlstein painted in the Abstract Expressionist idiom, but by the early 1960s, attempting to "rescue the human figure" from the distortions of the "Expressionists and Cubists", he had developed a distinctive style of unidealized nude painting. Dubbed perceptual realism, his approach focuses on the depiction of bodies exactly as they appear, without psychological, social or sexual interpretation. *Female Model on Eames Stool* (1978; Metropolitan Museum of Art, New York) is typical of his precise, objective approach. Unusual angles and compositions, highly finished surfaces, and hidden or cropped faces stress the abstract qualities of his works, though ironically they often also tend to raise rather than dispel questions of interpretation.

Pei Ieoh Ming 1917–

Born in China, the American architect Ieoh Ming Pei emigrated to the United States in 1935 and studied at Massachusetts Insti-

Charles Peale: Staircase Group; oil on canvas; 226×100cm (89×39in); 1795. Philadelphia Museum of Art

tute of Technology and at Harvard (under Walter Gropius). A prolific architect, he has worked on a broad range of public projects in the United States, his buildings often large scale and sharply geometrical. Pei is noted for the skill with which he relates design and materials to a specific environment. His work on urban renewal projects, such as Denver's Mile High Center (1952–56) illustrated his awareness of urban environments, while his design for the National Center for Atmospheric Research in Colorado (1961–67) demonstrated a sensitivity to a dramatic natural setting. He firmly established his career with innovative and confident buildings such as the John F. Kennedy Library, Boston, (1964–79) and East Building of the National Gallery, Washington, D.C., (1968–78), though it was with his controversial glass pyramid over a new entrance to the Louvre in Paris (1983–89) that he achieved international fame. Other works include the Xiangshan (Fragrant Hill) Hotel in Peking (1979–83) and the characteristically extrovert 70-story Bank of China building in Hong Kong (1990).

Further reading. Suner, B. *Ieoh Ming Pei*, Paris (1984)

Permeke Constant 1886–1952

The Belgian Expressionist painter and sculptor Constant Permeke was the son of an Antwerp marine painter. He studied at the art academies of Bruges (1903–6) and Ghent (1906–8). During the years 1909 to 1912 he stayed in Laethem-Saint-Martin with the painters Gust and Leon de Smet, Fritz van den Berghe, and Albert Servaes. Although he was still struggling with Impressionism at this time, he and his friends were apparently aware of German Expressionism. It was in England, where he had been evacuated during the First World War, that he finally broke through to his characteristically robust and earthy form of Expressionism (seen in *The Stranger*, 1916; Musées Royaux des Beaux-Arts de Belgique, Brussels). He returned in 1919 to Belgium, where he painted fishermen, peasants, and landscapes. These works are full of human sympathy, painted in somber colors with a broad impasto technique; the figures attain monumental proportions. He began to sculpt figures, mostly in plaster and clay, in 1936 (for example *Marie-Lou*, 1935–6; Middelheim Open Air Museum of Sculpture, Antwerp).

Perrault Claude 1613–88

Claude Perrault was a French doctor with an amateur interest in architecture. In 1667 he was appointed by Louis XIV to collaborate with Louis Levau and the painter Charles Lebrun on a design for the east front of the Louvre, Paris, to replace the scheme prepared by Bernini. Perrault's part in the final design is not clear. The Baroque rhythm of the coupled columns is probably Levau's, but the strict application of Roman forms, which made it a seminal work for the 18th century, reflects Perrault's archaeological interests. These led in 1673 to his edition of Vitruvius's *De Architectura*. He also designed the Paris Observatoire (1667) and a château at Sceaux for Colbert (1663–4; demolished). His brother Charles (1626–1703) was a theorist and chief assistant to Colbert in the *Surintendance des Bâtiments*.

Perréal Jean c1460–c1530

The French artist Jean Perréal has been identified (with little justification) both with the "Jehan de Paris, enlumineur" active in Bourges before 1480, and with the Maître de Moulins. He may have been born in Paris. By 1483 he was certainly in Lyons, where he held the post of painter, decorator, and *valet-de-chambre* to Charles VIII. He organized Charles' solemn entry into the city in 1489, and Anne de Bretagne's in 1493. Between 1499 and 1502 he followed the armies of Louis XII in Italy (where he met Leonardo da Vinci). His job was apparently to paint battles, but also, according to the chronicler Jehan Lemaire de Belges, to record "les villes conquises en Italie".

On his return to France in 1502, Perréal designed the tomb of François II and his wife Marguerite de Foix, commissioned by their daughter, Anne de Bretagne. The work, in Nantes Cathedral, is the masterpiece of the sculptor Michel de Colombe. In 1504 Perréal was appointed artistic adviser to Margaret of Austria, for whom he supervised at least part of the decoration of the splendidly exuberant monastery church at Brou (the fruit of a vow made by Margaret's mother-in-law, Marguerite de Bourbon). He also drew up plans for the tombs of Marguerite, and of Philibert II "Le Beau" de Savoie, Margaret of Austria's husband. He visited England at least once, in 1514.

Perréal's status as a painter is obscured by the circumstance that only three paintings—portraits of Charles VIII, of Anne de Bretagne, and of Pierre Sala—can safely be attributed to him. It has been suggested that he also illustrated the *Illustrations de Gaule et Singularitez de Troye* (1509) of Jean Lemaire de Belges, who was an admirer of Perréal and who also lived in Lyons.

Perret Auguste 1874–1954

The architect Auguste Perret was born in Ixelles, near Brussels. He studied at the École des Beaux-Arts in Paris but left in 1895 to join his father's building and contracting firm. His importance for the Modern Movement rests upon a handful of buildings in which he established reinforced concrete as an aesthetically acceptable material for architecture, as well as hinting at its structural potential. Nevertheless, Perret never overturned the academic tradition but preferred to fit concrete into it. He based his use of the material upon a system of columns and beams derived from wooden construction.

His first notable work was the block of flats at No. 25b Rue Franklin in Paris (1903), which displays its frame explicitly; it is also novel in plan, since the lightwell required by law is incorporated in the front of the building. In the Garage Ponthieu (1905) Perret left the structural concrete exposed. The structure that he conceived for the Théâtre des Champs Élysées (1911–14; with Henry van de Velde) anticipates the skeleton frames of the architecture of the 1920s.

The church of Notre Dame du Raincey (1922–3) was Perret's last influential work. It presented little that was daring in structural terms, except for its tall, attenuated columns; but it made a considerable impact upon younger architects in the utterly frank use of precast concrete units, and in the patterning of surfaces by means of the shuttering used to contain the concrete.

Perronneau J.-B. 1715–83

The French portrait painter Jean-Baptiste Perronneau was born in Paris and studied under Charles-Joseph Natoire and the engraver Laurent Cars. During his lifetime his reputation as a pastel portrait painter was overshadowed by that of Maurice-Quentin de La Tour (1704–88), whose greater virtuosity appealed more to Parisian taste. Perronneau found his patrons in the French provinces, and also abroad, in Italy, England, Russia, and especially Holland, where he died. Unlike La Tour, Perronneau was a successful painter in oils. His *Portrait of a Man* (National Gallery of Ireland, Dublin), for instance, has a directness and lack of flattery very rarely found in the French portraiture of his day.

Perugino c1448–1523

The Italian painter Pietro Vannucci was born at Città della Pieve, and was known as Perugino. In the late 1460s he may have been a pupil of Piero della Francesca; he then seems to have moved to Florence, where he worked in the studio of Verrocchio. Perugino's early career is somewhat obscure, but he was certainly an established master by 1479, when he was recorded as working in the Vatican. His earliest paintings in Rome are lost, but his frescoes in the Sistine Chapel of the Vatican, dating from 1481–2, already reveal the major characteristics of his mature style. The finest of them, *The Delivery of the Keys to St Peter* or *Christ's Charge to St Peter*, is notable for its spacious and clearly defined setting, which obviously shows the influence of Piero. But compared with those of Perugino's teacher the figures are rather timid and insubstantial, with gentle, rhythmic, and slightly monotonous poses.

J.-B. Perronneau: Portrait of Jacques Cazotte; oil on canvas; 92×73cm (36×29in); c1760–4. National Gallery, London

Perugino's style is always decorative rather than monumental or expressive. Virtually all his pictures have the same kind of sweetness of mood: the figures are stereotyped in pose and physical type, with an unvarying expression of vapid mildness, and they are set in ample landscapes which recall the work of Flemish artists such as Hans Memling. At his best, as for example in the fresco of the *Crucifixion with Saints* (1496; S. Maria Maddalena dei Pazzi, Florence) Perugino's supreme craftsmanship enabled him to produce an image of genuine power, in which the sense of subdued piety is entirely appropriate to the pathos of the subject. But the repetition of a well-worn repertoire of devotional formulae, for which he could always find a ready market, reveals the poverty of his invention as well as the excellence of his technique, especially in the rendering of space and light. Vasari's comment that "he always refused to accept the immortality of the soul" may be no more than malice, since it is not supported by any other evidence; but it is an understandable response to Perugino's apparent complacency.

In the later part of the 15th century Perugino enjoyed an immense reputation, not only in his native Umbria and in Tuscany, but even as far afield as Venice. He somewhat surprisingly undertook to paint a battle picture for the Doges' Palace, though he never actually delivered it. He was even employed by Isabella d'Este, the Marchioness of Mantua and one of the foremost patrons of the period, for whom he painted a *Combat between Love and Chastity* (1503–5; Louvre, Paris). During the 16th century his work began to seem old-fashioned beside the achievements of artists such as Leonardo, Michelangelo, and Raphael, who was for a time his pupil; but until his death Perugino remained singularly impervious to the influence of the younger generation.

Peruzzi Baldassare 1481–1536

Baldassare Tommaso Peruzzi was born in Siena, and may have trained as an architect and painter with Francesco di Giorgio. Before 1505, he designed for Sigismondo Chigi the Villa Le Volte, just outside Siena. He then moved to Rome, where he began the design of the Villa Farnesina for the rich papal banker, Agostino Chigi. The articulation of the walls, with doric pilasters, reflects Peruzzi's response to Rome.

Perugino: The Delivery of the Keys to St Peter; fresco; 335×550cm (132×217in); 1482. Sistine Chapel, the Vatican, Rome

The two loggias, which look out on to the Tiber and the garden, develop the Renaissance interest in opening buildings to the landscape. (This was a conscious revival of the effects described by Pliny the Younger in his account of his villas.) The "U" shape of the villa, which has its roots in the Quattrocento, was not continued in 16th-century Italy.

By contrast with his architecture, Peruzzi's paintings were provincial, and Agostino Chigi preferred Raphael's. Nevertheless, in 1517 Peruzzi returned to the Farnesina to enlarge the Sala delle Prospettive on the first floor. He decorated it with doric columns and pilasters (with a frieze above). They support the cornice, and extend the room to the balustrades that are set in front of the brilliantly conceived views of Rome. The illusionism of these views has no direct precedent in the Renaissance.

Baldassare Peruzzi: the Sala delle Prospettive; c1517. Villa Farnesina, Rome

Peruzzi's skills as an architectural painter were given full expression in his designs for the theater. This aspect of his work, together with his study of the Antique, influenced the treatise of his pupil, Sebastiano Serlio. Peruzzi's late work is best represented by the Palazzo delle Colonne, Rome, begun in 1532. The curve of the facade was suggested by the irregular site. The restriction of the pilasters and columns to the ground floor, with the mass of rustication above broken only by the window aedicules, shows his development of an inventive and expressive Mannerism, comparable to that of Giulio Romano and Michelangelo.

Pesellino Francesco c1422–57

Francesco di Stefano Pesellino was a Florentine painter. In 1455 he was commissioned to paint an altarpiece of *The Trinity with Saints* for a Pistoian church. Now in the National Gallery, London, it was unfinished at his death in 1457. Its completion, notably the painting of the *predella*, was entrusted to Filippo Lippi and his workshop. Pesellino's style owes much to Lippi, as seen in, for example, a *Madonna and Child with Saints* in the Metropolitan Museum, New York. Some *predella* panels attributed to him (for example, *A Miracle of St Sylvester*; Worcester Art Museum, Worcester, Mass.) and several *cassone* paintings (for example, *The Story of Griselda*; Galleria dell'Accademia Carrara, Bergamo), reveal skills in painting on a smaller scale.

Pettoruti Emilio 1895–1971

The Argentine painter Emilio Pettoruti studied in 1913 in Florence where he associated with the Futurists. From 1916 to 1917 he studied in Rome, where he became acquainted with Giacomo Balla, Enrico Prampolini, and Giorgio de Chirico. He spent 1919 in Milan, and 1921 in Vienna and Munich. In 1923 he exhibited at Herwarth Walden's center, "Der Sturm", in Berlin. He then went to Paris where he met Juan Gris and Gino Severini. In 1924 Pettoruti returned to Argentina where he remained for nearly 30 years, becoming director of the Museo Nacional de la Plata in 1930. Under Peron's dictatorship he was removed from his post, in 1947; he moved back to Paris in 1951.

Pettoruti's earliest work reflects his interest in Balla's Abstract pictures. After 1917 he painted figurative works in a late Cubist style (for example, *The Verdigris Goblet*, 1934; Museum of Modern Art, New York). He reverted to abstraction after 1950.

Pevsner Antoine 1886–1962

The Russian painter and sculptor Antoine Pevsner was born in Orel, Russia, and went to Paris in 1912 to paint; in 1915 he joined his brother Naum Gabo in Oslo. In 1917 they both returned to Russia, which was in a state of artistic as well as political ferment. In 1920 they published the *Realistic Manifesto* as their contribution to the debate about the future of art. During these years Pevsner's painting developed from a curvilinear Cubism to geometric abstraction.

In 1923 he moved to Paris, and began working in three dimensions. His earliest ventures are figures in relief, built up from curved sheets of plastic. He followed his brother in the use of synthetic materials and engineering techniques, although unlike Gabo he did not devote himself

Francesco Pesellino: The Triumph of David over Saul; detail; oil on panel; full size 45×180cm (18×71in). National Gallery, London

entirely to abstraction until the early 1930s. For all the superficial similarities between the work of the two brothers, Pevsner's sculpture is marked by a far more expressive quality. Even at his most abstract, the interplay between concave and convex surfaces gives form to sensations of stress and strain which inevitably become associated with muscular tensions.

After 1936 Pevsner began to construct his sculptures from bronze and copper rods, closely welded together. This gives rise to a richly textured surface that draws attention to itself, rather than, as with Gabo, to the void it delineates. The result impedes the apprehension of internal spatial relationships, reversing the principles of the *Realistic Manifesto* in favor of the traditional sculptural treatment of volume as mass.

Further reading. Duchamp, M. *Antoine Pevsner*, Paris (1947). Pevsner, A. *A Biographical Sketch of my Brothers, Naum Gabo and Antoine Pevsner*, Amsterdam (1964).

Pheidias 5th century BC

Pheidias was a Greek sculptor of the high Classical period from Athens, the son of Charmides, and related to the painter Panaenus. He was a pupil of Ageladas and a contemporary of Polycleitos. The Greeks considered him their greatest sculptor; he was also undoubtedly fortunate in being given the opportunity to realize his intentions. Supported by the Athenian statesman Pericles, Pheidias became the artistic agent of the political, financial, and cultural supremacy of Athens as head of a maritime empire.

He was appointed supervisor of the sculptural decoration of the temple of Athena (the Parthenon) on the Acropolis of Athens, employing some of the leading sculptors of the time, among them Agoracritus, Alcamenes, Cresilias, and Myron. In the Parthenon sculptures (448–432 BC) the naturalistic tendencies of the early Classical were invested with idealism, and the Classical style emerged as the expression of the conservative ideals of the enlightened aristocracy of the city. The forms created on the Parthenon lived to the end of the Classical world, and the temple itself has served as a model of imperial monuments both ancient and modern. The hand of Pheidias cannot be identified on the remaining fragments of Parthenon sculpture (British Museum, London; Acropolis Museum, Athens; Louvre, Paris), but his influence is manifest in their excellence.

The Greeks were much impressed by the colossal cult-statue of *Athena Parthenos* (Virgin) made by Pheidias for the *cella* of the Parthenon in ivory and gold (the gold in removable plating deposited by the state treasury). Although its significance was more political than religious, it settled the image of Athena for all time. The helmeted goddess was standing with her shield at her side, the snake Erichthonius curling within its concavity. She held a spear in the right hand and a flying Victory on the palm of the left hand, which was supported by a column. The statue was decorated with mythical scenes, like a temple: its base with the birth of Pandora, the first woman, and the sandals and shield with battle scenes. Popular tradition claimed that Pheidias had included portraits of himself and Pericles among the combatants on the shield.

Shortly after the statue's dedication in 438, Pheidias was indicted for embezzlement of some of the state gold from the *Parthenos* and fled to Olympia. There he created his second masterpiece in ivory and gold: a colossal cult-statue of *Zeus* for his temple at Olympia, financed from the spoils of the war between Elis and Pisa. The sublime figure carved by Pheidias had a deep theological significance and was acknowledged as a contribution to traditional religion. Zeus was shown as the benevolent king and father of gods and men, allegedly inspired by the imagery of the Homeric *Iliad*. He sat in an elaborate throne, holding a Victory in his right hand and a scepter crowned by an eagle in the left. Some of the clay molds used for sections of the golden drapery and other accessories (datable to the 430s) have been found in the workshop of Pheidias at Olympia, together with a mug incised with his signature as owner (Archaeological Museum, Olympia).

Before his work on the Parthenon, Pheidias had made a bronze colossus of *Athena Promachos* (Guardian) for Athens; it was erected on the Acropolis c456 BC, and financed by the spoils of the battle of Marathon. The top of her crest and spear were supposed to have been visible to sailors at Cape Sunion. His smaller bronze *Athena Lemnia* was dedicated on the Acropolis by the Athenian colonists of Lemnos, and was admired for the detailed treatment of the face (for once not covered by the helmet): she was not a warlike goddess but a graceful maiden. This statue has been reconstructed from copies as a bare-headed Athena holding her helmet in her right hand. The knowledge of the original is based on a head in the Museo Civico, Bologna, and on a torso in the Skulpturensammlung, Dresden.

Pheidias presented his own solution to the problem of stance and proportions by developing the quietly standing figure with both feet on the same level, one leg bent with the knee pointing to the side. He did not cultivate the animated rhythmical outline of Myron and Polycleitos, but achieved an effect of grandeur by means of elaborate drapery or detailed musculature combined with an idealized head. His ideas were at the root of a great many subsequent innovations. His experiments with statues, shifting their weight on to an external support, as in his *Amazon* in Ephesus, proved particularly fertile; they influenced Alcamenes, Cresilias, and Praxiteles. However, despite the enormous impact made by Pheidias on Greek and Roman art and taste, we know very little about his personality.

Further reading. Brommer, F. *Athena Parthenos*, Bremen (1957). Hekler, A. *Die Kunst des Phidias*, Stuttgart (1924). Richter, G. M. *A Handbook of Greek Art*, London and New York (1974).

Phillips Tom 1937–

The English painter and composer Tom Phillips was born in London. After reading English at Oxford University (1957–60) he studied painting at Camberwell School of Art with Frank Auerbach (1961–4). He taught art history at Ipswich School of Art (1965–6), painting at the Bath Academy of Art (1966–7), and then taught at Wolverhampton College of Art (1967–70). He has also been an instructor at the Royal College of Art and at the Slade School of Fine Art (1975).

Most of Phillips' imagery is derived from specially selected color postcards which he interprets in paintings made according to a preconceived program which combines figuration and abstraction. Since 1969 the paintings have included color catalogs of all the colors used in their making, painted in lines around the image, for example, *Benches* (1970–1; Tate Gallery, London). Other independent paintings called *Terminal Greys* are made from mixtures of

Tom Phillips: Benches; acrylic on canvas; 122×276cm (48×109in); 1970–1. Tate Gallery, London

colors used. A major series of paintings made between 1971 and 1975 reconstructs a wall of paintings shown in an old museum postcard. Since 1972 some of the paintings have been politically motivated by subjects like apartheid.

From 1966 Phillips has created many works, including paintings, prints, and an opera and ballet scenario from the pages of an obscure English novel, *A Human Document* (1892) by W. H. Mallock. Their collective title, *A Humument*, is also the title of a book published in 1980 in which every page of the novel has been painted over to produce a blend of painting and poetry.

Piazzetta Giovanni 1683–1754

In many ways the Italian painter Giovanni Battista (or Giambattista) Valentino Piazzetta stands apart from his Venetian contemporaries in his Bolognese training, in his slow working method, and in the fact that after 1711 he does not seem to have painted outside his native Venice.

His training under G. M. Crespi in Bologna was of fundamental importance. He inherited that city's famous tradition of fine academic drawing, becoming one of the greatest draftsmen of the 18th century. His use of strong chiaroscuro, especially in his early works, shows that he studied Guercino's paintings while in Bologna.

Piazzetta's early career in Venice is not clear. He was back in the city by 1711, but no dated paintings are known from before 1717 when he provided *The Martyrdom of St James* for S. Stae, Venice. With its harsh realism and zigzag composition, this work was one of the best of the similar canvases painted for the church by several prominent Venetian artists between 1717 and 1721. It is a measure of Piazzetta's success that when G. B. Tiepolo came to paint his own *Martyrdom* for S. Stae he followed Piazzetta's closely.

Realism remained throughout Piazzetta's career a hallmark of his art, and during the 1720s another became evident. This was his magnificent use of color, first apparent in the ceiling of a chapel in SS. Giovanni e Paolo, Venice, where pinkish browns, pale blues, greens, and grays lighten towards the center. Piazzetta was always reluctant to use too much color. At the end of the 1730s, a time when Venetian painting in general was getting lighter and brighter, he produced the altarpiece in the Gesuati, Venice. Here in complete contrast with contemporary fashion he carefully controlled his austere range of colors.

The slowness of his working method also set Piazzetta apart from his fellow artists and explains why he never tried fresco painting. His deliberations would also have proved disadvantageous in work at foreign courts and capitals. However, although he remained in Venice, many of Piazzetta's commissions came from abroad: not from the "advanced" centers of Rococo patronage like Paris, London, and Düsseldorf, but from the Electors of Saxony and Cologne, and other more conservative patrons.

During the 1740s Piazzetta produced several genre paintings where the subject matter and gentle afternoon light were unexceptional for contemporary painting. What sets these apart from mainstream Rococo work is their feeling of mystery and uncertainty. From the 1740s until his death, assistants became more and more important in his workshop, especially after 1750, when Piazzetta was made Director of the Venetian Academy. It was probably then, for the Academy, that he made most of his splendid nude drawings (most of which are now dispersed between private collections though a few remain in the Gallerie dell'Accademia, Venice). He remained the Director until his death four years later.

Picabia Francis 1879–1953

Francis Picabia was a painter and writer of mixed Spanish, Cuban, and French descent, who was one of the leaders of the Dada movement. He was born in Paris and began studying painting there in 1894. From 1898 to 1910 he worked with considerable success in an Impressionist style, but already by c1907 he had begun to experiment with abstraction. In 1911 he entered a Cubist phase, participating in the *Section d'Or* group and receiving encouragement from Apollinaire, who termed his type of Cubism "Orphic".

In 1913, under Duchamp's influence, Picabia embarked on a remarkable series of canvases—including *I See Again in Memory my Dear Udnie* (1913; Museum of Modern Art, New York). In these, within a basically Cubist structure, he expressed erotic themes by means of veiled, ironic allusions to mechanistic and natural forms.

Picabia lived in New York in 1915 and 1916 and, with Duchamp, was the center of a Dadaist group. In the dry, objective style of technical drawing, he produced works like *Machine, Turn Quickly* (1916; Galleria Schwarz, Milan), in which machine imagery is used with iconoclastic and satiric intent. From 1917 to 1921 Picabia was an active promoter of Dada in Barcelona, New York, Zurich, and Paris,

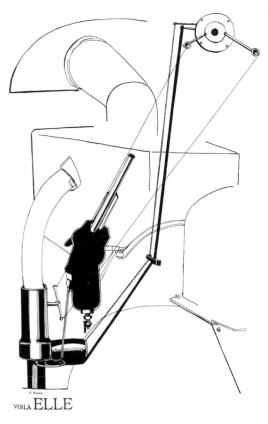

VOILÀ ELLE

Francis Picabia: Violà Elle!, the photograph of the original work (now lost) that appeared in "291"

Giovanni Piazzetta: Idyll on the Sea Shore; oil on canvas; 197×146cm (78×57in); c1741. Wallraf-Richartz-Museum, Cologne

editing his own Dada review, *291*.

Withdrawing from Dada in 1921, Picabia abandoned his machine style in favor of the expressionistic, figurative manner of *The Kiss* (1924; private collection). This phase was succeeded in 1927 by the so-called "Transparencies"—superimposed, transparent silhouettes of figures scattered over the picture. In the 1930s, he was associated sporadically with the Surrealists.

Further reading. Camfield, W. *Francis Picabia: His Art, Life and Times*, Princeton (1979).

Picasso 1881–1973

Born in Málaga, Spain, Pablo Ruiz Picasso was the son of a painter and art teacher, José Ruiz Blases. After active participation in the early-20th-century avant-garde—first in Barcelona and then in Paris—Picasso emerged as perhaps the most influential and vital single creative force in modern art. He remained at the forefront of European painting from the 1900s at least until the Second World War, if not until his death.

His prodigious ability was recognized in the Academies of Coruña, Barcelona, and Madrid (1895-6) and his personable originality led to his teenage entry into the bohemian avant-garde circles of Spain in the 1890s. He first went to Paris in 1900 and continued to pay visits there until 1904, when he finally settled in the city, taking a studio in the Montmartre tenement known as "le Bateau-Lavoir".

His early works of 1898 to 1905, full of adolescent eclecticism, are also powerfully individual. With remarkable facility and vivacity he assimilated ideas and techniques from Post-Impressionist and other *fin-de-siècle* art, as well as from older painting (for instance Classical art, Catalan art, and the works of El Greco). It was as though he were measuring himself against all available artistic terms of reference. (His friend Max Jacob remarked that Picasso made conscious pastiches after everyone, to make sure that he didn't do it unconsciously.) What distinguished him from the French avant-garde, with whom he became associated, was that he cast his net of inquiry so wide. He was not inhibited by the Parisian *belle peinture* tradition, and felt no allegiance to any one tradition of painting. He was more concerned with the making of things and images than with painting as such.

Picasso wrote later that he wanted "to get to the stage where nobody can tell how a picture of mine was done. What's the point of that? Simply that I want nothing but emotion given off by it." He did not want Parisian concerns for the painterliness of the activity to obstruct the power of the image. He was more involved as a painter with concepts and faiths than with the act of looking. He felt strong affinities with French Symbolist literature (with Mallarmé, Rimbaud, Verlaine). He had been closely associated with the Barcelona literary avant-garde, and his significant early contacts in Paris were also with writers (Apollinaire, Jacob, Gertrude Stein, Jarry). By 1905 his studio was known as "le rendezvous des poètes".

The content of Picasso's early work is about the reality of life more than art or nature. The intense melancholia of his "Blue Period" (*c*1901-4) is infected with *fin-de-siècle* obsessions with life and death, images of energy and the lack of energy. In art, he was interested in Munch, Van Gogh, and Gauguin. The *Tragedy* (1903; National Gallery of Art, Washington, D.C.), *The Old Guitarist* (1903; Art Institute of Chicago), and the etching *Frugal Repast* (1904; National Gallery of Art, Washington, D.C.) exemplify the period. *La Vie* (1903; Cleveland Museum of Art), perhaps the most ambitious, is typical in its dense blue palette and the brooding pessimism of its oblique allegory.

In the "Rose Period" (1904-6), his palette lightens towards pinks, grays, and ochers and the mood sweetens to a poignant sadness. Subjects come from circus and theater, the Montmartre acrobats and strolling players (many of them Spanish) that he had befriended. The autobiographical association of artist with isolated entertainer (especially with Harlequin) was to recur throughout his work. In *The Family of Saltimbanques* (1905; Art Institute of Chicago), the passive group in a desolate landscape has a muted pathos and dignity. It reflects Picasso's lifelong concern as man and artist with humanitarian values and with social and political inequality, but in a quiet understatement.

Subsequently, under the pervasive influence of French art, he concentrated more on formal problems and this muting of subject matter continued. Still monochromatic, but now less emotive in color (using browns and ochers), the paintings of 1906 seem devoid of sentiment (for example, *Portrait of Gertrude Stein* and *Two Nudes*, both in the Museum of Modern Art, New York). His concern is with sculptural and tonal oppositions, and he experiments with formal devices from various traditions, classical and archaic.

This conscious formal confrontation reaches a climax in *Les Demoiselles d'Avignon* (1907; Museum of Modern Art, New York). It is both a summation of his early work and the start of a revolutionary new phase in Picasso's art. The painting started in the mood of refined, stylized resolution that had made his early reputation. Its barely disguised allusions to the late works of Cézanne and to those of his contemporary, Matisse, suggest that it was some sort of conclusive answer to French traditions of monumental figure painting. But both the savageness of its change of mood and technique (apparently inspired by African tribal art) and Picasso's dramatic alterations to the work display the radical degree of enquiry to which he was to submit painting during the next decade.

Other 1907-8 works (*Landscape*, 1907, Musée Picasso, Paris; *Nude with Drapery*, Hermitage Museum, St Petersburg; and *Nude with Raised Arms*, Thyssen-Bornemisza Collection, Lugano, Switzerland) reflect the same aggressive urgency, and the same attack on the sanctity of European traditions of naturalism. Ritualistic art was uninhibited by either the High Art tradition of easel painting or Classical traditions of ideal beauty. Picasso was the first Western artist to bring this liberated vision to bear on the problems of European image-making.

In collaboration with Braque, whom he met in 1907, Picasso conducted an intensive overhaul of the practice of painting. The conceptual objectivity of his approach and the imaginative, often playful level of his improvisation and assimilation were the driving force behind each stage in the development of Cubism between 1907 and 1914. Once he had been drawn by Braque into an investigation of French traditions of painterliness and visual analysis—particularly of Cézanne's late work—Picasso produced a series of increasingly refined variations on the theme of Post-Impressionism. His portraits of the dealers Vollard, Uhde, and Kahnweiler (1909-10) are among the masterpieces of Analytical Cubism. They exploit a fine poise between the painting as a physical image (elusive but potent) and as an autonomous structure (a subtle monochrome fabric, lit like a crystal by internal reflection).

In his collages and in Synthetic Cubism (from 1912 onwards), Picasso's sharp and opportunist instincts for images and materials again came to the fore. After the almost classical reserve of Analytical Cubism, the latent Expressionism of his early art also reemerged. In a wide range of media—paintings like *Green Still Life* (1914; Museum of Modern Art, New York), constructions like the wooden *Still Life* (Tate Gallery, London), and sculptures like the painted bronze *Absinthe Glass* (edition of 6), all 1914—he improvised generously with the expressive and animistic properties of dislocated Cubist imagery. At the same time he revived a highly realistic idiom in a series of pencil portrait drawings: *Portrait of Vollard* for example (1915; Metropolitan Museum, New York). Such abrupt shifts as well as the range of simultaneous manners remained characteristic in his mature art.

Picasso: Three Dancers; oil on canvas; 215×142cm (85×56in); 1925. Tate Gallery, London

In 1917 Picasso visited Italy, invited by Jean Cocteau to design for Diaghilev's *Ballet Russe* in Rome. He worked on *Parade* in collaboration with Cocteau, Erik Satie, and Léonide Massine; he also met Igor Stravinsky. The drop curtain (Musée National d'Art Moderne, Paris) was in a naturalistic manner, but among the costumes the two Stage Managers wore enormous Cubist constructions, 10 ft (3.5 m) high. Picasso later designed for Diaghilev's *Le Tricorne* (1919), *Pulcinella* (1920), and *Cuadro Flamenco* (1921). While in Italy Picasso visited Naples and Pompeii and this may have precipitated the classical flavor that pervades his paintings of the early 1920s.

These include the large-scale "neo-classical" figure-paintings such as *Seated Woman* (Tate Gallery, London), and *Pipes of Pan* (Musée Picasso, Paris), both from 1923. He also painted some monumental and equally classical examples of late Synthetic Cubism, such as *Three Musicians* (1921; Philadelphia Museum of Art). The sense of menace or tragedy that seems to lurk behind even the calm somber simplicity of these images breaks out violently in others of the period. Finally, the *Three Dancers* (1925; Tate Gallery, London) relinquish all classical serenity for a ritualistic violence. Here the language of

Picasso: Nude Woman in a Red Armchair; oil on canvas; 130×97cm (51×38in); 1932. Tate Gallery, London

Picasso: Three Figures in an Interior; gouache; 40×80cm (16×31in); 1933. Private collection

Synthetic Cubism is openly converted into a vehicle for surreal fantasy.

This phase of his work coincides with the birth of the Surrealist movement. He met André Breton, became a close friend of Paul Éluard, and often contributed to Surrealist exhibitions and periodicals. To some extent he shared the political aspirations of the movement, but the connection is largely by virtue of the Surrealists' admiration for and assimilation of Picasso's inventive imagery. Paramount examples are the invented anatomies of Picasso's paintings and drawings in the early 1930s (*Seated Bather*, Museum of Modern Art, New York). Alongside such fantastic images he also painted the intimately beautiful *Woman in a Red Armchair* (1932; Tate Gallery, London). Here again are the two poles of life and death, love and violence.

In 1931 he moved south of Paris to Boisgeloup where he set up a sculpture studio and an etching workshop. With the technical help of a friend, the sculptor Julio González, he made a series of iron constructions that were often very linear in character, as well as a number of pieces incorporating *objets trouvés*. Others were carved in wood, and there are a few plaster heads. During this period he was active as an illustrator (for Balzac's *Chef d'Oeuvre Inconnu*, 1931; Ovid's *Metamorphoses*, 1931; and Bouffon's *Histoire Naturelle*, 1942). He also made the great series of etchings, *The Sculptor's Studio* (1933–4), in which the Minotaur succeeds Harlequin

as the artist's symbolic self-portrait.

In 1937 Picasso was invited to contribute to the Spanish section of the International Exhibition in Paris. *The Dream and Lie of Franco* etchings of 1936 had already shown the strength of his sympathies over the Spanish Civil War. The total devastation of the ancient Basque capital of Guernica by three hours' bombing focused his feelings and was the subject of the great mural *Guernica*, exhibited in the Spanish Pavilion in 1937 (now in the Prado, Madrid). Considered by many to be his masterpiece, it brings together not only many of the symbols and allegories he had evolved in the 1920s and 1930s, but also the expressive potency of his post-Cubist visual language. Monochromatic, and extraordinarily direct and simple in composition, it is one of the great symbolic images of European art. His later images of political protest (*The Charnel House*, 1945, Museum of Modern Art, New York; *Massacre in Korea*, 1951, Musée Picasso, Paris) do not achieve the same universality.

Picasso spent most of the Second World War in occupied Paris, making paintings and sculptures; many of these were exhibited at the first Salon d'Automne after the Liberation, in 1944, and in London in 1945. These exhibitions showed him at 63 to be the painter most capable of evoking massive public reaction and formed the basis for the remarkable popular reputation of his later years.

He devoted considerable time and energy in the late 1940s and early 1950s to a series of Peace Conferences around Europe. He had joined the Communist Party in 1944. Despite repeated condemnation of his art as degenerate by Communist leaders, he was suddenly awarded the Lenin Prize by Moscow in 1961. He said that his sympathy with Communism was "the logical outcome of my whole life"; it was humanitarian rather than political.

In 1945 he moved to the South of France, where he was to live for the rest of his life. He was in Antibes in 1946, moved to Vallauris in 1948, to Cannes in 1955, to Vauvenargues in 1958, and finally to Mougins in 1961. In this last long period between the Second World War and his death in 1973—he outlived most of his great friends and contemporaries by many years—he remained prolifically, if erratically, productive. An exhibition held in the Palais des Papes, Avignon, in 1970 of his previous year's output included 165 paintings and 45 drawings.

As always, he worked in many media concurrently. In the ceramics workshop that he set up in Vallauris he produced a large number of works, relaxed and joyful and full of the obvious relish he felt for the novelty of the medium. He spent several periods making linocut prints, equally light and inventive, and displayed continuous concern with sculpture. This concentrated in the 1950s on further improvisations with found objects (*She-Goat*, 1950, Museum of Modern Art, New York; *The Bathers*, 1956, National Trust for Historic Preservation in the United States, Washington, D.C.). In the 1960s he turned to freely-painted sheet iron works, again picking up a lead from the fertile period of 1912 to 1915. Several of these were enlarged—usually in sand-blasted concrete—for public sites in Europe and America (for instance the great *Head* in the Civic Center, Chicago, 1965–7).

He also undertook a few painting commissions: the *War* and *Peace* panels for the deconsecrated chapel in Vallauris (1952) and the mural for the UNESCO Building, Paris (1957–8). Other paintings include several sets of variations on motifs from other artists (from, for example, Delacroix's *Femmes d'Alger*, Velazquez's *Las Meninas*, works by Poussin, El Greco, Cranach, Courbet, and Manet). These are full of the dazzling virtuosity and improvisation displayed so clearly in Henri-Georges Clouzot's film of the artist at work, *Le Mystère Picasso* (1953).

His late work is epitomized in *The Artist and his Model* engravings (1968) and the many related paintings and drawings of the last years. They combine intimate autobiography with universal human allegory, as had his earliest paintings. They have an exuberant sensuality: sometimes lyrical, always erotic. Subtleties of facial and bodily expression are nailed with a sharp, almost caricatural perception. Above all they exude the energy and radiant lifeforce that is at the heart of Picasso's art and influence.

Major exhibitions of Picasso's work were held in Paris (1955), London (1960), New York (1962), and Paris (1966–7), as well as memorial exhibitions in 1973 and a major retrospective at the Museum of Modern Art, New York (1980). There are several museums devoted to his work in France (including the Musée Picasso in Paris) as well as the Museo Picasso in Barcelona which contains the complete *Las Meninas* variations. The enormous collection of his works still in his own possession at his death were bequeathed to the Louvre, Paris.

Further reading. Gilot, F. *Life with Picasso*, New York (1982). Leal, B. et al. *The Ultimate Picasso*, New York (2000). Penrose, R. *Picasso: His Life and Work*, Los Angeles, Calif. (1982). Picasso, P. *Picasso Erotique*, London (2001). Picasso, P. *The Time with François Gilot*, Bielefeld, Ger. (2003). Picasso, P., Picasso, B. and Rose, B. *Picasso: 200 Masterpieces from 1898 to 1972*, New York (2002). Richardson, J. *A Life of Picasso*, Vols. 1 and 2, New York (1991–). Spies, W. *Pablo Picasso: the Sculptures*, Stuttgart, Ger. (2000).

Piene Otto 1928–

The German Kinetic artist Otto Piene was born at Laasphe, Westphalia. After studying in Munich and Cologne he founded the utopian "Zero" group in 1957 with Heinz Mack, and in 1958 he produced a magazine of the same name which included a contribution from Yves Klein on monochrome painting.

Piene's work has concentrated on the phenomena of movement, space, and the articulation of light. Much of his time has been taken up with events and performances, for example those of his *Luminous Ballet*, developed in 1959 and 1960. Light projections, smoke, fire, and inflatables are some of the means and materials he employs. Piene has written and lectured extensively and his public commissions are many.

Piero della Francesca c1410/20–92

The Italian painter Piero della Francesca responded to a wide range of influences: the elegance of the International Gothic, the monumentality and control of light of Masaccio, and the innovations in landscape and technique of Flemish painting; but no artist of his generation combined these interests with such a mastery of clear, luminous color.

He was born Piero da Benedetto de' Franceschi in Borgo San Sepolcro, near Arezzo. We know neither his date of birth nor the reason why he was called Piero della Francesca. His early training is equally uncertain: the only document is the record of his presence in Florence in 1439 with Domenico Veneziano, who was working in S. Maria Novella. The disappearance of these frescoes means that we can only decide on Piero's status at this time by reference to his earliest work, the polyptych of *The Madonna of the Misericordia with SS. Sebastian, John the Baptist, Andrew, and Bernadino of Siena*, commissioned by the Confraternity of the Misericordia in Borgo in 1445. The contract specified it was to have been finished within three years. The comparative immaturity of the style suggests both that this was done and that in 1439 Piero had been an assistant of Domenico Veneziano: his influence can be seen in the bright, clear colors, in the drapery of the Madonna, and in her face with the swept-back hair and plucked eyebrows. The crumpled drapery of Saints John and Andrew reflect the influence of another Florentine artist, Andrea del Castagno, whose *Resurrection* provided the starting point for the *Resurrection* that Piero painted in Borgo (probably in the 1450s).

The immaturity of the Borgo polyptych can be brought out by comparing the exaggerated and clumsy contrapposto of St Sebastian with the refined and balanced pose of Christ in the center of *The Baptism of Christ* (National Gallery, London), probably painted in the early 1450s. The other flanking saints are developed in later works. St Andrew recurs in more solid and monumental form as St Sigismund in the 1451 *Pandolfo Malatesta before St Sigismund* in the Tempio Malatestiano, Rimini;

Piero della Francesca: The Baptism of Christ; panel; 167×116cm (66×46in); early 1450s. National Gallery, London

career in the early 1470s, is a last tribute to Masaccio. The interest in projecting the massive forms of the Virgin and Child in space is combined with a new sophistication in the contrasting costumes worn by the two flanking angels. The setting, with a view through to a window in a vestibule on the left of the panel, reveals a debt to Flemish painting. Flemish influence had transformed his handling of landscape from that in the National Gallery *Baptism*, where the green in the foreground is the same as that in the far distance, to that of the Portraits of *Federico da Montefeltro* and *Battista Sforza* (*c* mid 1460s; Uffizi, Florence) where there is an atmospheric handling of the misty distance behind the profile portraits (the format is Flemish).

Flemish painting served to transform the medium in which Piero painted from tempera in his early pictures, through a mixed medium with a combination of tempera and oil, to a full oil technique in his latest work. In the *Madonna Enthroned with Saints and Adored by Federico da Montefeltro* (Pinacoteca di Brera, Milan), the influence of Flemish painting is linked with Piero's mastery over perspective. This culminated in two treatises written at the Court of Urbino at the end of his career, when his sight had failed. Neither the Misericordia polyptych, nor that in Perugia, had afforded the opportunity to elaborate the settings. The *Madonna Enthroned* breaks with the Italian tradition of the *sacra conversazione*, and follows Flemish models by placing the figures in the nave of a church in front of the crossing and apse (which is dominated by a curious large egg, probably that of an ostrich). Such is the skill with which the figures are placed within the rich marble of the church that we overlook the discrepancy in scale—with the head of the seated Virgin on a line with that of the standing saints and angels.

Much about the picture remains uncertain. It cannot have been painted for S. Bernardino in Urbino, where it was first recorded, because that church was only built after 1483 and before 1491. The Brera altar must be earlier, because Piero gave up painting at the end of his career (when his sight failed), and because Federico da Montefeltro is not depicted with the ermine and the garter, both of which he was awarded in 1474, and which he wore in later portraits. Speculation connecting the ostrich egg in the background with the birth (after a number of

he is seen again, with a new range of color and richness of drapery, in the saint from the S. Agostino Altarpiece (1454–69) in the Frick Collection, New York. He is one of the four flanking saints in a polyptych commissioned for the main altar in S. Agostino, Borgo in 1454, but only executed at the end of the 1460s. The central *Virgin and Child* from this polyptych are lost. The other saints that survive are *St Augustine* in the National Gallery, Lisbon, *St Michael* in the National Gallery, London, and *St Nicholas of Tolentino* in the Museo Poldi Pezzoli, Milan.

This account of the Misericordia polyptych has so far failed to mention the

directness with which the light falls (the source is to the right), and the strength of the shadows cast. Piero looks beyond his immediate models in Florentine painting of the 1430s to the achievement of Masaccio. This interest is made explicit in the small Crucifixion on the top of the polyptych which is closely modeled upon that from Masaccio's polyptych formerly in the Carmine, Pisa, now in the Museo e Galerie Nazionali di Capodimonte, Naples. The link is important for Piero's greatest achievement, the Arezzo frescoes, but also for other later works; *The Madonna of Senigallia* (Galleria Nazionale delle Marche, Urbino), from the end of Piero's

daughters) of a son and heir for the Duke in 1472 seems misplaced: tradition records that the Duchess prayed at the shrine of S. Ubaldo, who is not included among the saints around the Virgin's throne.

The still calm that prevails in so much of Piero's work leaves us unprepared for the vividness with which he handles the narrative of *The History of the True Cross* in the fresco cycle in the main chapel of the church of S. Francesco, Arezzo. The decoration had been provided for by the Bacci family in 1416; but work was only begun in 1447 when Bicci di Lorenzo began the ceiling, most of which he had completed by his death in 1452. The date at which the commission was given to Piero is not known. He is referred to as the artist who had painted the cycle in a document of 1466, and it is possible that he only began it after 1459, a year he is documented as working in Rome. The debts to the Antique which suggest this dating occur both at the

bottom in *The Defeat of Chosroes*, where the leaping horseman on the right derives from a relief on the Arch of Constantine, and in *The Death of Adam* in the lunette of the south wall.

The frescoes are arranged in traditional manner on the side-walls of the chapel, with smaller frescoes flanking the lancet window. The light, which is taken as falling from this source, models the forms with an intensity that looks back to Masaccio, although Piero works with a brighter palette.

There may well have been a change in the original program. Both the choice of subject (from *The Golden Legend*) and its treatment connect with the call for a crusade against the Turks, made after the fall of Constantinople in 1453. This would explain why the narrative on the north wall is disrupted to show *The Defeat of Chosroes* (in a form not found in *The Golden Legend*). This is opposite *Constan-*

tine's Victory at the Milvian Bridge, where the introduction of the previous Byzantine Emperor, John Paleologus, as Constantine reinforces the reference to Constantinople. The contemporary overtones are brought out by the eagle of the Empire which flutters over the victors, and by the mixture of contemporary and classical armor. The notables of Arezzo crowd in to watch *The Meeting of Solomon and Sheba* and *The Death of Chosroes*.

The frescoes combine a feeling for variety with a sense of control. The courtly ritual of Sheba and her attendants is contrasted with the struggle of the laborers who have to bury the huge beam; and the night scene in which the angel appears to Constantine is set beside the clear, limpid morning light of his subsequent *Victory at the Milvian Bridge*. The perspective in *The Discovery of the Three Crosses* section of the S. Francesco frescoes is not an end in itself, but is used to differentiate between the discovery of the three crosses outside Jerusalem and the miraculous cure effected by the true cross within the city. Piero's achievement in S. Francesco can be compared with the outstanding monumental frescoes of the Quattrocento, those by Pisanello and Mantegna in the Palazzo Ducale, Mantua, and by Masaccio in the Brancacci Chapel, S. Maria del Carmine, Florence.

Further reading. Aronberg-Lavin, M. *Piero della Francesca's "Flagellation": the Triumph of Christian Glory*, Harmondsworth (1971). Clark, K. *Piero della Francesca*, London (1971). Fasola, N. (ed.) *Piero della Francesca: de Prospectiva Pingendi*, Florence (1942). Mancini, G. (ed.) *Piero della Francesca: Libellus de Quinque Corporibus Regularibus*, Rome (1915). Meiss, M. "Once again, Piero della Francesca's Montefeltro Altarpiece", *Art Bulletin*, New York (1966). Shearman, J. "The Logic and Realism of Piero della Francesca" in Kosegarten, A. and Tigler, P. (eds.) *Festschrift für Ullrich Middeldorf*, Berlin (1968).

Piero di Cosimo 1462–1521

The Florentine painter Piero di Cosimo was, as his name indicates, the pupil of Cosimo Rosselli. He was in Rosselli's shop by 1480, but it is not known when he left. According to Vasari, who provides the only documentation for his life and works, his early experience was with Rosselli in

Piero della Francesca: the train of the Queen of Sheba, a detail of The Meeting of Solomon and the Queen of Sheba; fresco; 1452–65. S. Francesco, Arezzo

Piero di Cosimo: The Forest Fire; panel; 71×203cm (28×80in); c1487–9. Ashmolean Museum, Oxford

Rome, where he helped his master with landscapes, and introduced portraits into the work on the walls of the Sistine Chapel (1481/2).

Piero was a strange man, who seems to have left his garden unkempt, saying that "nature ought to be allowed to look after itself ..." A mean man, he lived on hard-boiled eggs, cooking several days' supply at once in his glue-pot, to save on fuel costs. As an artist, he was certainly interested in the bizarre and the unusual. Vasari says "he stopped to examine a wall where sick persons had used to spit, imagining that he saw there combats of horses and the most fantastic cities and extraordinary landscapes ... He cherished the same fancies of clouds ..." Such Leonardesque ideas appear also in his work, and his style sometimes imitates that of his great compatriot. Although his portraits can be hard, in the manner of Baldovinetti, they often show Leonardo's delicacy and intimate intensity.

The best-known of Piero's works are a series of panels on *The Early History of the World*, including *A Fight between Lapiths and Centaurs* (National Gallery, London), *The Hunt* (Metropolitan Museum, New York), and *Prometheus* (Musée des Beaux-Arts, Strasbourg), based on stories deriving from Ovid. Although the exact meaning of these works is often unclear, their style is

startlingly vital, resting partly on the example of Luca Signorelli, who was also working in the Sistine Chapel in the 1480s. Piero's art might be used as an example of the variations that are possible within the Renaissance manner of art, which concentrates on the human body and shows great interest in Classical mythology. Instead of being monumental or heroic, Piero conjures up a poetic atmosphere which the intricacy and Flemish-style detailing of his landscapes helps to remove further from everyday life. His bodies are muscular and exciting in their sharp outline, but they do not blend with the landscape in any kind of unified perspective. Perspective is certainly present, however, as in *The Hunt*: here, a corpse dripping blood is placed in steep perspective, head lolling out of the picture—very much in the manner of Uccello's battle scenes, whose style Piero's work resembles.

Very different are works like his *Madonna and Child with a Dove* (Louvre, Paris), which attains a moral weight and physical dynamism most unlike his *poesie* (as the genre was to be called in the time of Titian). Like Leonardo (traces of whose *sfumato* are visible, in hardened form, in the *Madonna and Child with a Dove*), Piero was also apparently popular as a designer of festival ephemera. Possibly his morbid imagination was enhanced by Si-

gnorelli's scenes of death and damnation in *The Last Judgment* (c1499; Orvieto Cathedral). These may have inspired a particularly nasty triumphal chariot (in the Renaissance tradition, taken over from the Middle Ages, of Triumphs of Love, Fame, Chastity, Honor, and so forth). This is *The Triumph of Death* (1511) as described by Vasari: a "most realistic but a horrid and terrible sight ... this lugubrious spectacle, by its novelty and tremendous character ... at once terrified and amazed the whole city ..." This was only one of several contraptions he designed.

The importance of Piero, then, is twofold: his interest in the early history of the world was a reflection of contemporary appreciation of the notion of the Golden Age and its variations. Yet his landscapes, full of poetry, and described by Vasari as "very lovely and the coloring soft, graceful, harmonious and well blended", were well on the way to an interest in landscape for its own sake—to the creation of a new genre, which was to appear among the Venetians.

Pierre de Montreuil *fl.* 1231–67

Pierre de Montreuil was a French master mason. In 1231 he began rebuilding the Carolingian nave and transepts of the royal mausoleum of St-Denis, Paris, to link

the 12th-century choir, also partly rebuilt, and the narthex erected by Abbot Suger. The work is an early example of the Rayonnant style, characterized by a glazed triforium, large clerestory windows, transept rose windows, and tall, slim, vertical shafts from floor to vault. About 1265, he continued in this style at Notre Dame, Paris. He completed the additional bay of the south transept, with its rose window, as part of the enlargement of the cathedral that had been begun by Jean de Chelles.

Pietro da Cortona 1596–1669

Pietro da Cortona, one of the most influential artists of the Roman High Baroque, was architect, painter, decorator, and designer of monuments. He became the leading fresco painter in Rome; his superb control of complex iconographical schemes and richly diverse, large-scale compositions realized the full potential of the Baroque style.

His real name was Pietro Berrettini; he was known as da Cortona from the place of his birth, where his first teacher was Andrea Commodi. In 1612 he arrived in Rome and there developed his personal style from a study of Raphael and the Antique. He was also profoundly moved by a love for Titian, which was to make him a founder of the Neo-Venetian move-

ment. His earliest known works are frescoes in the Villa Muti at Frascati and in the Palazzo Mattei, Mantua (1622–3).

Cortona rapidly attracted powerful patrons such as the Sacchetti family and Cardinal Francesco Barberini, through whom he was commissioned to paint frescoes in the church of S. Bibbiana (1642–6). These paintings of the life of the saint reveal his profound response to the Antique; they include a profusion of meticulously observed classical ornament and backgrounds of grandiose imperial architecture. These are the result of Cortona's many drawings of vases, sarcophagi, arches, and Roman archaeological remains which he undertook for the famous antiquarian Cassiano dal Pozzo. Yet the boldness and drama of his style are new; his compositions depend on thrusting diagonals, and his touch is spirited.

For the Sacchetti family, Cortona decorated the chapel at the Chigi Palace at Castel Fusano with brilliant, freely painted landscape frescoes. A series of large mythological and historical paintings culminate in 1629 with *Rape of the Sabines* (Palazzo dei Conservatori, Rome). The powerful, almost sculptural groups of figures are organized in an energetic flow of movement both into and across the canvas; the color has a Venetian brilliance.

Between 1633 and 1639 Cortona frescoed the ceiling of the great hall of the Palazzo Barberini in Rome. The central theme is the glorification of Pope Urban VIII as the agent of Providence; the program was devised by the poet Francesco Bracciolini. An illusionistic architectural framework is created from a variety of intricate decorative details painted in simulated stucco. The ceiling is divided into five distinct areas. Painted figures float above and below the framework, giving the illusion of an airy space open to the sky. The rich diversity of subjects that subtly elaborate the central theme, and the swirling mass of brilliantly foreshortened figures, are orchestrated into a composition of overwhelming power focusing on the personification of Divine Providence. In 1637 Cortona had visited Florence and Venice; both in composition and in the beautiful effects of flickering light and atmosphere, his achievement owes much to a study of Veronese's ceilings. Between 1634 and 1638 his preeminence was recognized in Rome and he was elected *principe* of the Accademia di San Luca.

In Florence Cortona had begun to deco-

rate the Sala della Stufa in the Palazzo Pitti with frescoes of the Four Ages. In 1640 he returned to finish these frescoes, and between 1641 and 1647 he decorated a sequence of rooms in the grand ducal apartment. These rooms are unified by a vast iconographical program relating the virtues of Cosimo I to the signs of the planets. The painted scenes are framed by luxuriant stucco decoration; in them the artist reveals a new, highly sophisticated elegance. He also frescoed two small rooms in the Palazzo Pitti for Gian Carlo de' Medici.

Cortona's late compositions develop away from the passionate exuberance of the 1630s towards a calmer and more classical style. In the 1650s he painted many altarpieces and easel pictures and between 1647 and 1665 frescoed the dome, nave, and apse of S. Maria in Vallicella; the dome frescoes are a reworking of the illusionism of Giovanni Lanfranco and Correggio. Between 1651 and 1654 he decorated with fresco the ceiling of the long gallery in the Palazzo Pamphili Navona for Pope Innocent X. The ceiling shows a variety of scenes from *The Aeneid*. Influenced by Raphael and the Antique, it is a work of great elegance and delicacy, whose pale yet radiant colors anticipate the lightness of the Rococo.

Throughout his career Cortona was also occupied by large architectural commissions. The Villa del Pigneto near Rome was built for the Sacchetti family before 1630: here concave lateral wings framed a high central structure with a monumental niche, an idea that derived from the Belvedere in the Vatican. Between 1635 and 1650 Cortona was concerned with the rebuilding of SS. Martina e Luca, Rome. The plan is a Greek cross with apsidal endings, surmounted by a dome. The upper part of the church is richly decorated with a variety of different motifs that ultimately derive from Florentine Mannerism. In the dome, ribs are superimposed upon highly idiosyncratic and undulating recessed panels (coffers). The external facade is curved, seemingly in response to the pressures of internal space. This suggested movement is firmly halted by paired pilasters.

This contrast of concave and convex forms, a theme characteristic of the Roman Baroque, is further developed in Cortona's remodeling of the facade of S. Maria della Pace, Rome (1656–7). Here he placed a bold semicircular porch in front of the lower part of the facade. He emphasized its

Pietro da Cortona: The Apotheosis of Aeneas; detail; ceiling fresco; 1651–4. Galleria Doria Pamphili, Rome

outward thrust by setting it against a convex upper tier, framed by deep concave wings that seem to transform the whole area of the *piazza* into a stage. Yet in other ways the church is more sober than SS. Martina e Luca, and this tendency towards Roman grandeur and simplicity is further developed in the facade of S. Maria in Via Lata, Rome (1658–62). Here two stories are separated by a wide projecting entablature. In the lower story a Corinthian colonnade opens into a portico, in the upper story into a loggia. In the upper colonnade a round arch, enclosed by a triangular pediment, breaks into the entablature—a motive borrowed from Hellenistic or Roman Imperial sources.

In 1664 Cortona submitted plans for the completion of the Louvre. The most important project of his final years was the dome of S. Carlo al Corso, Rome, where the classic simplicity of the motifs contrasts sharply with the Mannerist intricacy of the dome of SS. Martina e Luca.

Further reading. Briganti, G. *Pietro da Cortona e la Pittura Barocca*, Florence (1962). Waterhouse, E. K. *Baroque Painting in Rome*, London (1937). Waterhouse, E. K. *Italian Baroque Painting*, London (1962). Wittkower, R. *Art and Architecture in Italy: 1600–1750*, Harmondsworth (1973).

Pigalle Jean-Baptiste 1714–85

The French sculptor, Jean-Baptiste Pigalle was born in Paris, the son of a joiner. He was to become the leading French sculptor of the mid 18th century, and the chief representative in sculpture of the Enlighten-

ment. The pupil first of Robert Le Lorrain and then of Jean-Baptiste Lemoyne, his beginnings were not auspicious. He failed to win a scholarship to Rome, and went there at his own expense. In his three years there (1736–9) he seems to have been little influenced by either Classical or Baroque sculpture. His phenomenal rise to fame began in 1744, when he exhibited his celebrated *Mercury* (Louvre, Paris) at the Academy: it was the most successful of all sculptural reception pieces.

Pigalle was a highly individual sculptor, whose style steers a middle course between classicism and the Baroque and is characterized by its regard for truth. An intellectual who avoided the seductive, he was closely associated with Voltaire and the Philosophes. He was a favorite sculptor of Madame de Pompadour, and received through Marigny in 1755 the commission for the great equestrian statue of Louis XV for Reims.

Pigalle's most original work is his extraordinary statue of the nude Voltaire (1770–6; Louvre, Paris) which caused a scandal in its day. His finest achievement is the monument to the Maréchal de Saxe at Strasbourg (1753–76; St Thomas), the outstanding French monument of the 18th century.

Jean-Baptiste Pigalle: the monument to the Maréchal de Saxe; marble; 1753–76. Church of St Thomas, Strasbourg

Pilon Germain c1525/30–90

The French sculptor Germain Pilon was born in Paris. In his early years he may have been responsible for the most famous and most mysterious of French Renaissance statues, *Diana of Anet* (Louvre, Paris), first mentioned in 1554. The first record of Pilon is in 1558, when he completed figures (now lost) for the tomb of Francis I. In 1560 he was working for Primaticcio, carving the well-known group of the *Three Graces* for the monument for the heart of Henry II (Louvre, Paris).

Between 1563 and 1570, as a member of Primaticcio's workshop, he provided most of the sculpture for the tomb of Henry II and Catherine de Medici (abbey of St-Denis, Paris), including two of the great bronze Virtues and the marble effigies and kneeling figures in bronze on the top. In these Pilon's individual mature style is first foreshadowed. From the 1570s date some superb portrait busts, of which the finest is perhaps that of the shifty-eyed *Charles IX* (Wallace Collection, London).

In the last ten years of his life, from 1580, Pilon emerged as the most powerfully emotive sculptor of the time. He reflected in his work the upheavals, the anxieties, and the strong religious feeling of the closing years of the Valois dynasty. From these years come sculptures for the never-completed royal mausoleum at St-Denis, including *The Virgin of Pity* (terracotta in the Louvre, Paris; marble in the church of St Paul and St Louis, Paris), which shows a return to the spirit of the late Gothic. Also from this period are the works that stand as his supreme masterpieces: the tombs of Chancellor René de Birague and his wife Valentine Balbiani, together with the associated bronze relief of *The Entombment*, all now in the Louvre, Paris.

Pintoricchio c1454–1513

The Italian painter Bernardino di Betto, known as Pinturicchio or Pintoricchio, was born in Perugia. His frescoes are his most important works, though he also painted altarpieces and portraits. He came to Rome in 1481 as Perugino's assistant, one of the group of Umbrian and Florentine artists (including Ghirlandaio, Rosselli, Signorelli, and Botticelli) Sixtus IV had summoned to fresco the Sistine Chapel.

Pintoricchio later secured important fresco commissions in Rome: for the decoration of the Bufalini Chapel in S. Maria in Aracoeli (c1485), the Borgia apartments in the Vatican Palace (1492–4), and Julius II's presbytery chapel in S. Maria del Popolo (1509–10). He also painted two important series outside Rome: the frescoes of the Baglioni Chapel in Spello (1501; S. Maria Maggiore) and those of the Piccolomini Library in Siena (1502–8).

Pintoricchio's many frescoes, and the many painted by contemporaries such as Ghirlandaio, show that increased opportunities for large-scale painting arose during the late 15th century. These stimulated Pintoricchio and other artists to try new approaches to mural decoration.

Pintoricchio's paintings often flamboyantly honor his patron. The Piccolomini Library in Siena was built to honor Aeneas Sylvius Piccolomini, the humanist Pope Pius II (1458–64), by preserving his collection of Classical texts. Pintoricchio's frescoes depict triumphant moments in the Pope's career, which he had recorded in his autobiography. (This was based squarely upon an ancient text: Julius Caesar's *Commentaries*.) References to Aeneas Sylvius extend even to the ceiling, where the Piccolomini *stemma* is at the center of the decoration.

Those paintings and others by Pintoricchio are effective decoration because of the charm of his seemingly naïve approach to monumental narrative. His paintings, both early and late, are stilted versions of those by his early master, Perugino. The space is more fragmented and the figures stiffer than in Perugino's suave creations. But Pintoricchio's awkwardness actually complements his pursuit of narrative pageantry. His paintings are tableaux in which he sought neither Peruginesque harmony nor dramatic intensity. Instead, he consistently transmuted events into innocent, beguiling pageants performed by pretty figures who pose before numerous picturesque props.

He developed a system of painted frames, fitting the narrative scenes into architectural settings in such a way that the scenes become illusionistic extensions of the room. For instance, he framed the scenes of the Piccolomini Library with fictive arches which seem to project forward. They thus make the narrative scenes appear to take place outside the room. Those painted arches also transform the room into an open loggia, reminiscent of the antique painted loggias described by Pliny the Elder (c AD 23–79).

Such Classical motifs pervade Pintoricchio's work. The rediscovery of the *Domus Aurea* (the "Golden House" of Nero) in Rome spurred him and other late-15th-century artists to imitate the painted and stucco ornament of its rooms. Patrons encouraged the development of such decoration *all'antica*. Pintoricchio's contract for the Piccolomini Library required him to include *grotteschi* in the decoration. He obliged, covering the applied pilasters of the Library's walls and its ceiling pendentives with polychrome grotesque ornament, copied from the decoration of the *Domus Aurea*.

Pintoricchio was a popular artist; he was innovative as well as prolific. The unfolding of his career in Rome, then the new artistic capital of Italy because of the Pope's return from Avignon, is in itself significant. His career established the pattern for later ambitious artists, from Raphael to Pietro da Cortona, who also came to Rome to paint monumental murals in its churches and palaces (*See* overleaf.)

Piranesi G.B. 1720–78

The Italian printmaker and architect Giovanni Battista Piranesi was born at Mogliano. He first trained with his uncle,

G.B. Piranesi: A Staircase before a Vaulted Hall; pen, brown ink, and wash over red chalk on paper; 38×26cm (15×10in); c1755. British Museum, London

the architect Matteo Lucchesi, then with another architect, Giovanni Scalfarotto, and with the engraver Carlo Zucchi. In 1740 Piranesi traveled to Rome as draftsman to Marco Foscarini, ambassador to the Papal Court of Benedict XIV. In Rome he was taught etching by Giuseppe Vasi, and took an interest in Roman Antiquity, history, and literature. In 1743 he visited Naples and the excavations at Pompeii and Herculaneum, then went on to Venice.

Returning to Rome, Piranesi began a successful series of print publications: the *Carceri* ("Prisons"), 1745; the *Vedute* ("Views"), 137 etchings of ancient and modern Rome, from 1745; *Le Antichità Romane*, 1756. He was supported by Pope Benedict XIV, and also by an Englishman, James Caulfield, Earl of Charlemont. His prints were popular among English connoisseurs; in 1757 he was made Honorary Fellow of the Society of Antiquaries, London.

Piranesi wrote an impassioned defence of the Etruscan (as opposed to the Greek) origin of Roman Antiquities in his *Magnificenza ed Architettura de' Romani* ("Magnificence and Architecture of the Romans"), 1761. His architectural works include improvements to the Papal Palace, Castel Gandolfo; S. Maria del Priorato, and the Piazza de' Cavalieri, Rome, 1764–9.

In his topographical prints, Piranesi infused a somber, even menacing, scale to the buildings he portrayed by the exaggerated use of perspective. By heavily shading certain areas of his compositions, he reinforced this dramatic mood.

Pisanello 1395–1455

The Italian artist Antonio Pisano, called Pisanello, was a fashionable court painter and medalist; he was a follower of Gentile da Fabriano, exponent of the International Gothic style.

Brought up in Verona, he was probably first trained under Stefano da Verona, whose influence distinguishes the early *Madonna della Quaglia* (c1420; Museo di Castelvecchio, Verona). Between 1415 and 1422 he worked in Venice, where he continued Gentile da Fabriano's fresco cycle (now destroyed) in the Grand Hall of the Doges' Palace under Gentile's direction. Later he is documented in Verona

and Mantua, and in 1423 may have traveled to Florence to help Gentile in the painting of his Strozzi Altarpiece (Uffizi, Florence).

From 1424 to 1425 Pisanello worked at the Gonzaga court in Mantua; during the same period he frescoed a signed *Annunciation* over the tomb of Niccolò Brenzoni in the Veronese church of S. Fermo. He either accompanied or followed Gentile da Fabriano to Rome in 1426, remaining there until 1432, and completing the fresco cycle in the Lateran Basilica left unfinished on Gentile's death (now destroyed). He also made drawings of Roman antiquities.

On returning to Verona, he frescoed the Pellegrini Chapel in the church of S. Anastasia (1436–8); only the *St George and the Princess* survives, demonstrating his predilection for animals. Indeed, in *The Vision of St Eustace* (1436–8; National Gallery, London) animals usurp all religious purport. Several preparatory drawings for both works exist among the numerous animal drawings attributed to Pisanello, many of which are in the Codex Villardi in the Louvre, Paris. They reveal him as one of the most observant depicters of fauna in Western art.

Pisanello went to Ferrara in 1438. It was at the Congress of Ferrara, attended by John VIII Paleologus, Emperor of Constantinople, that his career as a medalist began. His medallion of the Emperor (the first cast Renaissance medal made in Italy) must belong to the same year. It inaugurated a series of superb portrait medallions commissioned by the reigning tyrants of Italy, including those of Gianfrancesco Gonzaga (1439–40), Filippo Maria Visconti (1440), Francesco Sforza (1442), Lionello d'Este (1441–3), Sigismondo Pandolfo Malatesta (1445), Ludovico III and Cecilia Gonzaga (1447), and Alfonso of Aragon (1449). Pisanello's distinction as a portraitist is equally revealed in his paintings. These include the *Portrait of a Princess* (1435–40; Louvre, Paris), in which the subject is depicted against a background of pinks and columbines among which butterflies flit, and the similar profile *Portrait of Lionello d'Este* (1441; Galleria dell'Accademia Carrara, Bergamo).

In 1439 Pisanello returned to Mantua. During the following decade he moved between its Gonzaga court, the Este court in Ferrara, and his native Verona. In the Palazzo Ducale in Mantua he painted murals which were long believed to have

Above: Pisanello: Madonna and Child with St George and St Anthony Abbot; tempera on panel; 47×29cm (19×11in); c1445. National Gallery, London

Below: Pisanello: Study of Two Horses' Heads; pencil on paper; 29×19cm (11×7½in). Louvre, Paris

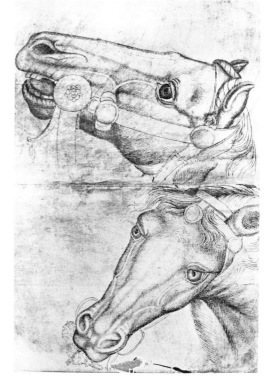

Pintoricchio: Pius II arrives at Ancona for the Crusade, a fresco scene in the Piccolomini Library, Siena; c1506–8

disappeared. But in 1969 the Sala del Pisanello was rediscovered. Extensive portions of *intonaco* painting (*Tournament Battle*) and *sinopie* (*Landscape with Episodes of Chivalrous Legend*) were revealed (c1436–42). The murals, commemorating King Henry VI's bestowal of the English Royal Livery on Gianfrancesco Gonzaga, were presumably abandoned on Pisanello's banishment from Mantua in 1442.

In 1448 Pisanello went to the Neapolitan court of Alfonso of Aragon, for whom he worked as a medalist. After 1449, we have no documentary evidence of his activities or whereabouts. He died in 1455.

Pisani 13th and 14th centuries

The group of Italian sculptors known as the Pisani included Nicola Pisano (*fl.* 1258–78) and his son Giovanni (*fl.* 1245/50–1314); Andrea da Pontedera, known as Andrea Pisano (*fl.* c1290–1348/9), and his son Nino (*fl.*1349–?68). The two families were not related.

Their name indicates their origins, and it was at Pisa that they founded and maintained the Pisan School which dominated Tuscan and to a lesser extent Italian sculpture over the century 1250 to 1350. Other artists of great accomplishment such as Arnolfo di Cambio and Tino di Camaino came from that circle. Their combined talents produced innovations in style, iconography, and sculptural programs that mark a major peak in the history of European art.

Pisa, at its heyday c1250, was one of several Tuscan city states (Florence, Siena, and Lucca being most notable among the others) that were in continuous rivalry during the later Middle Ages. Their rivalries, fueled by Guelph or Ghibelline loyalties, often spilled over into open warfare. But it was not a situation that prevented the movement of artists. Thus Nicola and Giovanni Pisano worked in Siena, the latter being a Sienese citizen for a number of years, and Andrea worked extensively in Florence.

An important factor in assessing the art of the Pisani is the presence in Naples from the 1260s onwards of the French Angevin monarchy. It prompted the appearance of French culture in Italy, particularly the Gothic style, of which there were to be many instances in the work of the Pisani. But this powerful influence was never able to extinguish the innate echoes of Classical Antiquity in Italian art, echoes that were to reverberate with great clarity in the sculpture of Nicola and Giovanni Pisano.

Knowledge of the lives of both Nicola and Giovanni is patchy, but much of their sculpture has survived in good condition, particularly the famous series of pulpits. These are the keystones of their work. Because of the advances they show in naturalistic representation—advances that precede the great achievements of Giotto—they are the basis for the claim that Nicola and Giovanni were the first Renaissance artists.

Nicola Pisano's date of birth is unknown, and his origins uncertain. While most documents refer to him as being "from Pisa", two say that he is from Apulia. Evidence to substantiate this possible south Italian origin is provided by his first pulpit, that at Pisa: the abundance of its quotations from antique art may have been inspired by work, deliberately Classical in style, carried out in southern Italy for the Emperor Frederick II (*ob.* 1250).

Nicola is first documented in 1258, and again in 1260 when he signed the pulpit in the Baptistery at Pisa. This hexagonal structure has three parts. The lower consists of seven columns. Their foliated capitals support the middle section, an archivolt of trilobe arches with prophets and evangelists in the spandrels, and statuettes of Virtues and St John the Baptist at the corners. The upper level, the casket, is decorated with five reliefs depicting incidents from the life of Christ and the Last Judgment, these being divided by clusters of three columns. The hard, solid forms of the reliefs are the result of Nicola's study of the Antique, and several figures can be traced to Roman sarcophagi that still survive. Though elements of the shape and arrangement follow south Italian and Tuscan traditions, the pulpit's originality lies in the new and highly sophisticated way these elements are handled.

After completing the Pisa pulpit, Nicola probably undertook two reliefs for Lucca Cathedral. These are neither documented nor signed, and the extent of his contribution is disputed. In 1265 he contracted to make a pulpit for Siena Cathedral. It was finished in 1268. Larger and more elaborate than the Pisa pulpit, it is octagonal, and has statuettes at the angles of the casket instead of columns. The relief scenes are smaller in scale than those at Pisa and their figures more numerous. In several places, particularly the angle figures of the casket, a softening of form and line introduces a Gothic flavor that was largely absent at Pisa. The pulpit's variety of styles and uneven quality is the result of workshop participation. Documents refer to four assistants, notably Giovanni Pisano and Arnolfo di Cambio. One reason for their involvement was the fact that Nicola was simultaneously supervising another major commission, the tomb of St Dominic at S. Domenico in Bologna. That work was finished by 1267, and again there is much evidence of studio participation.

The last documented work of Nicola's is the *Fontana Maggiore* at Perugia, undertaken with Giovanni and completed in 1278. It is on three levels: the lower basin is a 25-sided polygon decorated with 50 reliefs; above is a smaller 12-sided basin interspersed with statuettes. The upper level, all in bronze, consists of a column, surmounted by a basin and a caryatid from which gushes the water. The marble reliefs read like a medieval encyclopedia with carvings of, for example, the Labors of the Months and the Liberal Arts. The statuettes range from saints and prophets to city officials and personifications of local places. Style and iconography show French influence in parts, and may indicate Giovanni's hand.

Nicola's greatness lay in his ability to formulate large-scale sculptural programs, and his creation of a naturalistic relief style based on borrowings from Antiquity and northern Gothic. Suggestions that the latter are the result of a visit to France are entirely hypothetical.

Giovanni's date of birth is also unknown, though he was born a Pisan. After the completion of the Siena and Perugia projects he may have remained in Nicola's workshop, helping his father with the sculptural decoration of the outside of the Pisa Baptistery, a scheme that is not documented but is confidently assigned to this circle.

By 1285 he was resident in Siena and undertaking the design and decoration of the cathedral facade, though there is no direct documentary proof for this and he is first referred to as "capomaestro" (chief architect) only in 1290. By the time he left, probably in 1297, he had completed six animals and 14 large full-length biblical prophets and sages of Antiquity, all for the lower part of the facade. The badly weathered figures are now in the Museo dell'Opera del Duomo, Siena. Unlike such schemes in northern Europe, they were not incorporated in a rigid architectural framework,

pulpit than he was commissioned in 1302 to make another, this time for Pisa Cathedral. Completed in 1310, it is much larger than the other three and is octagonal in shape. The iconography of the upper sections is the same, though necessarily expanded. The main departure is the replacement of some columns by caryatids, two being accompanied by elaborate figure sculpture around the bases. Just as in Nicola's Siena pulpit, Giovanni's second version shows variations in quality that point to workshop participation, particularly in the angle figures. Some of the finest work—certainly done by Giovanni himself—is to be found in the caryatids. One, the "Prudence" figure, exemplifies the reappearance of Classical motifs in this pulpit. Other motifs, such as the acanthusleaf brackets replacing the pointed arches of Pistoia, help to emphasize the contrast with the earlier pulpit. The springy lightness of Pistoia has given way to a heavier, monumental, almost Baroque splendor.

In 1311–12 Giovanni carved his only surviving tomb sculpture, the monument to Margaret of Luxembourg, wife of Emperor Henry VII (fragments at the Palazzo Bianco, Genoa, and elsewhere). Other works that survive include some wooden crucifixes and a number of Madonna and Child groups, including one carved in ivory (Pisa Cathedral treasury). Most are undocumented and unsigned but are ascribed on firm stylistic evidence to various periods in Giovanni's life.

There is no concrete evidence for the claim, sometimes made, that Giovanni visited France, though the Gothic elements in his work are certainly considerable. Along with the borrowings from Antiquity, they are well assimilated in a way that his father's are not. Moreover, his work is marked by an easy confidence in the handling of gestures and groups of figures, and his narrative reliefs are extremely vivid. Giovanni's hallmarks include the long necks and jutting heads of his figures.

The massive achievements of Nicola and Giovanni Pisano overshadow the work of their namesakes in the 14th century. In the case of Andrea Pisano this is particularly regrettable, for his bronze doors for the Baptistery of Florence Cathedral are among the major monuments of Italian art. The doors, signed and dated 1330, provide the first mention of Andrea. Subsequent documents refer to various assistants and casting arrangements. The work was completed in 1336. Together the doors

Giovanni Pisano: the pulpit in Pisa Cathedral; marble; 1302–10

but seem to move around and interrelate with one another. To ensure that their powerful gestures and expressions were visible from the ground, Giovanni cut deeply into the marble and distorted both poses and features. The effect is awesomely impressive.

Probably soon after his return to Pisa, Giovanni began the third in the great series of pulpits, that for the church of S. Andrea at Pistoia. Completed in 1301, the pulpit differs little in arrangement and iconography from Nicola's at Siena, but returns to the hexagonal shape of that at Pisa. The

angle figures are larger in scale and now are carved to be seen from a number of viewpoints. Their thrusting, vigorous poses recall some of the Siena facade statues. In the five reliefs Giovanni stresses the human side of the stories, such as the tenderness of the Nativity or the violent emotions of the Massacre of the Innocents. In style the pulpit is in marked contrast to Nicola's works. It is essentially Gothic, with its pointed arches supporting the casket, its figure-style, and its general air of lightness and delicacy.

No sooner had Giovanni finished this

contain 20 scenes from the life of John the Baptist and eight personifications of virtues, each contained in a quatrefoil, a decorative element that enlivens the surface of the doors. There is no obvious source for the general arrangement though the quatrefoils, a French motif, were used by Giotto in the Capella dell'Arena, Padua. Giotto's figure and drapery style is employed with great beauty and gracefulness by Andrea, some of whose brilliant compositions are adapted from the painter's Peruzzi Chapel frescoes (in S. Croce, Florence). Where these fail to provide a prototype, Andrea uses the mosaics in the dome of the Baptistery. The format of the doors was copied by Ghiberti in his first set of doors for the same building.

In 1340 Andrea is mentioned as "capomaestro" of Florence Cathedral, a post he held until 1343. He was responsible for extending the campanile as far as the second main cornice. He is also generally held to have designed and executed most of the reliefs surrounding the lower half of the base, where again the style shows Giotto's influence. Some of the statues in the niches above have also been attributed to him on stylistic evidence.

He was appointed "capomaestro" at Orvieto Cathedral in 1347, being succeeded by his son in 1349. He may have died either then or at Florence in the following year.

Surviving references to Andrea's son Nino are very sparse. By 1353 he had left his post at Orvieto. In 1357–8 he is recorded as a silversmith at Pisa. By 1368 he was dead. His three surviving signed works are undated. Two of these, a *Madonna and Child* (S. Maria Novella, Florence) and some figures, including a *Madonna and Child*, surmounting the Cornaro monument (SS. Giovanni e Paolo, Venice), indicate a Gothic style close to contemporary French art. Their charm is exemplified by the sweet smiles of the Madonnas. On these works is hung a whole collection of homeless mid-14th-century sculpture. Few can be either attributed or dated with any certainty. Two of the more definite are a *Madonna and Child*

Left: Andrea Pisano: the south door of the Baptistery, Florence; bronze; height 564cm (222in); 1330–6

Right: Nino Pisano: Madonna and Child; marble; c1348. S. Maria Novella, Florence

where the Virgin is suckling the Child (Museo Nazionale di San Matteo, Pisa) and a pair of marble figures, *The Virgin and the Annunciatory Angel* (S. Catherina, Pisa) that were to be influential on later Annunciation groups.

Further reading. Crichton, G.H. and E.R. *Nicola Pisano and the Survival of Sculpture in Italy*, Cambridge (1938). Mellini, G.L. *Giovanni Pisano*, Milan (1970).

Pissarro Camille 1830–1903

The Impressionist painter Camille Jacob Pissarro was born on the island of St Thomas in the West Indies, the son of a Jewish father and a Creole mother. He settled in France in 1855, and studied landscape under Corot *c*1860; he met Monet at this time, and Cézanne in 1861. His early landscapes are in the tradition of the Barbizon School, quite subdued in color and simple in structure, for instance the large *Banks of the Marne at Chennevières*, shown at the 1865 Salon (National Gallery of Scotland, Edinburgh). The execution of this painting, largely by the palette-knife, shows a debt to Courbet. By 1870, Pissarro was painting smaller pictures, whose varied touch conveys the differing textures and effects in his landscape subjects, such as *The Diligence at Louveciennes* (Musée du Jeu de Paume, Paris).

In 1870 Pissarro took refuge from the Franco-Prussian War in London, where he found Monet, and had a chance to study the work of Constable and Turner. However, his paintings of London, and those painted between 1871 and 1873 after his return to France, show no direct influence of British painting. They continue the traits of his 1870 work, in their response to the variety of nature, as in *The Louveciennes Road* (1872; Musée du Jeu de Paume, Paris). Pissarro's concerns in this period were particularly close to those of Sisley.

Around 1874 Pissarro began to look for a greater surface unity in his paintings, perhaps as a result of his contact with Cézanne, with whom he worked regularly during the years 1872 to 1874. In paint-

Camille Pissarro: The Diligence on the Road from Ennery to L'Hermitage, Pontoise; oil on canvas; 47×55cm (19×22in); 1877. Musée du Jeu de Paume, Paris

Camille Pissarro: The Boieldieu Bridge at Rouen; oil on canvas; 74×91cm (29×36in); 1896. City of Birmingham Museums and Art Gallery

ings such as *Quarry at Pontoise* (c1874; Öffentliche Kunstsammlung, Kunstmuseum, Basel) he used the palette knife to give this unity, by comparatively broad strokes of paint. However, in 1876 and 1877 he began to seek homogeneity with small juxtaposed brush strokes, varied in color but often parallel in direction; these unified the picture surface but at the same time permitted him to introduce the varied atmospheric color he was increasingly seeking. This development, seen in a marked form in *Landscape at Chaponval* (1880; Musée du Jeu de Paume, Paris), is closely paralleled by the so-called "constructive stroke" adopted by Cézanne during the same years.

Pissarro lived in the Pontoise area, north of Paris, from 1872 to 1884; he then moved further north to the village of Eragny, and lived there for the rest of his life. He was a central figure in the organization of the Impressionist group exhibitions of 1874 to 1886, and was the only

artist to exhibit in all eight shows. Landscape, often with peasant figures, was his prime subject, apart from a sequence of townscapes of Rouen and Paris, which he began in 1896. His peasant subjects reflected his anarchist political beliefs; he felt that the future of society should lie in decentralization and in a return to the land.

Several members of the Neo-Impressionist group in the later 1880s were also anarchists, notably Paul Signac and Maximilien Luce. These shared beliefs, together with the increasing systematization in Pissarro's technique of 1877 to 1895, encouraged him in 1886 to adopt the Divisionist technique pioneered by Seurat, and to redefine the bases of his art in terms of the color theories of writers such as Michel-Eugène Chevreul and Ogden Rood. However, by 1888 Pissarro found that the rigors of pointillist execution prevented him from responding directly to the diversity of nature. *View from my Window,*

Eragny, completed in 1888 (Ashmolean Museum, Oxford), shows great variety of touch, though the individual brush strokes remain very small. Pissarro's handling and color effects became much broader in later paintings such as *The Boieldieu Bridge at Rouen* (1896; City of Birmingham Museums and Art Gallery). The rich color scheme of this work suggests that it was in the 1890s, rather than the 1870s, that Turner's color became relevant to Pissarro's art, when, in the works of his last decade, he sought to give his paintings an overriding unity of effect.

Further reading. Adler, K. *Camille Pissarro: a Biography*, London (1978). Lloyd, C. (*et al.*) *Camille Pissarro 1830–1903*, London (1980). Pissarro, C. (ed. Rewald, J.) *Letters to his Son Lucien*, London (1943). Rewald, J. *Camille Pissarro*, London (1963). Shikes, R.E. and Harper, P. *Pissarro, his Life and Work*, New York (1980).

Giambattista Pittoni: St Jerome and St Peter of
Alcantara; oil on canvas; 275×143cm
(108×56in). National Gallery of Scotland,
Edinburgh

Pittoni Giambattista 1687–1767

The reputation of the Venetian artist
Giambattista Pittoni was high in his lifetime, but has justifiably declined. His style.
an amalgam of the styles of many earlier
artists, was seldom infused with the
sparkle of originality that distinguished his
contemporaries G.B. Tiepolo and G.B.
Piazzetta. He is seen at his best in the
early altarpieces in the parish church at S.
Germano dei Berici, Vicenza (*Madonna
and Child with Saints*) and in the National
Gallery of Scotland, Edinburgh, where the
succulent paint and rich coloring are allied
with excellent draftsmanship. Like most of
his Venetian contemporaries, he received
many commissions from outside the city.

Pleydenwurff Hans c1420–72

A native of Bamberg, the painter Hans
Pleydenwurff became a citizen of Nuremberg in 1457. Apart from a brief stay in
Breslau in 1462, he worked in Nuremberg
until his death. He also supplied designs
for glass painters, and his style was developed from the Early Netherlandish

painters, in particular Rogier van der
Weyden.

Pleydenwurff's *The Descent from the
Cross*, painted for the High Altar of the
church of St Elizabeth in Breslau (1462;
Germanisches Nationalmuseum, Nuremberg), is the artist's earliest surviving major
commission; the exact means by which he
developed his mature style remains little
understood. However, his superb *Portrait
of George, Count of Löwenstein* (Germanisches Nationalmuseum, Nuremberg)
can be dated to c1456. It reveals the depth
of Pleydenwurff's understanding of the
Master of Flémalle/Rogier van der
Weyden tradition of portrait painting.
Indeed, this portrait is a major landmark in
the evolution of portraiture in Germany.

It is possible that Pleydenwurff spent
some time in the Netherlands. The clear
spatial organization and the detailed treatment of figures and landscape elements in
his *Crucifixion* (c1470; Alte Pinakothek,
Munich) demonstrate his continued debt
to Netherlandish models at the end of his
life. The town in the background is clearly
intended to be a realistic view of Bamberg;
the *Crucifixion* was probably painted for
Löwenstein, and formerly hung in Bamberg Cathedral.

After Pleydenwurff's death in 1472
Michael Wolgemut took over the
workshop, and thus the traditions of Pley-

denwurff's studio would have been transmitted to the young Albrecht Dürer.

Poelenburgh Cornelis van
c1586–1667

Cornelis van Poelenburgh, a painter from
Utrecht, was one of the first early-17th-
century Dutch landscapists to visit and
work in Rome. There he copied the small,
poetic landscapes of Adam Elsheimer
(1578–1610), and also admired the pictures of the Flemish landscapist Paul Bril
(1554–1626). During his Italian visit, and
after his return to Utrecht c1626, Poelenburgh painted much-admired and influential Italianate landscapes on copper, in
cool, enamel-like colors. These are often
arcadian in character, and exploit ancient
ruins and mythological personages to
evoke the Classical past. Poelenburgh
painted a few small-scale portraits, and
sometimes added the figures to the landscapes of other artists, for instance to those
of Jan Both (c1618?–52).

Poliakoff Serge 1906–69

The French painter Serge Poliakoff was of
Russian background. In 1919 he traveled
with his aunt, the singer Nastia Poliakoff,
as her accompanist. They went to Constantinople and from there via Sofia, Bel-

Cornelis van Poelenburgh: A Roman Landscape; oil on panel; 44×60cm (18×24in); c1620. Toledo
Museum of Art, Toledo, Ohio

grade, Vienna, and Berlin, to Paris. He settled in Paris in 1923, making his living playing the guitar, and studied painting at the Académie Frochot, Grande Chaumière. In 1935 he moved to London, studying at the Slade School of Fine Art. He returned to Paris, and in 1937 met Kandinsky. In the following year Poliakoff was a regular attender at the artists' gatherings at the home of Sonia and Robert Delaunay.

His mature work, from 1949 onwards, is characterized by the use of decisive abstract shapes and strongly contrasting color (for example, *Composition*; oil on plywood, 1950; Solomon R. Guggenheim Museum, New York). His work may be compared with that of other members of the School de Paris.

Polidoro da Caravaggio
1496/1500–43

Polidoro da Caravaggio was an Italian painter. His early years in Lombardy are obscure; Vasari says he began painting in the loggias of the Vatican under the influence of Giovanni da Udine. It was probably here that he discovered the type of *all'antica* fictive relief for the development of which he is perhaps best known. His resourcefulness lay in adapting it to the long, narrow areas on the facades of houses and palaces, mainly in Rome. The owners of such palaces required painted decorations whose subject matter would reflect the culture of ancient Rome. An example of his work is to be seen in the Palazzo Ricci, Rome. Most of these decorations have now faded away. After the Sack of Rome (1527) Polidoro went south, where the requirements of patronage led him to paint mostly altarpieces.

Pollaiuolo brothers 15th century

Antonio Pollaiuolo (1431/2–98) was a Florentine goldsmith, sculptor, painter, engraver and designer; his brother Piero (1441–94/6) was a painter. The brothers were sons of Jacopo di Giovanni Benci, a Florentine poulterer. According to tradition, Antonio trained under Lorenzo Ghiberti, and Piero under Andrea del Castagno. In 1466 Antonio entered the goldsmiths' guild. Both belonged to the Compania di San Luca, Piero being listed in 1472 as a painter and Antonio in 1473 as a goldsmith and painter. The two ran a joint workshop in which Antonio seems to have been the senior partner. As they

Piero Pollaiuolo: The Coronation of the Virgin; tempera on panel; 1483. S. Agostino, San Gimignano

frequently collaborated, it is often difficult to distinguish the work of one from that of the other. Antonio was undoubtedly a much more significant and versatile artist than Piero; but the common practice of attributing all the better productions of their workshop to the elder brother and all the worse to the younger is arbitrary and possibly misleading.

Several of Antonio's most important works were commissioned for Florence Baptistery and are still preserved in the Museo dell'Opera del Duomo, Florence. They are a large silver reliquary cross (1457-9; made with the assistance of Betto Betti), a silver relief of *The Birth of the Baptist* for the altar of S. Giovanni (1478–80), and a series of vestment embroideries of *The Life of St John the Baptist* (1469–80; executed by a team of embroiderers to Antonio's designs). Almost all of his numerous other pieces of goldsmith's work, parade armor, and jewelry have been lost.

As early as 1460 the two brothers collaborated on a series of large canvases of *The Exploits of Hercules* for Piero de' Medici for the Medici Palace, Florence.

Pallaiuolo brothers: The Martyrdom of St Sebastian; tempera on panel; 292×203cm (115×8oin); c1475. National Gallery, London

Although these are now lost, smaller variants record two of the compositions. They appear to have been the first monumental Florentine mythological compositions in the antique manner. The altarpiece of *St James between St Vincent and St Eustace* in the Uffizi was also a joint project, executed in 1466–7 for the chapel of the Cardinal of Portugal in S. Miniato al Monte.

Piero undertook a series of *Virtues* in the Uffizi for the Florentine Mercanzia in 1469 and an altarpiece of *The Coronation of the Virgin* in San Gimignano in 1483 (in the church of S. Agostino). These works are monumental and quite accomplished, although rather dry and monotonous in conception. A comparison of them with Antonio's large signed engraving of *The Battle of the Ten Nudes* (c1471–2) aptly demonstrates the superiority of the elder brother's powers of invention. This superb print has no apparent subject matter and was presumably intended as an illustration of the human body in motion. It proved enormously influential.

The large *The Martyrdom of St Sebastian* (c1475; National Gallery, London) was almost certainly a collaborative enterprise, and is the most impressive surviving painting produced by the Pollaiuoli. Its strangely rigid composition may reveal a deliberate exercise in the precepts of Alberti. The painting is particularly memorable for its representation of the human body from a wide variety of viewpoints, so it seems likely that Antonio played the more important part in its conception.

Although Antonio executed a number of small bronzes, it was only towards the very end of his life that he received large-scale sculptural commissions. These are the two bronze tombs of Pope Sixtus IV and Pope Innocent VIII at St Peter's in Rome. The former (c1484–93) is a freestanding monument, of a form unusual in Italy. The latter (c1492–8) is a more traditional type of wall tomb. It incorporates the interesting innovation of representing the Pope twice: as a recumbent corpse, and triumphantly enthroned, as if alive. Although Piero accompanied his brother to Rome (where both subsequently died), it is virtually certain that he played no part in the design of either monument. Both tombs indicate Antonio's training as a goldsmith—they are skillful assemblages of small bronzes arranged around dominant motifs, rather than truly monumental designs. However, his superb standards of craftsmanship and his profound interest in characterization and the human physique are equally apparent.

A number of other panel paintings, frescoes, and drawings survive, demonstrating the wide range of the Pollaiuoli's activities. Antonio's drawings are usually very vivacious and were clearly highly influential. In particular, they reveal his profound scientific knowledge of human anatomy. It was this aspect of his art that most impressed Antonio's contemporaries.

Further reading. Ettlinger, L.D. *Antonio and Piero Pollaiuolo*, Oxford and New York (1978).

Pollock Jackson 1912–56

The American painter Jackson Pollock was the leading figure of the New York School of the 1940s. Brought up in California, he moved to New York in 1929 and studied at the Art Students' League under Thomas

Graham, a Russian émigré who talked and wrote of Picasso, African art, symbolism, and the role of the unconscious in artistic creation. Pollock assimilated these elements to a great extent. They colored the obsessive symbols that appeared when he began drawing under psychoanalysis, as part of a psychiatric cure for alcoholism. The emphasis on the role of the unconscious was of particular importance for Pollock, who was to take the Surrealist principle of automatism to its furthest physical and artistic limits.

Pollock's work matured suddenly in 1943, aided by the example of Hans Hofmann, by the émigré artists in New York, and by the patronage of Peggy Guggenheim. The next decade saw the creation of all his most important work. *The Guardians of the Secret* (oil on canvas; 1943; San Francisco Museum of Art) synthesized Pollock's interests of the 1930s and looked forward to even more expressionist works. In this painting the "guardians", images both zoological and abstract, lurk around a central rectangle unified by a web of bright colors against a dark background, diversified by contradictory and frequently

Jackson Pollock: Don Quixote; oil on canvas; 74×46cm (29×18in); c1944. Peggy Guggenheim Foundation, Venice

Antonio Pollaiuolo: Apollo and Daphne; panel; 30×20cm (12×8in). National Gallery, London

Hart Benton, the American Regionalist. *Going West* (oil on gesso ground on composition board; 1934–5; private collection), with its exaggerated simplification of a folk subject, reflects Benton's championship of the American heartland as opposed to the artistic ideals of a decadent Europe.

For Pollock, as for all the New York School, the 1930s were years of vital experimentation and assimilation. Pollock's career was saved by employment in the easel division of the Works Progress

Administration from 1935 to 1943, years during which his work was in crisis and he was also suffering from acute alcoholism. Through Benton, Pollock met David Siqueiros, the Mexican muralist, who was running an experimental workshop in Union Square, New York. Siqueiros' influence introduced Pollock to a new scale of execution, and to new techniques such as spray painting and the use of enamel paint.

He also learned much from John

canceled depth.

The images disappear in *Mural* (oil on canvas; 1943; University of Iowa, Iowa City), commissioned by Peggy Guggenheim for her New York apartment. *Mural* is the essential Pollock: large scale, fluent and consecutive in execution, eliminating image in favor of an elaborate swirling web of inscription. At his best Pollock produced an overall rhythmic structure with an automatic intuitive technique. The process was intensified by the "drip" method of paint splashed over a canvas stretched on the floor. It was seen at its most grandiose in *Cathedral* (enamel and aluminum paint on canvas; 1947; Dallas Museum of Fine Arts). Here the intensity of the web of lines and color, consciously flattened by the enamel, produces a final stillness. *Cathedral* was the furthest point to which Pollock's Abstract Expressionist style could be taken. After six years of its practice, coupled with experimentation in various directions, the impetus went out of his work in 1953.

Pollock, the greatest of the Abstract Expressionists, was widely copied in America and Europe in the 1950s. But his followers, lacking his personal struggle and his innate control, rapidly reduced his style to a formula and a cliché.

Further reading. Emmerling, L. *Jackson Pollock 1912–1956*, Cologne, Ger. (2003). Friedman, B. *Jackson Pollock: Energy Made Visible*, New York (1972, reissued 1995). Landau, E. *Jackson Pollock*, New York (1980, reissued 2000). Varnedoe, K. *Jackson Pollock*, New York (2002).

Polycleitos 5th century BC

Polycleitos was a Greek sculptor of the high Classical period who came from Sicyon. He was a pupil of the Argive Ageladas, reputed master of Pheidias and Myron. He perfected the technique of bronze casting, and was the most distinguished representative of the Argive School, which specialized in bronze nudes of victorious athletes for the sanctuaries of southern Greece.

His contribution to sculpture consisted in the invention of the contrapposto. This was a pose suspended between walking and resting, with one side of the statue relaxed, the other tense, and the weight carried by one leg. He also devised a system of proportions aiming at the perfect scale, based on the quadrifacial nature of

Polycleitos: Doryphoros; marble; height 198cm (78in); a Roman copy of the 5th-century BC original. Museo Archeologico Nazionale, Naples

the Classical statue. He thus created a model type which exerted a formative influence on Greek and Roman sculpture. Its beauty depended on two apparently incompatible principles: the commensurability of parts, and a rather loose application of mathematical rules. This coincided with similar practices in architecture (for instance in the Parthenon) and was a development of earlier experiments.

Polycleitos explained his theory in a treatise, one of the first of its kind, and applied it to a statue: both treatise and statue are known as the *Canon* (Rule). The statue is a boyish *Doryphoros* (spear-bearer) standing on the right foot, the left drawn back on its toes. His left hand carries the spear on his shoulder, its line harmoniously incorporated into the balanced composition. (The best copies are in the Museo Archeologico Nazionale, Naples.) Roman critics complained that all the figures by Polycleitos were cut to one pattern. His works included a *Herakles* and a *Hermes* that have been identified in copies; and a figure with raised arms, the *Diadumenus* (*Youth tying his hair with a Band*), best known from a Hellenistic copy from Delos (National Museum, Athens; another marble copy is in the British Museum, London).

Like his contemporaries, Pheidias, Cresilas, and Phradmon, Polycleitos entered the competition to make a wounded *Amazon* for the temple of Artemis in Ephesus. According to the story about their competition, each of the other three sculptors ranked Polycleitos' *Amazon* second only to his own, so that he won the first prize. (Such stories were common in Antiquity, and have been told of Agoracritus and Pheidias, among others.) His *Amazon* is perhaps represented in copies showing her leaning on a spear while she uncovers her wounded breast (Museo Capitolino, Rome). The distribution of weight of the statue departs slightly from the *Canon*; it corresponds to that of the *Westmacott Athlete* (British Museum, London), a work thought to derive from Polycleitos' statue of the boy boxer Cyniscus. In both, the emphasis is shifted to one side, as they raise the right arm and bend the head under it.

Polycleitos also made a gold and ivory cult-statue of *Hera* for her temple at Argos, rebuilt after the fire of 423 BC. She was seated with a pomegranate in one hand and a scepter in the other, topped by a cuckoo, personifying her husband Zeus. She was accompanied by a standing *Hebe*, also in gold and ivory, by Naucydes, a member of Polycleitos' School. Naucydes was the brother of Polycleitos the Younger (4th century BC) who was both a sculptor and the architect of the Tholos and the theater at Epidaurus.

Polygnotus *fl.* 475–447 BC

The Greek artist Polygnotus, of Thasos and Athens, was the most famous painter of Antiquity. His name was borrowed by two vase painters in Athens, and in the

Jacopo Pontormo: Joseph in Egypt; oil on panel; 97×110cm (38×43in); 1517–18. National Gallery, London

view of Theophrastus he was the founder of the art of painting. His work represents a break with the Archaic tradition and the inception of the Classical, comparable with that of the master of the Olympia sculptures. Like the sculptures, his figures were remembered for the ethos and dignity that they portrayed. This was achieved by a technique of simple outline drawing with washes of color and effects of transparent dress, but no extensive use of shading, highlights, or any true perspective.

Polygnotus specialized in massed compositions for walls, dispersing the figures up and down the field to render depth. The device was copied on some Athenian vases and it is to these that we have to look for echoes of his compositions and figures, since no original works have survived. He painted *The Sack of Troy* and *The Underworld* for the Lesche (clubhouse) dedicated by the Cnidians at Delphi, with careful characterization of the individual heroes, described in detail by Pausanias. In Athens he executed another *Sack of Troy* in the Painted Stoa and his panels were long exhibited in the picture gallery in the north wing of the Propylaea on the Acropolis. He was a friend of the statesman Cimon and the poet Sophocles. Several of his themes were those also treated by the 5th-century dramatists, and he clearly played an important role in the intellectual life of early Classical Athens.

Pontormo Jacopo 1494–1557

The Italian painter Jacopo Pontormo was born Jacopo Carucci in Pontormo near Empoli outside Florence. Around 1507 he moved to Florence, and finished his training there in the workshop of Andrea del Sarto during the years 1512–14. His first work, the *Madonna and Saints* of c1514 painted for S. Rufillo, Florence (now in the Capella di S. Luca of SS. Annunziata), reveals his absorption of Andrea's figure-types, fluent grouping, and expressive gestures.

Pontormo's *Visitation* of 1515–16 (SS. Annunziata, Florence) is more personal in the figure-style and more independent in the use of the niche, which derives from Fra Bartolommeo (1472–1517). Andrea had experimented with the pyramidal grouping introduced by Leonardo, but none of his monumental works achieve the variety of Pontormo's fresco, where the spectators to the left are intended to distract attention from the Virgin in the center. The asymmetry is reinforced by the contrast between the small naked boy sitting on the second step and the large woman sitting on the other side of the step. She is closer to the spectator and suggests, in the elegance of her S-shaped curve, a distant derivation from the Libyan Sybil on the Sistine Chapel ceiling, Vatican, Rome. The ambiguities with which the figures interlock are developed by Pontormo in

the Visdomini Altar of 1518, whose dark tonality is conceived as a reaction against the brighter colors of Andrea's work (as also is the range of saints).

The drawings from this period and the drawings for the lost *St Michael* (c1519; Galleria della Collegiata, Empoli) reveal his profound study of Michelangelo. This underlies Pontormo's achievement in the years 1520 to 1530. His work ranges widely, from the light-hearted *Vertumnus and Pomona* of 1520 in Lorenzo de' Medici's villa at Poggio a Caiano, to the combination of emotional intensity and elegance in the *Deposition* of 1526–8 (S. Felicita, Florence). There is an expressive reinterpretation of Dürer in the frescoes at the Certosa di Val d'Ema (1523–4), where the grouping of the figures recalls Michelangelo's early *Entombment* (National Gallery, London).

The originality of these paintings is matched by that of his portraiture where, as in the portrait of the young man thought to be Alessandro de' Medici (Museo Nazionale di Villa Guinigi, Lucca) the stiffness of the pose and of the sitter's robes emphasize his effortless superiority. Other portraits combine this stiff elegance with an architectural setting that serves as an attribute, rather than as a space within which the figures are placed (for example, *Portrait of a Lady*, c1532; Städelsches Kunstinstitut, Frankfurt am Main). Pontormo's involvement with Michelangelo led, in 1530, to the commission to paint two pictures (neither of which has survived) from Michelangelo's cartoons. The contact with Michelangelo's work contributed to a change in his style: this is best documented in his drawings, since few of the paintings from this later period have survived. (The decoration of the Medicean villas at Careggi and Castello, and the frescoes in the choir of S. Lorenzo are all destroyed.) His studies for S. Lorenzo, where he was working from c1548 to 1557, show that the figures are still piled into the space with the intentional lack of logic of the *Deposition* in S. Felicita. But in style they combine the breadth and block-like form of late Michelangelo with the complexity of movement of earlier Pontormo, in a personal form of Mannerism— one that was very alien to Vasari.

Further reading. Berti, L. *L'Opera Completa del Pontormo*, Milan (1973). Nicco-Fasola, G. *Pontormo o del Cinquecento*, Florence (1947). Pontormo, J. *Diario*

INRI

1554–1556, Florence (1956). Reanek, J. C. *The Drawings of Pontormo*, Cambridge, Mass. (1964).

Poons Larry 1937–

Larry Poons is one of the leading American Post-Painterly Abstractionists, a group that includes Kenneth Noland, Jules Olitsky, Ellsworth Kelly, Jack Youngerman, Al Held, and Frank Stella. Poons' art demonstrates a tendency towards systems: his color-shapes—dots in ellipses floated on a field of strong, contrasted color—are worked out mathematically on graph paper. The sensation created by the pattern, and the contrast achieved, is intended to be more than merely optical: Poons aims to produce the maximum feeling of intensity commensurate with the retention of the integrity of the picture plane.

Pordenone Giovanni da
c1484–1539

Born in the Friulian town from which he took his name, Giovanni Antonio da Pordenone was a painter, formed in Venice, who—according to Vasari—consciously sought to rival Titian. About 1516 he seems to have visited Rome. His mature style combines a somewhat exaggerated apprehension of plastic form, derived from Michelangelo and Raphael, with Venetian color and bravura brushwork.

Uniquely among Venetian 16th-century artists he worked extensively in fresco. He painted major cycles in the Cappella Malciostro of the Duomo, Treviso (1520), in Cremona Cathedral (1520–2), where he displaced Romanino, and in the Pallavicini Chapel at Cortemaggiore, near Piacenza. All these, and particularly the last, show an extreme delight in illusionistic effects, which was not at all Venetian, but was related to his contemporary, Correggio. They also display a violent, aggressive emotionalism, conveyed through sweeping rhythms, large gestures, and contorted expressions.

His *Pietà* at Cremona Cathedral is typical of this style—the feet of Christ, for example, are thrust out at the spectator. The vast *Crucifixion* on the west wall above is a measure of both Pordenone's ambitions and his failure to realize them. Ill-drawn and hastily executed, its effect is over-inflated rather than truly grand.

His altarpieces in oil (for example, the *Madonna of Mercy with Saints and Donors*, 1516; Pordenone Cathedral) are gentler and more carefully executed than his frescoes, but show the same love of monumental effects. Their dark, smoky colors seem to reflect the light and tone of Pordenone's native Friuli. There are sometimes landscape backgrounds, although in his later works these are usually replaced by an imposing apparatus of columns.

The emotionalism as well as the illusionism of Pordenone's art were unusual in Venice, and had considerable influence in the second, "Mannerist" half of the century; notably on some of the works of Tintoretto. His synthesis of Roman and Venetian styles also appealed naturally to early Baroque artists, and his influence can be felt in the youthful work of Rubens.

Porta Giacomo della c1533–1602

The Roman architect Giacomo della Porta was a pupil of Michelangelo, and succeeded him as surveyor of works on the Capitol. He was also influenced by Vignola, whom he followed as architect in charge of St Peter's and the Palazzo Farnese. He also executed the facades of the Gesù, S. Maria ai Monti, and began S. Andrea della Valle.

By comparison with that of Vignola, the work of della Porta emerges as sober and simplified, much more in the tradition of late Michelangelo. Through his sympathetic understanding of his master's style, della Porta emerged as the most important Roman architect of the late 16th century. Competent rather than original, his genius lay in his ability to complete successfully the conceptions of greater men.

Porta Guglielmo della fl. 1534–77

The origins of the Italian sculptor Guglielmo della Porta are obscure. He was the most distinguished member of a Genoese family of sculptors, and is first recorded in Genoa in 1534. He worked there with his uncle, Gian Giacomo della Porta, on the sculptural decoration of the chapel of the Apostles Peter and Paul in the Cathedral. According to Vasari, he moved to Rome in 1537, although he is not recorded there until 1546, when he was working in the Vatican. In Rome he was profoundly influenced by Michelangelo. On the death of Sebastiano del Piombo in 1547 he succeeded to the papal sinecure of the "Piombo", and remained in Rome for the rest of his life. His most important surviving work is the tomb of Pope Paul III in St Peter's (1549–75).

Guglielmo della Porta: the altar in the chapel of Peter and Paul, Genoa Cathedral; marble; 1534–7

Giovanni da Pordenone: The Crucifixion; fresco; 1520–1. Cremona Cathedral

Paulus Potter: The Young Bull; oil on canvas; 236×339cm (93×133in); 1647. Royal Museum of Art (Mauritshuis), The Hague

Frans Pourbus II: Portrait of Claude de Lorraine, Duke of Chevreuse; oil on canvas; 198×123cm (78×49in); 1610. Althorp, Northants.

Portinari Candido 1903–62

The son of Italian immigrants, the Brazilian artist Candido Portinari was born in Sao Paolo. He began painting when he was eight, and in 1918 entered the Fine Arts School in Rio. In 1928 he won a journey to Europe, with an academic portrait of the poet Mariano, shown at the National Salon. In Europe his style was transformed, and he returned to Rio in 1930 to become the leader of the modern school. His monumental realism, indigenous subject matter, and prolific output, which have affinities with Mexican muralists like Diego Rivera, quickly won international recognition. In 1935, *Coffee* was exhibited at the Carnegie Institute, New York. From 1936 he executed a number of frescoes, including *War and Peace* (1953) for the United Nations General Assembly Building in New York. He also collaborated on the decoration of the Ministry of Education and Culture in Rio. In the 1940s he experimented with Cubism, but he never abandoned figuration.

Potter Paulus 1625–54

Paulus Pietersz. Potter was the most celebrated of Dutch animal painters. He devoted his short career almost exclusively to depictions of herds of cows, sheep, goats, and horses grazing in the lush green pastures of Holland. He painted a few subject pictures, but these are mainly of themes such as Orpheus taming the animals which allowed Potter to concentrate on his favorite motifs. Potter's most famous work is the life-size *The Young Bull* in The Hague (1647; Royal Museum of Art, Mauritshuis). His smaller pictures are superior, however, with their less labored detail, serene brownish-gold and light green landscape backgrounds, delicate light effects, and more thoughtful groupings. Potter produced the life-size *Equestrian Portrait of Dirk Tulp* (1653; Six Collection, Amsterdam) and a number of etchings of animals.

Pourbus family
16th and 17th centuries

The Pourbus were a family of Flemish painters active in the later 16th and early 17th centuries. Pieter Jansz. (1520–84) moved from his native Gouda to Bruges. There he executed religious works in a manner related to, but less florid than, that of his father-in-law, Lancelot Blondeel. He also produced portraits. He taught his son, Frans I (1545–81), who worked mainly in Antwerp. Frans I was an admirer of Frans Floris, whose niece he married. In addition to religious works, which reveal Floris' influence, he produced portraits, which owe a debt to Anthonis Mor. His son, Frans II (1569–1622), was the most inter-national of the family. He painted portraits of the aristocracy throughout Europe.

Poussin Gaspard 1615–75

Gaspard Poussin was originally called Gaspard Dughet. A French landscape painter active in Italy, he was born in Rome. He was the brother-in-law of Nicolas Poussin, in whose studio he served and whose surname he adopted. In 1635 he set up as an independent landscape painter; his classically structured views were strongly influenced by the compositions of Annibale Carracci and Domenichino. During the 1630s he visited Naples, Perugia, and Florence. The frescoes he painted between 1647 and 1651 in S. Martino ai Monti, Rome, made him famous, and led to commissions to decorate the Palazzo Colonna and the Palazzo Pamphili (Piazza Navona), Rome. He also painted numerous landscapes on canvas.

Poussin Nicolas 1594–1665

Nicolas Poussin was the greatest representative of Baroque classicism. His austere and profoundly moving style was the fruit of many years of intense intellectual effort. Imposing order and discipline on an ardent temperament, he sought to attain an ideal of beauty that he thought would be revealed by a passionate study of the laws of reason. He took as his guides the art of the ancients, and of Raphael (1483–1520), and of Annibale Carracci (1560–1609). He was a learned painter, unusually concerned with literary and philosophical problems. His art has none of the exuberance and extravagant emotion of his Baroque contemporaries, but is characterized above all by an attempt to appeal to the intelligence.

Poussin was born in a village in Normandy. He studied painting first in Rouen, and then in Paris from 1612 to 1624, where his masters were Ferdinand Elle and probably Philippe Lallemant. His earliest known works are a series of drawings illustrating Ovid's *Metamorphoses* (c1623); these were commissioned by the Italian poet G. B. Marino, whom he may have met at the Court of Marie de Medici. They show a gift for capturing, with directness and simplicity, the most dramatic moment in the classical stories. In 1624 Poussin arrived in Rome, after a few months in Venice on the way.

Later in the 1620s, after undergoing extreme poverty, Poussin was patronized by Cardinal Francesco Barberini. He experimented freely with different styles and subjects, military, religious, and mythological. He learned a great deal from other artists—from Domenichino, in whose studio he worked, from Raphael and Veronese, and from antique sculpture. His most important work from this period is a group of large religious paintings, in which the light and glowing color and rich, free handling of the paint suggest the influence of Titian and Veronese. In 1628–9 Poussin obtained a commission for an altarpiece in St Peter's, Rome, *The Martyrdom of St Erasmus* (Vatican Museums, Rome) and in 1629–30 he painted *The Virgin Appearing to St James the Greater* (Louvre, Paris) for the city of Valenciennes in Flanders. These two large altarpieces were the closest he ever came to the Baroque. *The Virgin appearing to St James* uses dramatic contrasts of light and shade, the composition depends on an ascending diagonal, and the dirty feet of the figure kneeling in the foreground was imitated from Caravaggio's *Madonna di Loreto* (Sant'Agostino, Rome).

More significant for the future than Baroque visions and ecstasies was Poussin's first fully mature work, the *Death of Germanicus* (c1627; Minneapolis Institute of Arts). The subject, from Roman history, is tragic and elevated; the color and texture have a Venetian brilliance and warmth; yet the composition, derived from an ancient relief, is austere and restrained. The space is shallow and figures and architecture are clearly arranged, in layers parallel to the picture plane. The gravity of the work introduced a new attitude to the stern ethics of the Romans, anticipated only by the austere classicism of Domenichino.

After his recovery from a serious illness in 1629–30, Poussin gave up his early attempts to secure public commissions for

Nicolas Poussin: Et in Arcadia Ego (The Shepherds of Arcadia); oil on canvas; 85×121cm (33×48in); 1638–9. Louvre, Paris

churches and palaces in Rome, and began to paint smaller pictures for a circle of learned connoisseurs who encouraged his study of Antiquity. Perhaps the most important of these was Cassiano dal Pozzo, who had commissioned a team of artists to make for him a large reference library of drawings after the Antique.

From 1629 to 1633 Poussin concentrated on themes from Classical poetry, particularly Ovid's *Metamorphoses*, and from Tasso. He painted the well-known stories of Diana and Endymion, Narcissus and Echo, Cephalus and Aurora, and subjects connected with Bacchus. At this period the dominant influence on his work was that of Titian. Poussin had studied Titian's great Bacchanals, which were then at the Villa Ludovisi: it is from them that he derived his wonderfully poetic light and color, his use of landscape motives, his Bacchic emblems, nymphs, satyrs, and river gods. Yet Poussin's treatment of the loves of the gods is tinged with a melancholy and pathos unknown to Titian. His ethereal figures are aware of the unhappiness and dangers of love, and of the ephemeral nature of human happiness; the dusky twilight and stormy light create an intensely elegiac mood.

Although many of these paintings contain allegorical allusions, the treatment of human emotion is direct and passionate. *Narcissus and Echo* (Louvre, Paris) shows with deep pathos the dying Narcissus, exhausted by desire for his own reflection. In *Diana and Endymion* (Detroit Institute of Arts), perhaps the most poetic of all 17th-century mythological paintings, Endymion kneels, desperate and pleading, at the feet of the departing Diana. Poussin seems to have been particularly attracted by Ovid's stories of metamorphoses into flowers. In *The Realm of Flora* (1631; Gemäldegalerie Alte Meister, Dresden) the goddess of flowers dances amid lovers, who, victims of their own tragic desires, have been turned into flowers. Her gaiety and serenity tempers the tragedy of their loves, from which a new form of beauty has sprung.

Poussin's *Adoration of the Magi* (1633; Gemäldegalerie Alte Meister, Dresden), indebted to Raphael rather than to Titian, presages another change in Poussin's style. After completing a series of Titianesque Bacchanals for Cardinal Richelieu in 1635–6, he had turned increasingly to Roman sculpture and ancient reliefs, and also to Raphael (1483–1520), particularly

the later Raphael of the tapestry cartoons. In this period Poussin was particularly interested in the problem of expressing emotion by means of gesture and facial expression. He tended to prefer scenes that showed many figures, each reacting in different ways to some dramatic crisis.

In 1639 he wrote of the *Israelite Gathering the Manna* (1638–9; Louvre, Paris) "I have found a certain distribution and certain natural attitudes ... which show the misery and hunger to which the Jewish people have been reduced, and also the joy and happiness which have come over them, the astonishment which has struck them, and the respect and veneration which they feel for their law giver ..." In *The Rape of the Sabine Women* (c1635; Metropolitan Museum, New York) the scene takes place in the carefully reconstructed forum of a Roman city. We are meant to study each group and each figure, and to appreciate the desolate grief of the old nurse, the terror of the abducted women, and the helplessness of the Sabine men. Each gesture and expression is held and crystallized at a moment of violent intensity. The light is cool and clear, and the figure groups, many indebted to ancient sculpture, are sharply and precisely modeled. By this date, the moral gravity and solemn stylization of Poussin's works were in open conflict with Pietro da Cortona's warm and romantic Baroque treatment of the fables of ancient Greece and Rome.

From 1640 to 1642 Poussin was in Paris, having at last succumbed to increasingly pressing invitations from Richelieu and Louis XIII. The kind of work they demanded from him was not suited to his talents. He was asked to decorate the long gallery of the Louvre, and to paint altarpieces and large allegories for Richelieu. The unhappy interlude was aggravated by the intrigues of threatened French artists, and Poussin must have left again for Rome with some relief.

In Paris he had made a new circle of intellectual friends and patrons—civil servants, bankers, and merchants—and it was for them that he painted after his return to Rome. They encouraged his interest in the philosophy of Stoicism, and after 1640 Poussin began to concentrate on themes that illustrated serious ethical problems. Many of his subjects are taken from Stoic writers, and he painted scenes from the life of Phocion, Diogenes, Scipio, and Coriolanus. Stylistically, he sought to

purge his works of their early sensuous charms, and to progress towards a greater clarity and intellectual precision. In 1642 he wrote, "My nature leads me to seek out and cherish things that are well ordered, shunning confusion which is as contrary and menacing to me as dark shadows are to the light of day".

In the period from 1642 to 1650 Poussin's art attained a new magnificence and gravity. His compositions tend to be clear and direct. There is little movement, and a few figures, whose gestures and expressions are full of significance, are arranged as if in a bas relief; space is exactly defined. Perhaps the most perfect embodiment of Poussin's classical style is the series of the *Seven Sacraments* painted for Chantelou between 1644 and 1648 (Collection of the Duke of Sutherland; on loan to the National Gallery of Scotland, Edinburgh). A scene from the life of the Virgin or Christ symbolizes each sacrament, and Poussin paid great attention to questions of archaeological accuracy. The architectural settings are restrained and severe, and the weighty figures, draped in long togas, have the gravity of ancient sculpture. The solemnity of the scenes is heightened by an aura of silence and stillness; each emotion is analyzed with great intellectual precision.

In these years Poussin sought for dramatic rhetoric and narrative vivacity. He was particularly indebted to the late works of Raphael, whose influence may be felt in *The Judgment of Solomon* (1649; Louvre, Paris) which Poussin considered to be his most perfect work. Violent emotion is communicated with heightened dramatic power, and the movement is extremely formalized. Solomon is enthroned in the center of the painting between the two mothers who claim the living child as their own. The two mothers respond to his judgment with wide-flung rhetorical gestures, and the onlookers with horror, conveyed by sharply turned heads and shoulders and emphatic use of the hands.

Between 1648 and 1651 Poussin created a new type of Holy Family, in which his principles of composition at this central period may be most lucidly appreciated. *The Madonna on the Steps* (1648; National Gallery of Art, Washington, D.C.) although indebted to Raphael and Andrea del Sarto, emphasizes the geometric structure of the composition in a new way: the figure-group is set into an elaborate architectural setting. The great beauty of the

Andrea Pozzo: The Apotheosis of St Ignatius; fresco; 1691–4; S. Ignazio, Rome

painting depends on the careful balance of horizontal and vertical, of cylindrical and rectangular blocks, of solid and void. Glowing fruits and foliage, rich draperies, and shining metal are set against the perfect forms and clear, hard surfaces of the stone. In Poussin's last decade the somber gravity that characterizes the Holy Families is developed still further; the colors become paler and softer.

In the same years Poussin turned his attention to landscapes; in these, space is as clearly and mathematically ordered as in his figure-paintings. Indebted initially to Venetian traditions, and, later, to the ideal landscapes of Annibale Carracci and Domenichino, he organized and controlled the world of nature. His most severe and elaborate landscapes are a pair, *The Ashes of Phocion Collected by his Widow* (1648; Collection of the Earl of Derby, Knowsley Hall, Lancashire) and *The Funeral of Phocion* (1648; Collection of the Earl of Plymouth, Oakly Park, Shropshire); Phocion was a Stoic hero unjustly executed for treason. In both works, a Classical city is spread out across the background, and the geometrical forms of the architecture set the pattern for his organization of trees, rocks, and clouds. Each detail is placed with care, and a sharp, bright sunlight

defines the forms. The world of nature is dominated and formed by man.

Towards the end of his life, in the mid 1650s, Poussin's style changed yet again. Landscape became still more important, but nature is wilder and more luxuriant, and Man is dwarfed by its immensity. Poussin returned to the Ovidian themes that had attracted him earlier in his career, but transformed them into symbols of cosmic significance. Many of them are iconographically very obscure. In *The Birth of Bacchus* (William Hayes Fogg Art Museum, Cambridge, Mass.) Mercury delivers Bacchus to Dirce, who, accompanied by a graceful group of naiads, sits before a cave overgrown with dense ivy and grapevines. In sharp contrast to this gaiety and fertility, Poussin included the pallid figures of the dead Narcissus and grieving Echo. The painting contrasts fertility and sterility, life and death; the theme fascinated Poussin, particularly in his last years. Between 1660 and 1664 he painted four canvases of *The Seasons* (Louvre, Paris) in which he uses an historical episode to symbolize each season. Marvelously clear and simple in form, they contain complex layers of meaning, and allude also to the four stages of Man's history and to pagan ideas of the seasons. Poussin's late works

no longer depend on the rational principles that had guided him in the 1640s; they attain a new and mysterious grandeur and sublimity.

Further reading. Blunt, A. *Nicolas Poussin*, London and New York (1967). Friedländer, W. *Nicolas Poussin*, London (1966).

Pozzo Andrea 1642–1709

The Italian painter Andrea Pozzo was born in Trent. He was educated by the Jesuits, whose Order he entered in Milan in 1685. He decorated many Jesuit churches, including the Gesù, Genoa; the Chiesa dei Gesuiti, Mondovì; and SS. Martiri, Turin. Called to Rome in 1680, he designed the high altar and the altar of St Ignatius in the Gesù, Rome, both of which were completed by 1700. His masterpiece, *The Apotheosis of St Ignatius* (S. Ignazio, Rome) was begun in 1691. His grandiose illusionistic decorations were inspired by those of Pietro da Cortona and Giovanni Battista Gaulli.

Praxiteles *fl. c*370–330 BC

A Greek late Classical sculptor from Athens, Praxiteles was the foremost representative of the Attic School in the middle years of the 4th century BC. He may have been either a son or a son-in-law of Cephisodotus. He spent most of his life in Athens, but is known to have traveled to Ephesus to decorate the altar of the temple of Artemis, rebuilt after 356 BC.

Praxiteles preserved the high Classical tradition of the Polycleitan stance and proportions; but he favored the languid variant, and tilted his statues a little off-balance by thrusting the hips sideways, creating an S-shaped body contour. His figures were often supported by a tree-trunk conceived as an element of landscape.

The surface treatment of Praxiteles' sculptures was famous for its luminosity and delicacy, and he was well-known for his rendering of emotion. His sculptures had a pictorial quality akin to the developments of painting. Significantly, he seems to have preferred those of his statues that were colored by Nikias, a diligent painter of the female form. Praxiteles represented certain aspects of the gods in a playful spirit tinted with eroticism; some of the deities he rejuvenated. The loveliness he imparted to his figures of boys and women had a perennial influence on Hellenistic and Roman art.

He had no special interest in portraiture, but he was reputed to have modeled his statues of Aphrodite on the courtesan Phryne. His only recorded portraits are of Phryne, one gilded in Delphi, another at her native Thespiae in Boeotia. He was responsible for the first major female nude that had any impact in the development of Greek sculpture, the marble *Aphrodite of Cnidos* (one Roman copy in the Vatican Museums, Rome). The goddess was shown placing her clothes on an urn in anticipation of a bath. She was described as smiling softly with inviting eyes. The Polycleitan proportions were here adapted to the female form, with broader hips and narrower shoulders; the knees were closer together. The statue made Cnidos a center of pilgrimage; it was placed in a temple with a back entrance in order to be visible from behind. The type was adapted by Praxiteles himself, emulated by Scopas, and later repeated with endless variations.

The *Hermes and the child Dionysos* (Archaeological Museum, Olympia) was found in the temple of Hera at Olympia in 1877. It had probably been brought there from another building, and had suffered reworking at the back. Whether it is in fact an original work of the sculptor is still a

Mattia Preti: St Andrew Bound to the Cross; fresco; c1651. S. Andrea della Valle, Rome

matter of dispute, but the style is unmistakably Praxitelean. The composition of adult and child is indebted to Cephisodotus' *Peace and Wealth*, with the weight of both here carried by a tree-trunk. The artist exploits textural contrasts between the delicate face of Hermes and his roughly blocked out hair, between the naturalistic drapery and his radiant skin.

The largest part of the relief base of his cult statues of Leto, Apollo, and Artemis at Mantinea survives in Athens (National Museum), carved by assistants to represent the musical contest of Apollo and Marsyas. The merging of the figures with the background illustrates the pictorial tendencies of Praxiteles' sculpture.

Further reading. Bieber, M. *The Sculpture of the Hellenistic Age*, London and New York (1961). Richter, G.M.A. *The Sculpture and Sculptors of the Greeks*, London and New Haven (1950).

Préault Antoine 1809–79

The French artist Antoine Augustin Préault was one of the most original sculptors of the Romantic school, a pupil of David d'Angers. He attempted to sculpt figures undergoing violent emotions; but he was cramped by insufficient technical knowledge, and by the difficulty of applying the Romantic doctrine of spontaneous expression to the slow creative process of sculpture. His work attracted official opposition, and he was excluded from the Salon between 1837 and 1849. His best-known works are *Massacre* (plaster; 1834; Musée Municipal, Chartres), *Silence* (marble; 1848; Père Lachaise, Paris), the *Gallic Horseman* (stone; 1853; Pont de Iéna, Paris) and *Ophelia* (bronze; 1876; Musée des Beaux-Arts, Marseilles).

Preti Mattia 1613–99

Born in Calabria, the Italian painter

Mattia Preti was in Rome by 1630. Later he worked in Venice, Rome, Modena, and Naples (1656–60), and in Malta (1661–99). He was a Caravaggesque painter of vigorous originality. His frescoes, with their restless, flickering movement, and vibrating light and shade, herald the stylistic change from High to late Baroque. For a period, notably in the frescoes in the apse of S. Andrea della Valle, Rome (1650–1), he was influenced by Bolognese classicism. His most powerful works were done in Naples, where he fused influences from the Neapolitan Caravaggisti with colors and compositions deeply indebted to Tintoretto and Veronese.

Primaticcio Francesco 1504–70

The Italian painter, decorator, and architect Francesco Primaticcio was born at Bologna, and brought up there in the surroundings of a minor Raphaelesque cult. Probably by 1527 he had joined the team of artists employed on the decoration of the Palazzo del Tè at Mantua, to designs by Giulio Romano. Recommended to Francis I of France, he joined Rosso Fiorentino at Fontainebleau in 1532. His first work as a decorator there (now lost) may have been prescribed by Giulio; he was Rosso's adjutant in the decoration of the Gallery of Francis I, and was responsible for the execution of the stucco work.

On the death of Rosso in 1540, Primaticcio came into his own as the leader of the enterprise at Fontainebleau under four successive kings. He created the essential figurative style of that place—one of finely cadenced physical grace (psychologically almost vacant), Raphaelesque by extraction, and influenced by Parmigianino and the Hellenistic Antique.

Little of his finished work survives; the best, if fragmentary, sample is in the stuccoes and frescoes for the *Chambre de la Duchesse d'Étampes* at Fontainebleau (c1541–4). Most is known through a substantial number of fluent chalk drawings (in the Louvre, Paris, and elsewhere). These are chiefly of mythological subjects, intended for translation into fresco, or sometimes into sculpture, by collaborators. One of these, Niccolò dell'Abbate, brought particular refreshment to his style.

Primaticcio worked occasionally and eclectically as an architect, his largest piece being the Vignolesque Aile de la Belle Cheminée at Fontainebleau (1568). He died at Paris.

Francesco Primaticcio: The Rape of Helen; oil on canvas; 155×188cm (61×74in); c1530–9. Bowes Museum, Barnard Castle, County Durham

Procaccini Giulio 1574–1625

Giulio Cesare Procaccini, one of a family of Bolognese artists who moved to Milan, was trained as a sculptor, but by c1602–9 was working as a painter on the decorations for S. Maria presso S. Celso, where he developed a dramatic and highly emotional style. In 1610 he was commissioned, as one of the three leading painters in Milan, to paint six scenes from the life of S. Carlo Borromeo (Milan Cathedral): his style now became more exaggerated and bombastic.

Later, probably in 1618, he visited Genoa. By 1612 the influence of Parmigianino became obvious in his elegant figure-style, dazzling colors, and crowded yet shallow compositions, as in *The Mystic Marriage of St Catherine* (Pinacoteca di Brera, Milan). His later work was stiffer and more academic.

Prud'hon Pierre-Paul 1758–1823

The French painter Pierre-Paul Prud'hon studied under François Devosge at the École de Dessin of Dijon. After spending three years in Paris he returned to Dijon, where he won the Prix de Rome of the États de Bourgogne in 1784. His stay in Rome was decisive in the formation of his highly individual style. Prud'hon absorbed the graceful art of Raphael (1483–1520), Leonardo (1452–1519), and Correggio (1490–1534), and was only minimally affected by the prevailing influences of J.-L. David and revolutionary Neoclassicism; he has, therefore, little in common with his contemporaries. Although he became an

Giulio Procaccini: The Mystic Marriage of St Catherine; oil on canvas; 145×149cm (57×59in). Pinacoteca di Brera, Milan

enthusiastic supporter of the Revolution, his allegories such as *The Union of Love and Friendship* (1793; Minneapolis Institute of Arts) and *Wisdom and Truth Come to Earth* (1799; Louvre, Paris), reveal a sentiment and harmony totally out of keeping with current expressions of heroism and Stoic morality.

His portraits show a grasp of the individual that heralds the psychological accuracy of Romanticism (for example, *M. Georges Anthony*, 1796, Musée des Beaux-Arts, Dijon; *Madame Anthony and her Children*, 1796, Musée des Beaux-Arts, Lyons). Although his art went against prevailing trends, Prud'hon attracted support and commissions. In 1799 he painted the decorations for the Hotel de Lanois. Napoleon commissioned the melancholy portrait of *The Empress Josephine* (1805; Louvre, Paris) and Prud'hon was later appointed drawing master and decorator to the new Empress Marie-Louise. His masterpiece was *Justice and Divine Vengeance Pursuing Crime* (1808; Louvre, Paris). Destined for the Court Room at the Palais de Justice, the painting shows a moonlit scene of grandeur and violence.

Puget Pierre 1620–94

The French sculptor Pierre Puget was born in Marseilles. He spent the years 1640 to 1643 in Rome and Florence working under Pietro da Cortona, largely on the decoration of the rooms in the Palazzo Pitti, Florence. From 1643 to 1656 he worked in Marseilles and Toulon, where he divided his time between designing the decoration of warships and producing paintings for local churches. In 1656 he gained his first important commission, the door of the Hotel de Ville at Toulon. The scheme of two supporting herms was current in Roman Baroque, and here perhaps derives from similar, painted supporters by Cortona on the ceiling of the Palazzo Barberini (now Galleria Nazionale), Rome. The figures are charged by Puget with an anguish far removed from the usual image of burden.

In 1659 Puget was called to Paris to execute two statues for Claude Girardin, who was assistant to Nicholas Fouquet, the *Surintendant des Bâtiments*. Following

Pierre-Paul Prud'hon: The Union of Love and Friendship; oil on canvas; 146×114cm (57×45in); c1793. Minneapolis Institute of Arts

Pierre Puget: Self-portrait; marble

this commission Fouquet himself commissioned a *Hercules Resting* (Louvre, Paris). Puget sensed the possibility of real success, but his hopes were dashed by Fouquet's fall from power before the statue was completed. Under Colbert, Fouquet's successor at the Surintendance, Puget received no Royal commissions for 20 years. His Baroque, individual, and Italianate style was alien to the hybrid, but carefully orchestrated classicism that had become the official Court style under the direction of Charles Lebrun.

Following this setback, Puget settled in Genoa, establishing a local reputation as a sculptor. His most important works during this period were two statues, *St Sebastian* and *The Blessed Alessandro Sauli*, for niches at the crossing of S. Maria di Carignano, Genoa. In these works Puget approaches Bernini more closely than ever before, but resists the full three-dimensionality of the High Baroque. Returning to Marseilles and Toulon in 1667, Puget resumed work on the decoration of ships and on architectural work in Marseilles; but he continued to produce sculpture. In 1670, with Colbert's permission, he carved the relief of *Alexander and Diogenes* and the *Milo of Crotona* (both Louvre, Paris) from two blocks of marble abandoned in the dockyards at Toulon.

The *Milo* is Puget's most significant work. It represents the moment when Milo, an athlete of the 6th century BC, has

become caught in the cleft of a tree while attempting to rend it asunder; he is attacked and eaten by wild animals. The anguish already seen in the Hotel de Ville at Toulon is restated. Puget's sources for the *Milo* are not unusual, though they are perhaps revealing. The head and mask are quotations from the *Laocoön*, the most baroque of all antique prototypes for physical torment, but important in this context for its restraint in terms of contemporary Roman Baroque. Puget again rejects the three-dimensionality of Bernini, choosing a single frontal viewpoint with rigidly controlled axes of movement, to create a style at once Baroque and classical. Taken to Versailles in 1683, the statue was approved by the King and placed prominently in the Gardens.

On Colbert's death some months later, Puget was given more commissions for Versailles by Colbert's successor Louvois; but the sculptor's last years were clouded by further failures at Court. The *Alexander and Diogenes* never reached Versailles; and his last work, a relief of *St Charles Borromeo in the Plague at Milan* (Musée des Beaux-Arts, Marseilles), was refused by the King.

Pugin A.W.N. 1812–52

Augustus Welby Northmore Pugin was an English architect, born in London. His father was Augustus Charles Pugin (1762–1832), an emigré Frenchman. The young Pugin attended his father's drawing school, where he developed as a skilled and sensitive draftsman, and helped to illustrate his father's books on Gothic architecture. In his teens, Pugin designed furniture for Windsor Castle, worked as a stage carpenter at Covent Garden, set up a short-lived cabinet-making enterprise, and designed stage-settings.

During the years 1832 to 1835 he was converted to Roman Catholicism, and established himself as an architect. He designed his own house (St Marie's Grange, near Salisbury; 1835), undertook architectural work for Charles Barry, and broadened his experience of medieval art. In 1835 his book of Gothic furniture designs appeared, and in 1836 he published a volume of the *Examples of Gothic Architecture* which his father had begun.

But it was *Contrasts* (1836) that established Pugin as an outstanding architectural critic. The book's reception foreshadowed the controversy that came to surround his career. The illustrations devastatingly satirized the meager standards of contemporary architecture, always using medieval buildings as the basis for comparison; while the text associated Christianity with Gothic architecture, and condemned all classical styles as pagan. The book's expanded second edition (1841) compared the fortunate social conditions of the Christian Middle Ages with grim images of 19th-century England. These extraordinary drawings and Pugin's radical argument were tremendously persuasive, and gave the Gothic Revival henceforth a distinctive sense of moral purpose.

After the success of *Contrasts* Pugin received an increasing number of commissions. Moving to London in 1837 he immersed himself in a frenzy of activity, designing numerous Roman Catholic churches, colleges, and convents. The cathedrals of St Chad, Birmingham (1839), St Barnabas, Nottingham (1841), and St Mary, Killarney (begun 1842) are impressive products of this period. All are correctly Gothic and boldly massed, tending to be plain externally and emphatically vertical within.

St Giles' Church, Cheadle (1841–6), is notable for its rich decorative scheme, and for heralding the change to asymmetry in church design. This asymmetry of plan and elevation is a feature of Pugin's later work (for example, St Augustine's Ramsgate; 1846). It was an extension of ideas that he formulated in *True Principles of Pointed or Christian Architecture* (1841), in which he employed rationalist arguments of "fitness for purpose" to justify the irregular or picturesque.

During the final years of his life Pugin received fewer commissions for churches, as younger Catholic architects gained success. But his consummate skill as a designer was given wide scope when, in 1844, Barry asked him to design most of the fittings and furnishings for the Houses of Parliament: this is one of Pugin's best-known memorials.

Pugin's last years were marked by recurring illness and eventual madness. He could not sustain the assertiveness of his earlier public encounters, and almost disowned some of his finest buildings. But of his enormous influence as a critic and theorist, even he had no doubt: he had "revolutionized the taste of England".

Puvis de Chavannes Pierre
1824–98

A contemporary of Gustave Moreau, Pierre Puvis de Chavannes admired the achievements of Théodore Chassériau as much as did Moreau himself. Puvis was born in Lyons and traveled to Italy to convalesce after illness in 1847. By the following year he had decided to become a painter. Chassériau's murals at the Cours des Comptes, which were destroyed in 1870, impressed Puvis with the possibility of reviving mural painting in 19th-century France. Puvis was to dedicate the greater part of his professional life as a painter to this pursuit, gathering to him in the process public success, civic commissions, and the admiration of a diverse number of younger painters.

Puvis first exhibited at the Salon in 1850, yet his work was frequently rejected during the following decade. Success was inaugurated with the showing of his allegorical paintings *Bellum* and *Concordia* at the Salon of 1861. These works were subsequently acquired for the Musée de Picardie, Amiens, and the Museum made further acquisitions from the Salons of 1864 (*Work* and *Rest*) and of 1865 (*Ave Picardia Nutrix*).

His paintings combined a mythological ambience with allegorical references that could be quite specific. His paintings were often colossal, consisting of canvases attached to the walls of buildings rather than murals painted upon the walls themselves. The composition of such huge paintings was evolved from numerous preparatory drawings. The design was established by focal figures or groups placed along the canvas according to a precise and rhythmic sense of interval. It was an influential achievement of Puvis' large paintings that they made full recognition of the flatness of

A.W.N. Pugin: design for a flagon; 1827. Victoria and Albert Museum, London

Puvis de Chavannes: The Sacred Wood; canvas mural; 460×1041cm (181×410in); 1884–6. Musée des Beaux-Arts, Lyons

the wall surface: as a result, areas of color were flattened and the color remained unmodulated and pale. Puvis' allegorical and mythological tendencies removed the daily world from the range of his subject matter. Within the fields and meadows of his large, bland paintings each element could be made to contribute towards the harmony of the whole. He was able to control minutely the shifts of hue and interval in his paintings. His paintings were so finely tuned in the relations of their parts one to another that he greatly impressed painters concerned with comparable questions of picture construction. His work was particularly admired by Post-Impressionists and Symbolists during the 1880s and 1890s.

His mural commissions continued throughout the Symbolist period. After showing paintings for Marseilles Museum (1869) and Poitiers (1872–5), Puvis undertook murals on the theme of St Geneviève for the Panthéon in Paris. Murals followed for, among others, the Palais des Arts at Lyons (1883–6), the Sorbonne (1887), and the Paris Hotel de Ville (1891–4). He painted a second series of murals for the Panthéon between 1896 and 1898. A major foreign commission also fell to

Puvis, for paintings to decorate the Boston Public Library (1894–6).

His paintings fulfilled a civic as well as a decorative role. They were much in demand, and his studio in Place Pigalle in Paris was extremely busy. Yet Puvis' reputation and achievement extends beyond the provision of public work, for his paintings impressed painters and writers as much as mayoral committees. If, on the one hand, public recognition led to a grand banquet in his honor in 1895, on the other he had received many homages from painters (among them Gauguin, Seurat, and the Symbolists Alphonse Osbert and Henri Martin), and from writers (including the Symbolists Mallarmé and Charles Morice).

To the Symbolists, his otherworldly love of the Antique, his rejection of the depiction of daily life, and his astute control over line, color, and rhythm to expressive and emotive effect, all made him a pioneer of the principles they embraced. Like Moreau, Puvis was adopted as both precursor and contributor to Symbolist art, and in this respect his easel paintings were of particular importance for their role as vehicles of emotional expression. *Hope* (1871; Louvre, Paris), dating from the Franco-Prussian War, and *The Poor*

Fisherman (1881; Louvre, Paris) were convincing examples of the art of ideas and of feelings that Symbolists were seeking.

Further reading. Brown Price, A. *Pierre Puvis de Chavannes*, New York (1994). *French Symbolist Painting: Moreau, Puvis de Chavannes, Redon and their followers*, London (1972). Vachon, M. *Puvis de Chavannes*, Paris (1895).

Pythagoras 5th century BC

The Greek early Classical sculptor Pythagoras of Rhegium was a contemporary of Myron and Calamis. The ancient sources sometimes divide his career between two artists, but in all probability there was only one. He was active in south Italy and Sicily, and also at the sanctuaries of Olympia and Delphi, for which he provided monuments to victorious athletes. He worked primarily in bronze, and was interested in the problems of the stance and proportions of the male nude in movement. His works included an *Apollo shooting Python with his Arrows*, a winged *Perseus, Eteocles and Polynices* killing each other, and a *Philoctetes* limping.

Q

Quarenghi Giacomo 1744–1817

The Italian Neoclassical architect Giacomo Quarenghi is best known for the buildings he designed in St Petersburg for Catherine the Great. He was born near Bergamo, and from 1763 lived in Rome working as a painter. He was influenced both by the work of Anton Mengs and by the buildings of Antiquity. After reading Palladio's *I Quattro Libri dell'Architettura* ("The Four Books of Architecture") he produced his only major work in Italy, the Benedictine Church at Subiaco (1772). Between 1779 and 1796 he was in Russia, where he designed important buildings in St Petersburg, such as the Hermitage Theater and the State Bank. His architecture combines Palladian concepts of Antiquity with Neoclassical detail.

Further reading. Reau, L. *L'Art Russe*, Paris (1922).

Quay Maurice c1779–1804

The French painter Maurice Quay was a pupil of J.-L. David. He was the leader of a group of fellow students known as the Barbus. Their aim was to return to the most ancient sources of inspiration, and to this end they cultivated an interest in Italian painters before Raphael (1483–1520). Though he died quite young, Quay's theories remained a strong influence on his companions. Their interest in "Primitivism" or "Etruscanism" eventually became respectable, and influenced the work of painters such as J.-A.-D. Ingres.

Quellinus Artus 1609–68

The Flemish sculptor Artus Quellinus was trained by his father, a sculptor in Antwerp. His first major works were paid for by the Stadholder of the northern Netherlands in 1634. He then traveled to Rome and spent five years there, probably as an associate of his elder countryman François Duquesnoy. He picked up many of the latter's stylistic traits and was impressed by Hellenistic sculpture, but was scarcely affected by the Baroque style of Bernini. In 1639 he was again working in Antwerp; he joined the guild there in the following year, falling under the strong influence of Rubens. An ivory *Sleeping Putto* dated

Artus Quellinus: the Royal Palace (formerly the Town Hall), Amsterdam; sculpture carved c1650–61 (architect: Jan van Campen)

1641 (Walters Art Gallery, Baltimore) betrays his continuing fascination with Duquesnoy and his modes of sculptural expression.

By 1646/7 Artus was engaged on the projected new Town Hall for Amsterdam, designed by Jacob van Campen, and from 1650 to 1664 he contracted to stay in that city, joining the guild there in 1651. In the ensuing decade he delivered a vast amount of sculpture in relief for the interior and exterior of the Town Hall which is still the glory of that building, now the Royal Palace. Artus' original models in terracotta (preserved in the Rijksmuseum, Amsterdam) betray a Rubensian amplitude and tactile quality in the modeling of naked flesh, while the drapery is loosely hung in a fashion derived from Duquesnoy. The

types of figure are Hellenistic, but their implied movement is slow and gentle, lacking the verve and drama produced by Bernini. There is a typically Netherlandish interest in incidental details—flora, fauna, and marine motifs, frequently composed into "still lifes". Artus also executed a few excellent portrait busts, based in format on Bernini's, with hands included among the lower drapery.

Under Artus the Elder, the sculptor Rombout Verhulst (1624–98) and Artus' nephew, Artus Quellinus the Younger (1625–1700), also worked on the Amsterdam Town Hall. The latter had a successful career in his native south Netherlands, specializing in religious sculpture and particularly in wood carving for church furnishings such as pulpits and confessionals.

Quercia Jacopo della 1367–1438

The Italian sculptor Jacopo della Quercia was born in Siena, the son of a goldsmith and wood carver. A singular genius, he belongs, together with Donatello and Ghiberti, among the founders of early Renaissance statuary and imagery. Nothing is recorded about his early training, but there are plausible reasons to believe he worked as an assistant in the Bologna workshop of Pierpaolo and Jacobello dalle Masegne, and that he was strongly influenced by the Northern Gothic sculpture.

Between 1401 and 1403 he participated unsuccessfully in the competition for the door of the Florentine Baptistery (his entry has been lost). A small marble *Madonna of Humility* (National Gallery of Art, Washington, D.C.) seems to date from these early years. His first documented and preserved work is the monumental marble *Silvestri Madonna* (Ferrara Cathedral), finished in 1406. The massive entity of this block-like, majestic figure marks a strikingly new aspect of sculpture in its relation to human space. The monument to Ilaria del Carretto (Lucca Cathedral) must have been executed shortly afterwards (*c*1408) and shows a significant interweaving of antique motifs, such as the frieze of winged putti ornamenting the sarcophagus, with the almost Burgundian recumbent figure of Ilaria.

In 1408 Quercia was commissioned to execute the city fountain, *Fonte Gaia*, in Siena (now replaced by a 19th-century copy; the original is in Palazzo Pubblico, Siena). Because of several interruptions, this enterprise lasted until 1419. The fountain forms an open trapezoid, surmounted at its ends by two freestanding statues of Acca Larentia and Rea Silvia (the latter carved from Quercia's model by Francesco da Valdambrino). Each of them is represented with the twins Romulus and Remus, elected by the proud city of Siena as its founders, in order to compete with Rome. The walls are decorated with shallow reliefs, depicting the creation of Adam and the expulsion from paradise, together with representations of the Virtues, with the Virgin in the center. Iconographically unique, the program of the *Fonte Gaia* shows a peaceful mingling of paganism and Christian salvation.

A freestanding, double-life-sized marble Apostle (*c*1420; S. Martino, Lucca) displays a new self-consciousness and a new comprehension of man as independent being, comparable only to the contemporary statuary of Donatello. Shortly afterwards, Quercia finished the marble altar for Lorenzo Trenta (S. Frediano, Lucca), probably executed with a great deal of assistance from his workshop. His only surviving wooden sculpture is an Annunciation group (*c*1421–5; Museo di Arte Sacra, S. Gimignano); executed for the Collegiata at S. Gimignano, it still bears the original polychromy. Between 1417 and 1431, della Quercia contributed towards the erection of the Siena baptismal font by providing the gilt-bronze relief of *The Annunciation to Zacharias*.

His last and most important work is the decoration of the *Porta Magna* at S. Petronio in Bologna (1425–38). This is one of the great landmarks of early Renaissance sculpture. Its lunette shows the freestanding figures of SS. Petronius and Ambrosius, the latter added in the 16th century. The jambs depict the history of the creation, including the sacrifice of Abraham, flanked by busts of prophets in the inner jambs. Here the new perception of man, already formulated in the goddesses from the *Fonte Gaia*, is brought to an unique culmination—one that greatly influenced Michelangelo.

Further reading. Pope-Hennessy, J. *Italian Gothic Sculpture*, London (1972). Seymour, C. Jr *Sculpture in Italy: 1400–1500*, Harmondsworth (1966). Supino, I.B. *Jacopo della Quercia*, Bologna (1926).

Jacopo della Quercia: Madonna and Child (Silvestri Madonna); marble; height 210cm (83in); 1406. Ferrara Cathedral

R

Raeburn Henry 1756–1823

The leading portrait painter of his generation in Scotland, Henry Raeburn was born at Stockbridge, near Edinburgh. He taught himself miniature painting before studying briefly with the portraitist David Martin. Two years of study in Rome, 1785 and 1786, had little effect on his subsequent development. After settling permanently in Edinburgh in 1787, his productivity increased dramatically. He developed a broad style of painting that relied on strong chiaroscuro for modeling and for the integration of figures and settings. He maintained this style, with only slight modifications, throughout his career. In 1815 he was elected Royal Academician, in 1822 he was knighted, and in 1823 appointed His Majesty's Limner for Scotland.

Raimondi Marc-Antonio c1480–c1534

The Italian engraver Marc-Antonio Raimondi probably learned metalwork in Bologna under Francesco Francia. The uncertainty of style of his engravings before 1505 is resolved during the period he spent in Venice, where he fell under the spell of Albrecht Dürer. He reproduced Dürer's woodcut series of *The Life of Mary* in copper (1506), also making signed copies of *The Small Passion*. Moving to Rome in 1509, he entered the circle of Raphael who provided designs for such engraved masterpieces as *The Massacre of the Innocents* and *The Judgment of Paris*. After the Sack of Rome in 1527, he probably passed the remainder of his life in Bologna.

Rainaldi Carlo 1611–91

The Italian architect Carlo Rainaldi was born in Rome. He was trained by his father, Girolamo Rainaldi (1570–1655), a mediocre architect. Father and son collaborated in the design of a number of buildings in north Italy and later, in 1652–3, in the design of S. Agnese, Rome (later completed by Borromini). Carlo's principal work is the church of S. Maria in Campitelli, Rome (1663–7), a Baroque masterpiece in which influences from Ber-

Henry Raeburn: Portrait of Sir John Sinclair; oil on canvas; 238×154cm (94×61in); c1794–5. National Gallery of Scotland, Edinburgh

nini are combined with qualities that derive from Mannerist and north Italian architecture. Carlo also designed the facade of S. Andrea della Valle, Rome (begun 1661).

Ramsay Allan 1713–84

The Scottish portrait painter Allan Ramsay was born in Edinburgh but practiced mainly in London. His first style was influenced by Imperiali and Francesco Solimena (1657–1747), with whom he

studied in Italy from 1735 to 1737. His early full-lengths, such as *Dr Mead* (1746; Foundling Hospital, London), exhibit strong characterization and a robust dignity. Returning to Italy in 1754, he renewed his friendship with the fashionable portraitist Pompeo Batoni, whose sophisticated style suggested the course of Ramsay's subsequent development. His recognized masterpiece, *Portrait of Margaret Ramsay* (1754–5; National Gallery of Scotland, Edinburgh), was painted during this visit. Its intimacy, graceful

Above: Marc-Antonio Raimondi: Raphael's Dream; engraving after a design by Raphael(?); 23×33cm (9×13in). British Museum, London

design, and delicate modeling introduce the traits of his best mature works.

In 1767 he became principal painter to George III, but after 1770 he virtually abandoned his profession, in order to write political essays and pamphlets. Ramsay was well educated, and numbered among his acquaintances the leading philosophers and writers of the period. He issued one important treatise, *Dialogue on Taste* (1754), but took no students and remained somewhat aloof from his colleagues. As a painter, he ranks with the best British portraitists of the 18th century and helped to inaugurate the Grand Style of English portraiture.

Raphael 1483–1520

Raphael was the common name of the Italian painter Raffaello Sanzio or Santi. He was born in the small hill town of Urbino, then ruled by the Montefeltro family, whose court was famous throughout Italy as a center of artistic and intellectual activity. His first teacher was presumably his father, Giovanni, a successful if mediocre local painter and a man of some cultural pretensions, who died in 1494.

Raphael was evidently a precocious artist: his first major altarpiece, *The Coronation of St Nicholas of Tolentino*, painted for a church in Città di Castello when he was only 17, is already extremely assured (1500–1; fragments in the Museo e Gallerie Nazionali di Capodimonte, Naples, and in the Pinacoteca Civica "Tosio Martinengo", Brescia). Throughout his career he showed himself exceptionally responsive to the work of other artists. His early style is a synthesis of the achievements of the major figures of the previous generation in central Italy—Melozzo da Forlì, Luca Signorelli, Pintoricchio, and above all Perugino, with whom he is known to have collaborated for a time soon after 1500.

By 1504, when he painted the masterpiece of his early period, *The Marriage of the Virgin* (Pinacoteca di Brera, Milan), Raphael had fully assimilated all these influences. His picture is closely based on another version of the same subject by Perugino (c1500–4; Musée des Beaux-Arts, Caen), but it is superior to its prototype in virtually every respect. The composition is much more spacious, with a

Left: Allan Ramsay: Portrait of Margaret Ramsay; oil on canvas; 76×64cm (30×25in); 1754–5. National Gallery of Scotland, Edinburgh

less rigid and schematic arrangement of figures; the poses are freer, more graceful and more varied; the color is richer and more harmonious; even the architectural background is an original creation, in contrast to the purely conventional design adopted by Perugino.

Raphael spent most of the period from 1504 to 1508 in Florence, where he had his first experience of the work of Leonardo da Vinci and Michelangelo, both of whom were then active in the city. As a result of his contact with Leonardo, drawings now began to play an increasingly important role in his creative process. Instead of attempting to give his ideas a definitive form at the first draft, as he had done previously, Raphael now learned to develop them gradually through a series of sketches. He used the different techniques of pen and chalk with an astonishing virtuosity, but virtually dispensed with the more precise and delicate medium of silverpoint. This new method of working enabled him to produce much more complex and unified compositions than he had achieved before. Michelangelo's influence was less significant. The two men seem to have been personally antipathetic, and Raphael never shared Michelangelo's single-minded obsession with the male nude—even though his figures now acquired something of the tension and vigor so characteristic of the latter's work.

While Raphael was in Florence his reputation was still insufficient to gain him important commissions. Most of the pictures that he produced in this period were relatively small compositions showing the Madonna and Child, often with one or two other figures, based on works by Leonardo and Michelangelo. Among the finest are the *Madonna of the Meadow* (1505/6; Kunsthistorisches Museum, Vienna), *Madonna of the Goldfinch* (*c*1506; Uffizi, Florence), and *La Belle Jardinière* (1507; Louvre, Paris). These Florentine *Madonnas* are probably Raphael's most famous works. They were particularly admired in the 19th century, when they were often reproduced in versions that exaggerated their somewhat sentimental religiosity. Indeed, their popularity as devotional objects has tended to obscure their real quality as an exceptionally brilliant and original series of variations on a single restricted theme. It was

Raphael: The Liberation of St Peter; detail; fresco; width of base of entire fresco 660cm (260in); 1513–14. Stanza di Eliodoro, Vatican, Rome

precisely the limitations of the subject that stimulated Raphael's powers of invention.

These paintings show that by 1508 he had fully mastered the problems involved in compositions with two or three figures. When he tried to produce an equally coherent design on a larger scale, in the *Entombment* (1507; Museo e Galleria Borghese, Rome), painted for a chapel in Perugia, the result was not entirely successful. The difficulties that he encountered in attempting to organize ten figures and to give them a sense of movement are all too evident. Despite the beauty of some of the individual poses, the composition as a whole is labored, frozen, and artificial.

Late in 1508 he was summoned to Rome by Pope Julius II, apparently at the suggestion of the papal architect Bramante, who was, like Raphael, a native of Urbino. He was employed in the redecoration of a series of rooms in the Vatican (known as the "Stanze"), at first merely as one of a team of artists, but very soon entirely on his own. He began work in the Pope's private library, now known as the Stanza della Segnatura. Besides a number of small scenes on the ceiling, the decorative scheme included a large fresco on each of the four walls symbolizing one of the four main topics of literature: theology, philosophy, poetry, and jurisprudence. For example, the so-called *School of Athens* shows Plato and Aristotle surrounded by a large number of other philosophers engaged in discussion or contemplation; while in the *Parnassus*, Apollo and the Muses are accompanied by the most famous ancient and modern poets.

In these frescoes Raphael succeeded in creating an ideal world, peopled with figures of superhuman nobility and grace, who were arranged in perfectly balanced compositions and linked to one another by a complex play of glances and gestures. His achievement was not just the culmination of a steady process of development, but to a great extent the reflection of his discovery of classical art, which he was able to see in quantity only after his arrival in Rome. Raphael's response to the Classical world was immediate, intense, and decisive. To a more marked degree than any artist before him, including even Michelangelo, he possessed the desire as well as the ability to recreate the style and the spirit of antique and especially of Hellenistic art with complete fidelity and consistency. This was an enterprise that was perfectly in tune with the contempo-

rary intellectual climate; it was just at this period that the Papacy was attempting to restore Rome to something of its former status by means of a conscious evocation of its Imperial past.

Immediately after completing the Stanza della Segnatura in 1511, Raphael began work in the next room, the Stanza d'Eliodoro. Here, during the next three years, he painted four large scenes showing instances of God's miraculous intervention on behalf of His Church, together with four smaller scenes on the ceiling. The style is different from that of the earlier frescoes, with more complex poses, a greater sense of movement, and a darker, more dramatic tonality. By now Raphael was a complete master of the fresco technique. He exploited it here with unprecedented brilliance, obtaining effects of color and lighting almost comparable to those of oil paintings.

From c1514 onwards, as a result of the pressure of commissions, he was forced increasingly to make use of assistants in carrying out his designs. This is first noticeable in the third of the Vatican Stanze, the Stanza dell'Incendio, painted between 1514 and 1517. Here the general quality is markedly lower than in the earlier rooms, and only one of the frescoes, *Fire in the Borgo*, seems to be substantially by Raphael's hand. Although he was usually able to exercise a high degree of control over the activities of his pupils, it must be admitted that in comparison with his best work, the actual execution of the majority of his later paintings leaves something to be desired. The extent of his participation varied greatly, depending on the nature of the commission. For instance, the series of nine large cartoons for tapestries to be hung in the Sistine Chapel was a highly important project in which Raphael found himself in direct competition with Michelangelo, who had already decorated the vault with frescoes. In this case he not only took immense pains with the compositions but was also personally responsible for much of the actual painting. On the other hand, the decoration of two large loggias in the Vatican, dating from c1518–19, was carried out almost entirely by assistants, who even provided some of the designs.

The tapestry cartoons, of which seven survive (1515–16; Victoria and Albert Museum, London, on loan from H.M. Queen Elizabeth II), are among Raphael's greatest and most influential works. They

established a pictorial convention that was to remain the norm for the presentation of historical narrative until the 19th century. The subjects were taken from the Acts of the Apostles. In each scene the content was expressed with absolute clarity and immediacy by a composition of monumental calm and simplicity, and by a highly rhetorical yet dignified vocabulary of gesture derived from Classical sculpture.

The major decorative projects for the Papacy comprised only a part of Raphael's artistic activity in Rome. His most important private patron was the banker Agostino Chigi. His villa, now known as the Farnesina, contained Raphael's fresco of *Galatea*, dating from 1511, as well as a series of scenes illustrating the story of Cupid and Psyche, which were painted by pupils from the artist's designs in 1518. Both works were imaginative recreations of Classical wall-paintings. They were to prove just as influential as models for the depiction of mythological subjects as the tapestry cartoons were for biblical and historical themes.

Raphael also designed two chapels for Agostino Chigi, one in the church of S. Maria della Pace, the other in S. Maria del Popolo. The latter, completed in 1516, was his first architectural project. It was remarkable both for the accurate rendering of motifs taken from Classical sources, notably the Pantheon, and for the lavish use of rich materials such as bronze and marble, which also followed antique precedents. In the later part of his career, and especially after he was put in charge of the reconstruction of St Peter's in 1514, Raphael became increasingly preoccupied with architecture. His buildings reflect his interest in the Classical world even more strongly than his paintings. Unfortunately, few of his projects have survived in the form that he intended.

One other particular noteworthy aspect of Raphael's immense output is portraiture. In Florence his portraits were still relatively stereotyped in pose and scarcely differentiated in mood, but in Rome he learned how to vary his compositions to express the personality and status of the sitter. For example, the apparent spontaneity of the portrait of his friend *Baldassare Castiglione* (c1514–15; Louvre, Paris), who is shown as if pausing momentarily in conversation, conceals the rigor and complexity of the pyramidal design. It is a perfect visual embodiment of the qualities of grace and facility that Castiglione defined as ideals in his book *The Courtier*. This and other Roman portraits, such as that of *Leo X with Cardinals Giulio de' Medici and Luigi de' Rossi* (?1518; Uffizi, Florence), were imitated by countless later artists.

Raphael's last major work, the altarpiece of the *Transfiguration* (1518–20; Vatican Museums, Rome), was still not quite finished at his death. The design, however, is entirely his responsibility, as is most of the execution. Compared with his earlier pictures, there is a greater use of chiaroscuro, a more complex narrative structure, and a more dramatic, artificial vocabulary of gesture. These are the essential characteristics of Mannerism, the style developed during the 1520s by his pupils, particularly Giulio Romano. Until recently, Raphael's Roman works up to the time of the tapestry cartoons were regarded as constituting a standard of perfection, while the late paintings such as the *Transfiguration* were seen either as symptomatic of a decline in his powers, or as embodying a reaction against his ideals on the part of his pupils. This analysis no longer seems convincing. There is no indication that he had reached an impasse *c*1515. In fact, his creativity was undiminished in his last years, and his work of this period established the direction taken by the next generation of artists in Rome and throughout most of Italy.

Further reading. Cocke, R. and de Vecchi, P. *The Complete Paintings of Raphael*, New York (1966, reissued 1987). Fischel, O. *Raphael*, London (1948, reissued 1964). Jones, R. and Penny, N. *Raphael*, New Haven (1983).

Rauschenberg Robert 1925–

The American painter and sculptor Robert Rauschenberg was born in Port Arthur, Texas. He studied at the Kansas City Art Institute (1947–8), the Académie Julian in Paris (1948), and Black Mountain College, North Carolina (1948–9).

After moving to New York in 1949, he created paintings that were completely white, black, or red. By the mid 1950s, working closely with Jasper Johns, he created painted assemblages of unexpected materials and objects—including Coca-Cola bottles, tires, and stuffed birds. These "combines" blurred the boundaries between art and sculpture. In 1962 he developed a method of combining oil paint with silk-screen techniques. Characterized

Robert Rauschenberg: Almanac; silkscreen and oil on canvas; 244×152cm (96×60in); 1962. Tate Gallery, London

by expressive brushstrokes and showing an interest in mass-media imagery, Rauschenberg's work from the mid 1950s to the early '60s is often seen as a bridge between Abstract Expressionsism and Pop art. In the 1960s Rauschenberg also participated in "Happenings." He designed sets and costumes for dance companies, even dancing in some performances. In the 1970s he worked with silk, cotton, and paper pulp, and in the 1980s he created sculpture from scrap metal in the "Gluts" series. He dedicated much of his time to the Rauschenberg Overseas Culture Interchange (1985–91), which aimed to create understanding among international artists. A tireless innovator, at the turn of the 21st century, Rauschenberg incorporated digital imagery into his work.

Further reading. Hopps, W. et al. *Robert Rauschenberg: A Retrospective*, New York (1997). Kotz, M. *Rauschenberg: Art and Life*, New York (2004). Mattison, R. *Robert Rauschenberg: Breaking Boundaries*, New Haven (2003).

Ray Man 1890–1976

Man Ray was the most important American Dada artist. Under the influence of Marcel Duchamp in New York, from 1915 onwards, he pioneered the construction of useless artifacts, such as *Object to be Destroyed* (destroyed), a metronome, and a painted eye. He also used the principles of chance in composition, as in *The Rope Dancer Accompanies Herself with Her Shadows* (1916); Museum of Modern Art, New York). By 1918 he was using a commercial airbrush in painting, 30 years before Abstract Expressionism or Tachisme. His main photographic achievement was the Rayograph, a technique for rendering a three-dimensional abstract world in a photographic print.

Further reading. Aragon, L., Arp, J., *et al.* *Man Ray: Sixty Years of Liberties*, Milan (1971). Bourgeade, P. *Bonsoir, Man Ray*, Paris (1972). Penrose, R. *Man Ray*, London (1975). Ray, M. and Eluard, P. *Les Mains Libres*, Paris (1937). Ray, M. *Self-Portrait*, Boston (1963). Schwarz, A. *Man Ray: the Rigour of Imagination*, New York (1977).

Above: Man Ray: Pisces; canvas; 61×73cm (24×29in); 1938. Tate Gallery, London

Read Herbert 1893–1968

Herbert Read was an English critic and poet, and a champion of modern art in the years between the First and Second World Wars. He became a neighbor of the painters Paul Nash and Ben Nicholson and the sculptors Henry Moore and Barbara Hepworth when he moved to Hampstead in 1933. With them he founded the group Unit One, "a point in the forward thrust of modernism in architecture, painting and sculpture". They were joined in Hampstead by Walter Gropius and other notable architects and artists who were refugees from the Continent. Read's most influential book of these years was the dogmatic *Art and Industry* (1934) which outlined a design aesthetic similar to that of Gropius and the Bauhaus. His other important works include *Education through Art* (1943) and *A Concise History of Modern Painting* (1959). He received a knighthood in 1953.

Below: Odilon Redon: Woman with Outstretched Arms; watercolor on paper; 15×20cm (6×8in); c1910–14. Musée du Petit Palais, Paris

Redon Odilon 1840–1916

The French artist and printmaker Odilon Redon developed an intensely personal visual vocabulary. Although he was held in high esteem by Symbolist writers and artists, he had few immediate followers.

Born in Bordeaux, he grew up on the family estate, Peyrelebade, amid the desolation of the flat, pine-covered Landes bordered by barren sand dunes and silent marshlands. This landscape haunted Redon throughout his life, providing a constant supply of visual images. Drawing lessons in Bordeaux were followed by studies in architecture and then painting in Paris. A mental breakdown forced him to return to Bordeaux, probably in 1862.

Apart from a careful study of Corot and Delacroix, it was his meetings with Rodolphe Bresdin, in 1863, and with Henri Fantin-Latour, in 1874, that were to shape the course of his artistic career. Bresdin taught Redon etching, enabling him during the 1860s to embark upon a series of small engravings whose subject matter consisted of memories of landscapes known in childhood, peopled with motifs taken from Corot and Delacroix. By 1870, however, Redon had discovered the more immediate technique of charcoal. Over the next nine years he evolved his own highly personal visual symbolism, which he translated into lithographs after 1879.

Redon was introduced to the lithographic technique by Fantin-Latour. Between 1879 and 1899 he produced 166 lithographs: 37 single plates (for example, *Brunnhilde*, 1886), 17 groups of book illustrations (for example, for Flaubert's *Tentation de St Antoine*, three sets 1888, 1889, 1896), and five groups of non-literary sequences of images (*Dans le Rêve*, 1879, and *Songes*, 1891). Most of the lithographs were complemented by deliberately ambiguous captions, usually invented by Redon himself.

In his diary-like autobiography, *À Soi-même* (1922; new edition 1961) Redon suggested that his lithographs summarized two concerns central to his art; the relationship between Man and Nature, and "suggestive" art. Influenced by his friend, the Bordeaux botanist Armand Clavaud, Redon frequently depicted images that expressed the interchangeability of Man and Nature, as in *The Marsh Flower* (plate II, *Hommage à Goya*, 1885). He proposed an alternative theory of evolution to that of Darwin, which he investigated more fully in his non-literary series, *Les Origines* (1883).

Like Mallarmé, who was his close friend and admirer from 1884 onwards, Redon believed in involving the spectator in the creative process. Rather than present a finite image or idea, he created a "suggestive art" in which the spectator was invited to enter into and complete the visual and mental images initially depicted by the artist. Redon achieved this by creating a world of visual ambiguities and absurdities, using for example an illogical juxtaposition of random objects and seemingly unrelated captions and images, a total disregard for unity of scale (*Sad Ascent*, plate 19 of *Dans le Rêve*, 1879) and a frequent reference to infinite space (*Blossoming*, plate 18 of *Dans le Rêve*).

Until c1895, Redon's life had not been happy. He was melancholic by nature, and the death of his first son and the tardiness of critical acclaim colored both the images and the media of his art. However, growing recognition of his work during the 1880s and early 1890s (from J.-K. Huysmans, Alfred Verhaeren and *Les Vingt*, Maurice Denis, and Émile Bernard), the sale of Peyrelebade, and the birth of another son caused light to flood into his work. He experimented with color in several ways. He translated the subjects of his lithographs into victorious images of explosive color (as in *Pegasus Triumphant*, 1905–10; Kröller-Müller Museum, Otterlo). He painted pastels of flower pieces and portraits in subtly balanced colors and textures. And he investigated the effects of mixed media in decorative cycles, screens, and easel paintings.

Redon's brilliant, non-naturalistic color presaged the art of the Fauves, and his use of illogical objects inhabiting an ambiguous world foreshadowed the art of the Surrealists.

Further reading. Bacou, R. *Odilon Redon* (2 vols.), Geneva (1956). Druick, D. (ed.) *Odilon Redon*, London (1994). Redon A. *Lettres de Gauguin, Gide, Huysmans, Jammes, Mallarmé, Verhaeren … à Odilon Redon*, Paris (1960). Redon, O. *À Soi-même, Journal: Notes sur la Vie, l'Art, et les Artistes*, Paris (1961). Wilson, M. *Nature and Imagination: the Works of Odilon Redon*, Oxford (1978).

Reinhardt Ad 1913–67

Ad Reinhardt emerged as the most relentless of American Minimalist painters, working with a logic that takes every theory of diminution and purity to its logical end. He painted geometrical abstractions in the 1930s and worked in a calligraphic style, related to that of Mark Tobey, in the 1950s. From there he progressed from studies of multiplicities of squares, to simple sequences, to the simple sequences, to the uncompromising *Untitled (Black)* (oil on canvas; 1960–6; Jewish Museum, New York)—an all-black, square canvas. Reinhardt was a vigorous polemicist of purity in art. He was an inspiration to the Minimalists, to whom the irreducible fact of color or shape in its simplest form is an expression of mystical value.

Further reading. Bois, Y.-A. *Ad Reinhardt*, New York (1991). Lippard, L. and Hunter, S. *Ad Reinhardt: Black Paintings 1951–1967*, New York (1990). Lippard, L. and Hunter, S. *Ad Reinhardt: Paintings*, New York (1966).

Rembrandt van Rijn 1606–69

Rembrandt Harmensz. van Rijn was the greatest painter of the Dutch School. He was born in Leiden, the son of a miller. After seven years at grammar school he enrolled at Leiden University, but left a few months later to begin an apprenticeship with a local artist. His first teacher has not been identified; his second, between 1620 and 1623, was a now little-known painter named Jacob van Swanenburgh. He completed his training with six months in the Amsterdam studio of the then famous Pieter Lastman (c1624/5). It was Lastman's work that inspired him to become a historical painter, and familiarized him with narrative techniques deriving from Italian Renaissance art.

In 1625 Rembrandt returned to Leiden, where he set up as an independent artist. Some genre paintings date from these early years, for instance *The Money-changer* (1627; Staatliche Museen, Berlin), a work influenced by Utrecht School nocturnal pictures, but Rembrandt's principal interest was, and remained, biblical history. His earliest surviving painting, the large *The Martyrdom of St Stephen* panel (1625; Musée des Beaux-Arts, Lyons) is an attempt to master dynamic physical action in a multifigured composition. This quickly gave way to more detailed work on a smaller scale, as in *The Presentation in the Temple* (1631; Royal Museum of Art,

Rembrandt van Rijn: Lady with a Fan; oil on canvas; 127×101cm (50×40in); 1633. Private collection

Mauritshuis, The Hague), with its numerous tiny figures, vast spatial effects, and use of chiaroscuro for dramatic ends.

Concurrently, Rembrandt painted a number of single-figure pictures which reveal his attraction to old people. Several of these are of biblical characters, for example *The Prophetess Hannah* (1631; Rijksmuseum, Amsterdam), in which the artist's mother was the model. In others the iconography is problematic, notably in several pictures of elderly sages who sit reading in dimly lit rooms. These are often regarded simply as philosophers or scholars, but allusions to prophets or saints may sometimes have been intended. The most important work from the Leiden period is the 1629 *Judas Returning the Thirty Pieces of Silver* (Lady Normanby Collection,

Mulgrave Castle, Yorkshire). Rembrandt's success in conveying emotion through gesture and facial expression in this work was admired by Constantin Huygens, the Secretary to the Stadholder, Prince Frederick Henry of Orange, who observed that he had already equaled the greatest painters and would soon surpass them.

Around 1631/2 Rembrandt settled permanently in Amsterdam, where he quickly established himself as a fashionable portrait painter among the prosperous bourgeoisie. The ensuing half, three-quarter, and full-length likenesses, each immensely varied in conception, are painted in a detailed and highly-finished technique; as much attention is given to costume as to the sitter's features. This style was related to the demands of pat-

rons, for in other paintings from this period (such as the artist's studies of both old men and models dressed in exotic Oriental costume) his brushwork was already much bolder. In one of the double portraits from these years, *The Shipbuilder and his Wife* (1633; Collection of H.M. Queen Elizabeth II) the apprehension of momentary action echoes the preoccupation of Frans Hals at this date.

Rembrandt's fame was consolidated by group portraits, in particular *The Anatomy Lesson of Dr Tulp* of 1632 (Royal Museum of Art; Mauritshuis, The Hague). The intent listeners in this painting are members of the Guild of Amsterdam Surgeons. The so-called *Night Watch* (1642; Rijksmuseum, Amsterdam), which shows the militia company of Captain Frans Banning Cocq about to form ranks, marks Rembrandt's high point in public esteem. This huge canvas (11 ft 9 in by 14 ft 4 in, 3.59 by 4.38 m; originally even larger) was a revolutionary variant on traditional versions of the commemorative group portrait. It had been customary to give each individual equal prominence, but Rembrandt sacrificed this in favor of common action and psychological unity. This was an application to portraiture of the principles governing his historical pictures. The misleading title of the painting dates from the time when it was darkened by discolored varnish.

The most notable religious pictures from the 1630s are the Passion scenes painted for Prince Frederick Henry (1633–9; Alte Pinakothek, Munich). The pathos of the Calvary scenes in this series distinguishes them from the glorification of Christ found in Rubens' interpretations of the Passion. The explicitly narrative intention reveals that Rembrandt's sources were didactic prints of the 16th century. He was well aware of Rubens' achievements, however, and the gruesome *The Blinding of Samson* (1636; Städelsches Kunstinstitut, Frankfurt am Main), which exhibits his youthful delight in themes of horrifying brutality, was conceived in emulation of the Flemish painter. Rembrandt's expressive range at this date can be seen in the mythological painting of *Danaë* (1636; Hermitage Museum, St Petersburg. This is a particularly beautiful example of his sensuous treatment of the female nude, and of his exploration of the possibilities of light as an agent of the supernatural.

Rembrandt was a wealthy man by the late 1630s. In 1639 he moved to a large

Rembrandt van Rijn: Portrait of Rembrandt's Mother Reading; oil on canvas; 74×62cm (29×24in); c1631? Wilton House, near Salisbury, Wiltshire

house in the Jodenbreestraat, where he lived with Saskia van Uylenborch, a well-connected girl whom he had married in 1634. The artist's awareness of his improved social status and of his celebrity as a painter is apparent in self-portraits from these years. An important consequence of prosperity was that it enabled Rembrandt to build up an extensive art collection; this played a vital role in his work as a source of pictorial and thematic ideas. The inventory of the collection reveals an enormous quantity of prints and drawings by other artists, many of them from the 16th century or earlier.

During the 1640s the mood of Rembrandt's work became quieter and more contemplative, a departure from the urgent physical dramas of earlier years. The change was to some extent related to the death of his wife in 1642—a bereavement that followed the death of three of their four children in infancy. The altered mood is especially evident in such small-scale devotional pictures as the *Adoration of the Shepherds* (1646; National Gallery, London). Rembrandt's conceptions in these intimate, somberly colored works are unaffectedly realistic, and this is typical of his general tendency to humanize rather than idealize biblical figures and scenes. The mystery and spiritual quality with which such works are imbued is achieved largely through the subtle manipulation of light and shade. Rembrandt's religious narratives are firmly rooted in assiduous reading of the Bible, and this is evident in the many other scenes from Christ's life painted during the 1640s. Departures from the text usually only arose when there was a need to extend the narrative scope, as in the famous *Hundred Guilder Print* etching (*Christ Healing the Sick*, c1642–5), where Rembrandt illustrated the whole of St Matthew, chapter 19.

The artist turned to landscape in the late 1630s and 1640s. He made many landscape drawings and etchings, works of incomparable luminosity and atmosphere which are predominantly naturalistic portrayals of the countryside around Amsterdam. The relatively few landscape paintings, by contrast, are intensely imaginative: romantic visions in which bleak mountain ranges, deserted river valleys, and mysterious ruins are momentarily flooded with light bursting through dark storm clouds. No other Dutch painter dramatized nature to this degree. But Rembrandt's interests lay primarily with

humanity, and after the mid 1650s he abandoned landscape as a subject in itself.

Although he received fewer commissions in the 1640s and 1650s, Rembrandt did not, as is often supposed, fall out of favor with patrons. It was the cumulative effects of living beyond his means that resulted in his eventual insolvency. His house and goods were auctioned between 1657 and 1658, and he moved to the Rozengracht, a poorer district of Amsterdam. He never completely cleared his debts; but he was partially protected from his creditors by Hendrickje Stoffels, who was his mistress from c1649, and by Titus (his only surviving son by Saskia), who formed an art-dealing firm and made him its employee.

The Anatomy Lesson of Dr Deijman (1656; Rijksmuseum, Amsterdam) is one of the more important late commissions. The surviving fragment of this group, which shows the corpse and two figures, has a poignancy normally associated with the *Pietà* theme. *The Syndics of the Drapers' Guild* (1662; Rijksmuseum, Amsterdam) is remarkable for Rembrandt's reversal of the customary relationship between sitter and spectator; it is the latter, not the former, who is the object of scrutiny here. In 1652 Rembrandt received his first known commission from abroad: an *Aristotle* (1653; Metropolitan Museum, New York) for which Don Antonio Ruffo, a Sicilian nobleman, was charged 500 guilders. Ruffo paid up, but remarked that this was eight times 'as much as an Italian artist would have received. A contract in 1661 for a painting to decorate the new Amsterdam Town Hall confirms that Rembrandt's reputation remained high, although the picture (*The Conspiracy of Julius Civilis*, National Museum, Stockholm), was ultimately replaced by a pupil's work. The reasons for this are not known.

Rembrandt is unique for his time in his practice of producing work independently of commissions. This practice increases in later years, with a number of single-figure pictures of Jews, old men, and members of the artist's family. Little or no church patronage existed in 17th-century Holland, and many of his religious paintings (for instance *Bathsheba*, 1654; Louvre, Paris) may also fall into this uncommissioned category. The majority of his later drawings are also private works—musings on historical themes, which are dissociated from such traditional functions as collecting pictorial ideas or serving as preliminary studies for paintings. Rembrandt's draw-

Rembrandt van Rijn: A Girl Sleeping; brush and wash on paper; 24×20cm (9×8in); c1655–60. British Museum, London

ings (only 1,500 or so survive) were not widely known in his lifetime; his 300 etchings, on the other hand, were much more familiar to the public than his paintings. They were an important source of income; it was in fact among the 17th-century connoisseurs who admired them that the history of print-collecting on a widespread scale began.

The unorthodox technique of Rembrandt's last paintings, in which broken touches of thickly impasted paint are worked with the brush handle and even the fingers, is accompanied by a greater degree of brilliance and warmth of color than before. This can be seen in such portraits as *The Jewish Bride* (c1666; Rijksmuseum, Amsterdam) and the *Family Portrait* (c1668; Herzog Anton Ulrich Museum, Brunswick). The consummate tenderness of these essays on the theme of human love is also manifested in such late religious paintings as *The Return of the Prodigal Son* (c1669; Hermitage Museum, St Petersburg), where the artist's reflections on the nature of human forgiveness are unmatched in Christian art for their depth of feeling. The choice of this particular episode from the parable (as opposed to scenes of debauchery) is consistent with Rembrandt's later preference for subjects involving emotional crises, as against those based primarily on physical action, and which have strong elements of sensuality or violence. Other examples are found in his later representations of the story of

Joseph and Potiphar's wife. These concentrate on the accusation scene, rather than on the scene of attempted seduction which Rembrandt had treated in the 1630s.

Themes involving stress arising from moral dilemmas—as in Rembrandt's representations of Bathsheba, and Peter at the time of his denial of Christ—are also characteristic of this tendency. An exception is found in the dark and tragic *Three Crosses* etching (completed c1661). Here the cataclysmic events of Christ's last hours are expressed in a purely pictorial way, by arresting contrasts of deep blacks and piercing lights.

Rembrandt's closing years were clouded by personal tragedies: Hendrickje Stoffels died in 1663, Titus in 1668. But knowledge of such biographical details is not necessary in order to appreciate the profoundly moving portrayal of the artist's careworn face in the final self-portraits.

Changes in taste since the 17th century have not always accommodated Rembrandt, but his greatness has rarely been questioned. The admiration of his contemporaries centered on the narrative scope and invention of the history paintings, the verve and characterization of the early portraits, and Rembrandt's technical facility as an etcher. This is also true of later generations of critics, although they invariably expressed reservations about his apparent indifference to ancient sculpture and to Italian Renaissance art, his rejection of precise, linear draftsmanship, and a certain lack of decorum. Today we are inclined to emphasize the content of Rembrandt's work, although our critical language is rarely equal to the descriptive tasks this involves.

Further reading. Schama, S. *Rembrandt's Eyes*, London (2000). Westermann, M. *Rembrandt*, London (2000). Wheelock, A. K. *Rembrandt's Late Religious Portraits*, Chicago (2005). White, C. and Buvelot, Q. (eds.) *Rembrandt by Himself*, London (1999).

Remington Frederic 1861–1909

Frederic Remington became famous for his heroic depictions of the American West. He studied at Yale University and briefly at the Art Students League, New York, achieving his first success with illustrations for journals such as *Harper's Weekly* and *Century*. Concentrating on heroic and glamorously rugged subjects, he made a major contribution to the myth of the Wild West, which was championed at the end of the 19th century by newspapers, dime novels and the Wild West shows featuring William F. "Buffalo Bill" Cody. Remington's paintings, spirited, colorful and full of authentic detail, became very popular. *Flight for the Waterhole* (c1895; Houston Museum, Texas) was one of the best known. His bronze sculptures, including *The Bronco Buster* (1895), were popular too, and often recast.

René of Anjou 1409–80

René of Anjou was the ruler of lands in southern France and Italy. He was also a patron of the arts, an author, and probably an illuminator—though there is no unequivocal evidence that René himself executed the illustrations to his writings. The artist's masterpiece is *Le Livre du Coeur d'Amour Épris* (1457; Nationalbibliothek, Vienna; MS. 2597) which employs dramatic lighting effects unprecedented in miniature painting. Other works by the same hand, like the *Livre des Tournois* (Bibliothèque Nationale, Paris; MS. Fr. 2695) and the *Mortifement de la Vaine Plaisance* (Bibliothèque Royale Albert I, Brussels; MS. 10308), are less striking and conform more to established genres of illumination. Nevertheless, they reveal an artist of originality, with elements of the mannered style of the Master of the Rohan Hours, whom René knew.

Rembrandt van Rijn: Self-portrait; oil on canvas; 53×44cm (21×17in); 1657. National Gallery of Scotland, Edinburgh (on loan from the Duke of Sutherland)

Guido Reni: St Cecilia; oil on canvas; 94×75cm (37×30in); 1606. Norton Simon Museum, Pasadena

Reni Guido 1575–1642

The Italian painter Guido Reni was born in Bologna, and from 1584 to 1593 was apprenticed to the Fleming Denys Calvaert (1540–1619). About 1595 he joined the Carracci Academy, where he was influenced by Annibale Carracci and by Raphael. He was essentially a classical artist who became increasingly devoted to the concept of ideal beauty. In his mature works, the inspiration of Classical sculpture and the importance of elegant line and flowing rhythms is clear. His classicism is personal and imaginative; it is sweeter, more nostalgic, and more melancholic than the classicism of the High Renaissance. Yet in one important way, Reni was a Baroque artist: he was concerned with the direct expression of charged religious emotion, an expression that modern spectators have often found distasteful.

Reni had already painted important altarpieces for churches in Bologna when he moved to Rome c1602. His early Roman works show the immediate influence of Caravaggio. He was patronized by Cardinal Scipione Borghese and by Pope Paul V, and a series of important commissions brought him immense success. These include frescoes in two rooms in the Vatican (1608–9), St Andrew led to Martyrdom in S. Gregorio, Rome (1608), frescoes in the Borghese chapel in S. Maria Maggiore (1610–12), and frescoes in the Cappella dell'Annunziata in the Palazzo del Quirinale (1609–12). The latter works reveal strongly the influence of the Florentine Renaissance. Their tenderness of feeling, and the radiant golden light that fills the painted dome, crowded with angels, make these some of the artist's most poetic works.

Between 1612 and 1614 Reni executed his famous fresco Dawn (Aurora), on the ceiling of the Casino Rospigliosi in Rome. This work, which makes no concessions to illusionism, shows how consciously Reni adapted the tradition of Classical art and of Raphael. It shows Dawn flying before Apollo in his chariot, accompanied by the maidens of the Hours, figures of ideal beauty who dance in graceful harmony. The colors are glowing and the landscape radiantly beautiful.

In 1611 Reni had visited Bologna and painted important works there. In 1614 he returned permanently to the city. He then painted a series of large altarpieces. In these his handling is broad, and his color rich, but the compositions are carefully balanced and even rigidly symmetrical. At this period he was also painting poetic reinterpretations of historical and mythological subjects for the nobility. In 1622 he went to Naples to fresco the Tesoro di S. Gennaro, but difficulties over the contract caused his departure for Rome. In his last years Reni developed a new style, distinguished by delicate silvery tonalities and ravishing combinations of oranges, pinks, and mauves.

Renier de Huy 12th century

Although the name of Renier de Huy has little historical foundation, it has been firmly connected with the creation of the 12th-century Mosan style of the Meuse River region of Flanders. The bronze font commissioned by Abbot Hellinus (1107–18) for his church of Notre-Dame-aux-Forts at Liège (now in the church of St-Barthélemy in Liège) has long been attributed to Renier. "Reinerus aurifaber" also appears as a witness on a charter of the church of Notre Dame at Huy, signed by Bishop Albero I of Liège in 1125—but the evidence for linking this goldsmith with the Liège font is very poor.

A contemporary rhymed chronicle written by a Canon of Liège Cathedral describes the font carefully, and states that it was made in the time of Abbot Hellinus and by him. It is not until the 15th-century chronicle of Liège that Renier's name is given as the craftsman responsible for the font ordered by Bishop Albero.

Renoir Auguste 1841–1919

The French Impressionist painter Pierre-Auguste Renoir was born at Limoges, but

Auguste Renoir: La Parisienne (Woman in Blue); oil on canvas; 160×106cm (63×42in); 1874. National Museum of Wales, Cardiff

temporary, for example *Lise with a Parasol* (1867; Museum Folkwang, Essen). Others fuse a naturalistic treatment of the figure with a mythological subject such as *Diana* (1867; National Gallery of Art, Washington, D.C.). This combination of modernity and timelessness has close parallels with Courbet's contemporary work, and became Renoir's central preoccupation in the later part of his career.

Renoir's brushwork of the later 1860s owes a debt to Manet's bold handling of paint, but always retains a delicacy of touch reminiscent of the French 18th-century masters, notably Fragonard. This appears even in Renoir's direct studies from nature, as can be seen by comparing his 1869 view of La Grenouillère (National Museum, Stockholm) with Monet's more broadly handled treatment of the same subject (Metropolitan Museum, New York).

After his Salon submissions were rejected in 1873, Renoir abstained from the Salon for four years, and exhibited in the first three Impressionist group exhibitions, in 1874, 1876, and 1877. His exhibits at these shows reveal the diversity of his aims and his work during the 1870s. In his small-scale paintings, he developed an extremely summary, spontaneous technique, evoking the presence of objects by apparently formless dabs and dashes of paint, as in *The Harvesters* (1873; Stiftung Sammlung E. G. Bührle, Zürich). He applied a similarly abbreviated technique to a female nude in *Woman in the Sunlight* (1875; Musée du Jeu de Paume, Paris). He clearly felt that these experimental studies were worth exhibiting, but he only showed them alongside far more ambitious and fully finished canvases, such as *La Parisienne* (*Woman in Blue*) (National Museum of Wales, Cardiff). This was an almost lifesize full-length portrait of a woman in blue, closely related in type to the fashionable portraiture of the day.

In his genre scenes of modern life, Renoir combined something of the spontaneity of his outdoor studies with—in the principal figures—the interest in characterization shown in his portraits. This is seen in *La Loge* (Courtauld Institute Galleries, London), and in Renoir's most ambitious modern-life painting of the decade, *Moulin de la Galette* (Musée du Jeu de Paume, Paris). The shadow effects in *Moulin de la Galette* are treated in rich blues, and its forms are modeled by persistent variations of color. In other, smaller paintings of this

he spent his childhood in Paris, where he was to live until he moved to the south of France in 1902. In the later 1850s he worked as a painter on porcelain, and then painted blinds, studying at the same time in the Louvre, where he became devoted to French 18th-century art. In 1862 he entered Gleyre's studio, where he met Monet,

Sisley, and Bazille; Monet and Bazille became particularly close friends.

During the 1860s, like the other Impressionists-to-be, Renoir sought success at the annual Salon exhibitions. In his landscapes of the period, he was indebted to the painters of the Barbizon School. Some of his figure-pieces are wholly con-

period, such as *Woman Reading* (*c*1876; Musée du Jeu de Paume, Paris), the modeling of the figure is almost entirely suppressed in favor of bold strokes of varied color; the patterns of light and shade on the woman virtually dissolve into those of the background.

In the later 1870s, Renoir began to gain a wider practice as a fashionable portraitist. This was largely through his contacts with Madame Georges Charpentier who was a society hostess and the wife of a leading publisher. He exhibited at the Salon again between 1878 and 1883, winning his greatest success with his *Portrait of Madame Charpentier and her Children* (1878; Metropolitan Museum, New

York), a picture tighter in handling and more conventional in color than *Moulin de la Galette*.

During the same years, probably as the result of the demands made on him by portrait commissions, he began to feel dissatisfied with the extreme formlessness of paintings such as *Woman Reading*. This dissatisfaction led him to a period of crisis in which he reexamined all the bases of his art, and began to seek ways of reintroducing tighter drawing and modeling into his paintings. He studied Ingres' oil paintings, for the clarity of their draftsmanship in paint. He also began to experiment with painting in thin, translucent glazes, on a dense white ground, instead of using a

dense impasto; this can be seen in *Young Girl with a Falcon* (1880; Sterling and Francine Clark Art Institute, Williamstown). Then in autumn 1881 he traveled to Italy; he visited Florence, Venice, Rome, and Naples.

He was particularly impressed by the more informal of Raphael's frescoes—those in the Villa Farnesina in Rome—and by the Pompeian mural paintings in the Naples Museum. He wrote to Madame Charpentier that in his own paintings he was seeking to emulate the grandeur and simplicity by which these earlier works suggested sunlight, by concentrating not on details, but on broad harmonies. He also found a relevance in the treatment of subject matters of the Renaissance masters and the Greco-Roman artists of Pompeii, in the way they treated mythological stories as lively genre scenes, in contrast to the idealizations and archaeological reconstructions characteristic of French 19th-century Neoclassical painting. In the 1870s, Renoir had been preoccupied with the most ephemeral modern scenes. But in the 1880s he began to treat more timeless subjects, and the informal treatments of mythology that he found on his Italian trip helped him to give spontaneity to such themes.

In the aftermath of his trip to Italy, his handling of paint became drier, and his drawing of forms very crisp. Sometimes he even tried to emulate in oils the dryness of fresco, as in *Woman Arranging her Hair* (1885; Sterling and Francine Clark Art Institute, Williamstown). This period of experiment culminated in *The Bathers* (1887; Philadelphia Museum of Art). Here, Renoir derived the figures in part from a 17th-century relief by François Girardon in the park at Versailles; the picture invites comparison with the similarly timeless treatments of the Bather theme by Boucher (*Diana Resting after her Bath*) and Fragonard (*Women Bathing*; both in the Louvre, Paris). Renoir's outlines are harsh, and some details meticulously defined, but the figures are frozen in the middle of apparently fleeting movements.

Renoir soon found this style too tight, and sought ways of regaining his spontaneity of brushwork without losing the fuller modeling of form which he had reached. He achieved this by *c*1890, adopting a type of handling in which fluent brushstrokes followed the contours of the form. It was the technique of Fragonard, in

Auguste Renoir: Woman Reading; oil on canvas; 47×38cm (19×15in); c1876. Musée du Jeu de Paume, Paris

particular, that helped him to attain this. Some of Renoir's canvases of *c*1890 are reminiscent of the French 18th century in feeling, as well as in handling, for example *In the Meadow* (Metropolitan Museum, New York). During the 1880s Renoir's color became richer and warmer as a result of two trips to Algeria, and of spells working on the Mediterranean coast. In his last period, after he had settled at Cagnes on the Mediterranean in 1902, his color became still more lavish and his handling more fluid. In the finest of his last paintings, such as *The Bathers* (1918–19; Musée du Jeu de Paume, Paris), form and color are married with unprecedented freedom, to create an idealized vision of womanhood far from the modern Parisian girls who had dominated his art in the 1870s. Renoir's greatest achievements lie at these two poles: as the painter of the modern life of the 1870s, and in the timeless visions created by his brush in his last years.

Further reading. Benjamin, R. *Renoir and Algeria*, Williamstown, Mass. (2003). Castellani, F. *Renoir: His Life and Works*, New York (2004). Feist, P. H. *Pierre-Auguste Renoir 1841–1919: a Dream of Harmony*, Cologne and New York (2000).

Repin Ilya 1844–1930

Ilya Efimovich Repin was a Russian Realist painter. Trained at the St Petersburg Academy, he subsequently spent two years in Paris (1873–4) where he was influenced by the Impressionists' use of color. In 1874 he joined the Abramtsevo artists' colony founded by S. I. Mamontov, and also became a member of the *Peredvishniki* ("Wanderers"). Both groups believed that art should be socially useful, and should concentrate on those subjects likely to elicit sympathy. Repin embodied these ideals in works with a strong idea-content, though he never neglected painterly qualities (for example, *Volga Boatman Hauling*, 1872; State Russian Museum, Leningrad). He painted portraits of many prominent Russians, including several of Tolstoy.

Repton Humphry 1752–1818

Humphry Repton was an English landscape gardener whose early life was spent as a country gentleman. It was not until 1788 that he turned an amateur interest into a profession and became a "landscape gardener" (he was the first to adopt the title). As such he fell heir to a tradition that had achieved, through the career of Lancelot ("Capability") Brown, a status equal to architecture, painting, and sculpture.

His first major publication, *Sketches and Hints on Landscape Gardening*, appeared in 1795. Criticizing the contrived informality of the Brownian setting, it argued the merits of a more rugged, natural landscape: one that his own enormous practice did more than anything else to popularize. He holds a prominent place in the development of the Picturesque aesthetic, although the emphasis he placed upon convenience and utility led him to preserve many features (including the balustraded terrace close to the house) that infuriated the more extreme exponents of the Picturesque.

Unlike Brown, Repton rarely practiced as an architect; but the list of architects with whom he worked includes Nash, Wyatt, Wilkins (senior), and his own sons, George and J.A. Repton. Despite his lack of practical experience, he held firm views on architecture. It was largely due to his writings that the "irregular Gothic style" of James Wyatt was popularized, as the architectural equivalent to the revolution that Repton had pioneered in landscape design.

No Reptonian landscapes have survived in an unaltered state, but good examples are still to be found at Tatton Park, Cheshire (1791), Cobham Hall, Kent (1790), and Corsham Court, Wilts. (1795).

Restout family
17th and 18th centuries

The French painter Jean Restout the Younger (1692–1768) was born in Rouen. His father, Jean Restout the Elder (1663–1702), and his grandfather, Marguerin Restout (*fl.* 1624), had both been painters. Jean moved to Paris in 1707 to work under his uncle, Jouvenet. He was received at the Académie in 1720, rising to become its Chancellor in 1761. The severity and integrity that marked both his life and his work were atypical of his age. His religious works have a seriousness lacking in the work of his contemporaries Coypel and J.-B. Lemoyne; his manner seems to have stemmed, through the influence of Jouvenet, from 17th-century artists like Hubert Le Sueur. His mythological sub-jects steer clear of the mildly erotic and the light-hearted, with an emotional commitment that presages J.-L. David. His son, Jean-Bernard Restout (1732–97), was also a painter, and his portrait of his father (*Portrait of Jean Restout*, Versailles) is revealing.

Rethel Alfred 1816–59

Alfred Rethel was a German painter and draftsman. He studied under the Nazarene artist W. von Schadow at the Düsseldorf Academy (1829–36). Schadow's style and ideals greatly influenced his early work, such as the Charlemagne Frescoes in the Kaisersaal, Aachen Town Hall (1840–7). Rethel is most famous for his drawings and for his woodcuts—a medium then enjoying a renaissance in Germany. Several of them show a medieval preoccupation with death (for example, *Death as Destroyer*, *c*1848); but the woodcut cycle *Also a Dance of Death* (1849) seems, more specifically, to be a reactionary ans-wer to the Revolution of 1848. Their power lies in the matter-of-fact inclusion of the figure of Death into a realistic setting. Rethel was mentally ill from 1853 until his death.

Reynolds Joshua 1723–92

An artist of refined intellect and taste, Sir Joshua Reynolds was the most celebrated and influential painter in England during the second half of the 18th century. His preeminence as a portrait painter was challenged only by Allan Ramsay in the 1750s and by Thomas Gainsborough after 1774. Through his paintings, which figured prominently in public exhibitions from 1760 onwards, and his 15 *Discourses on Art* delivered to the students of the Royal Academy (1769–90), he dictated the canons of taste and the methods of practice for successive generations of English artists. His collection of Old Master drawings and prints was one of the finest ever assembled by an English connoisseur, and he numbered among his intimate acquaintances the literary and political elite of his age.

Reynolds was born at Plympton in Devonshire. In 1740 he was apprenticed to the London portrait painter Thomas

Jean Restout the Younger: The Adoration of the Shepherds; oil on canvas; 400×330cm (157×130in); 1761. Church of St-Louis, Versailles

Hudson, but in 1743 he set up his own practice, working in Devon and London until his departure for Italy in 1749. In Rome, from 1750 to 1752, he studied assiduously the art works of Antiquity and of the High Renaissance. He was particularly inspired by the Bolognese classicists, Reni, Guercino, and the Carracci. After returning to London in 1753, he formulated his own version of the grand style, in which he sought to extend the limits of history painting to include the less honored category of portraiture. The "history" portrait, based on a solid appreciation of the aesthetic principles of past masters, and frequently quoting the poses and motifs of Classical statuary and paintings, was Reynolds' primary contribution to English portraiture. It was in the class of the heroic full-length, such as *Commodore Keppel* (1753/4; National Maritime Museum, London) and *Captain Robert Orme* (1756; National Gallery, London), that he registered his initial successes in this field.

Reynolds was never more dogmatic in his classicism than during the years immediately surrounding his election as first President of the Royal Academy in 1768. To this period belong the innovative *Garrick between Tragedy and Comedy* (1762; private collection), *Lady Cockburn and her Three Eldest Sons* (1774; National Gallery, London), and *Daughters of Sir William Montgomery as the Graces Adorning a Term of Hymen* (1774; Tate Gallery, London). In addition to the more formal commissions of the 1770s, he also painted so-called "fancy pictures", and became popular as a portrayer of children. His late work *Master Henry Hoare* (1788; Toledo Museum of Art, Toledo, Ohio) is one of his most sensitive pictures in this category.

In 1781, Reynolds toured Flanders and Holland where he made a careful study of Rubens' paintings. His approach to characterization in portraiture tends to be less intellectual after this date, although in his *Sarah Siddons as The Tragic Muse* (1784; Huntington Library and Art Gallery, San Marino) and *Lieutenant-Colonel Banastre Tarleton* (1782; National Gallery, London), the classical idiom is reiterated with increased vigor and insight. In the late 1780s he contributed three paintings to John Boydell's Shakespeare Gallery (*Macbeth and the Witches*, 1788, and *The Death of Cardinal Beaufort*, 1788, now at Petworth House, Petworth, Sussex: *Puck*, 1789, Collection of Earl Fitzwilliam, Milton Park, Peterborough, Cambridge-

Joshua Reynolds: Lt-Col. Banastre Tarleton; oil on canvas; 236×145cm (93×57in); exhibited 1782. National Gallery, London

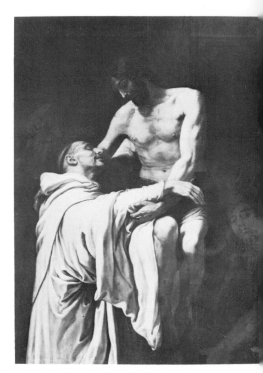

Francisco Ribalta: Christ Embracing St Bernard; oil on canvas; 158×113cm (62×44in). Prado, Madrid

Further reading. Cormack, M. *Exhibition of Works of Sir Joshua Reynolds, P.R.A.*, Birmingham (1961). Graves, A. and Cronin, W.V. *A History of the Works of Sir Joshua Reynolds* (4 vols.), London (1899–1901). Hudson, D. *Sir Joshua Reynolds*, London (1958). Wark, R.R. (ed.) *Sir Joshua Reynolds: Discourses on Art*, San Marino (1959). Waterhouse, E. *Reynolds*, London (1973).

Ribalta Francisco 1565–1628

The Spanish painter Francisco Ribalta was born in Solsona in Catalonia. In Madrid by 1582, he absorbed the style of the painters at the Escorial, especially the tenebrism of Juan Fernández de Navarrete (c1526–79).

By 1599 he was in Valencia, developing a strongly naturalistic Mannerist style similar to that of Bartolomé Carducho (1560–1680) in works for the church of Algemesí (1603) and for the Colegio del Patriarca at Valencia (1604–11).

Ribalta probably visited Italy between c1613 and 1615. This is suggested both by a signed copy of Caravaggio's *The Martyrdom of St Peter* and by the increasing realism and tenebrism of his later work. His masterpieces are luminous evocations of Franciscan legends (examples in the Prado, Madrid, and the Wadsworth Atheneum, Hartford, Conn.).

shire), and while he attempted serious history painting at this time, his efforts in this line were never entirely successful. After losing the sight of his left eye in 1789, he virtually stopped painting. He read his last *Discourses* to the Royal Academy in 1790. His last two years were not happy but he was given a sumptuous funeral and was buried at St Paul's in 1792 with unparalleled ceremony for an artist.